THE SOCIALIST REGISTER 1993

REAL PROBLEMS
FALSE SOLUTIONS

SOCIALIST
REGISTER
1 9 9 3

Edited by RALPH MILIBAND and LEO PANITCH

THE MERLIN PRESS
LONDON

First published in 1993
by The Merlin Press Ltd
10 Malden Road
London NW5 3HR

British Library Cataloguing in Publication Data

The Socialist Register. — 1993
    1. Socialism — 1993
    I. Miliband, Ralph   II. Panitch, Leo
355'.005

ISBN 0-85036-4272
ISBN 0-85036-4264 Pbk

Typesetting by
Computerset, Harmondsworth, Middlesex

Printed and bound in Great Britain by
Biddles Ltd, Guildford and King's Lynn

TABLE OF CONTENTS

PREFACE

Real Problems/False Solutions: this theme of the twenty ninth issue of *The Socialist Register* requires a brief explanation.

With the recent collapse of so much that formed socialist expectations in the twentieth century, and yet at the same time with a global capitalist order which is full of severe, massive and urgent problems, we live in a period of great political confusion. In such a period it is inevitable that nostrums are advanced both on the Right and on the Left which are incapable of tackling seriously the problems they are supposed to resolve.

We conceived this volume as addressing a broad range of 'dead-end' or 'morbid symptom' responses to various aspects of the current global disorder, offering analyses of why they arise as well as a critique and corrective to them. We deliberately cast our net widely: the essays in this volume highlight important aspects of our theme in relation to environmentalism, feminism, social democracy and revolutionary socialism; and they also address real problems and false solutions as they pertain to postmodernism, nationalism, constitutionalism and immigration.

We would have liked to have covered more ground still, not least in relation to the manifestly false solutions advanced in the name of 'competitiveness', 'free enterprise' and 'structural adjustment' to which, as our contributors attest, so many parties and governments, international bodies like the IMF and the World Bank, and a host of ideologues and commentators have ardently subscribed, and which they have successfully pressed on countries right around the globe.

Socialists like ourselves cannot reasonably claim to have ready-made blueprint solutions for the problems of the world: the time for such presumption is long gone. But we do believe that neo-liberalism, far from solving problems, is a recipe for their aggravation, at least for the vast majority of the population in all countries where that poisonous ideology holds sway; and we also believe that the control and regulation of economic life by progressive, democratic and accountable governments is the first condition for the alleviation of the ills plaguing the men and women who are not part of the small minority which prospers in conditions where the organising principle of social life is competition.

Our contributors range far and wide. David Harvey is Professor of Geography at Oxford University; Christopher Norris is Professor of English at Cardiff University; Marsha Hewitt is in the Department of Theology at Trinity College, University of Toronto; and Lynne Segal teaches in the School of Psychology at Middlesex University. John Griffith is Emeritus Professor of Public Law in the University of London; Michael Löwy is Research Director at the Centre National de la Recherche Scientifique, Paris; John Saul is Professor of Social Science at Atkinson College, York University, Toronto; K. S. Karol writes on Eastern Europe and the ex-Soviet Union for *Nouvel Observateur,* Paris; Stephen Hellman teaches in the Department of Political Science, York University, Toronto; Rudolf Meidner is a former Research Director of LO, the Swedish Confederation of Labour and is a Fellow of the Swedish Center for Working Life, Stockholm; Saul Landau is a Senior Fellow at the Institute for Policy Studies, Washington, D.C.; and Daniel Singer is the European Correspondent of *The Nation*, New York.

We are grateful to our contributors for their help, and to David Macey for his translation of K. S. Karol's essay. As usual, we must point out that neither our contributors nor the editors necessarily agree with everything that appears in the volume. We are also, once again, very grateful to Martin Eve of Merlin Press for his unfailing help.

March 1993

L.P.
R.M.

THE NATURE OF ENVIRONMENT: THE DIALECTICS OF SOCIAL AND ENVIRONMENTAL CHANGE*

David Harvey

I Prologue

Around 'Earthday' 1970, I recall reading a special issue of the business journal *Fortune* on the environment. It celebrated the rise of the environmental issue as a 'non-class issue' and President Nixon, in an invited editorial, opined that future generations would judge us entirely by the quality of environment they inherited. On 'Earthday' itself, I attended a campus rally in Baltimore and heard several rousing speeches, mostly by middle class white radicals, attacking the lack of concern for the qualities of the air we breathed, the water we drank, the food we consumed and lamenting the materialist and consumerist approach to the world which was producing all manner of resource depletion and environmental degradation. The following day I went to the Left Bank Jazz club, a popular spot frequented by African-American families in Baltimore. The musicians interspersed their music with interactive commentary over the deteriorating state of the environment. They talked about lack of jobs, poor housing, racial discrimination, crumbling cities, culminating in the claim, which sent the whole place into paroxysms of cheering, that their main environmental problem was President Richard Nixon.

What struck me at the time, and what continues to strike me, is that the 'environmental issue' necessarily means such different things to different people, that in aggregate it encompasses quite literally everything there is. Business leaders worry about the political and legal environment, politicians worry about the economic environment, city dwellers worry about

---

*This text was first presented in embryo at the Havens Center in the University of Wisconsin and as Ida Beam Visiting Fellow in the University of Iowa in March, 1991. It was subsequently presented at the School of Architecture and Urban Planning in UCLA, at Rutgers and Johns Hopkins Universities, as well as at Cambridge, Leiden, London, Oxford and Bristol Universities before being presented as the York University Lecture in Political Science in Canada in October, 1992. I want to thank the many people who, by way of criticisms and comments, have helped to both deepen and clarify my thinking on these occasions.

1

the social environment and, doubtless, criminals worry about the environment of law enforcement and polluters worry about the regulatory environment. That a single word should be used in such a multitude of ways testifies to its fundamental incoherence as a unitary concept. Yet, like the word 'nature', the idea of which 'contains, though often unnoticed, an extraordinary amount of human history . . . both complicated and changing, as other ideas and experiences change' (Williams, 1980, 67), the uses to which a word like environment is put prove instructive. The 'unnoticed' aspect of this poses particular difficulties, however, because it is always hard to spot the 'incompletely explicit *assumptions*, or more or less *unconscious mental habits*, operating in the thought of an individual or generation,' but which define 'the dominant intellectual tendencies of an age.' Lovejoy (1964, 7-14) continues:

> It is largely because of their ambiguities that mere words are capable of independent action as forces in history. A term, a phrase, a formula, which gains currency or acceptance because one of its meanings, or of the thoughts which it suggests, is congenial to the prevalent beliefs, the standards of value, the tastes of a certain age, may help to alter beliefs, standards of value, and tastes, because other meanings or suggested implications, not clearly distinguished by those who employ it, gradually become the dominant elements of signification. The word "nature," it need hardly be said, is the most extraordinary example of this.

The contemporary battleground over words like 'nature' and 'environment' is more than a matter of mere semantics, but a leading edge of political conflict, albeit in the realm of ideology where 'we become conscious of political matters and fight them out.' The fight arises precisely because words like 'nature' and 'environment' convey a commonality and universality of concern that is, precisely because of their ambiguity, open to a great diversity of interpretation. 'Environment' is whatever surrounds or, to be more precise, whatever exists in the surroundings of some being that is *relevant* to the state of that being at a particular moment. Plainly, the 'situatedness' of a being and its internal conditions and needs have as much to say about the definition of environment as the surrounding conditions themselves, while the criteria of relevance can also vary widely. Yet each and everyone of us is situated in an 'environment' and all of us therefore have some sense of what an 'environmental issue' is all about.

Over recent years a rough convention has emerged, however, which circumscribes 'environmental issues' to a particular subset of possible meanings, primarily focusing on the relationship between human activity and (a) the condition or 'health' of the bio or ecosystem which supports that activity (b) specific qualities of that ecosystem such as air, water, soil and landscapes and (c) the quantities and qualities of the 'natural resource base' for human activity, including both reproducible and exhaustible assets. But even mildly biocentric interpretations would quite properly challenge the implicit division between 'nature' and 'culture' in this convention. The consequent division between 'environmentalists' who adopt an external and often managerial stance towards the *environment* and 'ecologists' who view human activities as embedded in *nature*, is becoming politically contentious (see Dobson, 1990). In any case, there is increasing public acceptance of the idea that much of what we call 'natural', at least as far as the surface ecology of the globe and its atmosphere is concerned, has been significantly modified by human action (Marsh, 1965; Thomas, 1956; Goudie, 1986). The distinction between built environments of cities and the humanly-modified environments of rural and even remote regions then appears arbitrary except as a particular manifestation of a rather long-standing ideological distinction between the country and the city (Williams, 1973). We ignore the ideological power of that distinction at our peril, however, since it underlies a pervasive anti-urban bias in much ecological rhetoric.

In what follows I shall try to establish a theoretical position from which to try and make sense of 'environmental issues' in the rather circumscribed sense which we now attribute to that term.

II The Issue

I begin with two quotations.

> We abuse land because we regard it as a commodity belonging to us. When we see land as a community to which we belong, we may begin to use it with love and respect. (Aldo Leopold, *The Sand Country Almanac*)

> Where money is not itself the community, it must dissolve the community . . . It is the elementary precondition of bourgeois society that labour should directly produce exchange value, i.e. money; and similarly that money should directly purchase labour, and therefore the labourer, but only insofar as he alienates his activity in the exchange . . . Money thereby directly and simultaneously becomes the *real community*, since it is the general substance for the survival of all, and at the same time the social product of all. (Karl Marx, *Grundrisse*, pp. 224-6).

From Marx's perspective the land ethic that Leopold has in mind is a hopeless quest in a bourgeois society where the community of money prevails. Leopold's land ethic would necessarily entail the construction of an alternative mode of production and consumption to that of capitalism. The clarity and self-evident qualities of that argument have not, interestingly, led to any immediate rapprochement between ecological/ environmentalist and socialist politics; the two have by and large remained antagonistic to each other and inspection of the two quotations reveals why. Leopold defines a realm of thinking and action outside of the narrow constraints of the economy; his is a much more biocentric way of thinking. Working class politics and its concentration on revolutionising political economic processes comes then to be seen as a perpetuation rather than a resolution of the problem as Leopold defines it. The best that socialist politics can achieve, it is often argued, is an environmental (instrumental and managerial) rather than ecological politics. At its worst, socialism stoops to so-called 'promethean' projects in which the 'domination' of nature is presumed both possible and desirable.

My concern in this essay is to see if there are ways to bridge this antagonism and turn it into a creative rather than destructive tension. Is there or ought there to be a place for a distinctively 'ecological' angle to progressive socialist politics? And, if so, what should it be? In what follows I will concentrate on how *values* are assigned to 'nature' as the beginning point for consideration of how 'nature' and the environment can be socially used and construed as an aspect of socialist politics.

III Money Values

Can we put money values on 'nature' and if so how and why? There are three arguments in favour of so doing:

(1) Money is *the* means whereby we all, in daily practice, value significant and very widespread aspects of our environment. Every time we purchase a commodity, we engage with a train of monetary and commodity transactions through which money values are assigned (or, equally importantly, *not* assigned to zero-priced 'free goods') to natural resources or significant environmental features used in production and consumption. We are all (no matter whether we are ecologically minded or not) implicated in putting monetary valuations on 'nature' by virtue of our daily practices.

(2) Money is the only well-understood and *universal* yardstick of value that we currently possess. We all use it and possess both a practical and intellectual understanding (of some sort) as to what it means. It serves to communicate our wants, needs, desires as well as choices, preferences and values, including those to be put specifically upon 'nature', to others. The comparability of different ecological projects (from the building of dams to wild-life or biodiversity conservation measures) depends on the definition of a common yardstick (implicit or acknowledged) to evaluate whether one is more justifiable than another. No satisfactory or universally agreed upon alternative to money has yet been devised. Money, as Marx noted, is a leveller and cynic, reducing a wondrous multidimensional ecosystemic world of use values, of human desires and needs, as well as of subjective meanings, to a common objective denominator which everyone can understand.

(3) Money in our particular society is *the* basic (though by no means the only) language of social power and to speak in money terms is always to speak in a language which the holders of that power appreciate and understand. To seek action on environmental issues often requires that we not only articulate the problem in universal (i.e. money) terms that all can understand, but also that we speak in a voice that is persuasive to those in power. The discourse of 'ecological modernisation' is precisely about

trying to represent environmental issues as profitable enterprise (Hajer, 1992; Weale, 1992). Environmental economics is also a useful and pragmatic tool for getting environmental issues on the agenda. I cite here E. P. Odum's struggle to gain wetland protection legislation in his home state of Georgia, which fell upon deaf ears until he put some plausible but rather arbitrary money values on the worth of wetlands to the state economy (see Gosselink, Odum and Pope, 1974). This persuaded the legislature to formulate, at a relatively early date, extensive wetland protection legislation. There are enough parallel instances (e.g. Margaret Thatcher's sudden conversion to a shade of green politics in 1988) to make it quite evident that political clout attaches to being able to articulate environmental issues in raw money terms.

Exactly how to do that poses difficulties. Pearce, *et al* (1988), for example, operationalise the widely-accepted Brundtland Report (1987) view that 'sustainable' development means that present actions should not compromise the ability of future generations to meet their needs, by arguing that the value of the total stock of assets, both humanly produced (e.g. roads and fields and factories) and given in 'nature' (e.g. minerals, water supplies, etc.), must remain constant from one generation to another. But how can this stock be quantified? It cannot be measured in non-comparable physical terms (i.e. in actual or potential use values), let alone in terms of inherent qualities, so money values (exchange values) provide the only common (universal) denominator.

The difficulties with such a procedure are legion.

1. What, for example, is money? Itself dead and inert, it acquires its qualities as a measure of value by means of a social process. The social processes of exchange which give rise to money, Marx concluded, show that money is a *representation* of socially necessary labour time and price is 'the money name of value'. But the processes are contradictory and money is therefore always a slippery and unreliable representation of value as social labour. Debasement of the coinage, extraordinary rates of inflation in certain periods and places, speculative rages, all illustrate how money can itself be seriously unstable as a representation of value. Money, we say, 'is only worth what it will buy' and we even talk of 'the value of money' which means that we vest in whatever is designated as money some social qualities inherent in everything else that is exchanged. Furthermore, money appears in multiple guises – gold and silver, symbols, tokens, coins, paper (should we use dollars, pounds, sterling, yen, cruzeros, deutschmarks?). There have, furthermore, been historical instances when formal moneys have been so discredited that chocolate, cigarettes, or other forms of tangible goods become forms of currency. To assess the value of 'nature' or 'the flow of environmental goods and services' in these terms poses acute problems that have only partial recompense by way of sophisticated methods of calculation of 'constant prices', 'price deflators' and noble

attempts to calculate constant rates of exchange in a world of remarkable currency volatility.

2. It is difficult to assign anything but arbitrary money values to assets independently of the market prices actually achieved by the stream of goods and services which they provide. As Sraffa long ago observed, this condemns economic valuation to a tautology in which achieved prices become the only indicators we have of the money value of assets whose independent value we are seeking to determine. Rapid shifts in market prices imply equally rapid shifts in asset values. The massive devaluation of fixed capital in the built environment in recent years (empty factories, warehouses, and the like) to say nothing of the effects of the property market crash illustrates the intense volatility of asset valuation depending upon market behaviours and conditions. This principle carries over into valuing 'natural' assets in market economies (consider the value of a Texas oil well during the oil scarcity of 1973-5 versus its value in the oil glut of 1980). The attempt to hand on a constant stock of capital assets (both humanly constructed and naturally occurring) measured in such money terms then appears an unreliable enterprise.

3. Money prices attach to particular things and presuppose exchange-able entities with respect to which private property rights can be estab-lished or inferred. This means that we conceive of entities as if they can be taken out of any ecosystem of which they are a part. We presume to value the fish, for example, independently of the water in which they swim. The money value of a whole ecosystem can be arrived at, according to this logic, only by adding up the sum of its parts, which are construed in an atomistic relation to the whole. This way of pursuing monetary valuations tends to break down, however, when we view the environment as being constructed organically, ecosystemically or dialectically (Norgaard, 1985) rather than as a Cartesian machine with replaceable parts. Indeed, pursuit of monetary valuations commits us to a thoroughly Cartesian-Newtonian-Lockeian and in some respects 'anti-ecological' ontology of how the natural world is constituted (see below).

4. Money valuations presume a certain structure to time as well as to space. The temporal structure is defined through the procedure of dis-counting, in which present value is calculated in terms of a discounted flow of future benefits. There are no firmly agreed-upon rules for discounting and the environmental literature is full of criticism as well as defences of discounting practices in relation to environmental qualities. Volatility in actual interest rates and the arbitrariness of interest rates assigned on, for example, public projects makes valuation peculiarly difficult. Such valua-tion, furthermore, only makes sense if assets are exchangeable so that discounting the future value of, say, the state of energy fluxes in the ocean or the atmosphere is totally implausible. The multiple and often non-linear notions of time which attach to different ecological processes also pose

deep problems. While, for example, it might be possible to discover something about human time preferences (or at least make reasonable assertions about them), the multiple temporalities at work in ecosystems are often of a fundamentally different sort. McEvoy (1988, 222) cites the case of the (non-linear) reproductive cycle of sardine populations in Californian waters – the sardines adapted to 'ecological volatility' by individually 'living long enough to allow each generation to breed in at least one good year.' The stock suddenly collapsed when fishing 'stripped the stock of its natural buffer'. Of course, sensible policies and practices with respect to risk and uncertainty might have avoided such an outcome, but the point remains that the temporality defined by such ecological behaviours is antagonistic to the linear, progressive and very Newtonian conception of time we characteristically use in economic calculation. But even supposing some sort of valuation can be arrived at, profound moral questions remain for while it may be, as Goodin (1992, 67) points out, 'economically efficient for us to shortchange the future' it might well be 'wrong for us to do so' because it 'would amount to unjust treatment of future generations.' For this, and other reasons, 'green value theory' (as Goodin calls it) is deeply antagonistic to discounting practices. 'The concern for the future should add up towards infinity,' writes the deep ecologist Naess (1979, 127).

5. Property arrangements can be of various sorts. They look very different under conditions of, say, strong wetland preservation or land use controls. It is the task of much of contemporary environmental policy to devise a regulatory framework with which to cajole or persuade those holding private property rights to use them in environmentally benign ways, perhaps even paying attention to rather longer time horizons than those which the market discount rate dictates. Challenging though this theoretical, legal and political problem may be, it still presumes the environment has a clear enough structure so that some kind of cost-benefit argument concerning the relation between environmental goods and individualised property rights can be constructed. Appeal to money valuations condemns us, in short, to a world view in which the ecosystem is viewed as an 'externality' to be internalised in human action only via some arbitrarily chosen and imposed price structure or regulatory regime. This is precisely the mode of thinking which allowed Hardin (1986) to articulate the thesis of 'the tragedy of the commons' in which individual users of some common resource, seeking to maximize their individual utility, ultimately destroy that resource through overuse. Persuasive though that argument is on the surface, it breaks down not only when the model of individual utility maximizing behaviour is inappropriate, but also as soon as the sharp dichotomy between internal and external disappears, as occurs within ecosystems as well as in societies in which what we now rather patronisingly call 'respect for nature' is internalised in customary usages, religious beliefs, taboos, and the like (McCay and Acheson, 1987).

6. It is hard in the light of these problems not to conclude that there is something about money valuations that makes them inherently *anti-ecological*, confining the field of thinking and of action to instrumental environmental management. While the point of environmental economics (in both its theory and its practice) is to escape from a too-narrow logic of resource/environmental valuations and to seek ways to put money values on otherwise unpriced assets, it cannot escape from the confines of its own institutional and ontological assumptions (which may well be erroneous) about how the world is ordered as well as valued.

7. Money, lastly, hardly satisfies as an appropriate means to represent the strength or the manifold complexity of human wants, desires, passions and values. 'We see in the nature of money itself something of the essence of prostitution,' says Simmel (1978, 377) and Marx (1973) concurs. Freud took things even further, picking up on our penchant to describe money as something dirty and unclean ('filthy lucre' and 'filthy rich' are common expressions). 'It is possible the contrast between the most precious substance known to men and the most worthless . . . has led to the specific identification of gold with faeces,' he wrote, and shocked his Victorian readers by treating gold as transformed excrement and bourgeois exchange relations as sublimated rituals of the anus. Money, wrote his friend Ferenzci, 'is nothing other than odourless, dehydrated filth that has been made to shine' (Borneman, 1976, 86). We do not have to go so far as Freud and Ferenzci to recognise that there is something morally or ethically questionable or downright objectionable to valuing human life in terms of discounted lifetime earnings and 'nature' (for example, the fate of the grizzly bear and the spotted owl as species allowed to continue to dwell on earth) in monetary terms.

Capitalism is, from this last standpoint, beset by a central moral failing: money supplants all other forms of imagery (religion, traditional religious authority and the like) and puts in its place something that either has no distinctive image because it is colourless, odourless and indifferent in relation to the social labour it is supposed to represent or, if it projects any image at all, connotes dirt, filth, excrement, and prostitution. The effect is to create a moral vacuum at the heart of capitalist society – a colourless self-image of value that can have zero purchase upon social identity. It cannot provide an image of social bonding or of community in the usual sense of that term (even though it is the *real* community in the sense that Marx meant it) and it fails as a central value system to articulate even the most mundane of human hopes and aspirations. Money is what we aspire to for purposes of daily reproduction and in this sense it does indeed become the community; but a community empty of moral passion or of humane meanings. The sentiment that Leopold tried to articulate is, from this standpoint, correct.

At this point, the critic of money valuations, who is nevertheless deeply concerned about environmental degradation, is faced with a dilemma:

eschew the language of daily economic practice and political power and speak in the wilderness, or articulate deeply-held non-monetisable values in a language (i.e. that of money) believed to be inappropriate or fundamentally alien. There is, it seems to me, no immediate solution to the paradox. Zola hit it right in *L'Argent* when he has Madame Caroline say that:

> Money was the dung-heap that nurtured the growth of tomorrow's humanity. Without speculation there could be no vibrant and fruitful undertakings any more than there could be children without lust. It took this excess of passion, all this contemptibly wasted and lost life to ensure the continuation of life . . . Money, the poisoner and destroyer, was becoming the seed-bed for all forms of social growth. It was the manure needed to sustain the great public works whose execution was bringing the peoples of the globe together and pacifying the earth . . . Everything that was good came out of that which was evil.

Although the ultimate moral of Zola's novel is that acceptance of that thesis leads to speculative farce and personal tragedy, no less a theorist than Max Weber sternly and quite properly warned that it was an egregious error to think that only good could come out of good and only evil out of evil. Money may be profoundly inadequate, soulless and 'the root of all evil', but it does not necessarily follow that social and by extension all ecological ills result from market coordinations in which private property, individualism and money valuations operate. On the other hand, we also have sufficient evidence concerning the unrestrained consequences of what Kapp called *The Social Costs of Private Enterprise* to know that it is equally illusory to believe the Adam Smith thesis that good automatically arises out of the necessary evils of the hidden hand of market behaviours. Left to its own devices, Marx (1967, 474-5) argued capitalistic progress 'is a progress in the art, not only of robbing the labourer, but of robbing the soil,' while capitalist technology develops 'only by sapping the original sources of all wealth – the soil and the labourer.'

The conclusion is, then, rather more ambiguous than many might want to accept. First, all the time we engage in commodity exchanges mediated by money (and this proposition holds just as firmly for any prospective socialist society) it will be impossible in practice to avoid money valuations. Secondly, valuations of environmental assets in money terms, while highly problematic and seriously defective, are not an unmitigated evil. We cannot possibly know, however, how good the arbitrary valuations of 'nature' are (once we choose to go beyond the simple idea of an unpriced flow of goods and services) unless we have some alternative notion of value against which to judge the appropriateness or moral worth of money valuations. Nor can we avoid a deep connection between a Newtonian and Cartesian view of the biosphere (a view which many would now seriously challenge as inappropriate to confront ecological problems) and the very basis of economic thinking and capitalistic practices. It is important to stress that the Newtonian-Cartesian view is not in itself wrong, any more than is the parallel Smithian model of atomistic individualism, market behaviours, and property rights. But both are severely limited in their purchase and we are now wise enough to know that there are many spheres of decision and action, such as quantum theory and ecological issues, which cannot be captured in such a format. Newtonian mechanics and Smithian economics may be adequate to building bridges, but they are totally inadequate in trying to determine the ecosystemic impact of such endeavours.

IV Do Values Inhere in Nature?

There has been a long history within bourgeois life of resistance to and search for an alternative to money as a way to express values. Religion, community, family, nation, have all been proffered as candidates, but the particular set of alternatives I here wish to consider are those which in some manner or other see values residing in Nature – for romanticism, environmentalism and ecologism all have strong elements of that ethic built within them. And the idea is not foreign to Marxism either (at least in some of its renditions). When Marx (1971) argued in *The Jewish Question* that money has 'robbed the whole world – both the world of men and nature – of its specific value' and that 'the view of nature attained under the dominion of private property and money is a real contempt for and practical debasement of nature,' he comes very close to endorsing the view that money has destroyed earlier and perhaps recoverable intrinsic natural values.

The advantage of seeing values as residing in nature is that it provides an immediate sense of ontological security and permanence. The natural world provides a rich, variegated, and permanent candidate for induction into the hall of universal and permanent values to inform human action and to give meaning to otherwise ephemeral and fragmented lives (cf. Goodin, 1982, 40). 'It is inconceivable to me,' writes Leopold (1968, pp. 223-4), 'that an ethical relation to land can exist without love, respect and admiration for the land, and a high regard for its value. By value, I of course mean something far broader than mere economic value; I mean value in the philosophical sense' so that 'a thing is right when it tends to preserve the integrity, stability and beauty of the biotic community. It is wrong when it tends otherwise.' But how do we know and what does it mean to say that 'integrity, stability and beauty' are qualities that inhere in nature?

This brings us to the crucial question: if values reside in nature, then how can we know what they are? The routes to such an understanding are many and varied. Intuition, mysticism, contemplation, religious revelation, metaphysics, and personal introspection have all provided, and continue to provide, paths for acquiring such understandings. On the surface, at least, these modes of approach contrast radically with scientific enquiry. Yet, I shall argue, they all necessarily share a commonality. All versions of revealed values in nature rely heavily upon particular human capacities and particular anthropocentric *mediations* (sometimes even upon the charismatic interventions of visionary individuals). Through deployment of highly emotive terms such as love, caring, nurturing, responsibility, integrity, beauty, and the like, they inevitably represent such 'natural' values in distinctively humanised terms, thus producing distinctively human *discourses* about intrinsic values. For some, this 'humanising' of values in nature is both desirable and in itself ennobling, reflecting the peculiarities of our own position in the 'great chain of being' (Lovejoy, 1936). '*Humanity is nature becoming conscious of itself*' was the motto that the anarchist geographer Reclus adopted, clearly indicating that the knowing subject has a creative role to play at least in translating the values inherent in nature into humanised terms. But if, as Ingold (1986, 104) notes, 'the physical world of nature cannot be apprehended as such, let alone confronted and appropriated, save by a consciousness to some degree emancipated from it,' then how can we be sure that human beings are appropriate agents to represent all the values that reside in nature?

The ability to discover intrinsic values depends, then, on the ability of human subjects endowed with consciousness and reflexive as well as practical capacities to become *neutral* mediators of what those values might be. This often leads, as in religious doctrines, to the strict regulation of human practices (e.g. asceticism or practices like yoga) so as to ensure the openness of human consciousness to the natural world. This problem of anthropocentric mediations is equally present within scientific enquiry. But here too the scientist is usually cast in the role of a knowing subject acting as a *neutral* mediator, under the strictest guidelines of certain methods and practices (which sometimes put to shame many a Buddhist), seeking to uncover, understand and represent accurately the processes at work in nature. If values inhere in nature, then science by virtue of its objective procedures should provide one reasonably neutral path for finding out what they might be.

How neutral this turns out to be has been the subject of considerable debate. Consideration of two examples provide some insight into the nature of the difficulty.

(1) The Fable of the Sperm and the Egg

Feminist work has, over the years, revealed widespread resort to gendered metaphors in scientific enquiry. The effect is often to write social ideas about gender relations into scientific representations of the natural world and thereby make it appear as if those social constructions are 'natural'. Merchant (1980) highlights, for example, the gendered imagery with which Francis Bacon approached nature (in essence as a female body to be explored and a female spirit to be dominated and tamed by ruse or force) in his foundational arguments concerning experimental method (an imagery which sheds great light on what is happening in Shakespeare's *The Taming of the Shrew*). These are not, however, isolated or singular examples. Haraway, in an insightful essay on 'Teddy Bear patriarchy' in the New York Museum of Natural History, points out how 'decadence – the threat of the city, civilization, machine – was stayed in the politics of eugenics and the art of taxidermy. The Museum fulfilled its scientific purpose of conservation, preservation, and production of permanence in the midst of an urban world that even at the turn of this century seemed to be on the border of chaos and collapse.' It opposed to this world of troubled sociality a visual technology of exhibits deployed in part as a means to communicate to the outside world a sense of the true organicism of the natural order (founded on hierarchy, patriarchy, class and family) which ought to be the foundation of stability for any social order. In so doing, it explicitly used and continues to use primatology as a means to produce or promote race, class and gender relations of a certain sort.

Martin's (1991) example of the fable of the egg and sperm as depicted in the extensive medical and biological literature on human fertility is particularly instructive. Not only is the female reproductive process (particularly menstruation) depicted as *wasteful* compared to the immensely *productive* capacity of men to generate sperm, but the actual process of fertilization is depicted in terms of a passive female egg, tracked down, captured and claimed as a prize by an active, dynamic, and thrusting male sperm after a difficult and arduous journey to claim its prize. The sperm sounds oddly like an explorer looking for gold or an entrepreneur competing for business (cf Zola's parallel image cited above of financial speculation as the wasteful lust necessary to produce anything). It transpires, however, that the metaphor deployed in scientific studies of human fertility was fundamentally misleading; the sperm is by no means as directed, energetic and brave as it was supposed to be (it turns out to be rather listless and aimless when left to itself) and the egg turns out to play an active role in fertilisation. But it took time for researchers to lay their gendered predilections aside, and when they did so it was mainly by turning the egg into the equivalent of the aggressive *femme fatale* who ensnares, entraps and victimises the male (sperm) in an elaborate spider's web as 'an engulfing, devouring mother.' New data, Martin (1991, 498) suggests, 'did not lead scientists to eliminate gender stereotypes in their descriptions of egg and sperm. Instead, scientists simply began to describe egg and sperm in different, but no less damaging terms.' We plainly cannot draw any inferences whatsoever as to the values inherent in nature by appeal to investigations and enquiries of this sort.

(2) Darwin's Metaphors

Consider, as a second example, the complex metaphors that play against and alongside each other in Darwin's *The Origin of Species*. There is, firstly, the metaphor of stock breeding practices (about which Darwin was very knowledgeable by virtue of his farm background). This, as Young (1985) points out, took the artificial selection procedures which were well understood in stock breeding and placed them in a natural setting, posing the immediate difficulty of who was the conscious agent behind natural selection. There is, secondly, the Malthusian metaphor which Darwin explicitly acknowledged as fundamental to this theory. Entrepreneurial values of competition, survival of the fittest in a struggle for existence then appeared in Darwin's work as 'natural' values to which social Darwinism could later appeal and which contemporary 'common sense' continues to deploy. Todes (1989) in a detailed examination of how Darwin's ideas were received in Russia shows, however, that the Russians almost universally rejected the relevance of the Malthusian metaphor and downplayed intra-specific struggle and competition as an evolutionary mechanism:

> This unifying national style flowed from the basic conditions of Russia's national life – from the very nature of its class structure and political traditions and of its land and climate. Russia's political economy lacked a dynamic pro-laissez faire bourgeoisie and was dominated by landowners and peasants. The leading political tendencies, monarchism and a socialist-oriented populism, shared a cooperative social ethos and a distaste for the competitive individualism widely associated with Malthus and Great Britain. Furthermore, Russia was an expansive, sparsely populated land with a swiftly changing and often severe climate. It is difficult to imagine a setting less consonant with Malthus's notion that organisms were pressed constantly into mutual conflict by population pressures on limited space and resources . . . This combination of anti-Malthusian and non-Malthusian influences deprived Darwin's metaphor of commensensical power and explanatory appeal . . . (Todes, 1989, 168).

Though a great admirer of Darwin, this aspect of his work was not lost on Marx. 'It is remarkable,' he wrote to Engels, 'how Darwin recognises among beasts and plants his English society with its divisions of labour, competition, opening up of new markets, inventions and the Malthusian "struggle for existence."' (Marx and Engels, 1965, 128)

Had Darwin (and Wallace) not been so struck, as were many Englishmen of that era, by the extraordinary fecundity of tropical environments and oriented their thinking to the sub-Arctic regions, and if they had been socially armed with images of what we now call 'the moral economy of the peasantry,' they might well have downplayed, as the Russian evolutionists of all political persuasions did, the mechanisms of competition. They might have emphasised cooperation and mutual aid instead. When Prince Kropotkin arrived in London from Russia, armed with his theories of mutual aid as a potent force in both natural and social evolution, he was simply dismissed as an anarchist crank (in spite of his impressive scientific credentials), so powerful was the aura of social Darwinism at the time. But there is another interesting metaphor which flows into Darwin's work, to some degree antagonistic to that of competition and the struggle for existence. This had to do with species diversification into niches. The guiding metaphor here seems to have been the proliferation of the divisions of labour and the increasing roundaboutness of production occurring within the factory system, about which Darwin was also very knowledgeable given that he was married to Emma, the daughter of industrialist Josiah Wedgewood. In all of these instances, the interplay of socially grounded metaphors and scientific enquiry is such as to make it extremely difficult to extract from the scientific findings any non-socially tainted information on the values that might reside in nature. It is not surprising, therefore, to find Darwin's influential and powerful scientific views being appropriated by a wide range of political movements as a 'natural' basis for their particular political programmes (see Gerratana, 1973). Nor should we be surprised that others, such as Allee and his ecologist colleagues at the University of Chicago in the inter-war years, could use their scientific work on (in this case) animal ecology as a vehicle to support and even promote their communitarian, pacifist and coopera- tive views (Mitman, 1992).

The conclusion, it seems to me, is inescapable. If values reside in nature we have no scientific way of knowing what they are independently of the values implicit in the metaphors deployed in mounting specific lines of scientific enquiry. Even the names we use betray the depth and pervasive- ness of the problem. 'Worker bees' cannot understand the *Communist Manifesto* any more than the 'praying mantis' goes to church; yet the terminology helps naturalise distinctive social power relations and prac- tices (cf Bookchin, 1909b). The language of 'the selfish gene' or 'the blind watchmaker' provide equally vivid social referents of scientific arguments. Rousseau (1973, 65), interestingly, spotted the ruse long ago when he wrote of 'the blunder made by those who, in reasoning on the state of nature, always import into it ideas gathered in a state of society.' Ecologists concerned, for example, to articulate conceptions of equilibrium, plant succession and climax vegetation as properties of the natural world, have reflected as much about the human search for permanence and security as the quest for an accurate and neutral description or theorisation of ecological processes. And the idea of harmony with nature not as a human desire but as a nature-imposed necessity likewise smacks of the view that to be natural is to be harmonious rather than conflictual and contradictory both of which are quickly dubbed as artificial, the result of 'disturbance' and the like. We have loaded upon nature, often without knowing it, in our science as in our poetry, much of the alternative desire for value to that implied by money.

But the choice of values lies within us and not in nature. We see, in short, only those values which our value-loaded metaphors allow us to see in our studies of the natural world. Harmony and equilibrium; beauty, integrity and stability; cooperation and mutual aid; ugliness and violence; hierarchy and order; competition and the struggle for existence; turbulence and unpredictable dynamic change; atomistic causation; dialectics and principles of complementarity; chaos and disorder; fractals and strange attractors; all of them can be identified as 'natural values' not because they are arbitrarily assigned to nature, but because no matter how ruthless, pristine and rigorously 'objective' our method of enquiry may be, the framework of interpretation is given in the metaphor rather than in the evidence. From contemporary reproductive and cell biology we will learn that the world is necessarily hierachically ordered into command and control systems that look suspiciously like a Fordist factory system while from contemporary immunology we will conclude that the world is ordered as a fluid communications system with dispersed command-control-intelligence networks which look much more like contemporary models of flexible industrial and commercial organisation (Martin, 1992). When, therefore, it is claimed that 'nature teaches', what usually follows, Williams (1980, 70) remarks, 'is selective, according to the speaker's general purpose.'

The solution, here, cannot be to seek scientific enquiry without metaphors. Their deployment (like the parallel deployment of models) lies at the root of the production of all knowledge. 'Metaphoric perception,' say Bohm and Peat (1989, 35-41), is 'fundamental to all science' both in extending existing thought processes as well as in penetrating into 'as yet unknown domains of reality, which are in some sense implicit in the metaphor.' We can, therefore, only reflect critically upon the properties of the metaphors in use. And then we find that the values supposedly inherent in nature are always properties of the metaphors rather than inherent in nature. 'We can never speak about nature,' says Capra (1985, 77) 'without, at the same time, speaking about ourselves.'

V The Moral Community and Environmental Values

Deep ecologists have tended to abandon the idea of values purely intrinsic to nature in recent years (cf Dobson, 1990, 57-63). They have in part done so because of their readings in quantum theory and the translation of the ideas of Bohr and Heisenberg into a distinctive form of ecological discourse in Capra's highly influential *Tao of Physics* and *The Turning Point*. The parallel turn to metaphysics, hermeneutics and phenomenology as means to present and discover the values that should attach to nature emphasizes the powers of the knowing subject. Fox, for example, writes:

> The appropriate framework of discourse for describing and presenting deep ecology is not one that is fundamentally to do with the value of the non-human world, but rather one that is fundamentally to do with the nature and possibilities of the self, or, we might say, the question of who we are, can become and should become in the larger scheme of things.

The word 'should' here suggests that values do attach to the broader biotic community of which we are a part, but the means by which we discover them depend fundamentally on the human capacity for 'Self-realization' (as opposed to the narrower sense of 'ego-fulfilment' or 'self-realization' as understood in bourgeois society) within rather than without nature. The 'deep ecology' literature here tacitly appeals to the notion of a 'human essence' or a 'human potentiality' (or in Marx's language, a 'species being' whose qualities have yet to be fully realized) from which humanity has become fundamentally alienated (both actually and potentially) through separation from 'nature'. The desire to restore that lost connection (severed by modern technology, commodity production, a promethean or utilitarian approach to nature, the 'community' of money flows, and the like) then lies at the root of an intuitive, contemplative and phenomenological search for 'Self-realisation'. If values are 'socially and economically anchored,' Naess (1989, 45) argues, then the philosophical task is to challenge those instrumental values which alienate. Through 'elaboration of a philosophical system' we can arrive at a 'comprehensive value clarification and disentanglement,' so as to spark a collective movement that can achieve 'a substantial reorientation of our whole civilisation.'

All sorts of philosophical, metaphysical, and religious 'clarifications' are here available to us. Heidegger, for example, offers considerable sustenance to contemporary ecological thinking (Steiner, 1992, 136). Interestingly, his fundamental objections to modernity echo not only Marx's arguments against the fetishism of commodities, but also capture much of the sensibility that informs a broad spectrum of ecological metaphysics:

> the object-character of technological dominion spreads itself over the earth ever more quickly, ruthlessly, and completely. Not only does it establish all things as producible in the process of production; it also delivers the products of production by means of the market. In self-assertive production, the humanness of man and the thingness of things dissolve into the calculated market value of a market which not only spans the whole earth as a world market, but also, as the will to will, trades in the nature of Being and thus subjects all beings to the trade of a calculation that dominates most tenaciously in those areas where there is no need of numbers (Heidegger, 1971, 114-15).

Heidegger's response to this condition, as indeed is characteristic of much of this wing of the ecological movement, is to withdraw entirely into a metaphysics of *Being* as a way of *dwelling* that unfolds into a form of *building* that cultivates, cherishes, protects, preserves and nurtures the environment so as to bring it closer to us. The political project is to recover that 'rootedness' of 'man' which 'is threatened today as its core.' Instead of nature becoming 'a gigantic gasoline station' it must be seen as 'the serving bearer, blossoming and fruiting, spreading out in rock and water, rising up into plant and animal.' Mortals, Heidegger concludes, 'dwell in that they save the earth' but 'saving does not only snatch something from danger. To save really means to set something free into its own presencing.' The slogans of *Earth First* (e.g. 'set the rivers free!'), while they do not derive from Heidegger appeal to exactly such sentiments. All genuine works of art, Heidegger (1966, 47-8) goes on to argue, depend upon their rootedness in native soil and the way in which they are constructed in the spirit of *dwelling*. We are, he says, 'plants which – whether we like to admit it to ourselves or not – must with our roots rise out of the earth in order to bloom in the ether and bear fruit.' *Dwelling* is the capacity to achieve a spiritual unity between humans and things. Place construction should be about the recovery of roots, the recovery of the art of dwelling with nature.

Heidegger's 'ontological excavations' focus attention on 'a new way to speak about and care for our human nature and environment', so that 'love of place and the earth are scarcely sentimental extras to be indulged only when all technical and material problems have been resolved. They are part of being in the world and prior, therefore, to all technical matters' (Relph, 1989, 27-9). The relationship proposed here is active not passive. 'Dwelling,' writes Norberg-Schulz (1980, 15-21) 'above all presupposes *identification* with the environment' so that the 'existential purpose of building (architecture) is therefore to make a site become a place, that is to uncover the meanings potentially present in the given environment.' Human beings 'receive' the environment and make it focus in buildings and things that 'explain' it and 'make its character manifest' in a *place* that simultaneously acquires and imprints back on us a particular identity.

Heidegger's ideas are paralleled by movements in North America towards a bioregional ethic, in which Leopold's recommendation that we enlarge the boundaries of community 'to include soils, waters, plants, and animals, or collectively: the land,' is taken quite literally as a programme for living with nature in place. The ideals of a place-bound environmental identity are strong. Berg and Dasmann (cited in Alexander, 1990, 163) say this means:

> learning to live-in-place in an area that has been disrupted and injured through past exploitation. It involves becoming native to a place through becoming aware of the particular ecological relationships that operate within and around it. It means understanding activities and evolving social behaviour that will enrich the life of that place, restore its life-supporting systems, and establish an ecologically and socially sustainable pattern of existence within it. Simply stated it involves becoming fully alive in and with a place. It involves applying for membership in a biotic community and ceasing to be its exploiter.

Bioregionalism as a cultural movement therefore 'celebrates the particular, the unique and often indescribable features of a place. It celebrates this through the visual arts, music, drama and symbols which convey the *feeling* of place.' (Mills, cited in Alexander, ibid).

We arrive here at the core of what Goodin (1992, chapter 2) calls a *green theory of value*. It is a set of sentiments and propositions which provides a 'unified moral vision' running, in various guises, throughout almost all ecological and green political thinking. It has radical, liberal and quite conservative manifestations as we shall shortly see. And by virtue of its strong attachment of moral community to the experience of place, it frequently directs environmental politics towards a preservation and enhancement of the achieved qualities of places.

But the notion of a moral community also proves problematic. Consider, for example, how it plays in the work of an otherwise thoroughly liberal commentator like Sagoff (1988). While individuals often act as purely self-interested and atomistically constituted economic agents selfishly pursuing their own goals, he argues, they not only can but frequently do act in completely different ways as members of a 'moral community' particularly with respect to environmental issues. In the American case he concludes that:

> 'Social regulation most fundamentally has to do with the identity of a nation – a nation committed historically, for example, to appreciate and preserve a fabulous natural heritage and to pass it on reasonably undisturbed to future generations. This is not a question of what we *want*; it is not exactly a question of what we *believe in*; it is a question of what we *are*. There is no theoretical way to answer such a question; the answer has to do with our history, our destiny, and our self-perception as a people' (Sagoff, 1988, 17).

There are a variety of points to be made here. First, this is a strongly communitarian version of the 'Self-realization' thesis advanced by Fox (see above). Secondly, it has as much to say about the construction of a nation's identity as it does about the environment. And here we immediately hit upon a difficulty with the moral suasion and political implications of distinctively green values. For they are inevitably implicated in the construction of particular kinds of 'moral community' that can just as easily be nationalist, exclusionary and in some instances violently fascistic as they can be democratic, decentralised and anarchist. Bramwell (1989), for example, points out the Nazi connection, not only via Heidegger (whose role is more emblematic than real) but also via the building of a distinctively fascist tradition around German romanticism, themes about 'Blood and Soil' and the like, incidentally noting the extensive and often innovative conservation and afforestation programmes that the Nazis pursued. Even if Bramwell overstates the case, it is not hard to see how distinctive attitudes to particular environments can become powerfully implicated in the building of any sense of nationalist or communitarian identity. Sagoff's insensitivity in using the term America when he means the United States and his tendency to depopulate the continent of indigenous peoples and to ignore its class, gender and racial structure in his account of the nation's encounter with the environment contains many of the same disturbing exclusions.

Environmental politics then becomes caught up in handing down to future generations a sense of national identity grounded in certain environmental traits. Put the other way round, nationalism without some appeal to environmental imagery and identity is a most unlikely configuration. If the forest is a symbol of German nation, then forest die-back is a threat to national identity. This fact played a key role in sparking the contemporary German Green movement but it has also posed considerable difficulty for that movement in pointing up the way contemporary ecological sensibilities have their roots in traditions that also prompted the Nazis to be the first 'radical environmentalists in charge of a state' (cited in Bramwell, 1989, 11). Even an ecological radical like Spretnak (1985, 232) is then forced to recognize that 'the spiritual dimension of Green politics is an extremely charged and problematic area in West Germany.'

The point here is not to see *all* ideas about 'moral community,' bio-regionalism or place-bound thinking (e.g. nationalism and imagined community) as necessarily exclusionary or neo-Nazi. Raymond Williams, for example, builds elements of such thinking into his socialism. In his novels the whole contested terrain of environmental imagery, place-bound ideals, and the disruption of both by contemporary capitalism become meaningful arguments about the roots of alienation and the problematics of the human relation to nature. The task, then, is to try and articulate the social, political, institutional and economic circumstances that transform such place-bound sentiments concerning a special relation to 'nature' into exclusionary and sometimes radical neo-Nazi directions. The evocation of the Nazi connection by Bramwell (though itself a manifestation of conservative hostility to the Greens as 'new authoritarians antagonistic to free-market liberalism') is here very helpful, since it raises the question of the degree to which strong leanings towards reactionary rather than progressive trajectories might always in the last instance be implicated in green theories of value. In any case, it quickly becomes apparent that environmental values drawn from a moral community have as much to say about the politics of community as they do about the environment.

Political Values and Environmental-Ecological Issues

One of the more interesting exercises to undertake in enquiring into the environmental-ecological debate, is to inspect arguments not for what they have to say about the environment, but for what it is they say about the 'community' and political-economic organisation. In so doing, an impressive array of alternative forms of social organisation are invoked as seemingly 'necessary' to solve the issues at hand, along with an extraordinary display of disparate culprits and villains needing to be overthrown if our present ecodrama is to have a happy rather than tragic ending. 'Environmentalists,' notes Paehlke (1989, 194), not only 'occupy almost every position on the traditional right-to-left ideological spectrum,' but also can adapt to diverse political positions while simultaneously claiming they are beyond politics in the normal sense. Yet, again and again, 'the authority of nature and her laws' is claimed either to justify the existing condition of society or 'to be the foundation stone of a new society that will solve ecological problems.' (Grundmann, 1991b, 114). What is often at stake in ecological and environmentalist arguments,' Williams (1980, 71) suggests, 'is the ideas of different kinds of societies.'

Part of the problem here is that environmental-ecological arguments, precisely because of their diversity and generality are open to a vast array of uses to which environmentalists and ecologists would almost certainly object. Their rhetoric gets mobilized for a host of special purposes, ranging from advertisements for Audi cars, tooth pastes and supposedly 'natural' flavours (for foods) and 'natural' looks (mainly for women) to more specific targets of social control and investment in 'sustainable development' or 'nature conservation.' But the other side of that coin is that ecologists and to some degree even environmentalists of a more managerial persuasion, tend to leave so many loopholes in their arguments, litter their texts with so many symptomatic silences, ambiguities and ambivalences that it becomes almost impossible to pin down their socio-political programmes with any precision even though their aim may be 'nothing less than a non-violent revolution to overthrow our whole polluting, plundering and materialistic industrial society and, in its place, to create a new economic and social order which will allow human beings to live in harmony with the planet.' (Porritt and Winner, cited in Dobson, 1990, 7).

My intention in what follows is not to provide some firm classification or indeed to engage in critical evaluation of any particular kind of politics (all of them are open to serious objections), but to illustrate the incredible political diversity to which environmental-ecological opinion is prone.

A. Authoritarianism

Ophuls (1977, 161) writes: 'whatever its specific form, the politics of the sustainable society seem likely to move us along the spectrum from libertarianism towards authoritarianism' and we have to accept that 'the golden age of individualism, liberty and democracy is all but over.' Faced with escalating scarcities, Heilbroner (1974, 161) likewise argues, there is only one kind of solution: a social order 'that will blend a "religious" orientation and a "military" discipline (that) may be repugnant to us, but I suspect it offers the greatest promise for bringing about the profound and painful adaptations that the coming generations must make.' While their personal commitments are overtly liberal (and in Heilbroner's case so-cialistic) both authors reluctantly concede the necessity of some kind of centralised authoritarianism as a 'realistic' response to natural resource limits and the painful adaptations that such limits will inevitably force upon us. In the case of the strongly Malthusian wing of the ecological movement, and Garrett Hardin is probably the best representative, the appeal to authoritarian solutions is explicit as the only possible political solution to the 'tragedy of the commons.' Most of the writing in this genre presumes that resource scarcities (and consequent limits to growth) and population pressure lie at the heart of the environmental-ecological issue. Since these issues were paramount in the early 1970s, this style of argument was then also at its height. In recent years, however, authoritarian solutions to the environmental crisis have been abandoned by the movement (Dobson, 1990, 26). But there is always an authoritarian edge somewhere in ecological politics.

B. Corporate and State Managerialism

A weak version of the authoritarian solution rests upon the application of techniques of scientific-technical rationality within an administrative state armed with strong regulatory and bureaucratic powers in liaison with 'big' science and big corporate capital. The centerpiece of the argument here is that our definition of many ecological problems (e.g. acid rain, the ozone hole, global warming, pesticides in the food chain, etc.) is necessarily science-led and that solutions equally depend upon the mobilization of scientific expertise and corporate technological skills embedded within a rational (state-led) process of political-economic decision-making. 'Ecological modernization' (Hajer, 1992; Weale, 1992, chapter 3) is the ideological watchword for such a politics. Conservation and environmental regulation (at global as well as at national scale) would here be interpreted as both rational and efficient resource management for a sustainable future. Certain sectors of corporate capital, particularly those who stand to benefit from providing the technology necessary for global monitoring of planetary health, find the imagery of global management or 'planetary medicine' which can be derived from Lovelock's (1988) *Gaia* thesis very attractive, for example. It is perhaps no accident that Hewlett Packard funded much of Lovelock's research and that IBM has taken the lead in the 'greening' of corporate politics, since both corporations will likely play a leading role in providing the technology for global monitoring. 'Sustainability' here applies, however, as much to corporate power as to the ecosystem.

C. Pluralistic Liberalism

Democratic rights and freedoms (particularly of speech and opinion) are sometimes regarded as essential to ecological politics precisely because of the difficulty of defining in any omniscient or omnipotent way what a proper environmental-ecological policy might be. Open and perpetual negotiation over environmental-ecological issues in a society where diverse pressure groups (such as Greenpeace) are allowed to flourish is seen as the only way to assure that the environmental issue is always kept on the agenda. Whoever wants to speak for or about 'nature' can, and institutions are created (such as environmental impact statements and environmental law) to permit contestation over the rights of trees and owls. Consensus about environmental issues, and therefore the best bet for environmental protection, can best be reached only after complex negotiation and power plays between a variety of interest groups. But consensus is at best only a temporary moment in a deeply contested and pluralistic politics concerning the values to be attributed to nature and how to view ecological change.

D. Conservativism

In some of the ecological literature the principle of prudence and respect for tradition plays a a leading role. Human adaptations to and of natural environments have been arrived at over centuries and should not be unnecessarily disturbed. Conservation and preservation of existing landscapes and usages, sometimes argued for by explicit appeal to aesthetic judgements, give such a framework a conservative ring (see e.g. Collingwood, 1960). But arguments of this sort have a radical edge. They can be strongly anti-capitalistic (against development) and, when placed in an international setting, they can also be strongly anti-imperialistic. Tradition ought presumably to be respected everywhere, so that all-out modernisation is always regarded as problematic. Considerable sympathy can then be extended towards, say, indigenous peoples under siege from commodification and exchange relations. All of this has its romantic side, but it can also produce a hard-headed politics of place that is highly protective of a given environment. The issue is not non-intervention in the environment, but preservation of traditional modes of social and environmental interaction precisely because these have been found in some sense or other to work, at least for some (usually but not always elite) groups. The preservation of the political power and values of such groups is just as important here, of course, as environmental considerations.

E. Moral Community

The complex issues which arise when ideals of 'moral community' are invoked have already been examined. Many 'communities' evolve some rough consensus as to what their moral obligations are with respect to modes of social relating as well as to ways of behaving with respect to the 'rights of nature' (see Nash, 1989). While often contested, by virtue of the internal heterogeneity of the community or because of pressure towards social change, these moral precepts concerning, for example, the relation to nature (expressed increasingly in the field of 'environmental ethics') can become an important ideological tool in the attempt to forge community solidarities (e.g. nationalist sentiments) and to gain empowerment. This is the space *par excellence* of moral debate (see, e.g. Attfield, 1991) on environmental issues coupled with the articulation of communitarian politics and values that centre on ideals of civic virtues that carry over to certain conceptions of a virtuous relation to nature.

F. Ecosocialism

While there is a definite tendency in socialist circles to look upon environmentalism as a middle class and bourgeois issue and to regard proposals for zero growth and constraints on consumption with intense suspicion (see Benton, 1989, 52, for a good summary) there are enough overlaps in enough areas to make ecosocialism a feasible political project (though it is still a relatively minor current within most mainstream socialist movements). Some environmental issues, such as occupational health and safety, are of intense concern to workers, while many ecological groups accept that environmental problems can be 'traced back to the capitalist precept that the choice of production technology is to be governed solely by private interest in profit maximization of market share' (Commoner, 1990, 219). 'If we want ecological sanity,' assert Haila and Levins (1992, 251), 'we have to struggle for social justice.' This means social control of production technology and the means of production, control over the 'accumulation for accumulation's sake, production for production's sake' capitalist system which lies at the root of many environmental issues, and a recognition that 'the future of humanity simply cannot build on pleasant life for a few and suffering for the majority' (Haila and Levins, 1992, 227). This places the environmental issue firmly within the socialist orbit. Those socialists (see O'Connor, 1988) who accept that there is an ecological crisis, then argue that a second route to socialism is available; one that highlights the contradiction between the social organisation of production and the (ecological) conditions of production, rather than class contradictions. The necessity for socialism is then in part given because only in such a society can thorough, enduring and socially just solutions be found to the environmental crisis.

G. Ecofeminism

The nature-nurture controversy has been nowhere more thoroughly debated than in the feminist movement and in ecofeminism we find a diverse set of opinions on how to connect the environmental-ecological issue with feminist politics. In radical ecofeminism, for example, the devaluation and degradation of nature is seen as deeply implicated in the parallel devaluation and degradation of women. The political response is to celebrate rather than deny the web-like interrelations between women and nature through the development of rituals and symbolism as well as an ethic of caring, nurturing and procreation. In this equation, the feminism is as prominent, if not more so, than the ecology and solutions to ecological problems are seen as dependent upon the acceptance of certain kinds of feminist principles.

H. Decentralised communitarianism

Most contemporary ecological movements, Dobson, (1990, 25) argues, eschew authoritarian solutions on principle and 'argue for a radically participatory form of society in which discussion takes place and explicit consent is asked for and given across the widest possible range of political and social issues.' Their politics generally derive inspiration from 'the self-reliant community modelled on anarchist lines' (O'Riordan, 1981, 307) and writers like Bookchin, Goldsmith and a host of others (including the German Green party) have tried to articulate the form of social relations which should prevail within such self-reliant communities that could become, by virtue of their scale, 'closer' to nature. Egalitarianism, non-hierarchical forms of organisation and widespread local empowerment and participation in decision-making are usually depicted as the political norm (Dauncey, 1988). Decentralisation and community empowerment, coupled with a certain degree of bioregionalism, is then seen as the only effective solution to an alienated relation to nature and alienation in social relationships.

The array of ecological politics I have here outlined must be supplemented, however, by an ever vaster and much more complex array of special pleading, in which environmental/ecological issues or requirements are invoked for very particular social purposes. Scientists, for example, hungry for funding as well as for attention, may create environmental issues that reflect as much about the political-economy and sociology of science as they do about the condition of the environment. Robert May (1992), a Royal Society Research Professor writing on the evident urgency of taking measures to conserve biological diversity, focuses, for example, as much on the underfunding of taxonomy (relative to physics) as on how to define the importance of, or deal with, the issue. While on the one hand scientific ignorance is clearly a barrier to proper identification of what the relevant issues or solutions might be, the perpetual claims for more funding sometimes deservedly provoke scepticism.

Jacks and Whyte (1939, 261-2) provide another and even more insidious example. Writing in 1939, these two highly respected soil scientists, deeply concerned about soil erosion in Africa, argued that:

> A feudal type of society in which the native cultivators would be to some extent tied to the lands of their European overlords seems the most generally suited to meet the needs of the soil in the present state of African development. Africa cannot be expected to accept feudalism without a struggle; in parts of British Africa it would mean jettisoning the promising experiment of Indirect Rule, everywhere it would mean denying to the natives some of the liberty and opportunities for material advancement to which their labours should entitle them. But it would enable the people who have been the prime cause of erosion and who have the means and ability to control it to assume responsibility for the soil. Self-interest, untrammelled by fears of native rivalry, would ensure that the responsibility was carried out in the ultimate interests of the soil. At present, humanitarian considerations for the natives prevent Europeans from winning the attainable position of dominance over the soil. Humanity may perhaps be the higher ideal, but the soil demands a dominant, and if white men will not and black men cannot assume the position, the vegetation will do so, by the process of erosion finally squeezing out the whites.

Both blunt and startling, this statement illustrates how, in the name of the environment, all kinds of restrictions should be put upon the rights of 'others' while conferring rights (and obligations) on those who supposedly have the knowledge and the high technology to control the problem. While few would now dare to be so blatant, there is a strong strain of this kind of thinking in World Bank arguments and even in such a seemingly progressive document as the Brundtland report. Control over the resources of others, in the name of planetary health, sustainability of preventing environmental degradation, is never too far from the surface of many western proposals for global environmental management. Awareness of precisely that potentiality stimulates a good deal of resistance in developing countries to any form of environmentalism emanating from the West.

Similar issues arise whenever the environmental-ecological issues get converted into a purely aesthetic question. The special issue of *Fortune* devoted to the environment in 1970, for example, contained a strong argument for the redevelopment of the downtowns of the U.S.A., along what we would now call 'postmodern' lines, invoking environmental quality (usually depicted as user-friendly and as tree-lined or waterfront spaces) as its primary goal. The whole contemporary 'culture of nature' as Wilson (1992) calls it, is a very cultivated and hard-sold taste.

A cynical observer might be tempted to conclude that discussion of the environmental issue is nothing more than a covert way of introducing particular social and political projects by raising the spectre of an ecological crisis or of legitimising solutions by appeal to the authority of nature-imposed necessity. I would want, however, to draw a somewhat broader conclusion: all ecological projects (and arguments) are simultaneously political-economic projects (and arguments) and vice versa. Ecological arguments are never socially neutral any more than socio-political arguments are ecologically neutral. Looking more closely at the way ecology and politics interrelate then becomes imperative if we are to get a better handle on how to approach environmental/ecological questions.

VIII Historical-Geographical Materialism and the Political-Economy of Socio-Ecological Projects

There is an extraordinarily rich record of the historical geography of socio-ecological change that sheds much light on the ways in which socio-political and ecological projects intertwine with and at some point become indistinguishable from each other. The archive of such materials from archaeology (see, e.g. Butzer, 1982), anthropology (see e.g. Bennett, 1976; Ellen, 1982; Ingold, 1986), geography (Thomas, 1956; Goudie, 1986) and more recently history (cf. the debate in *Journal of American History*, 1990) is extensive indeed. Yet much of the contemporary debate on environmental-ecological issues, for all of its surface devotion to ideals of multidisciplinarity and 'depth', operates as if these materials either do not exist or, if they do, exist only as a repository of anecdotal evidence in support of particular claims. Systematic work is relatively rare and that which does exist (e.g. Butzer, 1982) has not been anywhere near as central to discussion as it should. The debate now arising within Marxism – between, for example, Benton (1989; 1992) and Grundmann (1991a and b) – operates at a level of historical-geographical abstraction that is most un-Marxist. Even a journal like *Capitalism, Socialism, Nature*, set up to explore green issues from a socialist perspective, is long on theory and anecdotal evidence and short on attempts to systematise across the historical-geographical record.

An impressionistic survey illustrates well how societies strive to create ecological conditions for themselves which are not only conducive to their own survival but also both manifestations and instanciations 'in nature' of their particular social relations. Since no society can accomplish such a task without encountering unintended ecological consequences, the contradiction between social and ecological change can become highly problematic, even from time to time putting the very survival of the society concerned at risk. This latter point was made long ago by Engels:

> Let us not, however, flatter ourselves overmuch on account of our human victories over nature. For each such victory nature takes its revenge on us. Each victory, it is true, in the first place brings about the results we expected, but in the second and third places it has quite different, unforseen effects which only too often cancel the first . . . Thus at every step we are reminded that we by no means rule over nature like a conqueror over a foreign people, like someone standing outside of nature – but that we, with flesh, blood and brain, belong to nature, and exist in its midst, and that all our mastery of it consists in the fact that we have the advantage over all other creatures of being able to learn its laws and apply them correctly.

This implies the sheer necessity of *always* taking the duality of social and ecological change seriously. The historian Cronon (1983, 13-14) argues, for example, that:

> An ecological history begins by assuming a dynamic and changing relationship between environment and culture, one as apt to produce contradictions as continuities. Moreover, it assumes that the interactions of the two are dialectical. Environment may initially shape the range of choices available to a people at a given moment but then culture reshapes environment responding to those choices. The reshaped environment presents a new set of possibilities for cultural reproduction, thus setting up a new cycle of mutual determination. Changes in the way people create and re-create their livelihood must be analysed in terms of changes not only in their *social relations* but in their *ecological* ones as well.

All of which is another way of stating Marx's and Engels' (1976, 55) adage that the 'antithesis between nature and history is created' only when 'the relation of man to nature is excluded from history.' Cronon's study of colonial settlements in New England raises another issue, however. It shows how an environment that was the product of more than 10,000 years of Indian occupation and forest use (promoting, through burning, the forest edge conditions which tend to be so species diverse and rich) was misread by the settlers as pristine, virginal, rich and underutilised by indigenous peoples. The implantation of European (i.e. Lockeian) institutions of governance and property rights (coupled with distinctively European aspirations towards accumulation of wealth) wrought, furthermore, an ecological transformation of such enormity that indigenous populations were deprived of the ecological basis for their way of life. The annihilation of that way of life (and thereby of Indian peoples) was, therefore, as much an ecological as military or political event. In part this had to do with the introduction of new disease regimes (smallpox in particular) but changes in and on the land also make it impossible to sustain a nomadic and highly flexible indigenous mode of production and reproduction.

One path towards consolidation of a particular set of social relations, therefore, is to undertake an ecological transformation which requires the reproduction of those social relations in order to sustain it. Worster (1985b) doubtless exaggerates in his flamboyant projection onto the American West of Wittfogel's theses on the relation between large-scale irrigation schemes and despotic forms of government, but his basic argument is surely correct. Once the original proposals for a communitarian, decentralised, 'bio-regional', river-basin-confined settlement system for the American west, drawn up by the geologist John Wesley Powell at the end of the nineteenth century, were rejected by a Congress dominated by large-scale corporate interests (Powell being thoroughly vilified in the process), those interests sought to assure their own reproduction through construction of dams, mega-water projects of all sorts and vast transformations of the Western ecosystem. Sustaining such a grandiose ecological project came to depend crucially upon the creation and maintenance of centralised state powers and certain class relations (the formation and perpetuation, for example, of large scale agribusiness and an oppressed landless agrarian proletariat). The consequent subversion of the Jeffersonian dream of agrarian democracy has ever since created intense contradictions in the body politic of states like California (see e.g. Gottlieb 1988 or Polanski's film *Chinatown*). But here another implication (notably absent in much of Cronon's work) follows: contradictions in the social relations (in Worster's case of class, but gender, religion, etc. can also be just as significant) entail social contradictions on the land and *within* ecosystemic projects themselves. Not only do the rich occupy privileged niches in the habitat while the poor tend to work and live in the more toxic and hazardous zones, but the very design of the transformed ecosystem is redolent of its social relations. Conversely, projects set up in purely ecological terms – one thinks of the so-called 'green revolution' for example – have all manner of distributive and social consequences (in the green revolution case the concentration of land holdings in a few hands and the creation of a landless agrarian proletariat).

Created ecosystems tend to both instanciate and reflect, therefore, the social systems that gave rise to them, though they do not do so in non-contradictory (i.e. *stable*) ways. This simple principle ought to weigh much more heavily than it does upon all angles of environmental-ecological debate. It is a principle which Lewontin (1982) argues has been forgotten as much in biology as in social science:

We cannot regard evolution as the "solution" by species of some predetermined environmental "problems" because it is the life activities of the species themselves that determine both the problems and solutions simultaneously . . . Organisms within their individual lifetimes and in the course of their evolution as a species do not *adapt* to environments; they *construct* them. They are not simply *objects* of the laws of nature, altering themselves to the inevitable, but active *subjects* transforming nature according to its laws.

It is pure idealism, for example, to suggest that we can somehow abandon in a relatively costless way the immense existing ecosystemic structures of, say, contemporary capitalistic urbanization in order to 'get back close to nature'. Such systems are a re-worked form of 'second nature' that cannot be allowed to deteriorate or collapse without courting ecological disaster for our own species. Their proper management (and in this I include their long-term socialistic or ecological transformation into something completely different) may require transitional political institutions, hierarchies of power relations and systems of governance that could well be anathema to both ecologists and socialists alike. But this occurs because, in a fundamental sense, there is in the final analysis nothing *unnatural* about New York City and sustaining such an ecosystem even in transition entails an inevitable compromise with the forms of social organisation and social relations which produced it.

To term urbanization a 'created ecosystem' may sound somewhat odd. But human activity cannot be viewed as external to ecosystemic projects. To view it so makes no more sense than trying to study pollination without bees or the pre-colonial ecosystem of the northeastern USA without the beaver. Human beings, like all other organisms, are 'active *subjects* transforming nature according to its laws' and are always in the course of adapting to the ecosystems they themselves construct. It is fundamentally mistaken, therefore, to speak of the impact of society on the ecosystem as if these are two separate systems in interaction with each other. The typical manner of depicting the world around us in terms of a box labelled 'society' in interaction with a box labelled 'environment' not only makes little intuitive sense (try drawing the boundary between the boxes in your own daily life) but it also has just as little fundamental theoretical and historical justification.

Money flows and commodity movements, for example, have to be regarded as fundamental to contemporary ecosystems, not only because of the accompanying geographical transfer of plant and animal species from one environment to another (see Crosby, 1986), but also because these flows form a coordinating network that keeps contemporary ecosystems reproducing and changing in the particular way they do. If these flows ceased tomorrow, then the disruption within the world's ecosystems would be enormous. And as the flows shift and change their character, so the creative impulses embedded in any socio-ecological system will also shift and change in ways that may be stressful, contradictory or harmonic as the case may be. Here, too, Cronon's (1992) consideration of Chicago as a city operating as a fundamental exchange point between and transformative influence within the ecosystems of North America provides an interesting case study. It in effect translates and extends Smith's theses (see Smith, 1990 and O'Keefe and Smith, 197) concerning 'the production of nature' through commodity exchange and capital accumulation into a detailed historical-geographical narrative.

The category 'environmental or ecological movement' may also for this reason be a misnomer particularly when applied to resistances of indigenous peoples to ecological change. Such resistances may not be based, as many in the West might suppose, upon some deep inner need to preserve a distinctive and unalienated relation to nature or to keep intact valued symbols of ancestry and the like, but upon a much clearer recognition that an ecological transformation imposed from outside (as happened in colonial New England or as has more recently happened to rubber tappers in the Amazon) will destroy indigenous modes of production. Guha (1989, xii), for example, in his study of the Chipko 'tree-hugging' movement in the Himalayas against commercial logging and high-tech forest yield management, shows that the 'most celebrated "environmental" movement in the Third World is viewed by its participants as being above all a *peasant* movement in defence of traditional rights in the forest and only secondarily, if at all, an "environmental" or "feminist" movement.' Yet, to the degree that a 'homogenizing urban-industrial culture' is generating its own distinctive forms of ecological and cultural contradictions and crises, the Chipko, precisely by virtue of their ecological practices, 'represent one of the most innovative responses to the ecological and cultural crisis of modern society' (Guha, 1989, 196).

Indigenous groups can, however, also be totally unsentimental in their ecological practices. It is largely a western construction, heavily influenced by the romantic reaction to modern industrialism, which leads many to the view that they were and continue to be somehow 'closer to nature' than we are (even Guha, it seems to me, at some point falls into this trap). Faced with the ecological vulnerability often associated with such 'proximity to nature', indigenous groups can transform both their practices and their views of nature with startling rapidity. Furthermore, even when armed with all kinds of cultural traditions and symbolic gestures that indicate deep respect for the spirituality in nature, they can engage in extensive ecosystemic transformations that undermine their ability to continue with a given mode of production. The Chinese may have ecologically sensitive traditions of Tao, Buddhism and Confucianism (traditions of thought which have played an important role in promoting an 'ecological consciousness' in the West) but the historical geography of de-forestation, land degradation, river erosion and flooding in China contains not a few environmental events which would be regarded as catastrophes by modern-day standards. Archaeological evidence likewise suggests that late ice-age hunting groups hunted many of their prey to extinction while fire must surely rate as one of the most-far reaching agents of ecological transformation ever acquired, allowing very small groups to exercise immense ecosystemic influence (Sauer, 1956).

The point here is not to argue that there is nothing new under the sun about the ecological disturbance generated by human activities, but to assess what exactly is new and unduly stressful, given the unprecedented rapidity and scale of contemporary socio-ecological transformations. But historical-geographical enquiries of this sort also put in perspective those claims typically advanced by some ecologists that once upon a time 'people everywhere knew how to live in harmony with the natural world' (Goldsmith, 1992, xvii) and to view with scepticism Bookchin's (1985, 97) equally dubious claim that 'a relatively self-sufficient community, visibly dependent on its environment for the means of life, would gain a new respect for the organic interrelationships that sustain it.' Much contemporary 'ecologically-conscious' rhetoric pays far too much attention to what indigenous groups say without looking at what they do. We cannot conclude, for example, that native Indian practices are ecologically superior to ours from statements such as those of Luther Standing Bear that:

> 'We are of the soil and the soil of us. We love the birds and the beasts that grew with us on this soil. They drank the same water as we did and breathed the same air. We are all one in nature. Believing so, there was in our hearts a great peace and a welling kindness for all living, growing things.' (cited in Booth and Jacobs, 1990, 27)

Such an inference would require belief in either some external and spiritual guidance to ensure ecologically 'right' outcomes, or an extraordinary omniscience in indigenous or pre-capitalistic judgements and practices in a dynamic field of action that is plagued by all manner of unintended consequences. 'The possibility of over-exploitation of a resource is perfectly compatible with our notion of peoples living close to nature, observing and acting accordingly' (Haila and Levins, 1992, 195). Furthermore, 'comparative studies have suggested that all high civilizations that incorporated intensification strategies were metastable and that their growth trajectories can be interpreted as those of accelerating energy extraction, to the point that both the ecosystem and the socioeconomic structures were stretched to capacity, with steady or declining absolute caloric productivity and input-output ratios' (Butzer, 1982, 320). All societies have had their share of ecologically-based difficulties and, as Butzer goes on to assert, we have much to learn from studying them.

Indigenous or pre-capitalist practices are not, therefore, necessarily superior or inferior to our own just because such groups espouse respect for nature rather than the modern 'promethean' attitude of domination or mastery (see Leiss, 1974). Grundmann (1991a) is surely correct in his argument contra Benton (1989; 1992) that the thesis of 'mastery over nature' (laying aside its gendered overtones for the moment) does not necessarily entail destructiveness; it can just as easily lead to loving, caring and nurturing practices. Uncritical acceptance of 'ecologically conscious' sounding statements can, furthermore, be politically misleading. Luther Standing Bear prefaced the thoughts cited above with the very political argument that 'this land of the great plains is claimed by the Lakota as their very own.' Native Indians may well have strong claims to land rights, but the creation of an 'ecologically conscious' rhetoric to support them is, as we have already argued, a familiar but dangerous practice.

We can, in the same vein, turn a critical eye upon the ideological, aesthetic and 'ecologically conscious' traditions through which the whole relation to nature is approached. Glacken's (1967) monumental *Traces on the Rhodian Shore* well illustrates some of the twists and turns that the history of the idea of nature has taken in a variety of historical-geographical contexts from the Greeks until the end of the eighteenth century. While he is not directly interested in how changes in such ideas connected to or might even have shaped the actual course of political-economic change, the connection is always tacitly present. In this regard even Marx was willing to countenance the way in which ideas could become a 'material force' for historical change when embedded in social practices. For this reason it appears vital to look upon ideas as well as practices in terms of the conflation of ecological and social projects.

In recent years, for example, we find Wordsworth at the centre of an interesting debate. On the one hand Bate (1992) interprets him as a pioneer of 'romantic ecology,' a purely 'green' writer whose concerns for restoring a relation to nature have been written out of discussion by those like McGann (1983) who see him solely as an apologist for certain class relations. In a sense, the debate misses the point. Wordsworth was seriously *both* at the same time. Even Bate is in no doubt as to the nature of the social relations Wordsworth sough to recover or reconstitute as part and parcel of his ecologism. And it was precisely because of the social relations he espoused in his ecologically-conscious literary project, that he pioneered in producing the kind of tourist guide genre of writing that invites nature to be consumed (in ultimately destructive ways, as contemporary visitors to the Lake District soon find) through what Urry (1991) calls 'the tourist gaze.' Contemporary British practices in relation to the consumption of nature as a cultural spectacle owe a great deal, therefore, to the ideas that Wordsworth pioneered.

Inspection of the historical-geographical record reveals much about why words like 'nature' and 'environment' contain 'such an extraordinary amount of human history' (Williams, 1980, 67). The intertwinings of social and ecological projects in daily practices as well as in the realms of ideology, representations, aesthetics and the like are such as to make every social (including literary or artistic) project a project about nature, environment and ecosystem, and vice versa. Such a proposition should not, surely, be too hard for those working in the historical materialist tradition to swallow. Marx argued, after all, that we can discover who and what we are (our species potential, even) only through transforming the world around us and in so doing put the dialectics of social and ecological change at the centre of all human history. But how should that dialectic be understood?

IX Dialectics

There are manifest dangers of imposing, as Engels did, a simple dialectical logic upon 'nature.' Yet the contemporary ecological literature is full of dialectical and quasi-dialectical modes of argumentation that parallel those that Marx practised. For this reason, there is, as Eckersley (1992, 53) points out 'a much greater potential for theoretical synthesis' between 'ecocentrism and communitarian and socialist political philosophies than there is between ecocentrism and individualistic political philosophies such as liberalism.' While I shall shortly dispute Eckersley's particular conclusions, I here want to explore briefly the implications of the vigorous denunciations within the ecological literature of the ontological presuppositions of Descartes, Newton and Locke and the reductionist (non-dialectical) forms of natural and social science (particularly economics) to which those ontological presuppositions give rise (see Capra, 1985). Ecological theory typically turns to quantum theory (Heisenberg, Bohr and David Bohm figure large in their writings) and various forms of ecological science for a quite different set of ontological propositions.

The Cartesian system to which ecologists object presupposes that there can be a strict separation between *res cogitans* and *res extensa* (between mind and body, fact and value, 'is' and 'ought') and that the materiality scientists study is no more affected by the scientific knowledge generated in the mind than the mind is affected in its capacity to represent 'objectively' by the materiality studied. Cartesianism, furthermore, builds a detailed picture of a universe structured according to certain basic principles. It presumes the existence of a 'natural' and self-evident set of entities (individuals or *things*) that 'are homogeneous within themselves, at least insofar as they affect the whole of which they are parts.' Such entities can be individuated (identified) in terms of an externally given and absolute space and time (this is the Newtonian presumption which carries over, as we have already seen, to the social theory of John Locke and contemporary economics). The entities are, furthermore, 'ontologically prior to the whole' and parts (individuals) 'have intrinsic properties, which they possess in isolation.' The whole (a society or an ecosystem) is nothing but the sum (or in complex cases a multiple) of its parts. Relations between entities are, furthermore, clearly separable from the entities themselves. The study of relations is then a study of the contingent way in which entities (e.g. billiard balls or people) collide. This poses the problem of the 'prime cause' and leads to the Cartesian-Newtonian vision of the universe as a clock-like mechanism which God wound up and set in motion. In this mode of thought, 'causes are separate from effects, causes being the properties of subjects, and effects the properties of objects. While causes may respond to information coming from effects (so-called "feedback loops"), there is no ambiguity about which is causing subject and which is caused object' (Levins and Lewontin, 1985).

This Cartesian view is widespread and it has proved an extraordinarily powerful device for generating knowledge and understanding of how the universe works. It also has intuitive appeal. We encounter 'things' (e.g. individuals) and systems (e.g. transport and communication nets) which appear to have a stable and self-evident existence so that it appears perfectly reasonable to build knowledge upon categorisations of them and upon the pattern of causal relations between them.

From the dialectical point of view, however, this is to look at matters in an unduly restrictive and one-sided way. Levins and Lewontin call the Cartesian view 'alienated' because it depicts a world in which 'parts are separated from wholes and reified as things in themselves, causes separated from effects, subjects separated from objects.' Marx was similarly critical of the 'common sense' view which whenever 'it succeeds in seeing a distinction it fails to see a unity, and where it sees a unity it fails to see a distinction' (cited in Ollman, 1991, 44). He would, doubtless, be equally scathing about the atomistic and causative reasoning which dominates in contemporary economics and sociology, the methodological individualism which pervades much of current political (including Marxist) philosophy, and the like.

Perhaps the most characteristic form that Cartesian thinking takes in the environmental field is to view 'society' as a bounded system in interaction with another bounded system called the 'biosphere'. Our present sense of environmental problems is then defined broadly in terms of the complex and problematic relations between these two systems. It is, in practice, hard to see where 'society' begins and 'nature' ends (try looking around you and figuring where the boundary lies), but even as an act of abstraction this configuration of thought looks precisely to be the product of alienated reason, having no historical or well-grounded scientific justification. And there is a strong consensus in the ecological literature that this convention together with its basis in a Cartesian form of reasoning is not only profoundly anti-ecological in itself but also, through its effects on social practices, the root of many of our ecological problems. If this is so, then analytical and rational choice Marxism, methodological individualism and perhaps even Marxist realism (though Bhaskar is now seeking to incorporate dialectics into his arguments) are also profoundly anti-ecological by virtue of their broadly Cartesian ontology. The debate between

Grundmann and Benton on Marxism and ecology would then appear to be an argument based within fundamentally flawed ontological presuppositions.

The alternative to the Cartesian-Newtonian-Lockeian view is given in a dialectical ontology which can perhaps unify the Marxian tradition with the emerging consensus about appropriate ontology in ecological theory. This might be done through elaboration of the following ten propositions:

1. Dialectical thinking prioritizes the understanding of processes, flows, fluxes and relations over the analysis of elements, things, structures and organised systems. The latter do not exist outside of the processes that support, give rise to, or create them. Money – a thing – cannot be understood outside of the processes of exchange and capital flow that support it, any more than organisms can be understood outside of the environmental relationships that constitute them (Eckersley, 1992, 49). Capital in Marx's definition is *both* the process of circulation *and* the stock of assets ('*things*' like commodities, money, production apparatus). Quantum theory similarly states that 'the same entity (e.g. an electron) behaves under one set of circumstances as a wave, and in another set of circumstances as a particle' (Bohm and Peat, 1989, 40). Yet it took many years for physicists to recognise that these two conceptions were not incommensurable or mutually exclusive. Only when they did so could modern quantum theory begin to take shape. It has likewise proven very difficult for social scientists to abandon what Ollman (1993, 34) calls the 'common sense view' – erected into a philosophical system by Locke, Hume and others – that 'there are things and there are relations, and that neither can be subsumed in the other.'

2. '*Things*', as a consequence, are always assumed 'to be internally heterogeneous at every level' by virtue of the processes and relations that constitute them (Levins and Lewontin, 1985, 272). A number of consequences then follow. Firstly, any '*thing*' can be decomposed into a collection of other '*things*' which are in some relation to each other. For example, a city can be considered as a '*thing*' in interrelation with other cities, but it can also be broken down into neighbourhoods which can in turn be broken down into people, houses, schools, factories, etc., which can in turn be broken down *ad infinitum*. There are, consequently, no irreducible building blocks of '*things*' for any theoretical reconstruction of how the world works. What looks like a *system* at one level of analysis (e.g. a city or a pond) becomes a part at another level (e.g. a global network of world cities or a continental ecosystem). There can be, as Levins and Lewontin (1985, 278) put it, 'no basement' to enquiry since experience shows that 'all previously proposed undecomposable "basic units" turn out to be decomposable, and the decomposition has opened up new domains for investigation and practice.' The implication is that it is legitimate to investigate 'each level of organization without having to search for funda-

mental units.' But this then poses a particular problem for enquiry: it is crucial to establish the *scale* (usually spatial and temporal) at which *processes, things* and *systems* are operative for what is relevant at one scale (e.g. the pond) may not be so at another (e.g. the continent). Secondly, if all 'things' are internally heterogeneous by virtue of the complex process (or relations) which constitute them, then the only way we can understand the qualitative and quantitative attributes of '*things*' is by understanding the very processes and relations which they internalize. We here find a very strong identity between Ollman's (1971; 1993) construction of the Marxian dialectic as internal relations and the ecological arguments set out by Eckersley (1992, 49-55), Birch and Cobb (1981), Naess (1989, 79) and Zimmerman (1988). There is, however, a limitation to be put upon this argument. I as an individual, do not in practice internalize everything in the universe, but absorb mainly what is relevant to me through my relationships (metabolic, social, political, cultural, etc) to processes operating over a relatively bounded field (my ecosystem, economy, culture, etc). There is no fixed or *a priori* boundary to this system. Where my relevant environment begins and ends is itself a function of what I do and the ecological, economic, and other processes which are relevant to that. Here, too, setting boundaries with respect to space, time, scale and environment becomes a major strategic consideration in the development of concepts, abstractions, and theories.

3. Space and time are neither absolute nor external to processes but are contingent and contained within them. There are multiple spaces and times (and space-times) implicated in different physical, biological and social processes. The latter all *produce* – to use Lefebvre's (1991) terminology – their own forms of space and time. Processes do not operate *in* but *actively construct* space and time and in so doing define distinctive *scales* for their development (see below).

4. Parts and wholes are mutually constitutive of each other. There is more to this than a mere feedback loop between thing-like entities. As, for example, I capture powers that reside in those ecological and economic systems that are relevant to me, I actively reconstitute or transform them *within* myself even before I project them back to reconstitute or transform the system from which they were initially derived (again, to take a trivial example, I breathe in, I reconstitute myself by virtue of the oxygen I transform within me, and I breathe out and transform the atmosphere around me). Reductionist practices 'typically ignore this relationship, isolating parts as preexisting units of which wholes are then composed' while some holistic practices reverse the preferential treatment (Levins and Lewontin, 1985).

5. The interdigitation of parts and wholes entails 'the interchangeability of subject and object, of cause and effect' (Levins and Lewontin, 1985, 274). Organisms, for example, have to be looked at as both the subjects

and the objects of evolution in exactly the same way that individuals have to be considered as both subjects and objects of processes of social change. The reversibility of cause and effect renders causally specified models (even when endowed with feedback loops) suspect. In practice, dialectical reasoning, precisely by virtue of its embeddedness in and representation of the flow of continuous processes, makes limited appeal to cause and effect argument.

7. 'Change is a characteristic of all systems and all aspects of all systems' (Levins and Lewontin, op. cit, 275). This is perhaps the most important of all dialectical principles and one which Ollman (1991; 1993) prioritises above all else. The implication is that change and instability are the norm and that the stability of 'things' or systems is what has to be explained. In Ollman's (1991, 34) words, 'given that change is always a part of what things are, (our) research problem (can) only be *how, when*, and *into what* (things or systems) change and why they sometimes appear not to change.'

8. Transformative behaviour – 'creativity' – arises out of the complementarities and contradictions which attach both to the internalised heterogeneity of 'things' and out of the more obvious heterogeneity present within systems. It is therefore omnipresent within the physical, biological and social worlds. This does not mean, however, that all moments within some continuous process are equally significant at a particular scale for understanding change or stability. The theoretical and empirical research task is to identify those characteristic 'moments' and 'forms' (i.e. '*things*') embedded within continuous flows which can produce radical transformations or, on the other hand, give a '*thing*' or system qualities of identity, integrity and relative stability. The question of 'agency' in social and biological as well as in physical systems has to be formulated broadly in these terms.

9. Dialectical enquiry is not itself outside of its own form of argumentation but subject to it. Dialectical enquiry is a *process* that produces *things* in the form of concepts, abstractions, theories and all manner of institutionalised forms of knowledge which stand in their own right only to be supported or undermined by the continuing processes of enquiry. There is, furthermore, a certain relationship implied between the researcher and the researched, a relationship which is not construed in terms of an 'outsider' (the researcher) looking in on the researched as an object, but one between two subjects each of which necessarily internalises something from the other by virtue of the processes that operate. Observation of the world is, Heisenberg argued, inevitably intervention in the world, in much the same way that deconstructionists will argue that the reading of a text is fundamental to its production. Marx similarly insisted that only by transforming the world could we transform ourselves and that it is impossible to understand the world without simultaneously changing it as well as ourselves. It is this principle that renders the duality of *anthropocentrism* and

ecocentrism, turned into mutually exclusionary principles by Eckersley (1992) into a false opposition (in exactly the same way that feminist theory, perpetually forced back to discuss the relation between nature and nurture, has broadly concluded – see Fuss (1990) – that the supposed opposition between essentialism and *social constructivism* is false because both are essential to each other). Dialectics cannot be superimposed on the world as an act of mind over matter (this was Engels' critical mistake, unfortunately replicated by Levins and Lewontin). The underlying unity of theory and praxis can, it seems, never be broken, only attenuated or temporarily alienated. Here lies, I would suggest, the true path towards that transcendence of the anthropocentric/ecocentric opposition that Benton (1992, 72) seeks.

10. *Eduction* – the exploration of potentialities for change, for self-realisation, for the construction of new totalities (e.g. social ecosystems) and the like – rather than deduction or induction is, as Bookchin insists, the central motif of dialectical praxis. Dialectical enquiry necessarily incorporates, therefore, the building of ethical, moral and political choices into its own process and sees the constructed knowledges that result as discourses situated in a play of power. Values, for example, are not imposed as universal abstractions from outside but arrived at through a process of enquiry embedded in forms of praxis and plays of power attaching to the exploration of this or that potentiality (in ourselves as well as in the world we inhabit). To the degree that a distinctively 'green value theory' has arisen in recent years, it must be seen as the product of socio-ecological processes and plays of power.

There is, evidently, a remarkable commonality of the dialectics (as both ontology and epistemology) present in Marx's argumentation in, say, *Capital*, (and as set out by Ollman, 1993) and those proffered, in one form or another, across a fairly wide spectrum of ecological writings. This commonality has not passed unnoticed (Parsons, 1977; Lee, 1980), nor can it be regarded as unproblematic (Clark, 1989; Dickens, 1992, 190-5). But it has not been creatively worked upon. In the same way (see Harvey, 1982; 1989) that Marxian theory can be extended dialectically to understand the production of both space and time – fundamental attributes of 'nature' after all – so the theoretical task of constructing a fuller and more coherent Marxian theory of the production of nature (see Smith, 1990) cries out for attention. There is, plainly, nothing in principle anti-ecological about Marx's dialectics. The prospects for creating a political economic ecology are therefore good, provided the dialectical imagination can be restored to that central position in Marxian theory from which it has been dislodged by many countervailing neo-Marxist currents of thought.

X Towards an Ecosocialist Politics

Benton (1989, 55) has recently argued that 'the basic ideas of historical materialism can without distortion be regarded as a proposal for an ecological approach to the understanding of human nature and history.' The difficulty, he asserts, is that there is a hiatus, 'internal to' the mature writings between this general commitment and Marx's political-economic conception of the labour process. I want to propose that a more dialectical reading of Marx, in which the labour *process* is seen as 'a form-giving fire' perpetually modifying other *processes* while passing through and giving rise to distinctive '*things*', eliminates much of that hiatus. Not only does it then become possible to explore the commonalities between Marx's project and some sectors of contemporary ecological thinking, but it also allows us to begin to construct more adequate languages with which to reflect upon the nature of socio-ecological activities and projects.

It is at this point useful to reflect for a moment upon the multiple languages – scientific, poetic, mythic, moral and ethical, economistic and instrumental, emotive and effective – in which ecological issues are typically addressed. For it is often argued that some kind of transdisciplinary language is required to better represent and resolve ecological problems and that the very existence of multiple discourses about 'nature' is a fundamental part of the problem. On the other hand, there is a deep reluctance to try to cram everything we want to say about 'nature' and our relation to it into one singular and homogeneous language. I want here to argue that a limited case can be made for both positions.

On the one hand we certainly need a much more unified language for the social and biological/physical sciences than we currently possess. The question of the unity of science has, of course, been broached many times – not least by Marx (1964). But serious problems have arisen on the social theory side whenever a biological basis has been invoked (familiar examples include the way social Darwinism founded Nazism, the profound social antagonisms generated in the debate over sociobiology). The response on the social science side has often been to retreat from any examination of the ecological side of social projects and act as if these either did not matter or as if they had to be construed as something 'external' to enquiry. I want to argue that this is not a satisfactory way to go about things and that ways have to be found to create a more common language. This is, however, dangerous territory – an open field for organicist or holistic rather than dialectical modes of thinking – and it may require deep shifts in ontological and epistemological stances on both the social and natural scientific sides, if it is to succeed.

On the other hand, the heterogeneity of discourses about 'nature' has to be accepted as not only an inevitable but also a very constructive and creative feature of ecological argumentation, provided that it is read not as fragmented and separate modes of thought and action embedded in isolated communities, but as the internalised heterogeneity, the play of difference, which all of us must surely feel and experience in our interaction with 'others' in both the human and non-human world. The pleasure of meaningful work and engagement with others is not irrelevant to the worker's life and the celebration of that in poetry and song has as much to convey as the more alienated representations of the world which science purveys.

Yet there is in this an omnipresent danger. Not only do different discourses lie uneasily side by side so that it becomes hard to spot the unity within the difference. But the careful analysis of the way power relations get embedded in distinctive discourses suggests that the vast conceptual muddle and cacophony of discourses is far from innocent in the reproduction of capitalism. Critical engagement with that is no trivial political task. If all socio-political projects are ecological projects and *vice versa*, then some conception of 'nature' and of 'environment' is omnipresent in everything we say and do. If, furthermore, concepts, discourses and theories can operate, when internalised in socio-ecological practices and actions, as 'material forces' that shape history (cf. Lovejoy, cited above; Ollman, 1971, 23-4), then the present battles being waged over the concepts of 'nature' and of 'environment' are of immense importance. All critical examinations of the relation to nature are simultaneously critical examinations of society. The incredible vigour with which ruling interests have sought to contain, shape, mystify and muddy the contemporary debate over nature and environment (for the most part within discourses of 'ecological modernisation', 'sustainability', 'green consumerism' or the commodification and sale of 'nature' as a cultural spectacle) testifies to the seriousness of that connection.

The danger here is of accepting, often without knowing it, concepts that preclude radical critique. Consider, for example, the way in which 'ecoscarcity' (and its cognate term of 'overpopulation') plays out in contemporary debate (see, for example, Benton, 1989, 1992). The emphasis is on the 'natural limits' to human potentialities. In Lee's (1989) case, the narrative proceeds as if the rules of human behaviour should be derived from the second law of thermodynamics and the inherent sustaining power of ecosystems(neither of which is helpful at all in explaining the shifting history of human social organisation let alone the genesis of life). But if we view 'natural resources' in the rather traditional geographical manner, as 'cultural, technological and economic appraisals of elements residing in nature and mobilised for particular social ends,' (see, e.g. Spoehr, 1956; Firey, 1960), then 'ecoscarcity' means that we have not the will, wit or capacity to change our social goals, cultural modes, our technological mixes, or our form of economy and that we are powerless to modify 'nature' according to human requirements (see Harvey, 1974). Even the short history of capitalism surely proves that none of these features are fixed, that all of them are dynamic and changing. It is one thing to say that capitalism, given its narrow fixations and rules of capital accumulation, is encountering a condition of ecoscarcity and overpopulation. Indeed, it can be argued with some force, *pace* Marx, that capitalism as a mode of production produces scarcity so that to focus on universal limitations is to completely elide the political-ecological point. In this regard at least, Benton (1989, 77) has it right:

> What is required is the recognition that each form of social/economic life has its own specific mode and dynamic of interrelation with its own specific contextual conditions, resource materials, energy sources and naturally mediated unintended consequences (forms of 'waste', 'pollution' etc). The ecological problems of any form of social and economic life . . . have to be theorized as the outcome of this specific structure of natural/social articulation.

Many of the terms used in contemporary environmental debates, it turns out, incorporate capitalist values without knowing it. While 'sustainability,' for example, means entirely different things to different people (see Redclift, 1987), the general drift of the term's use situates it against the background of sustaining a particular set of social relations by way of a particular ecological project. Imagine, for example, a highly simplified ecological-economic situation (along the lines of Lovelock's Daisyworld on *Gaia*) in which New York City has two species, international bankers and cockroaches. International bankers are the endangered species and so 'sustainability' gets defined in terms of organising the use of the earth (e.g. organising 'sustainable' agriculture in Malawi to facilitate debt repayments) to keep them in business. The model, though far-fetched in some ways, is also quite illuminating, since it indicates why and how it is that international finance, via the World Bank, is these days so interested in ecological sustainability. The duality of ecological and social projects here takes some interesting twists for while it is true that debt-repayment, as ecologists argue, is at the root of many ecological problems it is precisely the threat of debt default that forces international finance to recognise that such ecological problems exist.

But for exactly the same reasons that we cannot afford to limit options by internalising a capitalistic logic in which concepts of sustainability, ecoscarcity and overpopulation are deeply implicated, so socialists cannot simply be content to try and coopt the critical language of ecological discontent. The task is, rather, to both define and fight for a particular kind of ecosocialist project that extricates us from the peculiar oppressions and contradictions that capitalism is producing. Marx long ago summarised these succinctly enough:

> In our days, everything seems pregnant with its contrary. Machinery, gifted with the wonderful power of shortening and fructifying human labour, we behold starving and overworking it. The new-fangled sources of wealth, by some strange weird spell, are turned into sources of want. The victories of art seem bought by the loss of character. At the same pace that mankind masters nature, man seems to become enslaved to other men or to his

own infamy. Even the pure light of science seems unable to shine but on the dark background of ignorance. All our invention and progress seem to result in endowing material forces with intellectual life, and in stultifying human life into a material force (cited in Grundmann, 199b, 228).

It is then tempting , but not sufficient, to cite Engels' path towards an effective resolution to ecological as well as social dilemmas:

by long and often cruel experience and by collecting and analysing historical material, we are gradually learning to get a clear view of the indirect, more remote, social effects of our production activities and so are afforded an opportunity to control and regulate these effects as well . . . This regulation, however, requires something more than mere knowledge. It requires a complete revolution in our hitherto existing mode of production, and simultaneously a revolution in our whole contemporary social order.

I say this is insufficient because it leaves unresolved far too many dilemmas concerning the actual direction any ecosocialist project might take. And here the debate between Marxists and ecologists of all stripes has much to offer. That debate is largely a matter of articulating fixed positions, of course, but there are other, more dialectical ways, to go about reading it. 'One-sided representations are always restrictive and problematic,' Marx argued, and the best way to proceed when faced with a difficulty is 'to rub together conceptual blocks in such a way that they catch fire.' In that spirit I will conclude with the five key areas in which such a 'rubbing' might help ecosocialist conceptual politics catch fire:

1. Alienation, and Self-realisation

Ideals of 'self-realisation' are widespread in the ecological literature. They parallel in certain ways Marx's concerns, particularly in *The Economic and Philosophic Manuscripts of 1844* but also in later works such as the *Grundnisse*, for human emancipation and self-development through the working out of our creative powers. In the Marxist tradition, however, quite properly concerned as it has been with impoverishment and deprivation, the liberation of the productive forces came to be seen as the privileged and to some degree exclusive means towards the broader goal of human self-realisation (see Grundmann, 1990b, 54). As such, it became a goal in itself.

The ecologists' critique of socialist 'productivism' is here helpful, since it forces Marxists to re-examine the problematics of alienation (see, e.g., Meszaros, 1970; Ollman, 1971). Under capitalism, private property, class relations, wage labour, and the fetishisms of market exchange separate and alienate us from any sensuous and immediate contact (except in those fragmented and partial senses achievable under class-ordered divisions of labour) from 'nature' as well as from other human beings. But if 'man lives on nature' then 'that nature is his *body* with which he must remain in continuous interchange if he is not to die.' The health of that body is fundamental to our health. To 'respect' nature is to respect ourselves. To engage with and transform nature is to transform ourselves. This forms one side of Marx's theses. But estrangement from immediate sensuous engagement with nature is an essential moment in consciousness formation. It therefore is a step on a path towards emancipation and self-realisation (cf. Ingold, 1986, cited above). But herein lies a paradox. This never-ending estrangement of consciousness permits reflexivity and the construction of emancipatory forms of knowledge (such as science); but it also poses the problem of how to return to that which consciousness alienates us from. How to recuperate an unalienated relation to nature (as well as unalienated forms of social relations) in the face of contemporary divisions of labour and technological-social organisation, then becomes part of a common project that binds Marxists and ecologists ineluctably together. Where they split asunder is in the way that such a recuperation might be sought. For Marxists, there can be no going back, as many ecologists seem to propose, to an *unmediated* relation to nature (or a world built solely on face-to-face relations), to a pre-capitalist and communitarian world of non-scientific understandings with limited divisions of labour. The only path is to seek political, cultural and intellectual means that 'go beyond' the mediations such as scientific knowledge, organisational efficiency and technical rationality, money, and commodity exchange, while acknowledging the significance of such mediations. The emancipatory potential of modern society, founded on alienation, must continue to be explored. But this cannot be, as it so often is, an end in itself for that is to treat alienation as the end point, the goal. The ecologists' and the early Marx's concern to recuperate the alienation from nature (as well as from others) that modern day capitalism instanciates must be a fundamental goal of any ecosocialist project. The quest for meaningful work as well as meaningful play (making sure, for example, that 'victories of art' are not bought by 'loss of character') becomes a central issue through which the labour movement can grasp the nettle of ecological argumentation concerning alienation from nature, from others and, in the last instance, from ourselves.

This does not deny the relevance or power of phenomenological approaches in exploring the potentialities of more intimate and immediate relations to nature or to others. The depth and intensity of feeling implicit even in Heidegger's approach is not irrelevant, any more than is the search for adequate poetic languages, representations, symbolic systems. Sartre's existentialism owes as much, after all, to Marx as to Heidegger. The danger arises when such modes of thought are postulated as the sole basis of politics (in which case they become inward-looking, exclusionary and even neo-fascist), when it was surely Marx's intent to search for unity within the duality of *existential* and *mediated* experiences of the world. Exploring that duality has to be at the centre of ecosocialist politics, implying an uncomfortable but instructive duality of values between the purely instrumental (mediated) and the existential (unmediated).

2. Social Relations and Ecological Projects

Explorations of our 'species potential' and our capacity for 'self-realisation' require that we take cognizance of the relation between ecological projects and the social relations needed to initiate, implement and manage them. Nuclear power, for example, requires highly centralised and non-democratic power relations coupled with hierarchical command and control structures if it is to work successfully. Objections to it therefore focus as much on the social relations it implies as on the ecological problems of health and long-term hazardous wastes. The nature of many of the ecological projects undertaken in the Soviet Union likewise required social relations that were fundamentally at odds with the theoretical project of constructing a new society founded on egalitarianism and democracy. But this sort of critique is the easy part. For if we turn the equation around, and state that the only kinds of ecological projects to be undertaken are those which are consistent with non-hierarchical, de-centralised, highly democratic and radically egalitarian social relations, then the range of possible ecological projects becomes highly restricted, perhaps even life-threatening for substantial numbers of people. Adoption of such a stance certainly does not accord with the open exploration of our species potentiality and would probably militate against the alleviation of the tangible material misery in which much of the world's population lives.

There is, here, no resolution to what will always be a contradictory situation, save that of recognising fully the nature of the tension and seeking political ways to live with its effects. More immediately, we have also to recognise the effects that arise from the instanciation 'in nature' of certain kinds of social relations. If, for example, we view, as I think we must, contemporary ecosystems as incorporating the built environments of cities and the capital and commodity flows that sustain them, and if these ecosystems are instanciations of capitalist social relations, then what feasible (as opposed to catastrophically destructive) social and ecological transformations are available to us?

3. The Question of Technology

'Technology discloses man's mode of dealing with Nature, the process of production whereby he sustains his life, and thereby also lays bare the mode of formation of his social relations, and of the mental conceptions that flow from them' (Marx, 1967, 352). While it is plainly wrong to attribute any technological determinism to Marx ('discloses' cannot be read as 'determines'), the centrality of technology and of technological choices in embedding social relations in ecological projects (and vice versa) means that careful attention has to be paid to this issue. Grundmann (1990b) is here, surely on very strong grounds when he points to some of the deep tensions in Marx's own approach. If, for example, machinery not only dispossesses workers of their surplus value but also deprives them of their skill and virtuosity while mediating their relations to nature in alienating ways, then self-realisation (however much we insist on the collectivity of the project) may be in jeopardy for technological reasons. Some kinds of technologies run counter even to the aim of exercising greater control over nature. But the problem goes even deeper. The technological mixes that capitalism bequeaths us (with its particular mixes of socio-ecological projects) either have to be roundly rejected (as many ecologists now suggest) or gradually transformed in ways that better accord with socialist social relations, and of the mental conceptions (such as those concerning the relation to nature) that flow from them. Arguments over 'appropriate technology' and 'small-is-beautiful' here come into play, not as necessary technological principles or trajectories for the construction of socialism, but as a set of questions marks over the future technological organisation of a socialist society (cf. Commoner, 1990).

4. The Dialectics of Commonality and Difference, of Centralisation and Decentralisation

Since much of the radical ecological critique now in vogue has its roots in anarchism, it has typically taken the path of emphasising community, locality, place, proximity to 'nature', particularity and decentralisation (deeply antagonistic to state powers) as opposed to the more traditional socialistic concerns with the universality of proletarian struggles and the overthrow of capitalism as a world-historical system of domination. Any ecosocialist project has to confront that opposition. Here I think a more *geographical* historical materialism, one that is more ecologically sensitive, has much to offer, both in terms of analysis as well as in terms of prospective transformations. The *general* struggle against capitalist forms of domination is always made up of *particular* struggles against the specific kinds of socio-ecological projects in which capitalists are engaged and the distinctive social relations they presuppose (against commercial forestry and timber management in the Himalayas as against large scale water projects in California or nuclear power in France). The articulation of socialist principles of struggle therefore varies greatly with the nature and scale of the socio-ecological project to be confronted. And by the same token, the nature of the socialist transformation sought depends crucially upon the socio-ecological possibilities that exists in relation to particular projects, looking very different in Nicaragua or Zimbabwe from how it looks in Sweden and very different in terms of multinational finance from how it looks in terms of medical wastes dumped next to housing projects. But it is at this point that the *general* presumptions of the transition to socialism deserve to be reflected upon. Socialism is not necessarily about the construction of homogeneity. The exploration of our species potentiality can presumably also be about the creative search for and exploration of diversity and heterogeneity. Socio-ecological projects, much more in tune with resolving questions of alienation and opening up diverse pos-sibilities for self-realisation, can be regarded as fundamentally part of some socialist future. The failures of capitalism to produce anything other than the uneven geographical development of bland, commoditised, homogeneity is, surely, one of the most striking features of its failures.

The radical ecological literature that focuses on place construction, bioregionalism, and the like here has something creative to offer, partly as an excellent ground for the critique of capitalism's production of waste (do we really need to ship British beer to Australia and Australian beer to Britain?) as well as its production of serial conformity in urban design and the like. Mumford wishfully depicted the region, for example, 'like its corresponding artifact, the city, (as) a collective work of art' not found 'as a finished product in nature, not solely the creation of human will and fantasy.' Embedded in a socialist project of ecological transformation, such a way of thinking turns on the 'production of nature' as diverse localised works of art coupled with the creation of ecosystemic differences which can respect diversity as much of culture and of places as of eco-systems. The richness of human capacity for complexity and diversity in a context of the free exploration of the richness, complexity and diversity encountered in the rest of nature can become a vital part of any ecosocialist project. 'Each of us,' says a bioregionalist like Berg (cited in Alexander, 1990, 170) 'inhabits a "terrain of consciousness" determined in large part by the place we dwell in, the work we do, and the people with whom we share our lives.' And there is absolutely no reason not to follow him in arguing that 'the re-creation of caring and sustainable human cultures' ought to become 'part of the "real work" of our time.' In so doing he is echoing something that derives as much from Raymond Williams as from Heidegger.

But we also hit here the point of departure of ecosocialism from pure bioregionalist, place and local communitarian politics. The problem is that there is more than a hint of authoritarianism, surveillance and confinement in the enforced localism of such a decentralised politics and a naive belief that (1) respect for human diversity is compatible with the belief that all decentralised societies will necessarily construct themselves 'upon the (*enlightenment!*) values of democracy, liberty, freedom, justice and other such like *desiderata*' (Sale, 1985) rather than in terms of slavery, sexual oppression, and the like (see Dobson, 1990, 122), (2) that the 'impoverish-ment' which often attaches to communal autarky and strong restrictions on foreign trade can be overcome, and (3) that restrictions on population movements coupled with exclusions of disruptive 'foreigners' can some-how be squared with ideals of maximizing individual freedoms, democracy and openness to 'others.' Young's (1990) salutary warnings concerning the nightmare of communitarian politics in which community is defined as *against* others and therefore formulated in an entirely exclusionary, chau-vinistic and racist way, is not that easily avoided. When Goldsmith condescendingly writes (cited in Dobson, 1990, 97), for example, that 'a certain number of foreigners could be allowed to settle,' but that they would not 'partake in the running of the community until such time as the citizens elected them to be of their number,' the leaning towards a politics of exclusion that is neo-fascist becomes rather too close for comfort. The 'ecologism' of the right-wing Lombardy Leagues in Northern Italy, for example, shares exactly such a perspective not only with respect to the immigration of non-Italians but also with respect to movements from Southern Italy. Furthermore, there is in this thinking a presumption that bioregions are given, by nature or by history, rather than that they are made by a variety of intersecting processes operating at quite different temporal and spatial scales. In other words, bioregions get thought about, in a most undialectical fashion, as things rather than as unstable products of shifting processes. This then provokes the question: at what scale should a *bioregion, place, or human community* be defined?

Ecosocialist politics must, we can conclude, pay attention to a politics in which 'universality' has a dual meaning. This is best expressed in Young's (1990, 105) rule that 'universality in the sense of the participation and inclusion of everyone in moral and social life does not imply universality in the sense of adoption of a general point of view that leaves behind particular affiliations, feelings, commitments, and desires.' The perpetual negotiation of the relation between those two senses of universality, whether read across differences of gender, ethnicity or other social affiliation or across the diversity of socio-ecological projects that might be explored under socialism, must therefore remain at the heart of ecosocialist thinking.

5. The Question of Temporal and Spatial Scales

At first sight, the question of scale appears as a purely technical matter. Where, for example, do ecosystems (or socio-ecological projects) begin and where do they end, how does a pond differ from the globe, how is it that processes which operate with profound effect at one scale become irrelevant at another, and so on? 'Issues of appropriate scaling,' Haila and Levins (1992, 236) argue, 'are among the fundamental theoretical challenges in the understanding of society-nature interactions.' There is, they say, 'no single "correct" way' to define temporal and spatial scales: these are constituted by the organisms considered so that different scales are simultaneously present at any particular site in nature. If, as is the case in the dialectical view (see above), there are no basic units to which everything can be reduced, then the choice of scale at which to examine processes becomes both crucial and problematic. The difficulty is compounded by the fact that the temporal and spatial scales at which human beings operate as ecological agents have also been changing. Cronon (1983, 99) notes, for example, how even before colonial settlement began in New England, long-distance trade from Europe was bringing two hitherto largely isolated ecosystems into contact with one another in such a way as to commercialise the Indians' material culture and dissolve their earlier ecological practices. If we think these days of the scale defined by the commodity and money flows that put our breakfasts upon the table, and how that scale has changed over the last hundred years, then immediately it becomes apparent that there is an instability in the definition of scale which arises out of practices of capital accumulation, commodity exchange, and the like (Harvey, 1989, 1990).

Yet, as Smith (1992, 72) remarks, 'the theory of the production of geographical scale' (to which I would add also the production of temporalities) – 'is grossly underdeveloped.' It seems to imply the production of a nested hierarchy of scales (from global to local) leaving us always with the political-ecological question of how to 'arbitrate and translate between them.' The ecological argument is incredibly confused on exactly this point. On the one hand the Gaian planetary health care specialists think globally and seek to act globally, while the bioregionalist and social anarchists want to think and act locally, presuming, quite erroneously, that whatever is good for the locality is good for the continent or the planet. But at this point the issue becomes profoundly political as well as ecological, for the political power to act, decide upon socio-ecological projects and to regulate their unintended consequences has also to be defined at a certain scale (and in the contemporary world the nation states mostly carved out over the last hundred years maintain a privileged position even though they make no necessary politico-ecological sense). But this also says something very concrete about what any ecosocialist project must confront. On the one hand there will presumably be continuing transformations in human practices that redefine temporal and spatial scales, while on the other hand political power structures must be created that have the capacity to 'arbitrate and translate between' the different scales given by different kinds of projects. Here, too, it seems that an ecosocialist perspective has enormous impact for socialist thinking on how human potentialities are to be explored and what kinds of political institutions and power structures can be created that are sensitive to the ecological dimensions of any socialist project.

XI Epilogue

'At the end of every labour process,' Marx (1967, 174) once observed, 'we get a result that already existed in the imagination of the labourer at its commencement.' The purpose of the kind of labour that I have here engaged in, is to try and produce conceptual clarifications that might enter into the political practices of socialism. But to be realized, as Eckersley so acutely points out, the aspirations released by analyses of this sort 'must be

48   THE SOCIALIST REGISTER 1993

critically related to one's knowledge of the present, thereby uniting desire with analysis and (lead on) to informed cultural, social, and political engagement.' To bring my argument full circle, that means developing ways to conceptualise and represent ecological issues in ways that speak to the aspirations of the working class movement, certain segments of the women's and ecologists' movements, as well as to those African-Americans who, in the Left Bank Jazz Club in Baltimore more than twenty years ago, quite correctly defined their main environmental problem as the Presidency of Richard Nixon.

REFERENCES

Alexander, D., 1990, 'Bioregionalism: Science or sensibility,' *Environmental Ethics*, 12, 161-73.
Attfield, R. 1991 edition, *The ethics of environmental concern*, Athens, University of Georgia Press.
Bennett, J., 1976, *The ecological transition: Cultural anthropology and human adaptation*, New York, Pergamon Press.
Benton, T., 1989, 'Marxism and natural limits: An ecological critique and reconstruction', *New Left Review*, 178, 51-86.
Benton, T., 1992, 'Ecology, socialism and the mastery of nature: A reply to Reiner Grunmann,' *New Left Review*, 194, 55-74.
Birch, C. and Cobb, J., 1981, *The liberation of life: From the cell to the community*, Cambridge, Cambridge University Press.
Bohm, D. and Peat, F., 1987, *Science, order and creativity*, London, Routledge.
Bookchin, M., 1985, 'Ecology and revolutionary thought,' *Antipode*, 17, Nos 2 and 3, 89-97.
Bookchin, M., 1990a, *The philosophy of social ecology: Essays on dialectical naturalism*, Montreal, Black Rose Books.
Bookchin, M., 1990b, *Remaking society: Pathways to a green future*, Boston, South End Press.
Booth, A. and Jacobs, H., 1990, 'Ties that bind: Native American beliefs as a foundation for environmental consciousness,' *Environmental Ethics*, 12, 27-43.
Borneman, E. (ed.), 1976, *The psychoanalysis of money*, London, Urizen Books.
Bramwell, A., 1989, *Ecology in the twentieth century: A history*, New Haven, Yale University Press.
Brundtland Report, 1987, *Our common future*, World Commission on Environment and Development, Oxford, Oxford University Press.
Butzer, K., 1982, *Archaeology as human ecology*, Cambridge, Cambridge University Press.
Capra, F., 1975, *The Tao of Physics*, Berkeley, Shambhala.
Capra, F., 1982, *The turning point: Science, society, and the rising culture*, New York, Simon and Schuster.
Clark, J., 1989, 'Marx's inorganic body,' *Environmental Ethics*, 11, 243-58.
Collingwood, R., 1960, *The idea of nature*, Oxford, Oxford University Press.
Commoner, B., 1990, *Making peace with the planet*, New York, Pantheon.
Cronon, W., 1983, *Changes in the land: Indians, colonists, and the ecology of New England*, New York, Hill & Wang.
Cronon, W., 1991, *Nature's metropolis: Chicago and the Great West*, New York, Norton.
Crosby, A., 1986, *Ecological imperialism: The biological expansion of Europe, 900-1900*, Cambridge, Cambridge University Press.
Dauncey, G., 1988, *After the crash: The emergence of the rainbow economy*, Basingstoke, Green Print.
Dickens, P., 1992, *Society and nature: Towards a green social theory*, London, Harvester Wheatsheaf.
Dobson, A., 1990, *Green political thought*, London, Unwin Hyman.

Eckersley, R., 1992, *Environmentalism and political theory: Toward an ecocentric approach*, London, UCL Press.

Ellen, R., 1982, *Environment, subsistence and system: The ecology of small-scale social formations*, Cambridge, Cambridge University Press.

Engels, F., 1940, *The dialectics of nature*, New York, International Publishers.

Engels, F., 1940, 'The part played by labour in the transition from ape to man,' in Engels, *The dialectics of nature*, New York, International Publishers.

Enzensberger, H-M., 1974, 'A critique of political ecology,' *New Left Review*, 84, 3-31.

Firey, W., 1960, *Man, mind and the land*, Glencoe, Illinois, Free Press.

Fortune, Special Issue on the Environment, February, 1970.

Gerratana, V., 1973, 'Marx and Darwin,' *New Left Review*, 82, 60-82.

Glacken, C., 1967, *Traces on the Rhodian Shore*, Berkeley, University of California Press.

Goldsmith, E., 1992, *The way: An ecological world view*, London, Rider.

Goodin, R., 1992, *Green political theory*, Cambridge, Polity.

Gosselink, J., Odum, E. and Pope, R., 1974, *The value of the tidal marsh*, Baton Rouge, Center for Wetland Resources, Louisiana State University.

Gottlieb, R., 1988, *A life of its own: The politics and power of water*, New York, Harcourt Brace Jovanovich.

Goudie, A., 1986, *The human impact on the natural environment*, Oxford, Basil Blackwell.

Grundmann, R., 1991a, 'The ecological challenge to Marxism,' *New Left Review*, 187, 103-120.

Grundmann, R., 1991b, *Marxism and Ecology*, Oxford, Oxford University Press.

Guha, R., 1989, *The unquiet woods: Ecological change and peasant resistance in the Himalaya*, Berkeley, University of California Press.

Haila, Y. and Levins, R., 1992, *Humanity and nature: Ecology, science and society*, London, Pluto Press.

Hajer, M., 1992, 'The politics of environmental performance review: Choices in design' in Lykke, E., (ed.) *Achieving environmental goals: the concept and practice of environmental performance review*, London, Belhaven Press.

Haraway, D., 1989, *Primate visions: Gender, race and nature in the world of modern science*, New York, Routledge.

Hardin, G., 1968, 'The tragedy of the commons,' *Science*, 162, 1243-48.

Harvey, D., 1974, 'Population, resources, and the ideology of science,' *Economic Geography*, 50, 256-77.

Harvey, D., 1982, *The limits to capital*, Oxford, Blackwell.

Harvey, D., 1989, *The condition of postmodernity: An enquiry into the origins of cultural change*, Oxford, Basil Blackwell.

Harvey, D., 1990, 'Between space and time: Reflections on the geographical imagination,' *Annals, Association of American Geographers*, 80, 418-34.

Heidegger, M., 1971, *Poetry, language, thought*, New York, Harper and Row.

Heilbroner, R., 1974, *An inquiry into the human prospect*, New York, Norton.

Ingold, T., 1986, *The appropriation of nature: Essays on human ecology and social relations*, Manchester, Manchester University Press.

Jacks, G. and Whyte, R., 1939, *Vanishing lands*, New York, Doubleday.

Journal of American History, Vol. 76, (1990), 1087-1147.

Kapp, K., 1950, *The social costs of private enterprise*, New York, Schocken.

Lee, D., 1980, 'On the Marxian view of the relationship between man and nature,' *Environmental Ethics*, 2, 1-21.

Lee, K., 1989, *Social philosophy and ecological scarcity*, London, Routledge.

Leiss, W., 1974, *The domination of nature*, Boston, Beacon Press.

Leopold, A., 1968, *A Sand County almanac*, New York, Oxford University Press.

Levins, R. and Lewontin, R., 1985, *The dialectical biologist*, Cambridge, Mass., Harvard University Press.

Lovejoy, A., 1964 edition, *The great chain of being*, Cambridge, Mass., Harvard University Press.

Marsh, G., 1965, *Man and nature*, Cambridge, Mass., Harvard University Press.

Martin, E., 1991, 'The egg and the sperm: How science has constructed a romance based on stereotypical male-female roles,' *Signs*, 16, 485-501.

Martin, E., 1992, 'The end of the body?' *American Ethnologist*, 19, 121-40.

Marx, K., 1964, *The economic and philosophic manuscripts of 1844*, New York, International Publishers.

Marx, K., 1967, *Capital*, Volume 1, New York, International Publishers.

Marx, K., 1971, 'On the Jewish question,' in McClellan, D. (ed.), *Karl Marx: Early texts*, Oxford, Basil Blackwell.

Marx, K., 1973, *Grundrisse*, Harmondsworth, Middlesex, Penguin.

Marx, K. and Engels, F., 1965, *Selected Correspondence*, Moscow, Progress Publishers.

Marx, K. and Engels, F., 1975, *Collected works*, Volume 5, New York, International Publishers.

May, R., 1992, 'How many species inhabit the earth?' *Scientific American*, October, 1992, 18-24.

McCay, B. and Acheson, J., 1987, *The question of the commons: The culture and ecology of human resources*, Tucson, The University of Arizona Press.

McEvoy, A., 1988, 'Towards an interactive theory of nature and culture: Ecology, production and cognition in the California fishing industry,' in Worster, D. (ed.), *The ends of the earth*, Cambridge, Cambridge University Press.

McGann, J., 1983, *The romantic ideology: critical investigation*, Chicago, University of Chicago Press.

Merchant, C., 1980, *The death of nature: women, ecology and the scientific revolution*, New York, Harper & Row.

Meszaros, I., 1970, *Marx's theory of alienation*, London, Merlin Press.

Mitman, G., 1992, *The state of nature: Ecology, community, and American social thought, 1900-1950*, Chicago, University of Chicago Press.

Naess, A., 1989, *Ecology, community and lifestyle*, Cambridge, Cambridge University Press.

Nash, R., 1989, *The rights of nature: A history of environmental ethics*, Madison, University of Wisconsin Press.

Norberg-Schulz, C., 1980, *Genius loci: Towards a phenomenology of architecture*, New York, Rizzoli.

Norgaard, R., 1985, 'Environmental economics: An evolutionary critique and a plea for pluralism,' *Journal of Environmental Economics and Management*, 12, 382-94.

O'Connor, J., 1988, 'Capitalism, nature, socialism: A theoretical introduction,' *Capitalism, Nature, Socialism*, 1, 11-38.

Ollman, B., 1971, *Alienation: Marx's conception of man in capitalist society*, Cambridge, Cambridge University Press.

Ollman, B., 1990, 'Putting dialectics to work: The process of abstraction in Marx's method,' *Rethinking Marxism*, 3, 26-74.

Ollman, B., 1993, *Dialectical Investigations*, New York, Routledge.

Ophuls, W., 1977, *Ecology and the politics of scarcity: A prologue to a political theory of the steady state*, San Francisco, Freeman.

O'Riordan, T., 1981, *Environmentalism*, London, Pion.

Paehlke, R., 1989, *Environmentalism and the future of progressive politics*, New Haven, Yale University Press.

Parsons, H. (ed.) 1977, *Marx and Engels on ecology*, Westport, Conn., Greenwood Press.

Pearce, D., Markandya, A. and Barbier, E., 1989, *Blueprint for a green economy*, London, Earthscan.

Redclift, M., 1987, *Sustainable development: Exploring the contradictions*, London, Methuen.

Relph, E., 1989, 'Geographical experiences and being-in-the-world: The phenomenological origins of geography,' in Seamon, D. and Mugerauser, R., (eds.), *Dwelling, place and environment: Towards a phenomenology of person and world*, New York, Columbia University Press.

Rousseau, J-J., 1973, *The social contract and discourses*, London, Everyman.

Sagoff, M., 1988, *The economy of the earth: Philosophy, law, and the environment*, Cambridge, Cambridge University Press.

Sale, K., 1985, *Dwellers in the land: The bioregional vision*, San Francisco, Sierra Club Books.

Sauer, C., 1956, 'The agency of man on earth,' in Thomas, W. (ed.), *Man's role in changing the face of the earth*, Chicago, Chicago University Press.

DAVID HARVEY 51

Simmel, G., 1978, *The philosophy of money*, London: Routledge and Kegan Paul.

Smith, N., 1990 (second edition), *Uneven development: Nature, capital and the production of space*, Oxford, Basil Blackwell.

Smith, N., 1992, 'Geography, difference and the politics of scale,' in Doherty, J., Graham, E. and Malek, M. (eds.), *Postmodernism and the social sciences*, London, Macmillan.

Smith, N. and O'Keefe, P., 1985, 'Geography, Marx and the concept of nature,' *Antipode*, 12, No. 2, 30-39.

Spoehr, A., 1956, 'Cultural differences in the interpretation of natural resources,' in Thomas, W. (ed.), op. cit.

Spretnak, C., 1985, 'The spiritual dimension of Green politics,' in Spretnak and Capra, *Green politics: The global promise*, London, Paladin.

Spretnak, C. and Capra, F., 1985, *Green politics: The global promise*, London, Paladin.

Steiner, G., 1992 edition, *Heidegger*, London, Fontana.

Todes, D., 1989, *Darwin without Malthus: The struggle for existence in Russian evolutionary thought*, Oxford, Oxford University Press.

Thomas, W. (ed.), 1956, *Man's role in changing the face of the earth*, Chicago, Chicago University Press (two volumes).

Urry, J., 1990, *The Tourist Gaze*, London, Sage.

Weale, A., 1992, *The new politics of pollution*, Manchester, Manchester University Press.

Williams, R., 1973, *The country and the city*, London, Chatto and Windus.

Williams, R., 1980, *Problems in materialism and culture*, London, Verso.

Wilson, A., 1992, *The culture of nature: North American landscape from Disney to the Exxon Valdez*, Oxford, Basil Blackwell.

Worster, D., 1985(a), *Nature's economy: A history of ecological ideas*, Cambridge, Cambridge University Press.

Worster, D., 1985(b), *Rivers of empire: Water, aridity and the growth of the American West*, New York, Pantheon Books.

Young, I., 1990, *Justice and the politics of difference*, Princeton, NJ, Princeton University Press.

Young, R., 1985, *Darwin's metaphor: Nature's place in Victorian culture*, Cambridge, Cambridge University Press.

Zimmerman, M., 1988, 'Quantum theory, intrinsic value, and panentheism,' *Environmental Ethics*, 10, 3-30.

Zola, E., 1967, *L'argent*, Paris, Pleiade.

OLD THEMES FOR NEW TIMES: BASILDON REVISITED

Christopher Norris

This paper took shape during a period (1991-92) that witnessed, among other melancholy episodes, the return of the British Conservative government for a fourth consecutive term of office and the outbreak of a large-scale neo-colonialist war fought by the US and its coalition partners in the name of a 'New World Order' equated with Western economic and geo-strategic interests. I abandoned work on the original draft in order to write a book about the Gulf War which tried to explain how large sections of the erstwhile left or left-liberal intelligentsia had been won over to consensus-based doctrines of meaning and truth that left them unable to articulate any kind of reasoned or principled opposition.[1] Critical theory – or what passed itself off as such among postmodernists, post-structuralists, post-marxists and kindred schools – amounted to a wholesale collapse of moral and intellectual nerve, a line of least resistance that effectively recycled the 'end-of-ideology' rhetoric current in the late 1950s. Francis Fukuyama achieved overnight celebrity on the lecture circuit with his announcement that history had likewise come to an end, since the entire world – or those parts of it that counted for anything – had converted to capitalism and liberal democracy, thus rendering conflict a thing of the past.[2] Of course there would continue to be trouble-spots, those unfortunate 'Iraqs and Ruritanias' (in Fukuyama's phrase) where the winds of change had yet to penetrate, and where 'crazed dictators' like Saddam Hussein could still create problems for the New World Order.[3] But these regions were beyond the civilized pale, their conflicts 'historical' (or ideological) in the bad old sense, and therefore to be treated – not without regret – as scarcely 'the kind of place that we should wish to make our home'.

Meanwhile commentators in journals like *Marxism Today* – whose very title had by now become something of a standing joke – queued up to renounce any lingering attachment to such old-hat notions as truth, reason, critique, ideology, or false consciousness. Whatever their doubts with regard to Fukuyama and his end-of-history thesis, at least they were united in rejecting those ideas as having now been overtaken – rendered obsolete – by the passage to a postmodern ('New Times') outlook that acknowledged the collapse of any hopes once vested in Marxism or other such delusory 'meta-narrative' creeds.[4] This realignment of theoretical positions on the left went along with a widespread tactical retreat from socialist principles among Labour Party politicians, policy-makers, and (more or less) well-disposed media and academic pundits. Such thinking was presented as a victory for the 'new realism', for a programme that sensibly adjusted its sights to the horizon of a broad-based popular appeal defined in accordance with the latest opinion-poll feedback. On a range of issues – nuclear disarmament, trade union law, privatization, public sector funding etc. – it was thought to be in Labour's best electoral interests to adopt a more pragmatic line, or one more responsive to perceived changes in the currency of popular belief.

This involved a great deal of awkward (not to say devious and shuffling) argumentation, most of all with respect to Labour's erstwhile unilateralist stance, which had now to be presented – absurdly enough – as an option that somehow lacked credibility in the post-Cold War era. Better dump such commitments, it was felt, than carry on arguing a reasoned and principled case for this or that item of old-style socialist policy. For on one point at least the commentators were agreed: that elections were no longer won or lost on the strength of valid arguments, appeals to moral justice, or even to enlightened self-interest on the part of a reasonably well-informed electorate. What counted now was the ability to seize the high ground of PR and public opinion management by adopting strategies that faithfully mirrored the perceived self-image of the times. No matter if this led to a series of policy climb-downs that inevitably left the Labour leadership exposed to charges of inconstancy, tergiversation or downright cynical opportunism. No matter if it rested on a *false* consensus, a devalued and distorted version of the pragmatist appeal to what is 'good in the way of belief', more aptly characterized (in this case) as what is 'good in the way of consensus ideology as determined by those with the power and influence to shape popular opinion'. For to raise such objections was merely to demonstrate one's failure to move with the times, or one's attachment to hopelessly outworn ideas of truth, right, reason, or ethical accountability.

Small wonder that the end of all this pragmatist adjustment was a situation where many perplexed voters opted for the dubious comfort of sticking with the devils they knew. And on the intellectual left – among the pundits in journals like *Marxism Today* – the same orthodox wisdom prevailed. Thus it was taken as read that Labour's only chance was to update its image by adopting a rhetoric more consonant with these new (postmodern, post-industrial or 'post-Fordist') times.[5] In the process it would need to dump old alliances, among them its close relationship with the unions, its traditional reliance on a strong base of working-class support, and its claims to represent or articulate such interests in the name of a better, more just and egalitarian social order. These principles no longer held much appeal – it was argued – for an increasingly *déclassé* electorate whose allegiances had more to do with social aspiration – with Conservative talk of 'upward mobility', the 'classless society' and so forth – than with facts like unemployment, urban deprivation, the run-down of public services, or the emergence of something like a two-tier system in health care and education. To harp on such facts about the Tory record in office was a mistake, so the pundits urged, since it ignored the extent to which voters could identify with an upbeat rhetoric (however remote from their present situation and real future prospects) which clearly struck a responsive chord among many of Labour's erstwhile or potential supporters. Only by abandoning the moral high ground – by attuning its message to those same hopes and aspirations – could the party hope to win back the confidence of voters in its crucial target groups. What this advice came down to was a domesticated version of the wider postmodernist outlook, that is to say, a line of argument that renounced all notions of truth, principle or genuine (as opposed to imaginary) interests, and which counselled that those values henceforth be replaced with a straightforward appeal to whatever seemed best in the way of short-term electoral advantage. More specifically, it involved the four major premises: 1) that for all practical purposes truth is synonymous with consensus belief; 2) that ideology (or 'false consciousness') is an outmoded concept along with other such Marxist/enlightenment doctrines; 3) that any talk of 'class' or 'class-interests' was likewise a chronic liability, given the changed (and immensely more complex) conditions of present-day social experience; and 4) that these conditions required a complete re-thinking of Labour's claims to 'represent' any actual or emergent community of interests. What might be left of 'socialism' at the end of this revisionist road was a question that the pundits preferred not to raise, unless by according it – as many now advised – the dignity of a decent burial.

When the results came through one might have expected some modification of this line, or at least some acknowledgement that pragmatism had not paid off, and that maybe it was time for a long hard look at matters of policy and principle. On the contrary: the first postmortem articles were off on exactly the same tack, arguing (as in a *New Statesman* piece by Stuart Hall) that Labour had betrayed its own best interests by *not going far enough* along the revisionist path.[6] The litmus-test here was the issue of tax reform and redistribution of wealth, since it offered the sole instance of an election pledge (higher taxes for those who could afford to pay) where Labour had – albeit very cautiously – ventured to challenge the consensus wisdom. Indeed there was heartening evidence from interviews and polls during the run-up campaign that this policy enjoyed support even among voters in the projected high-tax band who agreed ('in principle') that the extra burden would be more than offset by the wider benefits of improved health care, increased spending on education, investment in public transport, social services, welfare provision etc. In the event it appears that many people switched votes at the eleventh hour, or perhaps (more depressingly still) that they had intended to vote Conservative all along, but concealed the fact as simply too shameful to acknowledge. Anyway the post-election consensus was that this had been yet another great mistake on Labour's part, a piece of high-minded (but pragmatically disastrous) policy-making which once again revealed the widening gap between socialist principle – or principled politics in whatever form – and the 'realities' of life as currently perceived by voters in the crucial interest-groups. As Stuart Hall put it:

> [t]he shadow budget's tax bands gave Labour the look of punitive vindictiveness. It drew the line where, realistically, it reckoned people could afford it, forgetting that in post-Thatcher Britain, people calculate their tax liabilities not on what they actually earn, but how much they hope, desire or aspire to earn in the very near future. Labour was playing the economics of realism and fiscal rectitude. The Tories played the 'sociology of aspirations'.

The language of this passage would repay close analysis in the style of Raymond Williams' *Keywords*, that is to say, a socio-cultural anatomy of the times based on the semantics (or the structures of compacted meaning) contained within certain ideologically loaded terms.[7] To be 'realist' in such matters, on this account, was to abandon that other (more pragmatic or efficacious) kind of 'realism' which might have carried Labour to victory had its strategists only taken heed of the opinion-polls and not indulged their old, vote-losing fondness for values like truth, reason and principle. For such values count for little – so the argument runs – as compared with those 'hopes and aspirations' (however ill-founded) which the Conservatives were much better able to exploit by appealing to a highly seductive realm of imaginary wish-fulfilment.

Stuart Hall would most likely reject any comparison between this kind of hard-headed 'realist' assessment and Baudrillard's wholesale postmodernist espousal of a 'hyperreality' that negates all distinctions between truth and falsehood, fact and fiction, real human needs and their simulated counterparts as purveyed by the opinion-polls, market-research agencies, voter-group profiles and so forth.[8] His essay is after all a serious contribution to debate, written from a standpoint of sober diagnostic hindsight, and hence worlds apart from Baudrillard's style of puckish nihilist abandon. But this does seem to be where his arguments are headed, especially in view of the way that 'realism' shifts over, in the course of his article, from a usage that signifies something like 'old-fashioned socialist respect for the truth-telling virtues' to a sense much more within the Baudrillard range, i.e. 'willingness to play the postmodern game and make the most of one's chances through a "realist" appeal to the current self-images of the age'. It is hard to know how else one should interpret passages like the following:

Bland and colourless as he is, Mr. Major may indeed be finely tuned, as a political symbol, to these intricate (and perhaps self-deceiving) attempts to square the circle, and to the other underlying sociological and aspirational shifts in the electorate that have taken place. His meritocratic 'decency' registers with extraordinary precision exactly that balance between the desire for a more 'caring' self-image, which led committed Thatcherites, with heavy hearts, to ditch Mrs. Thatcher, and that deeply self-interested calculation, which remains her enduring contribution.

On the one hand this acknowledges the specious character of John Major's electoral appeal, his continuation of Thatcherite policies under a different (more 'caring' and 'decent') rhetorical guise, and the extent to which voters had been taken in by this superficial switch of style. On the other it veers away from any such realist judgment, 'realist' (that is to say) in the strong sense of maintaining the distinction between truth and falsehood, or allowing that those electors were actually *wrong* – deceived by the rhetoric of their own 'aspirational' self-image – into voting as they did. What Hall cannot countenance is any hint of a return to notions like 'ideology' or 'false consciousness', terms that might provide at least the beginning of an answer to the questions posed by his article.

Thus Hall's talk of 'squaring the circle' applies most aptly to his own attempt to explain this phenomenon while denying himself recourse to the only adequate explanatory concepts. For on a postmodernist reading of the signs there is simply no escaping the closed circuit – the pseudo-logic of specular misrecognition – which accounts for John Major as a 'finely tuned' (albeit a 'bland and colourless') symbol of voter aspirations, while viewing the electorate as a passive reflector of those same imaginary interests. 'Imaginary', that is, for the majority of voters who would surely lose out (on any realist reckoning) once the Tories were returned to power. Of course there were others – relatively few – whose 'real' (if selfish and short-term) interests John Major could plausibly claim to represent, and who thus had cause (if not justification) for welcoming the outcome. But Hall is in no position to remark such differences, resting as they do on a prior set of distinctions – real/imaginary, true/false, knowledge/ideology etc. – which he regards as simply obsolescent. Not that he wishes to dump the whole baggage of socialist aims and principles. Indeed he goes so far as to acknowledge that these are still 'decent' values, that Labour fought a 'decent' campaign, and that even its fiscal policy was justified – in real if not in 'realist' terms – by the existing maldistribution of wealth. Nor is the reader left in any doubt as to Hall's grim prognosis for the coming electoral term. Thus:

> under his [Major's] benign regime, Thatcherism as a model of social transformation will continue to work its way through the system. By the time we are allowed to vote again, education, public transport and the welfare state will have been reconstructed along the two-track lines of the National Health Service, and broadcasting will have succumbed to the new brutalism. Everything in life will be 'private' ('I have, of course no intention of privatising the NHS') – in the sense of privately owned, run, or managed, driven by the short-term model or powered by the self-interested, profit-motivated goals of British

bosses, the most philistine and least successful ruling class in the Western World. In this sense, Mr. Major is child and heir of Thatcherism, smile and smile as he may.

One could hardly wish for a clearer, more forthright and impassioned statement of the social evils likely to follow from another five years of Conservative rule. Certainly Stuart Hall has no desire to line up with the chorus of ideologues, tabloid commentators, business analysts, captains of industry and the like, all of them greeting the election result as yet another chance to proclaim the demise of socialism East and West. But they could well take comfort from his other, more 'realist' line of argument concerning the need for Labour to move with the times and adapt its image to current ideas of what is good – pragmatically warranted – in terms of consensus belief. For in the end this amounts to a vote of no confidence in any kind of reasoned or principled socialist case that would counter the drift towards a politics based entirely on the workings of (real or illusory) self-interest.

II

It seems to me that the lessons to be learned from Labour's defeat were precisely the opposite of those proferred by Stuart Hall and other commentators of a 'New Times'/postmodernist persuasion. One has to do with the inbuilt limits (or the self-defeating character) of a pragmatist approach that goes all out for electoral appeal by abandoning even the most basic standards of reason, consistency, and truth. In this sense there was justice in the charge against Labour – exploited to maximum effect in the Tory press – that its turnabout on the issue of nuclear disarmament was merely a tactical ploy, having nothing to do with any change of conviction or (still less) any realist assessment of the altered geopolitical state of affairs. By taking the line of least resistance (very much in accordance with 'New Times' wisdom) Labour relinquished not only the moral high ground but also its chance to argue a case much strengthened by this turn in real-world events. For their policy shift was all the more absurd when set against the obvious benefits to be gained by sticking to the unilateralist case *on pragmatic as well as principled grounds* and thus pointing a sensible way forward from the deadlock of entrenched Cold War attitudes. On fiscal policy, by contrast, Labour came up with a justified (fully workable and right-minded) set of arguments, despite all the sage advice from opinion-poll watchers, media pundits, and those – like Stuart Hall – who counselled a more 'pragmatic', 'realist' or consensus-based line of approach. Quite possibly this cost them dear in the election, though the case is by no means proven. What seems more likely is that various things combined to sway people's voting intentions at the last moment, among them the distorted press coverage, the 'aspirational' factor (as Hall defines it), and no doubt a measure of greed and self-interest on the part of those high-bracket earners who wished only to protect their own pockets. But none of this touches the central issue, that is to say, the question whether Labour was right to adopt such a policy, or whether – on a more 'realistic' assessment – it should have switched course and fine-tuned its message to the signals coming back with each new opinion-poll or latest media sounding. For on this account what is right (pragmatically effective) in any given context just *is* what produces the required results by appealing to the widest possible range of in-place values and beliefs. That the voters might actually be wrong – and that a 'failed' policy might none the less be *justified* on reasoned and principled grounds – is simply inconceivable, along with all that old-style enlightenment talk of 'ideology', 'false consciousness' and the like.

Let me quote one further passage from Hall's article which exemplifies some of the moral and intellectual contortions produced by this effort to analyse Labour's defeat from a post-ideological standpoint.

> Choice, opportunity to rise, mobility within one's lifetime, the power to decide your own fate, where anyone, whatever his or her background, can become anything, provided they work hard enough; this is what Mr. Major means by 'classlessness' and 'a society at ease with itself'. The claim appears ludicrous to more egalitarian folk. But it is exactly the kind of 'accessible classlessness' that millions believe to be desirable and realistic, and exactly the kind of low-powered motor that takes Majorism beyond traditional Tory areas into a new arena where new constituencies are there to be won. This is the voice that was heard in Basildon and a thousand new 'classless' working-class and suburban communities across the country, the heartland of the new 'sociology of aspirations'.

Stuart Hall knows full well how bogus was this appeal to a 'classless' society that existed only as a figment of the social imaginary, projected on the one hand by shrewd Tory strategists with an eye to the electoral main chance, and on the other by those 'millions' who doubtless believed such a prospect to be both 'desirable' and 'realistic'. He also knows that there is a difference between wish and reality; that this gap is not closed (though it may be kept from view) by pragmatic talk of what is 'good in the way of belief'; that voter 'aspirations' were expertly played upon in the course of the election campaign; and that they bore no resemblance – outside this imaginary realm – to anything that might reasonably be expected from a further term of Conservative rule. More precisely: Hall knows all this at the level of straightforward knowledge-by-acquaintance, or on the basis of certain well-documented facts (unemployment, social deprivation, high-income tax breaks, cutbacks in the health service, in public transport, education etc.) which gave the lie to those illusions so sedulously promoted by the Tory propaganda machine. But when it comes to drawing the relevant lessons there are things that Hall either chooses to ignore or somehow cannot bring himself to 'know'. Among them are the three most salient points: that many people voted against their own and the country's best interests, that they did so for ideological reasons, and – following from this – that despite being out of fashion as a concept among present-day critical theorists 'false consciousness' still has some useful explanatory work to do.

Hall's reluctance to concede these facts gives rise to some curious argumentative and rhetorical shifts. The symptoms appear in those queasy quote-marks around phrases like 'accessible classlessness', 'sociology of aspirations', and 'a society at ease with itself'. For the passage simply won't let on as to whether we should take them at face value (i.e., as both 'desirable' and 'realistic') or whether, on the contrary, they are best treated from a critical, diagnostic, or socio-pathological standpoint. To opt for the first and reject the second reading would amount to a line of unresisting acquiescence in whatever the opinion-polls happened to say, or whatever people could be brought to accept through forms of manufactured consensus belief. It would thus mark the end of any socialist hopes for a better, more just or humane social order achieved by criticizing false beliefs and exposing their imaginary (ideological) character. But from a 'New Times' perspective this looks too much like the old Marxist or enlightenment line, the arrogant idea that intellectuals are somehow entitled to speak up for truth, reason or principle as against the current self-images of the age. Thus Hall winds up in the odd position of recognizing 'Majorism' for the hollow fraud that it is – a re-run (so to speak) of Marx's *Eighteenth Brumaire*, with Thatcher and Major standing in for Napoleon and *Napoléon le petit* – while denying himself the conceptual and ethical resources to come straight out and acknowledge the fact. And this despite his often clear-eyed perception of the means by which voters were persuaded to endorse a mystified version of their own real interests as purveyed by the Tory media.

One could make the same point about Hall's passing nod to the standard 'left' analysis, his remark that such popular hopes and aspirations must appear ludicrous 'to more egalitarian folk'. For this prompts the obvious question: does Hall still count himself among their number, or has he now moved on with these postmodern times to the stage of abandoning all such high-toned (unrealistic) talk? Hence what comes across as the tonal insecurity, the sense of an irony that somehow misfires and hits the wrong target. For *either* Hall believes (as surely he does) that egalitarian and socialist principles are still worth upholding, *or* (to judge solely by the passage in hand) he has redefined 'socialism' in such a way as to sever its links with any principled commitment to notions of equality, social justice, or redistribution of wealth. This is the real irony of Hall's analysis: that in leaning so far toward consensus-values (or refusing to endorse a critique of those values in ideological terms) he effectively denies any prospect of escaping from the goldfish-bowl of imaginary misrecognition. And if the message is directed primarily at old-style left intellectuals – or 'egalitarians' who have failed to register the postmodern signs of the times – then it also rebounds on those other, more representative types for whom

'Majorism' exerted a genuine (if in some sense illusory) appeal. For theirs, as Hall reminds us, 'was the voice that was heard in Basildon and a thousand new "classless" working-class and suburban communities across the country'.

With a little decoding this last sentence has a good deal to say about the problems and perplexities that beset Hall's diagnosis. Again he resorts to quote-marks in order to soften that otherwise oxymoronic conjunction of terms ('"classless" working-class') required by an argument which in effect wants to have it both ways, conceding the reality of social class as a matter of everyday experience, while renouncing such ideas – from a 'New Times' perspective – as nominal definitions that no longer correspond to anything in the nature of current social trends. Then there is the reference to Basildon, a place-name that will surely be fixed in the memory of anyone who stayed up late on election night to see the results come in. For Basildon was a Conservative-held seat high on the list of Labour's looked-for gains if it was to stand much chance of forming the next government. What made this result even more crucial as an index of the way things were going was the fact that Basildon presented such a challenge to conventional (income- or class-based) demographic methods for predicting electoral trends. Situated in the border-zone between London and Essex, home to a great many upwardly mobile or hard-to-classify voters, representing as it did (and as Hall rightly notes) the very heartland of the 'new sociology of aspirations', Basildon was indeed a feather in the wind for psephologists and other watchers of the pre-election scene. In the event it was among the first results to be declared and marked the turn from predictions (however guarded) of a workable Labour majority to predictions (increasingly confident) that the Conservatives were back in power.

So Stuart Hall has good reason, on these grounds at least, for his choice of Basildon as something of a test-case in light of the election result. But again there is a difference – a crucial difference – between analysing the causes (socio-economic, psychological, demographic etc.) which conspired to produce that result, and holding it out as an object-lesson, a model instance of the kinds of voter-appeal that Labour would have done well to cultivate. For in that case pragmatism (in its 'Majorite' form) would define the agenda of political debate not only for the Basildon electorate but also for those others – professing socialists or Labour campaign managers included – who sought to learn the lessons of electoral defeat and adapt more successfully the next time around. After all, John Major 'embodies the growing number of people who, though not mystified about their humble class origins, no longer believe they should remain, as he puts it, "boxed in" to them forever'. And moreover, according to Hall, 'he articulates this attitude, not in terms of the reality of, but the *aspiration to*, social mobility, and the ethic of personal achievement'. This passage would again bear a lot of conceptual unpacking, but a few salient points must suffice. What can it mean to be non-mystified about issues of class and social origin if this promotes a mind-set perfectly attuned to John Major's spurious *déclassé* rhetoric, or a groundswell of imaginary identification with class-interests so remote from those of even the most upwardly-mobile Basildon voter? How should we interpret such talk of an 'ethic of personal fulfilment' if not by realistically translating it back into the language of straightforward Thatcherite greed, self-interest, or acquisitive individualism? What remains of the socialist argument against these values if one adopts a new 'realism' (or a 'new sociology of aspirations') which models itself so closely on the style and techniques of Tory campaign management? And again: why assume that Basildon (of all places!) points a way forward to the only kind of future – or the only 'realistic' policy options – for a re-think of Labour strategy in light of its latest electoral defeat?

One might have thought – on the contrary – that any lessons to be learned from 'Basildon 1992' had to do not so much with Labour's need to back down on yet more of its socialist principles as with its need to stand by those principles, communicate them more effectively, and (above all) combat their malicious and distorted presentation in the organs of Tory propaganda. It would indeed be cause for despair if the 'voice of Basildon', as heard on election-night, were taken as a truly representative sample, an instance of those 'heartland' communities that Labour has to win by ditching its every last policy commitment and espousing a rhetoric of '"classless" working-class' values. This message may perhaps carry credence with analysts – especially cultural critics of a post-Marxist 'New Times' persuasion – whose main interest is in seeking out evidence to support their reading of the signs. Otherwise there would seem little merit in resting one's case for policy review very largely on the vagaries of a localized melting-pot constituency where voting behaviour can better be analysed in causal-symptomatic than in rational terms. Stuart Hall of course draws the opposite conclusion, lamenting Labour's failure to press far enough with its revisionist line. Thus: 'the adaptation has been too shallow, painful without cutting deep . . . More the kind of face-lift marketing men give an old product when launching it with a new package, less a shift of political culture and strategy rooted in the configurations of modern social change'. In effect this attempts to turn the tables on all those old-fashioned, high-toned moralists by suggesting that the *principled* course would have been for Labour to conduct such a wholesale policy review, as contrasted with a shiftily compromise approach or a kind of half-way revisionism that lacked the courage of its own pragmatist convictions. Nothing could be further from the truth, at least to the extent that 'truth' is still in question (as distinct from its suasive or imaginary substitutes) for anyone adopting this line. What the election results bore home with painful clarity – and nowhere more so than in Basildon – was the fact that

Labour could only lose out by playing the Tories at their own cynical game, or adjusting its image to whatever seemed currently good in the way of belief.

On Stuart Hall's account the best, most courageous (as well as effective) electoral strategy would have been one that pushed right through with this revisionist programme and denied itself the recourse to such old-left palliatives as 'ideology', 'false consciousness' and the like. Such is at any rate the message implicit in his call for a thoroughgoing 'shift of political culture and strategy' responsive to – or dictated by – the 'configurations of modern social change'. In fact Hall's phrase is 'rooted in', which suggests something more like a Gramscian organic relation, a quasi-naturalized elective affinity between socio-economic structures and their articulation at the level of cultural values and political beliefs. But there is no room here for the role that Gramsci attributes to 'critical' intellectuals, that is to say, those thinkers who challenge the dominant ideology from a dissident standpoint identified with interests that are marginalized by the current consensus.[9] For they could exercise this role only in so far as such interests achieved articulate expression *over and against* the prevailing set of values, beliefs, or cultural self-images. And this would in turn require a stronger (more adequately theorized) account of 'ideology' than anything allowed for by Hall's consensualist model, i.e. his understanding of 'political culture and strategy' as a matter of finely-tuned feedback response, or rapid adjustment to the latest opinion-poll findings. What drops out of sight on this analysis is the difference (again) between real and imaginary interests, or the extent to which people can be swung into accepting a false – systematically distorted – view of those interests through various well-tried suasive techniques.

Clearly there would be small hope of success for any future socialist strategy which ignored the 'Basildon factor', or which failed to take account of the demographic shifts – the new 'sociology of aspirations' – noted by observers like Hall. Such data provide the indispensable starting-point for a politics aware of the problems it confronts in overcoming those forms of imaginary investment (or ideological misrecognition) so effectively exploited by Conservative Central Office and its allies in the tabloid press. But this is not to say – far from it – that the only 'realistic' way forward for Labour is to tailor its appeal to the image given back by those same (however accurate or in some sense representative) findings. For it is a counsel of despair, a no-win policy even in tactical terms, to adopt this pragmatist line of least resistance and thus offer nothing but a softened-up version of Tory electoral strategy. Given such a choice many voters will feel that they might as well opt for the genuine article – for a politics frankly wedded to the values of self-interest and appetitive individualism – rather than one that concedes those values in a shamefaced or opportunist manner. This was how it appeared with Labour's climb-down on the unilateralist issue, and also (contrary to Hall's post-mortem) with its rush to abandon other such policies without the least show of reasoned or principled argument.

Of course there is the danger of arrogance, complacency, or worse in the use of terms like 'ideology' and 'false consciousness', terms that may connote an offensively us-and-them attitude, a presumption of superior (undeluded) knowledge on the part of enlightened leftist intellectuals. In Terry Eagleton's words, 'I view things as they really are; you squint at them through a tunnel vision imposed by some extraneous system of doctrine'. Or again: 'His thought is red-neck, yours is doctrinal, and mine is deliciously supple'.[10] After all, as Eagleton bluntly remarks, 'nobody would claim that their own thinking was ideological, just as nobody would habitually refer to themselves as Fatso . . . Ideology, like halitosis, is in this sense what the other person has'.[11] No doubt the desire not to strike such an attitude plays its part in current variations on the pragmatist, postmodernist or end-of-ideology theme. It is likewise a factor in commentaries on the British political scene which understandably back off from imputing 'false consciousness' to a sizable portion of the electorate, or from setting themselves up as somehow in possession of a truth denied to those other, more benighted types. But one should also bear in mind Stuart Hall's reference to the illusions suffered by well-meaning 'egalitarian folk' who continue to believe – despite all the signs – that socialism cannot or should not make terms with the reality of social injustice. For it is they (Hall implies) who must nowadays be seen as the real dupes of ideology, that is to say, of an attitude which vainly persists in distinguishing truth from its various 'imaginary' or 'ideological' surrogates. What thus starts out as a decent respect for the other person's viewpoint – or a dislike of high-handed moralizing talk – in the end becomes a kind of reverse discrimination, a refusal to conceive that anyone could have grounds (reasoned and principled grounds) for adopting such a dissident stance. And this would apply not only to left intellectuals hooked on notions like truth, critique, or ideology but also to those credulous old-guard types – among them the majority of Labour voters – who persist in the sadly deluded belief that 'socialism' means something other (and more) than a shuffling adjustment to the signs of the times.

III

The debate around postmodernism in philosophy, criticism and cultural theory may appear far removed from the doldrums of present-day British and US politics. All the same I think it is worth pursuing the connection – at the very least the elective affinity – between this *au courant* talk of 'New Times' on the post-Marxist left and that strain of ultra-nominalist sceptical thought for which the sublime figures as a limit-point of language or representation, a point where (according to theorists like Lyotard) philosophy comes up against a salutary check to its truth-telling powers and prerogatives. These are specialized concerns, sure enough, and unlikely to rank very high on the list of anyone seeking a persuasive diagnosis of contemporary social and political ills. But the connection may appear less remote if one considers (for instance) some of Lyotard's claims with regard to the Kantian sublime, a topos whose extraordinary prestige and prominence in recent critical debate can hardly be explained without taking stock of that wider cultural context.[12] For what the sublime gives us to reflect upon – in Lyotard's account – is the absolute 'heterogeneity' of phrases-regimes, the gulf (or 'differend') that exists between judgments in the cognitive or epistemic mode and judgments of an ethical, political, or evaluative nature.[13] These latter cannot (should not) be subjected to the same kinds of validity-condition that standardly apply with phrases in the domain of factual or historical knowledge. That is to say, they belong to a realm quite apart from that of theoretical understanding, where the rule is that phenomenal intuitions must be 'brought under' concepts by way of ascertaining its operative powers and limits. For there is always the danger (so Kant warns us) that philosophy will overstep those limits, pursuing all manner of metaphysical ideas which may be perfectly legitimate in themselves – i.e., as bearing on the interests of reason in its pure or speculative modes – but which can have no basis in our knowledge of the world as given by the forms of sensuous cognition and adequate conceptual grasp.[14]

To confuse these realms is moreover a mistake which leads on to some large and damaging consequences. On the one hand it exposes theoretical enquiry (science and the cognitive disciplines) to a range of bewildering distractions, projects that begin by aiming beyond their epistemological reach, and which end up – most often – by reactively adopting some posture of extravagant sceptical doubt. On the other it tends to annul the distinction – so vital for Kantian ethics – between *determinate* judgments (having to do with matters of causal consequence, factual truth or logical necessity) and *reflective* judgments that issue from the sphere of 'suprasensible' ideas or principles, and which thus secure a space for the exercise of freely-willed autonomous agency and choice. Any confusions here are apt to produce the worst of both worlds, an illusory freedom (or unrestrained speculative licence) in the realm of theoretical understanding and a bleakly reductive (determinist) outlook with regard to ethical issues. Hence the significance of the Kantian sublime as a name for that which somehow 'presents the unpresentable', or which calls forth an order of affective response beyond what is given us to think or understand at the level of cognitive judgment. Hence also its attraction for Lyotard and other revisionist readers of Kant, anxious as they are to play down his attachment to the philosophic discourse of modernity and to stress those aspects of his thinking which supposedly prefigure our current 'postmodern condition'.

But the result of such readings – as I argue – is a perverse misconstrual of the Kantian project which elevates the sublime to absolute pride of place, and which does so solely in pursuit of its own irrationalist or counter-enlightenment aims.

This emerges most clearly in Lyotard's extreme version of the incommensurability-thesis, his idea that there exists a multiplicity of language-games (or 'phrase-regimes') each with its own *sui generis* criteria of meaning, validity or truth. From which it follows – again by analogy with the Kantian sublime, or Lyotard's reading thereof – that the cognitive phrase-regime not only has to yield up its privileged truth-telling role, but must also be seen as committing a form of speech-act injustice (a suppression of the narrative 'differend') whenever it presumes to arbitrate in matters of ethical or political justice. What this amounts to, in short, is a postmodern variant on the drastic dichotomy between fact and value standardly (though wrongly) attributed to Hume, allied to a strain of out-and-out nominalism which denies that statements can have any meaning – any truth-value, purport or operative force – aside from the manifold language-games that make up an ongoing cultural conversation. Only by seeking to maximize narrative differentials – by cultivating 'dissensus' or 'heterogeneity' – can thinking be sure to remain on guard against those kinds of coercive (and potentially totalitarian) phrase-regime that have so far exerted their malign hold upon the discourse of 'enlightened' reason.

Thus it is wrong, so Lyotard would argue, to adduce historical or factual considerations when assessing the significance of 'great events' like the French Revolution, the Nazi death-camps, or other such charged and evocative phrases whose meaning eludes such criteria. For this is to confuse the two distinct orders of truth-claim, on the one hand those that properly have to do with issues of empirical warrant, eye-witness testimony, archival research etc., and on the other hand those that can only find expression in a language whose evaluative character precludes any straightforward appeal to the facts of the case. The crucial point here is the way that certain *names* are taken up into a range of contending discourses which then set the terms – or establish their own criteria – for what should count as a truthful, relevant, or good-faith assertion. Those names would be 'rigid designators' (in Kripke's parlance) only to the extent that they served to pick out persons, places or dates whose reference – in some minimal sense of the word – could be taken pretty much for granted.[15] Beyond that they would evoke such deep-laid disagreement that the names would function more as surrogate descriptors, nominal points of intersection for a variety of language-games, narrative paradigms, imputed attributes, ethical judgments etc., each of them assigning its own significance to the term in question. Such names might include (to mix some of Lyotard's examples with some of my own) 'Napoleon', 'Marx', 'Lenin', 'Hitler', 'Auschwitz', 'Leningrad', 'Dunkirk', 'October 1917', 'Berlin

1953', 'Prague 1968', 'Berlin 1990', 'Baghdad 1991' and others of a kindred character.[16] In every case – according to Lyotard – their utterance gives rise to a strictly irreducible conflict of interpretations, a dispute (or differend) between rival claims as to their 'true' historical meaning.

Least of all can such issues be resolved through an attempt to establish what actually occurred, or to offer more adequate (factual or evidential) grounds for arriving at a properly informed estimate. For on Lyotard's account there is simply no passage – no possible means of translation – from the phrase-regime of cognitive (or factual-documentary) truth to the phrase-regimes of ethics, political justice, or other such evaluative speech-act genres. And this rule must apply, he maintains, even when confronted with apparently outrageous instances, like Faurisson's right-wing 'revisionist' claim that for all we know the gas-chambers never existed, since there survive no witnesses who can vouch for the fact on the basis of first-hand experience or knowledge-by-acquaintance. Of course it may be said that such arguments amount to nothing more than a vicious sophistry, an effort to obscure or deny the truth by adopting criteria grossly inappropriate to the case in hand. But this is to miss the point, according to Lyotard, since Faurisson has not the slightest interest in getting things right by the normative standards of responsible (truth-seeking) scholarly inquiry. Nor, for that matter, is Faurisson much concerned with issues of right and wrong as conceived by most historians of the Holocaust, those for whom the interests of factual truth are indissociable from questions of moral account-ability or good-faith ethical judgment. On the contrary: 'the historian need not strive to convince Faurisson if Faurisson is "playing" another genre of discourse, one in which conviction, or the attainment of consensus over a defined reality, is not at stake'.[17] Opponents may have good reason – at least by their own disciplinary or moral lights – for denouncing Faurisson as a rabid ideologue, a sophistical perverter of the truth, or a pseudo-historian whose 'revisionist' project is a cover for the crudest kinds of anti-semitic propaganda. But they will be wrong so to argue, Lyotard thinks. For quite simply there is *no common ground* between Faurisson and those who reject his views, whether professional historians affronted by his cavalier way with the documentary evidence or non-specialists appalled by his indifference to the manifest evils of Nazism and the suffering of its victims.

This is where the sublime comes in, once again, as an index of the gulf between factual truth-claims and judgments of an evaluative or ethico-political order. For what the death-camps signify (according to Lyotard) is an event beyond all the capacities of rational thought, an event that stands as the ultimate rebuke to 'enlightenment' aims and principles. At this point, he writes,

> something new has happened in history (which can only be a sign and not a fact) which is that the facts, the testimonies, which bore the traces of *heres* and *nows*, the documents

which indicated the meaning or meanings of the facts, and the names, finally the possibility of diverse kinds of phrases whose conjunction makes reality, all this has been destroyed as much as possible.[18]

If 'reality' (or historical truth) were indeed just a matter of 'phrases' – a construct out of various descriptions, vocabularies, language-games, tropes, narratives, etc. – then one might (just about) make tolerable sense of Lyotard's argument. And of course such ideas are pretty much *de rigueur* among the adepts of postmodern and post-structuralist theory, those for whom the referent is a fictive postulate, a redundant third term whose role has been eclipsed (since Saussure) by our knowledge of the 'arbitrary' relation between signifier and signified. Otherwise the passage will serve as an index – a cautionary reminder – of the sceptical extremes to which 'theory' may be driven when divorced from any sense of real-world cognitive and moral accountability. For it is a *fact* (not an 'idea' in Lyotard's quasi-Kantian usage of the term) that Auschwitz existed, that it became one of the sites for the Nazi programme of mass-extermination, that the gas-chambers functioned as a part of that programme, and moreover – as will surely be agreed by any but the most blinkered of 'revisionist' ideologues – that there exists an overwhelming mass of evidence to prove that case. Nor would Faurisson's lies (or Lyotard's scepticism) be in any way justified even if it were true that 'all this' (i.e. all the documentary evidence) had in fact been 'destroyed as much as possible'. For witness to the event would still be borne by those material traces – relics of various kinds – that were not (or could not be) so destroyed, together with the archives, the depositions of death-camp survivors, the testimony of convicted war-crime defendants, and so forth.

The same confusions are visible (albeit in less spectacular form) when Lyotard addresses political issues of class, ideology, and representation. Here again he falls back on the sublime as a kind of postmodernist shibboleth, a reminder – if any were needed – of the problems confronted by left intellectuals who still seek to make sense of history from a standpoint of class-based *Ideologiekritik*. His response to Terry Eagleton during a 1985 debate at the Institute of Contemporary Arts in London is a fair enough sample of Lyotard's reflections in this quasi-Kantian vein.

Nobody has ever seen a proletariat (Marx said this): you can observe working-classes, certainly, but they are only part of the observable society. It's impossible to argue that this part of society is the incarnation of the proletariat, because an Idea in general has no presentation, and *that is the question of the sublime* . . . I'm sure we have to read and re-read Marx, but in a critical way: that is, we must say that the question of the proletariat is the question of knowing whether this word is to be understood in terms of the Hegelian dialectic (that is to say, in the end, in terms of science), expecting to find something experiential to correspond to the concept, and maybe to the concept itself; or is the term 'proletariat' the name of an Idea of Reason, the name of a subject to be emancipated? In the second case we give up the pretension of presenting something in experience which corresponds to this term.[19]

In some details of phrasing – e.g., its talk of a 'subject to be emancipated' – this passage might seem true to its Kantian lights and even to that critical 're-reading' of Marx that Lyotard here recommends. But the postmodern scepticism shows up clearly in other, more decisive and symptomatic ways. Thus his nominalist language ('the term "proletariat"', 'the *name* of a subject') betokens Lyotard's refusal to acknowledge that such words could possess any reference outside the discourse of speculative reason. So it is that the sublime does duty, yet again, as an analogue for those strictly unrepresentable 'Ideas of Reason' whose significance lies beyond the furthest bounds of conceptual or experiential knowledge. For the only alternative – as Lyotard would have it – is an Hegelian reading of Marx on history according to which Ideas become incarnate in the form of a universal class (the Proletariat) whose advent marks the definitive transcendence of all such ontological distinctions.

This shows, to say the least, a somewhat limited grasp of debates within the Marxist theoretical tradition since Lukacs's *History and Class-Consciousness*. And as a reading of Kant it is even more skewed and tendentious, chiefly on account of Lyotard's desire to aestheticize ethics and politics by deploying the sublime as a figure of ultimate heterogeneity, a wedge (so to speak) or a deconstructive lever that can always be driven between the cognitive and evaluative phrase-regimes. Such ideas thus serve to immaterialize the language of any class-based social analysis or any account of knowledge and human interests that would assign a more than notional (speculative) content to terms like 'society' and 'class'. This whole line of argument bears a striking resemblance to other variations on the end-of-ideology theme, among them Margaret Thatcher's celebrated claim that 'society' doesn't exist, that 'individual' interests, motives, or talents are the only ones that count, and that talk of 'class' is just a tedious irrelevance in present-day social and economic terms. For whatever their express political allegiance – no matter how remote from the numbing banalities of Thatcherite rhetoric – these theorists must be seen as effectively endorsing the same ultra-nominalist position.

It is here that postmodernism feeds back into the 'New Times' thinking of an otherwise shrewd and perceptive commentator like Stuart Hall. Such, after all, is the message implicit in his article on the 1992 election campaign and the reasons for Labour's defeat at the polls. If there is any way forward for socialism in the wake of this defeat then clearly it doesn't lie through the old left country of class-politics, collective social values, or appeals to enlightened interest on the part of an informed and responsible electorate. Rather it must take full account of those factors – upward mobility, the 'classless society', free enterprise, individual 'empowerment' and so forth – whose appeal may be largely or wholly bogus when set against all the evidence to hand, but which have none the less managed to set the agenda for now and the foreseeable future. Such phrases have a ready-made suasive power – an ability to chime with the 'new sociology of aspirations' – which leaves no room for the old left analysis, based as it was on obsolete notions like truth, reality, ideology, critique, and genuine (as opposed to false or distorted) consensus values. If words (styles of talk) are indeed all we have, and if those old language-games are now hopelessly outdated, then socialists had better move with the times and adapt their rhetoric accordingly.

Hall is not much given to philosophical excursions in the manner of Lyotard and kindred spirits on the postmodern cultural scene. But his view of current domestic political 'realities' has a good deal in common with that strain of nominalist thinking which claims a starting-point and justification in Kant's idea of the sublime. Thus the language of class, of real human interests or the 'subject to be emancipated' may still (for Lyotard or Hall) possess a certain ethical resonance, a power to evoke 'Ideas of Reason' whose meaning cannot be wholly exhausted by setbacks on the socialist road. But we shall be wrong – both agree – if we think that there is 'something experiential' that could ever 'correspond' to such ideas, or if we cling to the cognitivist illusion of 'presenting something in experience' that might actually bear them out. Now of course there is some truth in these arguments, both as a matter of social observation and (albeit more debatably) in so far as Lyotard would claim to derive them from a reading of the Kantian sublime. Thus it can hardly be denied that class predicates (or socio-economic terms of analysis) become more difficult to apply – at least in any straightforward representationalist mode – at a time of rapid and complex demographic change when so many of the old class indicators no longer seem to have much purchase. To this extent Hall is fully justified in arguing that any workable socialist politics will need to take account of these factors when considering its future electoral strategy. And there is also a sense in which Lyotard is right to invoke Kant by way of controverting any simple correspondence-theory of history, politics and class-interests. Thus he can cite various passages in the third *Critique* which do indeed proffer the sublime as a token of the gulf between cognitive and evaluative phrase-regimes, the existence of a 'suprasensible' realm beyond the bounds of phenomenal self-evidence, or the confusions that arise when 'Ideas of Reason' are wrongly referred to the cognitive tribunal whose competence extends only to matters of theoretical understanding, i.e. those cases where sensuous intuitions may be 'brought under' adequate concepts. In short, there are good reasons for maintaining that the interests of justice – or the hopes of social and ethico-political progress – are not best served by a direct appeal to those interests as embodied in the actual experience of some existing class or group. Of course one might well have arrived at this conclusion without benefit of Lyotard's repeated and circuitous detours via Kant on the sublime. For Stuart Hall it is largely a matter of inductive observation, of remarking those current social trends and demographic shifts that pose a problem for more traditional (class-based) modes of analysis and critique. But for other theorists on the post-Marxist left there is a plausible (though by its very nature somewhat fugitive) connection to be drawn between the Kantian sublime and issues of a present-day political or socio-cultural import.[20]

Where this connection breaks down – as I have argued – is with the further move that presses such scepticism well beyond the point of a argued appeal to the evidence of demographic change. For it then becomes a pretext for the kind of wholesale nominalist approach that denies what should surely be apparent to any commentator, that is to say, the continuing *facts* of unemployment, social deprivation, unequal opportunities, two-tier health care, educational underprivilege and the rest. No doubt these data have then to be interpreted with a due regard to all the complicating factors – upward mobility, imaginary investment, Hall's 'new sociology of aspirations' – which will strike any reasonably sensitive observer of the current electoral scene. But there is little purpose in pursuing such analyses if they end up (like Lyotard's obsessive ruminations on the Kantian sublime) by denying both the relevance of class predicates and, beyond that, any version of the argument that would link those predicates – however refined or qualified – to the lived *experience* of class divisions in an unjust social order. It is for this reason, I would suggest, that the sublime has come to play such a prominent role in the thinking of postmodern culture-critics who are otherwise largely unconcerned with issues of a specialized philosophical nature. What it serves to promote – whether overtly or implicitly – is a sceptical ethos which simply takes for granted the collapse of all realist or representationalist paradigms, the advent of a postmodern 'hyperreality' devoid of ontological grounding or experiential content, and the need henceforth to abandon any thought of criticizing social injustice from a standpoint of class solidarity based on communal perceptions and interests. In short, there is a strong elective affinity between this strain of post-Marxist/'New Times' thinking and the current high vogue for invocations of the Kantian sublime.

IV

In his book *Protocols of Reading* Robert Scholes has some pertinent thoughts with regard to this issue of experience, class and representation as treated by various schools of post-structuralist theory.[21] His point, very briefly, is that critics cannot have it both ways, on the one hand proclaiming their 'radical' credentials and their concern with questions of politics, race and gender while on the other adopting a nominalist (or 'textualist') stance which denies any possible ground of appeal in the realities of oppression as *known and experienced* by members of the relevant class, community, or interest-group. For theory then becomes just a play-off between different (incommensurable) language-games, an affair of multiple competing 'discourses' or 'subject-positions' devoid of any real-world consequence. Feminism, conversely, 'is based upon the notion of a gendered reader, and is driven by a perception of injustice in the relations between men and women in specific social, economic, and political terms'.[22] Scholes's main target here is the claim advanced by some (mostly male) critics: that since gender is after all a discursive product, a position constructed within language, or according to the roles 'arbitrarily' assigned by this or that set of cultural codes, *therefore* it must be possible for good-willed male feminists to 'read as women', or adopt the kinds of viewpoint typically accorded to the female 'implied reader'. Such arguments understandably possess great appeal for theorists who would otherwise feel themselves *de facto* excluded from having anything relevant to say. But they are none the less mistaken, Scholes contends, since they ignore the manifold differences – the real and material (not just 'discursive') differences of interest – that characterize women's experience as subjects and readers.

This is not to say that males have nothing to learn from the encounter with feminist criticism or with work by women writers that foregrounds the issue of gender-role representation. Where the fallacy appears – as Elaine Showalter argues in her well-known essay on critical 'cross-dressing' – is with the notion that such roles go all the way down, so that male critics can somehow divest themselves of masculine attributes and espouse the other viewpoint through an act of (however well-meaning) readerly choice.[23] For this ignores the stubborn *facticity* of sexual difference, its inscription in a history (collective and individual) which cannot be so blithely transcended in pursuit of some notional view from elsewhere. As Scholes puts it:

> Both texts and readers are already written when they meet, but both may emerge from the encounter altered in some crucial respect. Feminist critics have made this semiotic process concrete and intelligible for us all, for gender – if not destiny – is one of those rough spots by which necessity, in the form of culture, grasps us and shapes our ends. Because women in this culture have been an underprivileged class, they have learned lessons in class consciousness that many men have not. Because it cuts across social class, gender brings the lessons of class consciousness into places normally so insulated by privilege as to be unconscious of the structure that supports and insulates them. Feminism, then, has drawn its strength from the ethical-political domain, by showing that women, as a class, have been regularly discriminated against by a cultural system that positions them as subordinate to men.[24]

This clear-headed passage is important to my argument for two connected reasons. First, it brings out the point that *difference* can only be a fashionable buzzword – like Lyotard's rhetoric of sublime 'heterogeneity' – so long as it is conceived in ideal abstraction from the contexts of real-world experience or the lived actualities of class and gender oppression. Second, it shows how such predicates of class-membership (e.g. 'women as a class') still play a vital descriptive and explanatory role, even – or especially – at times like the present when gender issues must be seen to 'cut across' other, more traditional modes of class analysis.

Scholes's argument here is partly a matter of empirical observation and partly – though he doesn't deploy such terms – the result of what amounts to a Kantian deduction on transcendental or *a priori* grounds. Thus practical experience is enough to confirm that any effective critique of social injustice, oppression, unequal opportunities and so forth will need to identify the particular group whose lives, prospects or conditions of existence have been consequently damaged or curtailed. Such criticism may indeed come from non-members of the group, from male feminists who strive (so far as possible) to 'read as a woman', or from left intellectuals and cultural theorists who adopt a standpoint markedly at odds with their own class-interests narrowly conceived. Even so, they will be working on the prior assumption – *contra* the postmodern sceptics and nominalists – that such a group exists, that its name corresponds (in however complex or overdetermined a way) to certain facts of shared or communicable human experience, and furthermore that criticism can best represent the interests of justice and truth by attempting to identify (and identify with) the experiences thus conveyed. At this point the empirical arguments join with the question as viewed under a Kantian (or 'conditions of possibility') aspect. For just as understanding (in its cognitive or theoretical mode) requires always that the manifold of sensuous intuitions be 'brought under' adequate concepts, so here it is the case that one cannot begin to grasp the lived realities of class or gender oppression without using terms (like 'gender' and 'class') which render that experience intelligible. And this holds – to repeat – despite all the problems (of an empirical *and* a theoretical nature) that are nowadays confronted by anyone seeking to apply such terms in a non-reductive or sufficiently 'flexible' manner.

One can therefore see why Scholes thinks it important to 'clarify the notion of *class*' as deployed in his argument, and to explain that the term is 'not restricted to socio-economic class, even though that remains as a central type or model for the concept'.[25] His point is not (or not only) that we need such enabling categories in order to wrest form from chaos, or to represent what would otherwise be lost to the flux of inchoate experience. More specifically, he is arguing *on ethico-political as well as on cognitive grounds* that we cannot do justice to these truths of experience – to the record of human suffering and waste brought about by various discriminative practices – unless we acknowledge the applicability of class predicates in this wider sense. The problem about post-structuralism is that it denies the pertinence of all such categorical descriptions, and thus contrives to block the appeal to any kind of real-world knowledge or experience. For if everything is ultimately constructed in discourse – truth, reality, subject-positions, class allegiances and so forth – then *ex hypothese* we could only be deluded in thinking that any particular discourse (for instance, that of feminism) had a better claim to justice or truth than the others currently on offer. And there is also a sense – a quite explicit and programmatic sense –

in which post-structuralism works to undermine the very bases of critical or oppositional thought. That is to say, it takes the view (the nominalist view) that 'opposition' is itself just a product of discursive differentials, a term whose meaning inevitably fluctuates with the passage from one discourse to the next, and which therefore cannot be assigned any content – any real-world experiential truth – aside from its role in this or that (wholly conventional) signifying practice. And this applies not only to those aspects of inter-cultural linguistic difference (e.g., the various colour-term vocabularies or other such discrepant semantic fields) which post-structuralists often adduce in support of their claims for ontological relativity. Instances of this sort, though striking enough, need pose little problem for a theory of translation that views them as localized exceptions to be set against the broader regularities of human understanding within and across cultures.[26] But post-structuralism goes much further in its drive to relativize meaning and truth to the structures of linguistic representation or the force-field of contending discourses. For it operates on an abstract (quasi-systemic) model of 'opposition' and 'difference' whereby those terms are deprived of all specific historical or experiential content, and treated – in effect – as linguistic artefacts or products of discursive definition.

Such is of course Saussure's account of language as a system of structural contrasts and differences 'without positive terms', a system that requires (among other preconditions for achieving theoretical consistency) the positing of an 'arbitrary' link between signifier and signified.[27] This explains his well-known lack of interest in the referential aspect of language, justified as a matter of working convenience or methodological priority. But there is no warrant whatsoever in Saussure for extending this strictly heuristic principle to the point where any mention of the referent – any appeal beyond the self-enclosed domain of signification – is regarded as a lapse into naive ('positivist' or 'metaphysical') ways of thought, to be dismissed briefly with a sigh.[28] What such ideas amount to is a form of specular misrecognition, a confinement to the structural-linguistic imaginary which mistakes its own theoretical preconceptions for the limits of language, thought, and experience in general. (Lacan is perhaps the most egregious example of the way that ontological distinctions – the imaginary, the symbolic, the real – can be so redefined as precisely to invert the order of relationship between them).[29] Hence post-structuralism's dogged attachment to a nominalist thesis which treats the Saussurian 'arbitrary' sign – or the bar between signifier and signified – as a pretext for rejecting any notion that language might give access to the realm of cognitive or experiential knowledge.

It is at this point that some theorists have perceived a kinship with current readings of the Kantian sublime, a sense in which post-structuralism might be seen as engaged with the same problematic of radically disjunct or 'heterogeneous' discourses.[30] But in both cases such scepticism follows from a failure (or refusal) to grasp Kant's argument in the first *Critique* regarding the conceptually mediated character of all empirical truth-claims, or the requirement of 'bringing intuitions under concepts' in order to establish their cognitive validity. By ignoring this requirement – switching their sights to the more seductive prospects of the Kantian sublime – these theorists end up with an aestheticized reading of Kant that reduces all forms of knowledge (and knowledge-constitutive interests) to the level of so many subject-positions constructed in and through language. It is worth quoting Scholes at some length here since he offers some particularly telling examples of the confusion engendered by a textualist approach to issues of class- and gender-politics.

> Readers who read as members of a class can be distinguished from those who are members of what Stanley Fish has called an 'interpretive community' . . ., in that membership in a class implies both necessity and interest. A member of the class *Jew* in Hitler's Germany or of the class *Black* in South Africa at present is a member of those classes by necessity and has an interest in the situation of the class as a whole . . . A class, in this sense, is a cultural creation, part of a system of categories imposed upon all those who attain subjectivity in a given culture . . . One may choose to be a feminist or not, but one is assigned one's gender and may change it only by extraordinary effort. The relationship between being female and being a feminist is neither simple nor to be taken for granted, but there is no comparable relationship between being a deconstructionist and belonging to a class – which is of course not to say that deconstruction is free of interest or beyond ideology . . . A feminist literary critic writes for other critics, to be sure, but she also writes on behalf of other women and, as a critic, she is strengthened by the consciousness of this responsibility. A male critic, on the other hand, may work within the feminist paradigm but never be a fully-fledged member of the class of feminists.

My one minor quarrel has to do with Scholes's idea that deconstruction is chiefly to blame for dissolving those various categories – among them (as he argues) the interlinked concepts of class-membership and cognitive representation – which alone make it possible to render such experience intelligible. In fact one could say more accurately – at least with reference to Derrida's work – that deconstruction continues to operate with those concepts and respect their rigorous necessity, while at the same time resisting any premature appeal to the binary structures (or logics of exclusion) on which they customarily depend.[32] This is not to deny that there are some texts of Derrida that do give credence to Scholes's charge. Among them are those essays where he touches on the topic of sexual difference and the imagined possibility of 'reading as a woman' – or exploring all manner of polymorphous gender-roles – as a strategy for contesting received ('phallogocentric') discourses of meaning and truth.[33] But elsewhere, that is to say, in the bulk of his more considered and analytical work, Derrida is at pains to disavow any notion that difference – as a concept and a fact of experience – can be somehow transformed through the utopian 'freeplay' of a writing that blithely rejects such irksome constraints. Scholes's criticism applies more justly to that facile strain of postmodern and post-structuralist thought which takes it as read –

with no philosophical qualms – that truth *just is* what we are given to make of it according to various textual strategies, gender-role constructs, signifying practices or whatever. In which case it would follow (logically though absurdly) that 'there is no significant difference between reading about an experience and having an experience, because experience never simply occurs'.[34]

The switch from 'never simply' to 'simply never' – from deconstruction to postmodernism, or Derrida to Baudrillard – is one that occurs with remarkable ease among thinkers of a 'New Times' persuasion. This is why it is important to address some of the muddles and misreadings (especially misreadings of Kant) that currently exert such widespread appeal. For these issues have a relevance – as I have argued here – outside and beyond the specialized enclaves of cultural and critical theory. In fact they are within reach of the single most urgent question now confronting left thinkers in Britain and the United States: namely, what remains of the socialist project at a time when distorted consensus values have gone so far toward setting the agenda for 'informed' or 'realistic' political debate. It might seem extravagant – just a piece of academic wishful thinking – to make such claims for the importance of getting Kant right on the relation between epistemology, ethics and aesthetics, or for pursuing the question 'What is Enlightenment' as raised once more in Foucault's late writings on the politics of truth.[35] But for better or worse it has been largely in the context of 'theory' – that capacious though ill-defined genre – that these issues have received their most intensive scrutiny over the past two decades. It is unfortunate that so much of this debate has been characterized by a proneness to the vagaries of Francophile intellectual fashion, as well as by a skewed and superficial grasp of its own formative prehistory. Philosophical confusions can often go along with disastrous failures of political judgment, as recent cases (Heidegger's among them) have demonstrated plainly enough. All of which tends to support the idea that postmodernism is more a symptom of the present malaise than a cure for modernity and its manifold discontents.

NOTES

1. Christopher Norris, *Uncritical Theory: postmodernism, intellectuals and the Gulf War* (London: Lawrence & Wishart and Amherst, Mass.: University of Massachusetts Press, 1992).

2. Francis Fukuyama, 'The End of History', *The National Interest* (Washington D.C.), Summer, 1989. See also Fukuyama, *The End of History and the Last Man* (London: Hamish Hamilton, 1992).

3. Fukuyama, 'Changed Days for Ruritania's Dictator', *The Guardian* (London), April 8, 1991.

4. See for instance Jonathan Steele, Edward Mortimer and Gareth Stedman Jones, 'The End of History?' (a discussion of Fukuyama's essay), in *Marxism Today*, November 1989, pp. 26-33.

5. See the essays collected in Stuart Hall and Martin Jacques (eds.), *New Times: the changing face of politics in the 1990s* (London: Lawrence & Wishart, 1989).

6. Stuart Hall, 'No new vision, no new votes', *New Statesman and Society*, 17 April 1992, pp. 14-15. This issue also carried a number of other 'post-mortem' articles on the reasons for Labour's electoral defeat and the best way forward for British socialism.

7. See Raymond Williams, *Keywords: a vocabulary of culture and society* (London: Fontana, 1976).

8. See for instance Jean Baudrillard, *Selected Writings*, ed. Mark Poster (Cambridge: Polity Press, 1989); also *America* (London: Verso, 1988), *Fatal Strategies* (London: Pluto Press, 1989) and *Revenge of the Crystal: a Baudrillard reader* (London: Pluto Press, 1990).

9. Antonio Gramsci, *Selections from the Prison Notebooks*, ed. and trans. Quintin Hoare and Geoffrey Nowell Smith (London: Lawrence & Wishart, 1971).

10. Terry Eagleton, *Ideology: an introduction* (London: Verso, 1991), p. 3.

11. Ibid, p. 4.

12. See for instance Peter de Bolla, *The Discourse of the Sublime: readings in history, aesthetics and the subject* (Oxford: Basil Blackwell, 1989); Neil Hertz, *The End of the Line: essays on psychoanalysis and the sublime* (New York: Columbia University Press, 1985); Hugh Silverman (ed.), *The Textual Sublime* (Albany, NY: State University of New York Press, 1990); and Slavoj Zizek, *The Sublime Object of Ideology* (London: Verso, 1990).

13. See Jean-Francis Lyotard, *The Differend: phrases in dispute*, trans. Georges van den Abbeele (Manchester: Manchester University Press, 1988); also *The Inhuman: reflections on time*, trans. Geoffrey Bennington and Rachel Bowlby (Cambridge: Polity Press, 1991).

14. Immanuel Kant, *Critique of Pure Reason*, trans. N. Kemp Smith (London: Macmillan, 1933); *Critique of Practical Reason*, trans. Lewis W. Beck (Indianapolis: Bobbs-Merrill, 1977); and *Critique of Judgment*, trans. J. C. Meredith (Oxford: Clarendon Press, 1978).

15. Saul Kripke, *Naming and Necessity* (Oxford: Basil Blackwell, 1980).

16. See Lyotard, *The Differend* (op. cit.), p. 179.

17. Ibid, p. 19.

18. Ibid, p. 19.

19. Lyotard, 'Complexity and the Sublime', in Lisa Appignanesi (ed.), *Postmodernism* (London: ICA Documents/Free Association Books, 1989), pp. 19-26; p. 23.

20. See for instance Dick Hebdige, 'The Impossible Object: towards a sociology of the sublime', *New Formations*, No. 1 (Spring 1987), pp. 47-76 and *Hiding in the Light: on images and things* (London: Routledge, 1988).

21. Robert Scholes, *Protocols of Reading* (New Haven: Yale University Press, 1989). For a wide-ranging treatment of these issues from a socio-philosophical viewpoint, see Margaret Gilbert, *On Social Facts* (London: Routledge, 1989).

22. Scholes, *Protocols of Reading* (op. cit.), p. 91.

23. Elaine Showalter, 'Critical Cross-Dressing', *Raritan*, Vol. 3, No. 2 (Fall 1983), pp. 130-49. See also Marjorie Garber, *Vested Interests: cross-dressing and cultural anxiety* (New York & London: Routledge, 1992); Stephen Heath, *The Sexual Fix* (London: Macmillan, 1982); Mary Jacobus, 'Reading Women (Reading)' and 'The Difference of View', in *Reading Women: essays in feminist criticism* (New York: Columbia University Press, 1986), pp. 3-24 and 27-40; and Alice Jardine and Paul Smith (eds.), *Men in Feminism* (London: Methuen, 1987).

24. Scholes, *Protocols of Reading* (op. cit.), p. 92.

25. Ibid, p. 92.

26. For further discussion of this and related topics, see especially W. V. O. Quine, *'Ontological Relativity' and Other Essays* (New York: Columbia University Press, 1969) and Donald Davidson, *Inquiries into Truth and Interpretation* (Oxford: Clarendon Press, 1984).

27. Ferdinand de Saussure, *Course in General Linguistics*, trans. Wade Baskin (London: Fontana, 1974); also translated by Roy Harris (La Salle, Ill.: Open Court, 1986) with significant changes of terminology and detail.

28. For a vigorously-argued critique of these ideas, see Raymond Tallis, *Not Saussure* (London: Macmillan, 1988). There is also some useful commentary to be found in Jonathan Culler, *Saussure* (London: Fontana, 1976); Roy Harris, *Reading Saussure*

(London: Duckworth, 1987); and David Holdcraft, *Saussure: signs, systems and arbitrariness* (Cambridge: Cambridge University Press, 1991).

29. See Jacques Lacan, *Ecrits: a selection*, trans. Alan Sheridan (London: Tavistock, 1977).

30. See for instance Hebdige, *Hiding in the Light*; Hertz, *The End of the Line*; Silverman (ed.), *The Textual Sublime*; and Zizek, *The Sublime Object of Ideology* (op. cit.).

31. Scholes, *Protocols of Reading* (op. cit.), pp. 92-3.

32. See especially Jacques Derrida, 'Afterword: toward an ethics of discussion', in *Limited Inc* (2nd. edn., Evanston, Ill.: Northwestern University Press, 1988), pp. 111-60.

33. See for instance Derrida, 'Women in the Beehive: a seminar with Jacques Derrida', in Jardine and Smith (eds.), *Men in Feminism* (op. cit.), pp. 189-203.

34. Scholes, op. cit., p. 99.

35. See Michael Foucault, 'What is Enlightenment?', in Paul Rabinow (ed.), *The Foucault Reader* (Harmondsworth: Penguin, 1984), pp. 32-50.

A slightly different version of this essay has appeared in the journal *New Formations*. I am grateful to the editors and publishers for permission to reprint it here.

ILLUSIONS OF FREEDOM: THE REGRESSIVE IMPLICATIONS OF 'POSTMODERNISM'

Marsha A. Hewitt

Any critical assessment or discussion of 'postmodernism' requires a common, if tentative understanding, of what the concept means; 'tentative,' because the term, 'postmodernism' surfaces in any number of academic disciplines, from architecture, to philosophy, aesthetics, literary criticism, and theology. As well, the very word 'postmodernism' contains the implicit claim that modernity is finished and done with, which is itself open to debate on two counts: first, is modernity over, and, if so, is the condition of 'postmodernity' as desirable as its exponents would have us believe? As the title of this paper indicates, the concept is itself problematic, not only because of the wide range of subjects to which it is being applied, but also because of its formulations concerning human experience, at least in contemporary Western cultures, as well as the questions postmodernism raises about the intellectual and political traditions of modernity. What most postmodernist theories share is a sustained critique, and at times, even outright repudiation of the Enlightenment and the modernist traditions that developed from it.

Some of the most cherished humanist ideals of the Enlightenment and the modern age contained in concepts such as the autonomy of the human individual, the capacity for independent judgement and reason oriented toward the pursuit of justice, freedom and human happiness, are condemned by postmodernism as 'metadiscourses' of power and knowledge whose social, cultural and political implications serve to suppress difference by subjecting all particularity and 'otherness' to the relentless, imperialist logic of identity. Against the 'totalizing' cultural practices and philosophical systems of the West, postmodernism proclaims its commitment to the 'death' of the subject, understood as an autonomous, self-reflective agent; the 'death' of history, understood as the unifying narrative of Man's progress toward self-realization; and the 'death' of Western metaphysics and ontology with their attendant claims to knowledge of Being and Truth. In place of these totalizing discourses of Western civilization, postmodernism offers a multiplicity of local narratives whose self-justification is rooted in an immanent appeal to their own specificity.

All claims to universality as a legitimate means of adjudicating values and deciding among possible strategies as authentically oriented toward justice and the satisfaction of human needs, are dismissed as further ploys of domination and the drive to mastery that is understood to be characteristic of modernity.

There are two important questions that arise in any attempt to evaluate the validity of the postmodernist claims sketched above: one involves the justification of the postmodernist critique of modernity, while the other inquires into the emancipatory or regressive implications of postmodernist theory. Hal Foster differentiates two types of postmodernism which he identifies as one of resistance, which issues in a critical 'deconstruction' of modernity, and one of 'reaction', which he describes as little more than an uncritical 'repudiation' of modernity.[1] The argument to be advanced here is that the 'deconstructive' and 'reactionary' elements of postmodern thought are not as clearly distinguishable as Foster believes, and that what appears as emancipatory critique in postmodern discourse is often little more than a 'verbal radicalism'[2] that conceals a latent, but nonetheless insidious political conservatism which undermines, rather than contributes to, the possibility of human liberation in either theory or practice.

As it is impossible to engage in a full-scale critique of postmodernism within the scope of an essay, I will restrict my argument to a critique of the postmodernist theme of the 'death' of the subject. In particular, I wish to discuss the ways in which this theme has been appropriated by feminist versions of postmodernism in order to show how the postmodernist repudiation of autonomous subjectivity works against the emancipatory interest of feminist theory and practice. The acceptance on the part of an increasing number of feminist theorists of the postmodernist version of the Enlightenment and modernity is resulting in a premature closure of discussions as to how concepts of subjectivity, autonomy, and reason may be reconstructed and expanded to advance the liberation of women. In confining the discussion to the impact of postmodernism on feminist theory, I hope at the same time to show that the 'anti-Enlightenment polemic'[3] characteristic of most expositions of postmodernism has regressive implications that extend beyond feminism.

In his essay, 'An Answer to the Question: What is Enlightenment?' (1784), Immanuel Kant wrote that,

> *Enlightenment is man's [sic] emergence from his self-imposed immaturity. Immaturity* is the inability to use one's understanding without guidance from another. This immaturity is *self-imposed* when its cause lies not in lack of understanding, but in lack of resolve and courage to use it without guidance from another. *Sapere Aude!* 'Have courage to use your own understanding!' – that is the motto of enlightenment.

This definition of Enlightenment understands that human beings are rational, self-conscious subjects with the capacity for autonomous action as agents free to make their own decisions about how to live. This concept of individuality and freedom presupposes notions of truth, justice and equality, all of which are central ideals of the modern age and deeply associated with it. Feminism, as a theory and praxis whose goal is the liberation of women from all forms of domination, is a thoroughly modern movement insofar as it claims these ideals as legitimate and necessary for women. More accurately, feminism emerges as a counterdiscourse within modernity when it interrogates the ways in which women have been excluded from the project of Enlightenment humanism, thereby demonstrating how this tradition has betrayed itself by degenerating into an exclusivist, male-centred, bourgeois, racist ideology that legitimates the material interests of a particular group at the expense of virtually the rest of humanity.

In doing this, feminism exposes the false universalisms of abstract humanism so that a concrete humanism may emerge, thereby opening the possibilities of the performative enactment of Enlightenment ideals within the material conditions of life. In this sense, feminism contributes to the political task of the reconstruction and transformation of the ideals, values and goals of modernity. Feminism is a 'modern movement',[5] and is inconceivable prior to, or outside modernity. In this sense, as far as feminism is concerned, modernity is not over, it remains unfinished.[6]

The realization of Enlightenment ideals in the cultural and political practices of daily life is impossible in the absence of rational, autonomous subjectivity. One of the most troubling themes of postmodern feminism concerns the repudiation of the concept of the subject under the rubric of 'The Death of Man'. According to Jane Flax:

> Postmodernists wish to destroy all essentialist concepts of human being or nature. They consider all concepts of Man to be fictive devices that acquire a naturalistic guise both in their construction and in repeated use within a language game or set of social practices. . . . In fact Man is a social, historical, or linguistic artifact, not a noumenal or transcendental Being. . . . Man is forever caught in the web of fictive meaning, in chains of signification, in which the subject is merely another position in language.

In disclaiming all 'essentialist concepts of human being', Flax perhaps inadvertently, reveals the presence of another essentialism behind that which postmodernism seeks to liquidate when she tells us that '*In fact* Man is a social, historical, or linguistic artifact.' (Italics added.) While I can readily agree with the critique of abstract notions of 'Man' with their consequent androcentric, imperialist, epistemological and political implications, I have great difficulty with the concept of the human being as 'artifact'. There must be an alternative notion of subjectivity that lies somewhere between the false abstraction, 'Man', and the inhuman concept, 'artifact.' Not only has one 'essentialism' given way to another, but material structures of power and domination seem to have dissolved into mere webs of 'fictive meaning', and 'chains of signification'. Oppression by signification? We should be so lucky. One of the unsettling aspects of postmodernist language is its remote impersonality and unreal tone, a typical example of which is contained in the passage quoted from Flax.[8]

A much more intensified and sustained feminist attack on the concept of subjectivity along postmodernist lines has been advanced by Judith Butler. Butler is largely concerned with deconstructing gender categories which oppress women by inscribing them with a series of fixed, 'natural' attributes which are culturally constructed devices of social control. As part of her analysis, Butler quite rightly questions the female counterpart to abstract notions of Man in the equally abstract category, 'Woman'. Part of her critique focuses on the way in which feminism implicitly adopts this category as the 'stable subject' of the feminist movement. Butler effectively exposes the repressive and authoritarian implications of a feminist theory that assumes the existence of a unitary category, 'Woman', behind the experience of individual, concrete women.

The concept of a universal female subject functions, in Butler's view, as a regulatory mechanism that dissolves and reduces the multiple differences between women into a compulsory, abstract unity in whose name political goals are defined. The result is that all women become coerced into accepting these predetermined goals as their own, whether they address the actual conditions of their lives and are accurate reflections of their particular experiences or not. It is quite true that the ways in which women suffer oppression and marginalization are specific to their particular life conditions, such as race, class, sexual orientation, and so on. As Butler writes, the unitary category of woman excludes the 'multiplicity of cultural, social and political intersections in which the concrete array of "women" are constructed'.[9] This is why feminism requires a materialist theory that is flexible enough to address the specific nature of women's oppression in given historical and cultural contexts, so that appropriate strategies capable of effectively abolishing their condition as oppressed people may be devised. Given the diversity of women's experience, a feminist theory built on an abstract concept of 'Woman' can only end up producing reifications of *women* that are not only severed from reality, but reinforce their oppression.

At the same time, Butler's critique is highly problematic, not because of her rejection of totalizing, 'identitary'[10] discourses that obliterate all distinction between concepts of female essence and living, individual women. It is precisely this critique that leads to a repudiation of no less totalizing political practices that sacrifice the plurality and multiplicity of human experience in the name of a singular movement motivated more by its own interests disguised as unified goals than by the actual needs of those it pretends to serve. Rather, what is disconcerting about Butler's analysis in the extreme is its profoundly anti-humanist tenor, which becomes clear in her treatment of subjectivity. And no less disturbing is the suggestion that the emancipation of women from gender oppression is to be achieved in changes of *style*, or gender performances. Butler's work attests to the influence of a postmodernism that values style over politics, and betrays an underlying logic that fits neatly with the demands of consumerism.

In an essay heavily influenced by (and critical of) Lacanian psychoanalytic theories, Butler explains how the interrogation of subjectivity by
those theories offer feminist theorists,

> a way of criticizing the disembodied pretensions of the masculine knower and exposing the
> strategy of domination implicity in that disingenuous epistemological gesture. The de-
> stabilization of the subject within feminist criticism becomes a tactic in the exposure of
> masculine power and, in some French feminist contexts, the death of the subject spells the
> release or emancipation of the suppressed feminine sphere . . . the political critique of the
> subject questions whether making a conception of identity into the ground of politics,
> however internally complicated, prematurely forecloses the possible cultural articulations
> of the subject-position that a new politics might well generate.
>
> This kind of political position is clearly not in line with the humanist presuppositions of
> either feminism or related theories on the left.[11]

Butler's legitimate concern with deconstructing ossified gender identities in order to expose their repressive and regulatory function that restricts
women's lives does not require 'the death of the subject', as she comes very
close to asserting here. For Butler, gender identity is discursively and
performatively constituted, a 'performatively enacted signification'[12] 'behind' which there is no subject, no identity, no 'doer behind the deed'.
Since gender acts are performative, 'there is no pre-existing identity by
which an act or attribute might be measured'; there is no 'locus of agency'
from which various acts follow, but rather gender is 'an identity tenuously
constituted in time, instituted in an exterior space through a stylized
repetition of acts'.[13] Given that 'the gendered body is performative', it has
'no ontological status apart from the various acts which constitute its
reality, and if that reality is fabricated as an interior essence, that very
interiority is a function of a decidedly public and social discourse, the
public regulation of fantasy through the surface politics of the body'.[14]

For Butler, fixed and repressive gender identities can only be abolished
with the extinction of the subject who is nothing more than performance. It
comes as no surprise, then, that in the place of concrete freedom, Butler
offers the drag performer as the model image of freedom, momentarily
achieved in the 'perpetual displacement [that] constitutes a fluidity of
identities that suggests an openness to resignification and recontextualiza-
tion [thereby depriving] hegemonic culture and its critics of the claim to
essentialist accounts of gender identity'. For Butler, the drag performer's
performances expose the 'radical contingency in the relation between sex
and gender',[15] thereby breaking the conflation of the 'referent' and the
'signifier' which inscribes a set of meanings understood to 'inhere in the
real nature of women'. The 'deconstruction' of the abstract subject of
feminism opens to 'a future of multiple significations' whereby 'unantici-
pated meanings'[16] may come into being at the site of perpetually shifting
identities. What Butler proposes is neither more nor less than privatized,
life-style changes, which is the logical consequence of freedom reduced to
resignification, politics to surfaces, and where multiple abstractions stand
in for the old repressive one.

The work of Judith Butler is representative of feminist appropriations of postmodernist themes that draw heavily on Foucauldian philosophy and Lacanian psychoanalysis. As well, her work is typical of the treatment of subjectivity and autonomous agency found in expressions of feminist postmodernism, which is one reason why her work deserves attention. The postmodernist dismissal of the possibility of a rational, self-conscious, autonomous, intersubjective subject as the agent of emancipatory change, itself reflects a totalizing theory that collapses all possible notions of subjectivity into the absolute, Cartesian Ego. In disallowing transformative reconstructions of modern concepts of subjectivity that are both situated and relational, yet rational and autonomous, postmodernism preserves the concept of the mastering ego which has long been exposed as a transparent caricature of authentic subjectivity. Moreover, the concept of subjectivity has not been uncontested by Enlightenment and modern philosophies, as can be readily seen, for example in comparing Descartes, Kant, Hegel, Marx, Freud, Horkheimer, Adorno, or Habermas.

It is indisputable that such Western notions of 'the commanding self' bent on pursuing the dream of 'acquiring absolute mastery over nature, of converting the cosmos into one immense hunting-ground',[17] is bound up with the transfiguration of reason as purposive, instrumental and manipulative, and that this concept of reason emerged as the prevalent one. The notion of instrumental reason is accompanied by an abstract form of humanism that celebrates and justifies the self-creating, ruling, all-knowing subject who subdues other human beings and nature to (usually) his dominating control. The critique of such distorted and mutilating notions of subject, reason, and humanism in the name of a concrete humanism, remains as a significant counterdiscourse of modernity, finding its most incisive expressions in the critical social theories of Karl Marx and the Frankfurt School. Postmodernist writers tend toward superficial dismissals of critical theorists such as Marx, subsuming his thought under the by-now ubiquitous label of 'master-narrative',[18] that destructive admixture of power and knowledge which reproduces domination on the level of thought. Such attributions, most notably in the case of Marx, derive from an outright misunderstanding of his concept of labour, which becomes reduced to a justifying ideology of the domination of nature by a self-inventing subject. This is a misreading of Marx that betrays an inability to attend to the subtleties of his concept of labour as *objectification*, a means of positing one's humanity to and for another. These distortions have their roots in deeper levels of misunderstanding that confuse and conflate the concept of *objectification* with *reification*, which although related, are quite distinct terms.[19] Perhaps the postmodernist obsession with perpetual 'de-centering' has gone too far, with the result that meaningful concepts lose coherence and integrity.

The task of all theories of emancipation, including and especially feminism, is to develop and reconstruct the counterdiscourse of modernity that also conceives of reason as the possibility of justice, freedom and human happiness. It is theoretically insufficient and politically dangerous to abandon these ideals which derive from and are made possible by modernity with blanket proclamations of the 'death' of the subject, history and Western metaphysics in the name of pluralism, difference and 'local narratives' for their own sake. In severing the particular from the universal, in absolutizing difference and diversity without linking them to justice, freedom and happiness as universally valid ideals for all human beings, we risk a turning inward that threatens to elevate and privilege specific groups at the expense of others, the horrifying implications of which we are now witnessing in the ethnocidal disintegration of Eastern Europe. There is a real danger in the postmodern negation of reason and subjectivity that tends to over-valorize the 'irreducible plurality of incommensurable life-worlds and forms of life' apart from all universal ideals. In this sense I can only agree with Thomas McCarthy's assessment of the need for a reconstruction of modernity:

> The undeniable 'immanence' of the standards we use to draw . . . distinctions – their embeddedness in concrete languages, cultures, practices – should not blind us to the equally undeniable 'transcendence' of the claims they represent – their openness to critique and revision and their internal relation to intersubjective recognition brought about by the 'force' of reasons. The ideas of reason, truth, justice *also* serve as ideals with reference to which we can criticize the traditions we inherit; though never divorced from social practices of justification, they can never be reduced to any given set of such practices. *The challenge, then, is to rethink the idea of reason in line with our essential finitude – that is, with the historical, social, embodied, practical, desirous, assertive nature of the knowing and acting subject – and to recast accordingly our received humanistic ideals.*[20] (Italics added)

Rather than remaining with the self-creating, absolute subject that can only be rejected, we need to conceive of an autonomous subjectivity that is at the same time communitarian and intersubjective, and which is fully aware of its social, situated and historical character. A reconstruction of the subject along the lines of the humanist ideal of modernity is especially urgent for women in their efforts toward self-emancipation. In turn, this will entail the transformation of modernity by challenging the very alienation that has resulted in twisted notions of subjectivity connected with material, political structures of domination and oppression. In this sense I can only endorse the views of feminist theorists like Rita Felski: 'Rather than announcing the death of rationality, subjectivity, or history, feminist practices indicate that such concepts must be thought differently in relation to the interests and struggles of a gender politics. The eschatological themes and motifs of exhaustion interspersed throughout much postmodernist thought seem in this context to have little relevance to the present concerns of the women's movement'.[21]

I referred earlier to the deeply anti-humanist tenor of postmodernist theorists such as Judith Butler, but which applies to most postmodern thought. In commenting on the anti-humanist tenor of postmodernist discourse in general, I am referring to the absence of acting human beings in the world, who are displaced so that we may focus our attention on the struggles of 'artifacts', 'signifiers', and 'signifying processes'. Similarly, women dissolve into an 'undesignated field of differences'[22] that constitutes 'another position in language',[23] The concept of 'critique' gives way to 'resignification', unaccompanied by efforts to distinguish between emancipatory and oppressive 'resignifications'.[24] Perhaps the concept of critique is too evocative of humanist traditions, insofar as it is associated with intentionality, accountability, and self-reflexivity, thereby presupposing a subject capable of critical thought. 'Resignifications' seem more appropriate to postmodern ideas, in that they are uncontaminated by human agency, and are much more compatible with changes that occur as repositioning in language games. Not only Butler, but much postmodernist writing 'seems to valorize change for its own sake',[25] which is likely due to the concern that nothing be excluded, except of course, the subject, which must finally be dispensed with, since subjects are 'constituted through exclusion'.[26]

In the context of postmodernism's 'simple evocation of the extinction of the subject',[27] feminists need to pose sobering questions, such as asked by Nancy Hartsock: 'Why is it, exactly at the moment when so many of us who have been silenced begin to demand the right to name ourselves, to act as subjects rather than objects of history, that just then the concept of subjecthood becomes "problematic"?'[28] Or, with Seyla Benhabib we might also ask if the critique of identity politics and theory is 'only thinkable via a complete debunking of any concepts of selfhood, agency and autonomy?'[29] Benhabib's question is especially relevant, as it challenges postmodernism with the suggestion that the critique of subjectivity does not require its simple repudiation. The critical theorists associated with the Frankfurt School (the philosophical tradition out of which Benhabib comes) recognized that concepts of subjectivity as the commanding self are little more than clichés designed to console a humanity for whom the experience of authentic subjectivity and individuality has been little more than illusory.[30] Max Horkheimer and Theodor Adorno, building on the philosophy of Hegel and Marx, were fully aware of the social nature of individuals, writing that there is no such thing as 'the pure individual in his ineffable singularity'.[31] At the same time, their critique of abstract subjectivity did not lead them to reject the individual or rational agency altogether. Their reinterpretation of psychoanalytic insights resulted in a view of subjectivity as thoroughly objective, and that what is often misunderstood as 'human nature' is the sedimentation of social, cultural and historical experience within the human psyche. Adorno's remark that the psychology of individuals 'points back . . . to social moments'[32] means that analysis of subjectivity inevitably devolves into objectivity, until it reveals 'the social and historical events that preformed and deformed the subject'. In other words, 'Before the individual can exist, before it can become an individual, it must recognize to what extent it does not yet exist. It must shed the illusion of the individual before becoming one.'[33]

For critical theory, the notion of the absolute individual not only inhibits the potential of real individuals of coming into being, it also reinforces and preserves the social status quo whose interests do not coincide with possibilities for self-actualization. In the view of Horkheimer and Adorno, Western capitalist societies' reverence for ideological 'individualism' conceals a callous disregard for real individuals, whose interests are not in line with those of the prevailing social and economic order: 'the human being is capable of realizing himself as an individual only within a just and humane society'.[34] In the absence of the very possibility for the emergence of authentic individuality under current conditions, the notion of the transcendental subject assumes the political function of a compensating illusion that disguises the degradation of real human beings: 'The more individuals are really degraded to functions of the social totality as it becomes more systematized, the more will man [sic] pure and simple, man as a principle with the attributes of creativity and absolute domination, be consoled by exaltation of his mind.'[35]

Such insights into the contradiction between abstract and concrete subjectivity is part of a critique of society which acknowledges that social transformation can only come about through the intentional, self-conscious actions of human agents. Without such individuals, 'evolution toward the humane [becomes] increasingly difficult'.[36] In the view of critical theory, human beings, while both agents of society and derivative of it, are not identical with it, leaving open the possibility for 'resistance that is always the core of true individuality'.[37]

One of critical theory's most valuable insights concerning the individual lies in its recognition of the concrete relationship between the individual and society, and that changes in the social realm, such as the intensification and proliferation of structures of domination, effect changes within human beings as well. At the same time, their consistent refusal of total identity between subject and object on the theoretical level allowed them to maintain the non-identity of individuals and society, thus leaving open possibilities for social transformation which are in turn predicated upon the capacity of individuals for critique and resistance. At the same time, critical theory saw that the hope for 'true individuality', with its capacity for critique and resistance, was fast disappearing with the intensified encroachment of capitalism into all areas of human existence, or what Habermas would call 'lifeworlds'. The brutalizing conditions necessary to the preservation and expansion of capitalism have perhaps already 'deconstructed' the subject more efficiently than was ever dreamed possible by postmodernist theories.

The question of the crisis of subjectivity and the dissolution of the individual is particularly urgent for feminist theory. The critical task of feminism is to expose and account for the dynamics of power and its effects throughout the society down to the most mundane practices of everyday life, with the purpose of constructing a 'wide-ranging critique'[38] of domination in all its diverse and different manifestations. This requires nothing less than a critical social theory that is conscious of, and continually interrogates, the materiality of its own positions and discourse, which is strikingly absent from most postmodernist discussions, and marks one of its greatest failures.

The degree to which postmodernist theories sever themselves from material reality and concrete experience is strikingly illustrated in the field of contemporary theology, which has proved no less immune to postmodernist applications than other disciplines. I will conclude this essay by turning to one of Christian theology's best known postmodernist exponents, Mark C. Taylor, whose *Erring: A Postmodern a/theology*, offers one of the clearest examples of the more problematic implications of postmodernist thought for both feminist theory and the struggles of contemporary women against the oppressive patriarchal structures of the Christian churches and the theological systems that justify them. Some problems in Taylor's approach apply to postmodernist thought in general, and its appropriation by feminism in particular. In many respects, Taylor is quite typical in the way he applies postmodernist critiques to a specific discipline, and this is the point of referring to his work. Like many other postmodernist writers, he too uses deconstructionist techniques in order to integrate fairly standard postmodernist themes into his discussions of Christian theology, which leads him, predictably, to jettison the subject and celebrate the loss of self. He writes:

> . . . I explore the possibility that the dissolution of the individual self gives rise to anonymous subjectivity, in which care-less sacrifice takes the place of anxious mastery and unreserved spending supplants consuming domination. The expropriation of personality presupposes the appropriation of death. This loss of self is not, however, simply nihilistic. The disappearance of the subject is at the same time the emergence of the trace. The trace concretely embodies the ceaseless interplay of desire and delight.[39]

Taylor's 'delight' in the disappearance of the subject leads him to embrace the rather traditional religious values of 'self-mortification', 'sacrifice of the self', 'dismemberment' and 'homelessness', which he presents as valid existential options leading to more authentic experiences of the divine. What is missing in his thought is a conscious awareness of the materiality of his own discourse, along with its consequent political implications. There is an unsettling sense of unreality that increases with each deconstructive move, becoming most apparent in his treatment of the homeless person, and, later, 'woman'. As for the homeless person, he writes:

> Free from every secure dwelling, the unsettled, undomesticated wanderer is always unsettling and uncanny. Having forsaken the straight and narrow and given up all thought of return, the wanderer appears to be a vagrant, a renegade, a pervert – an outcast who is an

irredeemable outlaw. The outlaw is forever liminal, marginal; he is curiously ambivalent, shifty, and slippery. Insofar as the outlaw is not only a heretic who transgresses but also a subversive who breaks the (power of the) law, erring points to the ways of grace.[40]

Taylor returns to the image of the homeless wanderer at various points in the book, but at no point does it become anything more than an abstract fragment, disconnected from reality. The image loses all poetry if one recalls the actual existence of destitute, discarded human beings whose numbers are vastly increasing as a result of the inhuman and cruel effects of a global capitalism that generates impoverishment and misery for the majority of the world's population. The idealized image of the homeless wanderer presented here has the political effect of rendering the concrete, suffering homeless person invisible in a romantic image which not only leaves the material conditions that create poverty and homelessness unquestioned, but implicitly accepts them. Without a real homeless human being, and the conditions that produce her or him, there would be no one to idealize. As everyone knows, the existence of the homeless and the outcast as such is the direct result of injustice. These are issues that postmodernism appears incapable of, or uninterested in confronting. This is perhaps the inevitable result of a theory that having dispensed with all concepts of transcendence, including transcendence of specific social conditions, contents itself with the 'delight in the superficiality of appearances'.[41]

There are equally disquieting implications for feminism and the question of women's liberation in Taylor's unthinking celebration of the inherent affinities between 'woman' and 'superficiality'. His rather brief treatment of 'woman' is as unreal as is his treatment of the homeless, as he whimsically weaves together quotations from Nietzsche and Derrida that link 'woman' with the 'untruth of truth', the 'superficiality of experience'. Taylor's comments on the superficial nature of 'woman' leads him into further acts of intellectual free association, where he somewhat enigmatically considers the occupation of tailors, since they too are 'after all . . . profoundly interested in surfaces and completely preoccupied with appearances'.[42] For Taylor, 'Appearance and nothing more' is the concern of woman, 'for she suspects (but only suspects, since she is never certain about anything) what man refuses to admit: there is nothing other than appearance'.[43] A feminist reading of such texts must inquire into their social and historical contexts, raising questions about the ways in which such attitudes continue to legitimate the violence, sexual abuse, discrimination, degradation and inequality that have long marked the specific history of the domination of women in many societies. Are these phenomena merely appearances? What are the political consequences for women in societies whose cultural practices and institutional structures presuppose that women are 'naturally' associated with superficiality rather than depth, suspicion rather than reason, and untruth rather than truth? The unreflective manner in which Taylor quotes Nietzsche and Derrida on women has the political effect of endorsing some long-standing theological prejudices toward women, the harmful effects of which they still suffer. Such assumptions about women are neither new to Christian theology nor to the philosophical traditions of the West, and it is surprising that Taylor can in fact repeat them without critical comment. But perhaps it doesn't matter if women are, after all, mere positions in a language game.

Not only feminism, but any social theory with conscious emancipatory goals needs to seriously consider the regressive implications of postmodernism. As argued here, one of the most serious issues in need of critical scrutiny is postmodernism's dismissal of subjectivity and the Enlightenment values associated with it. As for feminism, the example of Taylor illustrates that the repudiation of subjectivity connected with affirmations of self-sacrifice that reduce human agency to the status of a 'trace' threatens to ultimately relocate women within the old, debilitating associations that have traditionally undermined their full humanity.[44]

To tell women, for whom the issue of subjectivity and autonomy has always been historically and socially problematic, to give up the struggle since the whole concept is by now passé, is to abandon hope not only in the future liberation of women, but in the possibility of reclaiming and reconstructing the best Enlightenment traditions inherited by modernity that hold the ideals of justice, freedom and human happiness as valid for *all* human beings. There is some truth to postmodernist charges that these ideals have become distorted and mutilated, resulting in the deformation of reason into mastery and instrumentality, while relegating justice to the private preserve of privileged groups. Nonetheless, the formation of a negative critique that accounts for the twisted processes that inform all areas of modernity remains the greatest service that a feminist critical theory can render modernity, let alone itself. To reduce feminist theory and praxis to a 'localized strategy of subversion in a postmodern era'[45] not only trivializes feminism, it threatens to divest it of its critical and emancipatory power.

NOTES

1. Hal Foster (ed.), *The Anti-Aesthetic: Essays on Postmodern Culture*, Port Townsend: Bay Press, 1983, p. xii.
2. Russell A. Berman, 'Troping to Pretoria: The Rise and Fall of Deconstruction', *Telos* No. 85, Fall 1990, p. 5.
3. Sabina Lovibond, 'Feminism and Postmodernism', *New Left Review*, No. 178, November – December 1989, p. 5.
4. Immanuel Kant, *Perpetual Peace and Other Essays on Politics, History and Morals*, trans. Ted Humphrey, Indianapolis/Cambridge: Hackett Publishing Company, 1983, p. 41. For a critique of this essay that contains several postmodern concerns vis-a-vis the Enlightenment, see Michel Foucault, 'What Is Enlightenment?', in *The Foucault Reader*, ed. Paul Rabinow, New York: Pantheon Books, 1984.
5. Sabina Lovibond, 'Feminism and Postmodernism', p. 11.
6. Here I have in mind the essay by Jürgen Habermas, with which I am largely in agreement: 'Modernity – An Incomplete Project', in Hal Foster, *The Anti-Aesthetic*.

7. Jane Flax, in *Thinking Fragments: Psychoanalysis, Feminism, and Postmodernism in the Contemporary West*, Berkeley: University of California Press 1990, p. 32.
8. While generally sympathetic to postmodernist accounts of subjectivity, Flax is not altogether uncritical: 'the postmodernist narratives about subjectivity are inadequate', because they do not incorporate to the 'specificity of women's experiences or desires'. (p. 210) While there is some truth to this, Flax's critique does not address the deeper problems attached to the postmodernist caricature of a unitary Master Self that remains impervious to change and revision throughout all forms of Enlightenment discourse. In fact the nature of 'subjectivity', 'human essence', and 'epistemology' have always been contested in modern philosophy, from Descartes to the present.
9. Judith Butler, *Gender Trouble: Feminism and the Subversion of Identity*, New York: Routledge, Chapman & Hall, Inc., 1990, p. 14.
10. The term 'identitary', or 'identitarian' is used by Theodor Adorno in one of his most important, yet highly compressed essays, 'Subject and Object', in *The Essential Frankfurt School Reader*, Andrew Arato and Eike Gebhardt, eds., New York: Continuum Publishing Company, 1982, p. 505.
11. Judith Butler, 'Gender Trouble, Feminist Theory, and Psychoanalytic Discourse', in *Feminism/Postmodernism*, Linda J. Nicholson (ed.), New York: Routledge, Chapman & Hall, 1990, p. 327.
12. Ibid., p. 33.
13. *Gender Trouble*, p. 141; 140.
14. Judith Butler, *op. cit.*, p. 336.
15. Ibid., p. 338.
16. Judith Butler, 'Contingent Foundations: Feminism and the Question of "Postmodernism"', *Praxis International*, Volume 11, No. 2, July 1991, p. 160. In this article Butler defends herself from the charge that her critique of the subject is identical with calling for the annihilation of the subject. However, the negativity of her critique of the subject is such that I remain unconvinced by her disclaimer.
17. Max Horkheimer and Theodor W. Adorno, *Dialectic of Enlightenment*, trans. John Cumming, New York: The Seabury Press, 1972, p. 35; 248.
18. Jean-François Lyotard, *The Postmodern Condition: A Report on Knowledge*, trans. Geoff Bennington and Brian Massumi, Minneapolis: University of Minnesota Press, 1984.
19. Marx elaborates his concept of labour as objectification in the 'Economic and Philosophic Manuscripts of 1844', in Karl Marx and Frederick Engels, *Collected Works*, Volume 3, New York: International Publishers, 1975. The distinction I have in mind between 'objectification' and 'reification' follows Herbert Marcuse's interpretation of Marx's concept of alienated and unalienated labour. According to Marx, objectification is a social activity that occurs within labour as a free activity and the universal self-realization of human beings. Objectification is not necessarily tied to domination. Within the alienated conditions of capitalism, objectifying activity unfolds into reifying activity, in that the products of human labour, along with their social relationships, have little to do with humanity's real needs and creative capacities, becoming estranged to the point that they are experienced as having a 'life of their own' that is often hostile to humanity. It is essential that the distinction between the two concepts is maintained; in many critiques of Marx, including those from feminist perspectives both postmodernist and not, objectification is employed when the sense of the text more accurately implies reification. See for example, Seyla Benhabib's and Drucilla Cornell's 'Introduction: Beyond the Politics of Gender', in *Feminism as Critique*, Minneapolis: University of Minnesota Press 1988, p. 2, and Linda Nicholson in the same volume, p. 18. For Marcuse's interpretation of Marx which offers one of the best clarifications of the distinction between objectification and reification, see 'The Foundation of Historical Materialism', in *Studies in Critical Philosophy*, trans. Joris De Bres, London: NLB, 1972.
20. Thomas McCarthy, 'Introduction', Jürgen Habermas, *The Philosophical Discourse of Modernity*, trans. Frederick Lawrence, Cambridge: The MIT Press, 1990, p. x.
21. Rita Felski, 'Feminism, Postmodernism, and the Critique of Modernity', *Cultural Critique*, Number 13, Fall 1989, p. 53.
22. Judith Butler, *op. cit.*, p. 160.

23. Seyla Benhabib, 'Feminism and Postmodernism: An Uneasy Alliance', *Praxis International*, Volume 11, No. 2, July 1991, p. 139.

24. Nancy Fraser, 'False Antithesis: A Response to Seyla Benhabib and Judith Butler', *Praxis International*, *op. cit.*, p. 170.

25. Nancy Fraser, *op. cit.*, p. 171.

26. Judith Butler, *op. cit.*, p. 158. I agree that 'exclusion' is a necessary part of self-conscious subjectivity, because it involves choice. People choose, for example, to embrace democracy by excluding fascism, or choose peace by excluding war as a desirable means for resolving conflicts. Indeed, 'I am' implies that 'I am not' something or someone else, and so on. Such 'exclusionary' acts however do not negate or even necessarily impede the establishment of intersubjective relationships and mutual respect between human beings who understand themselves as subjects.

27. Jürgen Habermas, *The Philosophical Discourse of Modernity*, p. 310.

28. Nancy Hartsock, 'Rethinking Modernism: Minority vs. Majority Theories', *Cultural Critique*, Number 7, Fall 1987, p. 196.

29. Seyla Benhabib, 'Feminism and Postmodernism', *op. cit.*, p. 140.

30. Max Horkheimer and Theodor W. Adorno, *Aspects of Sociology*, trans. John Viertel, Boston: Beacon Press, 1972, p. 48.

31. Ibid., p. 41.

32. Theodor W. Adorno, 'Sociology and Psychology', *New Left Review*, Number 46, November – December 1976, p. 73.

33. Russell Jacoby, *Social Amnesia: A Critique of Conformist Psychology from Adler to Laing*, Boston: Beacon Press, 1975, p. 79; 81.

34. Max Horkheimer and Theodor W. Adorno, *Aspects of Sociology*, trans. John Viertel, Boston: Beacon Press, 1972, p. 46.

35. Theodor W. Adorno, 'Subject and Object', p. 500.

36. Max Horkheimer, *Eclipse of Reason*, New York: Continuum, 1974, p. 156.

37. Ibid., p. 161.

38. Rita Felski, *op. cit.*, p. 56.

39. Mark C. Taylor, *Erring: A Postmodern A/theology*, Chicago: The University of Chicago Press, 1984, p. 15.

40. Mark C. Taylor, *Erring*, p. 150.

41. Ibid., p. 15 – 16.

42. Ibid., p. 171 – 172; 180.

43. Ibid., p. 171 – 172.

44. For a fuller discussion of the ways in which the intellectual traditions of the West have failed to recognize the full humanity of women, see my 'The Politics of Empowerment: Ethical Paradigms in a Feminist Critique of Critical Social Theory', in *The Annual of the Society of Christian Ethics*, November, 1991, pp. 173 – 192.

45. Rita Felski, *op. cit.*, p. 56.

FALSE PROMISES – ANTI-PORNOGRAPHY FEMINISM

Lynne Segal

Few political movements sprung into life with more confidence and
optimism than the Western women's liberation movements of the late
Sixties and early 1970s. 'Sisterhood', as Sheila Rowbotham, enthusiastically declared back in 1973, 'demands a new woman, a new culture, and
a new way of living'.[1] Men, perhaps reluctantly, would be swept along as
well, she continued: 'We must not be discouraged by them. We must go
our own way but remember we are going to have to take them with us.
They learn slowly. They are like creatures who have just crawled out of
their shells after millennia of protection. They are sore, tender and afraid.'[2]
But today many people, women and men alike, are urging all of us to crawl
right back into our shells – it's safer, we are told, to stay put, to seek
protection, because there is no change in men's eternal and ubiquitous
oppression of women. 'Our status as a group relative to men has almost
never, if ever, been changed from what it is'[3], Catharine MacKinnon tells
us, in 1992. After all these years, what has feminism achieved? Nothing.

The End of Optimism

Yet women's liberation unquestionably *did* expand everybody's horizons,
forcing a redefinition of what is personal and what is political. And of
course most things have changed for women, much of it due to the
persistent pressure of organised feminism. As I argued in *Is the Future
Female?*, however uneven and complicated the general achievement of
feminist goals seeking women's autonomy and equality with men, they are
now widely supported and respectable. A mere twenty years ago women
lacked even the words to speak in our own interests, and when attempting
to do so invariably met with ridicule.[4] Campaigns against sexual harass-
ment and violence against women, for childcare provision, abortion rights
and women's equality generally are all now familiar on trade union and
council agendas, however much recession and cutbacks in welfare have
further entrenched working-class and ethnic minority women in increasing

impoverishment. Women today are more aware of their rights, less ready to be exploited and more aggressive.

Despite its own success, however, despair is the theme of much contemporary feminist writing. Once optimism starts to wane, former ways of seeing can quickly become obscured, even disappear altogether. Victories are no longer visible. With confidence in decline, new theoretical frameworks start replacing the old, frameworks which transform memory itself, the stories we tell of our own past, our ideas for the future. We have seen it happen in one radical movement after another since the close of the 1970s. Within feminism, nowhere is this more apparent than in the area of sexual politics.

Only two decades ago, although it feels more like two lifetimes, it was common for women who were politically aware and active to declare themselves both sexual liberationists and feminists. In the early years of the Women's Liberation Movement, women's rights to sexual pleasure and fulfilment, on their own terms, symbolised women's rights to autonomy and selfhood. Despite all its sexism, all its unexamined (pre-Foucauldian) acceptance of drives and their repression, all its complications for women at the time, it was the liberation rhetoric of the New Left of the 1960s, around notions of emancipation and participatory democracy, which provided the inspiration for the emergence of second-wave feminism. Today, however, there has been a shift away from any type of sexual radicalism towards a bleaker sexual conservatism. The same notions of autonomy and selfhood are turned around, used against the very idea of sexual pleasure, at least in its heterosexual varieties, as being incompatible with women's interests. Sexual discourses and iconography are seen as ineluctably linking female sexuality (and hence identity) with female submission.

It is true that there has been some powerful yet positive women's writing on female sexuality, but it comes from and addresses lesbian desire and practice – in terms of its specific challenge to the 'heterosexual matrix' linking sex and gender. Lesbian and gay studies and writing are beginning to blossom in academic institutions and popular publishing outlets. In scholarly texts they introduce a heterogeneous range of discourses, debates, research and analyses which constitute a rich and exciting new field of cross-disciplinary theoretical work on sexuality. This development comes out of the still confident and campaigning sexual politics created by the last twenty years of lesbian and gay struggles and self-reflection. Once merely the object of a medical gaze and elaborate scientific classification, lesbian and gay people increasingly set the agenda for a reversal in which the interrogators are interrogated, and compulsory heterosexuality, heterosexism and the roping of sexuality to gender themselves become the problem.5

Two decades of campaigning feminism, however, have yet to produce the same level of confident and diverse reversals which might begin to turn around the traditional male gaze and phallic construction of the heterosexual woman. Instead, contemporary feminist debate and discourses around heterosexuality remain engulfed by the anti-pornography campaigns and politics of the 1980s. The rhetoric of sexual liberation which featured so prominently in the idealistic politics of the 1960s, inspired many women as well as men to dream of a different world of love and freedom. The early women's liberation movement of the 1970s emerged out of that era, both using and contesting its notions of 'sexual liberation' and 'freedom', while organizing around abortion, childcare and men's domestic responsibilities, to build the power of women. All too soon, however, feminist awareness of both the extent of men's violence against women (much of it sexual) and the cultural ubiquity of discourses linking sexuality and female submission produced new depths of pessimism over the possibilities for any sexual liberation on women's terms.

With denunciation rather than celebration the growing mood of the moment, a type of political lesbianism became the sexual ideal for one influential strand of feminism: 'Women who make love to women are more likely to express their sexuality in a more equal way.' Most feminists simply stopped writing about sex altogether, refocussing on the problem of men's violence. Not to focus thus, in Britain, was to court aggressive attack from the 'revolutionary feminist' faction, increasingly active from 1978. Coincidentally, in the United States, Women Against Pornography groups grew rapidly from 1978. Not coincidentally, as Ann Snitow was later to write, this was the time when the mood of the women's movement changed – especially in the US where the feminist anti-pornography campaigns first flourished, and which has always had a profound influence on feminism in Britain.[6] Having just witnessed the defeat of women's rights to state-funded abortion, won only four years earlier, the Equal Rights Amendment (ERA) was coming under serious attack from the growing strength of the New Right, soon to sweep Reagan to power and to derail the ERA. With poorer women facing greater hardship, welfare services being removed, and the conservative backlash against radical politics in the ascendancy everywhere, 'pornography' came to serve as the symbol of women's defeat in the US. From then on, feminists were less confidently on the offensive, less able to celebrate women's potential strength, and many were now retreating into a more defensive politics, isolating sexuality and men's violence from other issues of women's inequality. Today many feminist writers, in tune with the age-old voices of conservatism, insist like Susanne Kappeler, that 'sexual liberation' merely reinforces women's oppression.[7]

There certainly are formidable obstacles which continue to block women's moves towards empowering political perspectives, sexual, social and economic, but anti-pornography feminism is, in my view, increasingly one of them. It accompanies, and resonates with, the rise of pre- and post-feminist traditionalisms found, for example, in the assertion of Islamic fundamentalism or the recent western 'pro-family' backlash against feminism. Because of the place of sex in our culture and our lives, however, it has always been tempting to displace personal and social crises and discontent onto sexuality. It's not so much that sex can drive us crazy, as Victorians once thought, fearing masturbation as the source of all vice and degeneracy, but the reverse. Sex has been given such a central place in our culture and narratives of personal identity that all our craziness – our wildest dreams and worst fears – are projected onto it.

The Focus on Pornography

To the bewilderment of many of second-wave feminism's founding members (who were often ridiculed for their concern with their own orgasms in seeking to liberate 'the suppressed power of female sexuality' from centuries of male-centred discourses and practices), pornography seemed to become *the* feminist issue of the 1980s. The critique of the sexism and the exploitation of women in the media made by women's liberation in the 1970s had indeed always been loud and prominent. After picketing the Miss World beauty contest as the decade kicked off, pin-ups, pornography, advertising, textbooks and religious beliefs and imagery, all – with spray gun and paint – were declared 'offensive to women'. In the 1970s feminists had not, however, sought legal restrictions on pornography, nor seen it as in any way uniquely symbolic of male dominance – the virgin bride, the happy housewife, the sexy secretary, were all equally abhorrent. With the state and judiciary so comprehensively controlled by men, obscenity laws were known in any case to have always served to suppress the work, if not jail the organisers, of those fighting for women's own control of their fertility and sexuality. Objecting to all forms of sexist representations, feminists then set out to subvert a whole cultural landscape which, whether selling carpet sweepers, collecting census information or uncovering women's crotches, placed women as the subordinate sex.

Representatively, Ruth Wallsgrove, writing for *Spare Rib*, declared in 1977 'I believe we should not agitate for more laws against pornography, but should rather stand up together and say what we feel about it, and what we feel about our own sexuality, and force men to re-examine their own attitudes to sex and women implicit in their consumption of porn.'[8] This type of feminist emphasis on women's need to assert their own sexual needs and desires, however, and force men to discuss theirs, came to be overshadowed by, and entangled with, feminist concern with the issue of male violence by the close of the seventies. As I have described elsewhere, it was the popular writing of Robin Morgan and Susan Brownmiller in the USA in the mid-1970s which first made a definitive connection between pornography and male violence.[9] It was in their writing that men's sexuality was made synonymous with male violence, and male violence was presented as, in itself, the key to male dominance. With pornography portrayed as the symbolic proof of the connection between male sexuality and male violence, anti-pornography campaigning was soon to become emblematic of this strand of feminism. It re-defined 'pornography' as material which depicts violence against women, and which is, in itself, violence against women.

Andrea Dworkin's *Pornography: Men Possessing Women* is still the single most influential text proclaiming this particular feminist view of pornography, in which 'pornography' not only lies behind all forms of female oppression, but behind exploitation, murder and brutality throughout human history.[10] Following through such logic to draft model feminist anti-pornography legislation – the Minneapolis Ordinance – Andrea Dworkin and Catharine MacKinnon define pornography as 'the graphic sexually explicit subordination of women through pictures or words'.[11] Armed with this definition, they propose that any individual should be able to use the courts to seek financial redress against the producers or distributors of sexually explicit material if they can show it has caused them 'harm'.

And yet, despite the growth and strength of the feminist anti-pornography movement during the 1980s, particularly in the United States and in Britain (where we have seen the emergence of the Campaign against Pornography and a similar Campaign against Pornography and Censorship), some feminists, and I am one of them, (represented in Britain by the Feminists Against Censorship) passionately reject its analysis and its related practice. We see it as a mistake to reduce the dominance of sexism and misogyny in our culture to explicit representations of sexuality, whatever their nature. Men's cultural contempt for and sexualization of women long pre-dated the growth of commercial pornography, both stemming from rather than uniquely determining the relative powerlessness of women as a sex. (Other subordinated groups are somewhat similarly sexualized and exploited, whether as Black Stud, Saphire, 'effeminate' male, or working-class wanton.) Narrowing the focus on women's subordination to the explicitly sexual downplays the sexism and misogyny at work within all our most respectable social institutions and practices, whether judicial, legal, familial, occupational, religious, scientific or cultural.

More dangerously (in today's conservative political climate) we risk terminating women's evolving exploration of our own sexuality and pleasure if we form alliances with, instead of entering the battle against, the conservative anti-pornography crusade. These are alliances which Dworkin and MacKinnon have unhesitatingly pursued in the USA, collaborating almost exclusively with the extreme Right: Presbyterian minister

Mayor Hudnut III in Indianapolis, anti-ERA, anti-feminist, Republican conservative Bealah Coughenour in Minneapolis, far right preacher Greg Dixon and, of course, pro-family, anti-feminist Reagan appointee responsible for removing funds from Women's Refuges, Edwin Meese.[12] Certainly, the most effective opponents of pornography, have traditionally been, and remain, men. The men of the Moral Right (like Jesse Helms in the USA) are as deeply horrified by the feminist idea of women as sexually assertive, autonomous and entitled to sex on their own terms, as they are by gay sex or indeed any display of the male body as the object of desire rather than the subject of authority.

Any type of blanket condemnation of pornography will discourage us all from facing up to women's own sexual fears and fantasies, which are by no means free from the guilt, anxiety, shame, contradiction, and eroticization of power on display in men's pornographic productions. And even here, those few scholars, like Linda Williams in *Hard Core*, who have chosen to study rather than make their stand over pornography, point to changes in its content which are worth studying, rather than simply dismissing. There is, to be sure, little change in the monotonous sexism of soft-core pornography. But this is increasingly *identical* with the come-on, passive and provocative portrayal of women in advertising, or many other clearly non-pornographic genres – except for the explicit crotch shot. William's research suggests that the most significant change in hard-core pornography (one of the few genres where women are not punished for acting out their sexual desires), is its increasing recognition of the problematic nature of sex, with clearer distinctions being made between good (consensual and safe) and bad (coercive and unsafe) sex. She attributes this shift to more women now seeing, discussing, buying, and – just occasionally – producing pornography.[13] The changes in contemporary pornographic production mean that more women are beginning to use it. In the USA, 40% of 'adult videos' are said to be purchased by women. Nevertheless, it is men who predominantly still produce and consume pornography, which means that it is *men's* fears and fantasies which pornography primarily addresses. (Even though more women are now hoping to enter that restricted country – if they can find the right backing and the images which turn women on.)

Uninterested in the particulars of any such shifts, the basic feminist anti-pornography argument sees all pornography as very much of a piece, and its very existence as central to the way in which men subordinate women. Pornography, on this view, both depicts and causes violence against women. Fundamental to anti-pornography feminism, most recently and comprehensively presented in Britain in Catherine Itzin's new collection, *Pornography: Women, Violence and Civil Liberties*, is thus the connection made between pornography, violence and discrimination against women. Itzin opens her collection, for example, with the claim that the US Attorney General's Commission on Pornography (carefully selected by

Edwin Meese III in 1985 to seek stronger law enforcement against sexually explicit images) was 'unanimous in its finding of a causal link between pornography and sexual violence'. In fact, as Itzin must know, there were only two feminists on the Commission, Ellen Levine and Judith Becker, both of whom rejected the Commission's findings and published their own dissenting report, claiming: 'To say that exposure to pornography in and of itself causes an individual to commit a sexual crime is simplistic, not supported by the social science data, and overlooks many of the other variables that may be contributing causes.'[14]

Itzin's own collection, despite its numerous essays claiming to provide consistent and conclusive proof of links between pornography and violence, itself unwittingly undermines any such claim. For here, the psychologist James Weaver overturns what little consistency there was in the previous experimental data which had suggested that it was *only* sexually explicit *violent* material which could, for certain individuals, in specific laboratory conditions, be correlated with more calloused responses from men towards women. Weaver's data, however, 'proves' that it is exposure to any sexually explicit images, but in particular to 'consensual and female instigated sex', which produces the most calloused responses from men to women.[15] It is not hard to imagine just what the conservative right might conclude using this data – from banning sex education to banning any feminist representation of sex.

What we might more reasonably conclude from the existing experimental muddle, which provides anything but clear and consistent proof of anything at all, is not really so hard to see. It is never possible, whatever the image, to isolate sexuality out, fix its meaning and predict some inevitable pattern of response, independently from assessing its wider representational context and the particular recreational, educational or social context in which it is being received. Men together can, and regularly do, pornographise any image at all – from the Arab woman in her chador to any coding of anything as female (nuts and bolts, for example) – while the most apparently 'violent' images of S & M pornography may be used in only the most consensual and caring encounters between two people. Context really does matter. This might help to explain why inconsistency is the only consistency to emerge from empirical research which ignores both the semiotic and the social context of images of sexual explicitness. As the most recent Home Office report on pornography commissioned in the UK concluded: 'inconsistencies emerge between very similar studies and many interpretations of these have reached almost opposite conclusions'.[16]

Women's Experience of Harm

Some anti-pornography feminists who are more aware of both the inconsistency and possible irrelevance of the experimental proof of pornography's harm have preferred to call upon the testimony of women's own experience of the harm they feel pornography has caused them. A typical example is the evidence provided by one woman at the Minneapolis public hearings. There she described how, after reading *Playboy*, *Penthouse* and *Forum*, her husband developed an interest in group sex, took her to various pornographic institutions and even invited a friend into their marital bed. To prevent any further group situations occurring, which she found very painful, this woman had agreed to act out in private scenarios depicting bondage and the different sex acts which her husband wanted her to perform, even though she found them all very humiliating.[17] It was only after learning karate and beginning to travel on her own that this woman could feel strong enough to leave her husband. This is indeed moving testimony, but surely all along there was only one suitable solution to any such woman's distress: having the power and confidence to leave a man, or any person, who forced her into actions she wished to avoid, and who showed no concern for her own wishes. Pornography is not the problem here, nor is its elimination the solution.

Another type of gruesome evidence frequently used by anti-pornography feminists to establish links between pornography and violence draws upon the myth of the 'snuff movie', first circulated in New York in 1975 about underground films supposedly coming from South America in which women were murdered on camera apparently reaching a sexual climax. On investigation such movies, like the classic film Snuff itself, released in the US in 1976, have always turned out to be a variant of the slasher film, using the special effects of the horror genre, and thus distinct from what is seen as the genre of pornography.[18] There is, however, also the personal testimony of some former sex workers, exemplified by that of 'Linda Lovelace'/Marchiano. Linda Marchiano in her book *Ordeal* has described how she was coerced, bullied and beaten by her husband, Chuck Traynor, into working as a porn actress. (Interestingly, however, although coerced into sex work by a violent husband, the book actually describes how it was her success as a porn actress in *Deep Throat* which gave Linda Traynor the confidence to leave her husband, re-marry and start campaigning for 'respectable family life' and against pornography.)[19]

The more general problem here is that other sex workers complain bitterly about what they see as the false and hypocritical victimization of them by anti-pornography feminists, whose campaigns they believe, if successful, would serve only to worsen their pay and working conditions, and increase the stigmatization of their work.[20] (I am not referring here, of course, to the production of child pornography, which is illegal, along with other forms of exploitation of children.) Some sex workers declare that they choose and like the work they do, and the type of control they believe it gives them over their lives. Indeed, it has been suggested that the feminist anti-pornography campaign itself primarily reflects the privileges

of largely white and middle-class women who, not being as exploited as
many other women, can self-servingly present the issue of women's sexual
objectification by men as the source of oppression of all women.[21]

Whether it is from abused women or abused sex workers, however, what
we hear when we do hear, or read, women's testimony against pornography or the pornography industry, are stories of women coercively pres-
surised into sex, or sexual display, which they do not want – varying from
straight, to oral, anal, bondage and group sex. But we would be more than
foolish if we saw the harm we were hearing about as residing in the
pornographic images themselves, or in the possibility of enacting them
(all, without any doubt, practices which certain women as well as men, at
certain times, freely choose), and not in the men's (or possibly, although
very rarely in heterosexual encounters, women's) abuse of power. The
harm, it is important we should be clear, is contained not in the explicitly
sexual material, but in the social context which deprives a woman (or
sometimes a man) of her (or his) ability to reject any unwanted sexual
activity – whether with husband, lover, parent, relative, friend, acquain-
tance or stranger. And this is one fundamental reason feminists opposed to
anti-pornography campaigning are so distressed at each attempt to bring in
some new version of the Minneapolis Ordinance, like the so-called Pornography Victims' Compensation Act first introduced into the US Senate
in 1989, and cropping up against in New York, in 1992, or Itzin's own
proposals taken up by MPs like Dawn Primarolo and Clare Short in
Britain.

It is not just that these bills, quite contrary to the self-deceiving rhetoric
of their advocates (Itzin and Dworkin claim to be 'absolutely opposed to
censorship in every form') would suppress sexual and erotic materials by
opening up the threat of quite unprecedented levels of censorship through
harassing lawsuits and financial penalties against producers, distributors,
booksellers, writers, photographers and movie makers. It is also that,
again quite contrary to the stated goals of their supporters, such legislative
proposals cost nothing and do nothing to provide real remedies against
men's violence. State funding for women's refuges, anti-sexist, anti-
violence educational initiatives, and above all empowering women more
fundamentally through improved job prospects, housing and welfare
facilities, would seem to be the only effective ways of enabling women to
avoid violence.

Instead, however, the idea that pornographic material causes men's
violence tends to excuse the behaviour of the men who are sexually
coercive and violent, by removing the blame on to pornography. Men who
rape, murder and commit other violent sex crimes against women, children or other men may (or may not) have an interest in violent pornography. However, as overviews of all the available empirical data suggest, the
evidence does not point to pornography as a cause of their behaviour[22].

When Itzin, along with so many of the authors in her collection, weirdly but repeatedly cite as 'evidence' for pornography's harm the final testimony of serial killer Ted Bundy before his execution, they surely do more to expose rather than to support their argument. Today both the rapist and, even more hypocritically, tabloid wisdom, has learnt to lay the blame for sex crimes on 'pornography' (whereas once, with the same sort of certainty, they would lay the blame on 'mothers').

Meanwhile, although Dworkin, MacKinnon, Itzin and their supporters continue to argue that it is pornography which violates women's civil rights by increasing discrimination against them, studies in the USA and Europe have tended to reverse the picture. In the US it is in states with a preponderance of Southern Baptists (followers of leading anti-pornography campaigner Jerry Falwell) that the highest levels of social, political and economic inequality between women and men can be found – despite the lowest circulation of pornography.[23] Indeed Larry Baron discovered a positive correlation between equal opportunities for women in employment, education and politics and higher rates of pornography which he attributed to the greater social tolerance generally in these states. Such findings are consistent with those from Europe, where we find far higher levels of overall economic, political and other indices of gender equality in Sweden and Denmark compared to either the USA or Britain, and lower levels of violence against women – coupled with more liberal attitudes towards pornography.[24] Baron's survey, interestingly, also found that gender inequality correlated with the presence and extent of legitimate use of violence in a state (as measured by the numbers of people trained to work in the military, the use of corporal punishment in schools, government use of violence – as in the death penalty), as well as with mass-media preferences for violence, as in circulation rates of *Guns and Ammo*).

Beyond Pornography

It is time for feminists, and their supporters, who want to act against men's greater use of violence and sexual coercion, and against men's continuing social dominance, to abandon anti-pornography feminism. It was, after all, a type of feminist anti-pornography rhetoric which facilitated Jesse Helms successful attack on state funding for exhibitions of gay artists like Robert Mapplethorpe in the US, on the grounds that it 'denigrates, debases or reviles a person, group or class of citizens', in this case straight men. And the frightening truth is that the type of legislation anti-pornography feminism has proposed encourages new and far wider forms of censorship than anyone has yet admitted. Feminists are surely well aware that censorship does not operate simply through any single legal act or institution. Feminist anti-pornography legislation, if passed, would enable women and men to seek financial redress, through the courts, against publishers or distributors of sexually explicit material if they felt they had been 'harmed' by it. Given the current encouragement of rapists today (and certain 'experts') to point the finger of blame at 'pornography' for sexual and violent crimes, such legislation could entail all kinds of self-imposed censorship on anyone trying to market sexually explicit material – particularly material transgressing prevailing heterosexual sexist norms. (Using similar legislation in Canada, the lesbian sex magazine, *Bad Attitudes* was recently condemned and fined.)

One fundamental theoretical disagreement in the debate between anti-pornography feminists and their opponents is over the question of fantasy. In defining pornography as 'sexually explicit subordination', anti-pornography feminists want to condemn all representations which in any way erotize power. Within any erotic power relation, they assume that men always line up as the subjugator, women as the subjected. But, whether looking at the pleasures some men find in the pornography they consume, or the enjoyment women gain from romance novels (*both* charac-teristically portraying the erotization of power), it is far from clear where precisely women and men do line up. (In s/m or bondage pornography there are more portrayals of men as submissive and women as dominant than the other way around.)

Even were it possible to detect some fixed positioning of identification in a person's enjoyment of fantasy, we could never generalize from that to predict that person's public status or behaviour in everyday encounters. The indulgence of heterosexual masochistic fantasies of spanking and subordination, for example, once a favourite pastime of the Victorian gentleman, neither undermined his accompanying social and sexual domi-nation of women nor dented his sense of superiority to any other type of person, black or white. There is an autonomy to fantasy life which, if consuming pornography, may provide the setting for us to take up any number of volatile and impossible positions: active and passive, strong and weak, male and female, desired and repulsive, sacred and contemptible, pleasure-filled and suffering, and anything else as well and its opposite, all at one and the same time.

It is the social *context* of pornographic consumption which is all import-ant. Men may use pornography as a form of male bonding, in the boys night out to the sex arcades. The very same pornographic stimulation, however, may serve quite different functions when consumed in, perhaps guilty, isolation. And boys, of course, have countless other ways of male bonding. A man may also force a woman against her will to enact some sexual act he has seen in pornographic material. This is a situation, however, quite distinct from one where such material is used as a stimulus to some freely chosen sexual encounter – whether heterosexual, gay or lesbian. And of course a man, or occasionally a woman, can easily force a person to do their bidding without pornography, if that person lacks the power to refuse.

Before we start to proscribe any type of representation as in itself unquestionably harmful, we do need to raise all manner of questions about fantasy, what it means and how it works. Just as we do need to raise all sorts of questions about men and women's actual freedom to lead sexual lives of their own choosing, and seek ways of empowering women both socially and sexually. Without a more measured view on pornography, we are in danger of forfeiting the setting of sexual agendas to the right, with its traditionally repressive attitudes towards women, and towards sexuality generally.

Some men are, as they always have been, quite capable of using violence without the assistance of pornography. We are, it is true, ubiquitously surrounded by images and discourses which represent women as passive, fetishised objects; men as active, controlling agents, devoid of weakness, passivity or any type of 'femininity'. They saturate all scientific and cultural discourses of the last hundred years – from sexology, embryology and psychoanalysis to literary and visual genres, high and low – and they construct the dominant images of masculinity to which so many men, inevitably, fail, in any way, to match up. Women provide the most available scapegoats for the shame and anxiety this failure causes them.

Men don't need pornography to encounter these 'facts' of crude and coercive, promiscuous male sexualities; helpless and yielding, nurturing female sensitivities. The anxious mirrorings of these narratives of male transcendence and female passivity (as well as occasional challenges to them) are, it is true, on offer in the culturally marginal and generally disparaged genre of 'pornography'. Women (or men) may well choose to pull down or deface the sexist pin-ups or pornography which men together may use to create their own exclusionary space or to try to taunt the women around them. (Some women have preferred to paste up their own images of penile display, which usually bring down the pin-ups). From the Bible and Desmond Morris, to Roger Scruton and the *Sun* newspaper, we see messages of male transcendence which we can and should attack. There are a variety of tactics which we can use to discredit, mock or remove images we find offensive from the personal and public spaces of our lives. It is a battle which has only just begun. But there is no compelling reason to focus upon sexually explicit material alone, unless as feminists we do wish to throw in our lot with the initiatives and goals of the Moral Right.

In the end, anti-pornography campaigns, feminist or not, can only enlist today, as they invariably enlisted before, centuries of guilt and anxiety around sex, as well as lifetimes of confusion and complexity in our personal experiences of sexual arousal and activity. In contrast, campaigns which get to the heart of men's violence and sadism towards women must enlist the widest possible resources to empower women socially to seek only the types of sexual encounters they choose, and to empower women sexually to explore openly their own interests and pleasures. We do need the space

to produce our own sexually explicit narratives and images of female desire
and sensuous engagement if we are even to begin to embark upon that
journey. And there are certain to be people who will feel harmed and
provoked by our attempts.

There are lessons to be learned from the current flowering of lesbian and
gay studies and politics. They are that it is time for feminists everywhere to
expand our horizons and re-build our hopes. Even in these economically
depressed and politically conservative times, we can still recognize our
victories and attempt to surmount the real obstacles which stand in the way
of building upon them. This will return us to some of the former insights
and strategies of socialist feminism, now, however, enriched by the perspectives which black and other more specific feminist priorities can add to
them. It will return us, as well, to the need to forge alliances with any
progressive – not reactionary – forces, working against all forms of
political, economic and cultural domination.

NOTES

1. Sheila Rowbotham, *Women's Consciousness, Men's World*, Penguin, 1973, p.xi.
2. ibid, p.38.
3. Catherine MacKinnon, 'Pornography, Civil Rights and Speech' in Catherine Itzin ed. *Pornography: Women, Violence & Civil Liberties* Oxford Univ. Press, 1992, p.456.
4. Lynne Segal, *Is the Future Female: Troubled Thoughts on Contemporary Feminism*, Virago, 1987.
5. Diana Fuss, *inside/out: Lesbian Theories, Gay Theories*, Routledge, 1992, Jonathan Dollimore, *Sexual Dissidence*, Oxford Univ. Press, 1992.
6. Ann Snitow, 'Retrenchment Vs Transformation; the Politics of the Anti-pornography Movement' in *Caught Looking*, Caught Looking Inc, 1986.
7. Susanne Kappeler, *The Pornography of Representation*, Polity Press, 1986, p.160.
8. Ruth Wallsgrove, 'Pornography: between the devil and the true blue Whitehouse', *Spare Rib*, 1977, no. 65, p.15.
9. Lynne Segal, *Slow Motion: Changing Masculinities, Changing Men* Virago, 1992, ch. 8, and Lynne Segal and Mary McIntosh, eds. *Sex Exposed: Sexuality and the Pornography Debate*, Virago, 1992, introduction.
10. Andrea Dworkin, *Pornography: Men Possessing Women,* Women's Press, 1981.
11. Catharine MacKinnon, *Feminism Unmodified: Discourses on Life and Law*, Harvard, 1987, p.176.
12. Lisa Duggan 'Censorship in the name of feminism' in *Caught Looking*, Caught Looking Inc. 1986, p.63.
13. Linda Williams, *Hard Core: Power, Pleasure and the 'Frenzy of the Visible'*, Pandora, 1990.
14. In Philip Noble and Eric Nadler, *United States of America Vs. Sex*, Minnesota Press, 1986, p.311.
15. James Weaver, 'The Social Science and Psychological Research Evidence: Perceptual and Behavioral Consequences of Exposure to Pornography', in Itzin ed. op cit.
16. Dennis Howitt and Guy Cumberbatch, *Pornography: impacts and influences*, Home Office Research and Planning Unit, 1990, p.94.
17. In Everywoman, Pornography and Sexual Violence: Evidence of Links, Everywoman, 1988, p.68.
18. See Linda Williams, op cit, 1990, pp.189–195.
19. See Anne McClintock, 'Gonad the Barbarian and the Venus Flytrap; Portraying the female and male orgasm' in Segal and McIntosh eds., 1992 op cit p.129.

20. See F. Delacoste and P. Alexander, eds. *Sex Work: Writings by Women in the Sex Industry*, Virago, 1988.
21. Clarla Freccero, 'Notes of a post-Sex War Theorizer', in M. Hirsch and E. .Fox Keller eds., *Conflicts in Feminism*, Routledge, 1991, p.316.
22. See D. Howitt and G. Cumberbatch, op cit, 1990, p.94.
23. Larry Baron, 'Pornography and Gender Equality: An Empirical Analysis' *Journal of Sex Research*, 1990, vol. 27, no. 3.
24. B. Kutchinsky, 'Pornography and Rape: Theory and practice: Evidence from Crime data in Four Countries where Pornography is Easily Available', *International Journal of Law and Psychiatry*, 1990, vol. 13, no. 4, 1990.

THE RIGHTS STUFF

John Griffith

As part of its search for new and popular policies, the Labour leadership is proposing constitutional changes. Before the general election, there was conflict over the desirability of adopting a Bill of Rights and, in the event, the manifesto merely listed a number of specific reforms including a freedom of information statute and control over the security services. More recently a much wider and more comprehensive set of proposals has been advocated.

Changes in the system of government look attractive, especially after the experience of the 1980s. But the dangers are very great. The consequences of what is now proposed are, as I shall seek to show, likely to result in the serious weakening of centralised power (essential to a Labour Government) and the considerable strengthening of private interests.

A Bill of Rights, interpreted and enforced by appointed judges, an elected second chamber, devolution to regional assemblies, proportional representation, all these constitutional proposals will diffuse political power and leave a Labour Government without the means to achieve its political ends.

It is commonplace today to decry the achievements of the Attlee administrations between 1945 and 1951. Yet nothing in the last 40 years has more importantly advanced the cause of the public good. Under our constitution, electoral success gives legitimacy and authority to strong Government. That strength, in the socialist cause, must not be jeopardised.

Since 1950 the United Kingdom has been a signatory of the European Convention on Human Rights along with some 20 other countries. The Convention contains 11 substantive articles. The articles proscribing torture, inhuman or degrading treatment or punishment and slavery or servitude are absolute in their terms, while others are defined with reference to exceptions or conditions. Petitions may be lodged complaining that a country by its laws or practices has contravened an article. This is first considered by the Human Rights Commission which, if it finds that there has been a contravention, may send the case to the Human Rights

Court. If that Court upholds the Commission, the 'guilty' country must bring its law or practice into conformity with that finding.

Since the late 1960s, campaigns have been conducted seeking to incorporate the ECHR into UK domestic law. The result of so doing would be to provide that law with a Bill of Rights which would then be wholly applicable in UK courts and override or 'trump' existing laws which were inconsistent with it. In 1974 Lord Scarman joined this campaign, followed in 1977 by the Northern Ireland Standing Advisory Committee on Human Rights and in 1978 by a narrow majority in a select committee of the House of Lords. Lord Hailsham and Lord Denning have supported the campaign at times and withdrawn their support at other times. Other eminent judges have taken sides. Most members of most of the recent Liberal parties have been in favour. The Conservatives have been against, and the Labour Party prefer some specific remedies but not the general prescription.

In 1988 was launched a new campaign under the pretentious title of Charter 88. Within two years it had been supported by some 20,000 people. It called for 'a new constitutional settlement, with an enshrined Bill of Rights plus freedom of information and open government, proportional representation, a democratic House of Lords, a reformed judiciary, and certain other changes all to be incorporated in a written constitution which would 'place the executive under the power of a democratically renewed parliament and all agencies of the state under the rule of law'. The document says: 'Our central concern is the law. No country can be considered free in which the government is above the law. No democracy can be considered safe whose freedoms are not encoded in a basic constitution.'

No doubt partly because of the imminence of a general election, 1991 produced more documents. The Labour Party concentrated on freedom of information, privacy, the security services, equal opportunities, immigration, citizenship and asylum, children's rights, legal rights, and rights in employment and to assembly. Otherwise there were some constitutional changes such as the creation of elected regional authorities. The Second Chamber of Parliament would be elected, with negligible legislative powers except for an ability to hold up constitutional bills, particularly affecting fundamental rights. Presumably as the result of a compromise between opposing opinions within the party top brass, the absurd proposal is made that this delaying power would be exercised for the whole period until the next general election, under the artificial pretext that this would enable the electorate to decide.

Two much more ambitious publications followed. The National Council for Civil Liberties put forward 'A People's Charter' subtitled 'Bill of Rights: A Consultation Document'. This was an elaborate document of over 100 pages, well researched and well presented. The authors said that the Bill could form part of wider changes but did not put forward proposals for other constitutional reforms.

Also in 1991 was published 'The Constitution of the United Kingdom' the product of the Institute for Public Policy Research, a body established in 1988 and closely connected with the Labour Party though this document acknowledges help and advice from several liberals of various party allegiances.

One common belief links all these documents. It is that the principal antagonist in the battle for the enlargement of civil liberties and freedoms is the State, and its agent the Government of the day. The rights to be protected are political and modelled on the ECHR and on the United Nations International Covenant on Civil and Political Rights. Social and economic rights are listed in the IPPR Constitution but made 'not enforceable'. The UK Courts would be empowered to declare invalid any Act of Parliament or administrative practice that conflicted with the Bill of Rights.

The NCCL proposal provides that an Act of Parliament, passed after the Bill of Rights comes into effect, which is held by the courts to conflict with the Bill of Rights, may nevertheless be effective if a special Committee of the House of Commons so declares by a two-thirds majority supported by a vote in both Houses. Clearly the NCCL is worried by the criticism that Bills of Rights vest final decision-making in the appointed judiciary and wants in exceptional cases to draw the process back into ultimate Parliamentary adjudication. The result is a clumsy and elaborate device which does little to meet the principled criticism.

Because of its much broader scope, embracing not only a Bill of Rights but other constitutional reforms, the IPPR document deserves the fuller examination.

> There has over the last twenty years been a growing chorus of complaint about aspects of British government which in any other system would be recognised as constitutional.

The words are taken from the commentary introducing the written constitution for the United Kingdom proposed by the IPPR. The 'aspects' include the electoral system, the weakness of Parliament, excessive secrecy, a political police. For these defects, the IPPR recognises that there are available remedies: select committees could be strengthened, secrecy greatly reduced, freedom of information and protection of privacy made statutory requirements, and so on.

But it is such ad hoc solutions that the IPPR wishes to get away from. For they have found 'a growing interest across the political spectrum in bringing these separate complaints together'. This interest, we are told, 'reflects a common understanding of the underlying problem which is best expressed in Dunning's famous motion of 1780: 'the power of the executive has increased, is increasing and ought to be diminished'.[1] So a 'growing chorus' inspires a 'growing interest' in a 'common understanding' of an underlying problem which provides its own solution: the curtailment of the power of Government. And this is to be achieved by binding rules and precepts set down in writing, incorporated and entrenched in a new covenant. The proposal is, in some respects, radical even revolutionary. The commentary continues:

> The essential question is whether the time has come not to change the historical constitution incrementally as has been done in the past, but to change the basis of the Constitution. That is, to change from a single fundamental principle, the supremacy of Parliament, which is founded in custom and usage as recognised by the courts, to a fundamental law which is prior to, independent of and the source of authority for the system of government.

This fundamental law is a written constitution here set down in 129 clauses and 6 schedules.

The primary proposition that the Executive has too much power is extended significantly to include not only power 'in relation to individuals' but also 'in relation to its political opponents'. So 'other collectivities' have to be protected against the Government. The argument is extended further by taking 'a radically different view' from those who are suspicious of entrenched 'rights' and who prefer political decisions always to be taken by the political decision of the representatives of the people. The written constitution, which most importantly includes a Bill of Rights, prevails over Acts of Parliament and all other rules of law.

Apart from the provisions relating to the Bill of Rights, the more important reforms contained in the written constitution include fixed four year terms for the Houses of Parliament with possibility of dissolution if the Government loses the confidence of the Commons (but the newly elected House would continue only until the expiry of the four year term); proportional representation for election to both Houses; the second chamber to have equal powers with the Commons on constitutional matters, including the Bill of Rights; and 15 elected regional assemblies.

These regional assemblies are to have powers to legislate over all major domestic functions and services. As was found during the discussions on the abortive Scotland and Wales Bills, the key problem is how to resolve disputes between the rival jurisdiction of the assemblies on the one hand and Parliament on the other. The IPPR draft runs away from any attempt at a solution. It provides that Parliament may make laws with respect to any matter within the legislative power of the assemblies if (1) that matter cannot be adequately regulated by an individual assembly or (2) the regulation of a matter by an assembly would prejudice the interests or interfere with the rights of residents of other parts of the United Kingdom.

This passes the buck directly to the Supreme Court (under the proposed constitution) which has exclusive jurisdiction in any proceedings brought by the central Government seeking a ruling that any assembly Act is wholly or partly invalid; or brought by the executive of an assembly seeking to invalidate an Act of Parliament. This will give rise to litigation of a quality so horrendous (except to lawyers) that nothing like it has been seen since Franklin Delano Roosevelt struggled, in not dissimilar circumstances, to get his New Deal legislation past the Supreme Court.

Some of the regional assemblies will be controlled by political parties opposed to the party of the central Government. They will wish to implement policies which the central Government strongly disapproves of or which will directly affect those in neighbouring regions. Examples from education, energy, environment, health, housing, social welfare, trade and industry and transport (all these being within the jurisdiction of assemblies under the Constitution) are easy to imagine. So the central Government asks the Supreme Court to rule that the assembly cannot 'adequately' regulate this matter or that what the assembly proposes will 'prejudice the interests or interfere with the rights' of those neighbouring regions. Or perhaps the central Government legislates in the matter and the assembly asks the Supreme Court to invalidate the Act of Parliament. Once again we see how unwise and productive of continuing animosity it is to seek to solve a political problem by calling in the judiciary. Such litigation would quickly destroy the working of the Constitution.

Elected local authorities are to be set up within each region; and a new structure is to be created for UK courts, with a judicial appointments commission.

All this means that the top level of Government is largely unaltered. The role of the Royal Family and the honours system are made explicit and strengthened. Individual Ministers are to be relieved of responsibility for what happens in their Departments except for matters of 'general direction and control'. Parliamentary opposition is weakened by the dissolution provisions. The stage is set for major conflicts between the regions and the Departments. And the role of the judiciary is greatly enlarged.

But the principal purpose of the exercise is to establish the new constitution as 'the sole foundation for the exercise of executive, legislative and judicial power', and to set down a list of fundamental rights and freedoms.

A Supreme Court is to have jurisdiction over the interpretation and effect of the constitution. If it is shown to the satisfaction of the Supreme Court that any law, convention, practice or usage in force immediately before the coming into force of the constitution, is inconsistent with any provision of the constitution, or that any decision or act of the Government or of any public body is so inconsistent, then the Supreme Court may declare any such law (including any Act of Parliament), decision or act to be invalid. In particular, the Supreme Court may so declare whenever it finds that any such law, decision or act is inconsistent with any provision of the Bill of Rights. So the provisions are retrospective as well as prospective.

A Human Rights Commission would be set up with the power, amongst other things, to investigate any act or practice that might be inconsistent with the Bill of Rights, to assist individual complainants in legal proceedings, itself to institute such proceedings whether or not it had received a complaint, to challenge the validity of any provision of an Act of Parliament, to intervene in any proceedings that involved human rights issues, to report to Parliament and to publicise guidelines for the avoidance of acts or practices inconsistent with the Bill of Rights. This is a most formidable collection of powers to bestow on a public body.

One other quotation from the IPPR commentary on its proposed constitution is significant.

> We need rules to govern the exercise of power. It is in the interest of the less powerful that those rules should be clear and explicit, to lessen their manipulation by the more powerful. We need rules that we can accept as fair in general, though we object to their application in particulars. We need rules to protect ourselves and others against ourselves.

And when faced with the argument that all this hands over too much power to judges, the commentary adds 'And we need referees, *even bad referees*, to interpret and enforce the rules'. The words I have here emphasised show how far the drafters of this constitution are prepared to go in defence of their own dogma.

The IPPR constitution lists 18 'fundamental rights and freedoms' including rights to life, to liberty and security, to fair and public hearing, to education, to enjoyment of possessions and to asylum; and freedoms from torture, slavery, and of thought, expression, assembly and association; and others. The constitution does not attempt to justify the inclusion of those rights and freedoms or the exclusion of others, being content to assert that these are 'equal and inalienable rights with which all human beings are endowed'. We are left to suppose, along traditional lines, that 'each person is to have an equal right to the most extensive liberty compatible with a similar liberty for others' a form of words which over the years has given political philosophers a bad name. For the truth is, as Bentham said:

> It is impossible to create rights, to impose obligations to protect the person, life, reputation, property, subsistence, liberty itself, except at the expense of liberty.

In the application of a bill of rights in a case before a court of law (and no other forum is proposed) the knife of interpretation has to cut and the winners will fall on one side, the losers on the other. Some rights are indeed more equal than others. Where a provision of the bill of rights is judged to trump an existing law, 'the word *right* is the greatest enemy of reason, and the most terrible destroyer of governments' (Bentham again). But, then, under the proposed constitution, it is meant to be.

The creation of political rights in a constitution or elsewhere is a political act. How the rights are defined, with what exceptions and on what terms, how rights relate to each other, are all political statements. If we favour a strong executive because, for example, we believe that for our country, at this period, major reforms need to be introduced, then we will not wish to construct a system where the countervailing forces can easily frustrate the executive. In time of war or national emergency we may prefer to have a strong Government with judicial controls at a low level, as happened from

1939 until the late 1940s. If we wish to curtail executive powers, as does the IPPR in its constitution, we will make appropriate provision and one way of doing this is to create rights legally enforceable against the Government.

Mystification follows and these rights are presented in metaphysical or transcendental wrappings. Words like 'natural', 'inalienable', and 'endowed' conceal what is no more than a particular statement about the exercise of political power. Some philosophers and some lawyers have long sought extra-legal principles or standards by which legal relationships may be judged. But, not surprisingly in our conflictual society, they have not progressed beyond phrases like a sense of justice, or the morality of the community.

In the event it is inevitable that when such general rights are given legal form, interpretation will follow. The founding fathers of the United States constitution did not attempt detailed definition. 'Congress shall make no law', they said 'abridging the freedom of speech, or of the press.' No person, they said, shall 'be deprived of life, liberty, or property, without due process of law.' Later they added that no State should 'deny to any person within its jurisdiction the equal protection of the laws.' For many years, little happened to explain what was the impact of such words on civil rights. Then at the end of the nineteenth century, the Supreme Court ruled that inequality between black and white people was permissible if the two groups were segregated. In the middle of the twentieth century this was reversed and from that time the Supreme Court has been continuously engaged in sometimes broadening and sometimes narrowing the bill of rights in a multiplicity of judicial opinions, veering this way and that according to the views of the Chief Justice and his eight colleagues. Most recently, much controversy has centred on the role of the Court, how far it should reinterpret the constitution in the light and darkness of today, how far it should stay clear of matters (like abortion) which did not directly engage the attention of Madison and his contemporaries.

That is certainly one way of going about it. State the principle and let the courts decide what it means. In any event the courts will be obliged to impose their own interpretations and perhaps it is better not to seek to spell out the exceptions as to do so will only give the courts more words to play with. This looks like a paradox for if the draftsman itemises the exceptions, surely (one might think) this will reduce the scope for interpretation. But this is not so. Or not necessarily so, as we shall see.

The IPPR followed the European Convention of Human Rights in spelling out the exceptions. When the ECHR was drafted and ratified, the UK representatives had no thought of its provisions trumping Acts of Parliament. That was strictly for foreigners.

The IPPR Bill of Rights places first in its list 'Right to Life'. This provides:

2.1 Everyone's right to life shall be protected by law.

2.2 No one shall be deprived of life intentionally.

Para 2.3 allows exceptions for self defence and the quelling of riot or insurrection, where the taking of life is 'absolutely necessary'. Para 2.4 rejects capital punishment.

Both the statement of the principle and the statement of the exceptions give rise to considerable problems of interpretation which are to be determined by the courts. It seems to allow for a considerable extension of any right to shoot to kill to suppress disorder. But it also raises one of the most divisive issues in modern society: abortion. Is the unborn embryo or foetus entitled to the protection of this article? If so, does this depend on how advanced is the pregnancy? A majority of the Supreme Court of the USA in *Roe v Wade* (1973) famously declared that abortion was legal. But it laid down terms which provided that (1) prior to the end of the first trimester of pregnancy, the State might not interfere with or regulate an attending physician's decision, reached in consultation with his patient, that the patient's pregnancy should be terminated (2) from the end of this trimester until the point in time when the foetus became viable, the State might regulate the abortion procedure only to the extent that such regulation related to the preservation and protection of maternal health (3) that after viability, the State might prohibit all abortions altogether, except those necessary to preserve the life or health of the mother. Subsequently the Supreme Court limited the applicability of this decision but has not, so far, overruled it. The suitability of persons nominated for appointment to the Supreme Court in recent years has been widely challenged on the basis of their attitude to the decision in this case.

Nothing in the Bill of Rights of the USA bore directly on abortion, neither the founding fathers nor their successors having considered the matter. But the majority in the Supreme Court decided that the right to privacy encompassed a woman's decision whether or not to terminate her pregnancy and that this right to privacy, though itself not mentioned in the Bill of Rights, was to be inferred from it.

The legal right to an abortion and the conditions limiting that right are defined by an Act of Parliament in the UK and much argument takes place from time to time, inside and outside Parliament, about these statutory rules and whether they should be amended. The policy decision is taken by Parliament. If a Bill of Rights were part of UK domestic law, the policy decision would be taken by the courts who could strike down the present and any future legislation. Perhaps the UK courts would imitate the Supreme Court of the USA and lay down similar rules based on trimesters or some other criteria. The courts would certainly need to decide whether the unborn child was a person for these purposes and, if so, at what stage of pregnancy it acquired that status.

To take another example: in what circumstances is the withdrawal of medical treatment which it is known will result in the patient's death to be regarded as 'intentional' deprivation of life? More generally, are the variations of what is popularly known as euthanasia permissible (if ever)? During the *Bland* case, which established the right to withhold artificial feeding and antibiotic treatment in certain circumstances even though this would result in the patient's death, Anthony Lester QC (a well known Bill of Rights draftsman) is reported to have argued that human life was valueless without 'a minimal capacity to experience, to relate with other human beings, for life is surely valued only as a vehicle for consciousness', and so the court should allow Bland to die. That is one view though I believe many people less sensitive than Mr Lester might be surprised to know that they valued life only because it was a vehicle.

So. Is it better for these difficult questions of abortion and euthanasia to be answered definitively and finally by QCs and judges after argument in a law court, even one having the advantage of advice from Mr Lester as amicus curiae? Or to be answered after public debate by the representatives of the people? My view is that such social matters are best kept away from senior judges who (in fairness) have never shown much enthusiasm for them.

Article 3 of the IPPR model states: No one shall be subjected to torture or to cruel, inhuman or degrading treatment or punishment. This looks straightforward enough though the same words in the ECHR have caused problems. The security forces in Northern Ireland used five dubious methods of interrogation: wall-standing, hooding, subjection to noise, deprivation of sleep, and reduction of diet. Combined they could amount to torture, said the Commission. So could bastinado (in Greece). Again, a fourteen year old girl was caned by her headmistress for eating potato crisps in class, leaving three red weals across her buttocks with pain and discomfort for several days, the scars remaining for two months. No marks are given for guessing in which country that was perpetrated. Treatment of convicts (e.g. solitary confinement), and aspects of deportation and extradition, give rise to cases under this head. More interesting, especially for liberals, are the rights of sado-masochists, who voluntarily inflict or suffer pain for their own pleasure. The UK courts have recently decided against them. All these matters are better dealt with by legislative rules than by judicial interpretation.

Forced or compulsory labour (Article 4) is outlawed by the IPPR though they feel obliged to exclude from protection 'any service exacted in case of an emergency threatening the wellbeing of the community' which could be a dangerous weapon in some circumstances not difficult to imagine and not a category I would entrust judges to interpret. Here, as so often, one feels safer without the protection supplied by the Bill of Rights.

Similarly what is one to say of the express power under Article 6 of the IPPR model to exclude press and public from hearings in court, 'to the extent strictly necessary', 'where publicity would prejudice the interests of justice'. There certainly are occasions when it is necessary for cases to be heard in private but they should be carefully defined and not left in a category so general that the presiding judge has an absolute discretion.

The provisions of articles 8, 9, 11 and 12 lie at the heart of the IPPR Bill of Rights (as they do in the ECHR). Article 8 concerns the right to privacy; 9 concerns freedom of thought; 11 concerns freedom of expression; 12 concerns freedom of assembly and association. But, as before, the catch is in the authorised restrictions on the principles, the legitimised grounds on which the principles can be set aside. In every case the grounds are those provided by law and deemed 'necessary in a democratic society' for the prevention of disorder or the preservation of order; for the protection of health or morals; for the protection of the rights and freedoms of others. The interests of national security are protected by articles 8, 11, 12 and those of public safety by articles 8, 9, 12. The 'reputations' of others are protected by article 11.

In the face of this list, it is difficult to think of any unprotected interests. The restrictions on rights and freedom are wider than those enjoyed under statute or common law. When therefore an action is brought claiming a breach of the Bill of Rights, the Government or other defendant can resist by establishing that the alleged infringement was provided by law (very few would not be), protective of one of those listed interests (not difficult to show) and necessary in a democratic society. It is on this last that the principal argument is joined. Article 8 declares the right to respect for private and family life, home and correspondence. The present concern over press intrusion and the real difficulties faced in formulating rules that would be protective of privacy but not enable wrongdoings, especially by public persons, to be covered up, demonstrate the social and political nature of the problem. Whether self-regulation by the press or statutory rules laid down by Parliament are the answer, it is clear that individual judges sitting on individual cases with nothing to guide them but the generalities of a Bill of Rights do not provide a workable alternative. Once again, social and political problems require social and political solutions.

Article 11 of the IPPR draft on freedom of expression is based in part on article 10 of ECHR. The European Court, to its credit, albeit by the narrowest majority of 11 judges to 9, overturned the injunction obtained in UK courts banning the publication by the *Sunday Times* of a piece strongly supportive of the thalidomide children in the struggle to obtain compensation from the manufacturers of the drug. But most recently the European Court upheld the injunction imposed by UK courts on the *Guardian* and the *Observer* preventing the publication of extracts for Peter Wright's *Spycatcher* until after the book had been published in the USA. In the UK courts, Lord Templeman was of opinion that the ECHR would not have helped the newspaper had the Convention then been part of UK democratic law. Certainly the record of the UK courts on freedom of speech and on protection of journalists' sources is deplorable.

The living conditions of the great majority of people are determined not by the politics of Government but by the economics of corporations. And civil liberties are curtailed more by employers than by the State. The restraints on free speech are imposed more by the threat of demotion or dismissal than by public censorship. Wherever, before expressing criticism, we pause to consider who might be offended by what we say, what might be the result of speaking out, the fear is not likely to be that we shall commit a breach of the peace, or be found guilty of obscenity or blasphemy or of offending the Official Secrets or the Race Relations Acts, or of being sued for defamation of character. What we are likely to be concerned about is whether our job or our career is likely to be imperilled. We may have contracted with our employer not to discuss publicly any matter relating to the corporation and we will under the common law be under an implied obligation to act 'in good faith or fidelity'. This threat is a far greater constraint on activity both inside and outside the workplace especially when the remedy for unfair dismissal is seldom reinstatement and often inadequate compensation. Rules against making public complaints about terms and conditions of work even when made to protect others are strict and enforced. Whistle-blowers can, at best, expect their dismissal to be delayed for a short time. These powers at the disposal of the employer (who may be a public authority) are in no way challengeable under a Bill of Rights.

Article 12 of the IPPR draft on freedom of association follows article 11 of the ECHR. It includes the right to join a trade union. But an additional restriction on the right excludes members of the armed forces or of the police or persons charged with the administration of the state. The European Commission under this restriction upheld the banning by the UK Prime Minister and the Foreign Secretary of trade union membership at GCHQ in December 1983. The UK courts had refused to interfere with the Ministerial decision.

Keith Ewing in his pamphlet on a Bill of Rights for the Institute of Employment Rights (1990) surveyed the practice overseas. The Privy Council in London, sitting as a court, is composed almost entirely of Law Lords. In *Collymore* v *Attorney General of Trinidad and Tobago* (1969) the Privy Council held that an Act which effectively removed trade union bargaining rights as well as the right to strike was not unconstitutional although there were guarantees of freedom of association in the Trinidad Tobago constitution. This decision was followed by three Canadian cases in 1987. The legislation suspended the right to collective bargaining, denied the right to strike to public sector employees: and in one case ordered striking workers to return to work. This was upheld, despite freedom of association guarantees in the Canadian Charter of Rights and Freedoms.

The European Convention, says Ewing, 'has been a deep disappointment for British trade unions'. It left the GCHQ staff defenceless and the

Commission and the Court 'appear more concerned with the right not to belong to a union than with the right to belong'.

Article 10 of the IPPR Bill of Rights provides: No person shall be denied the right to education. These words are the same as those used in the ECHR. The IPPR draft article goes on to require public authorities to respect the right of parents to ensure that education and teaching are in conformity with their religious and philosophical convictions. The question has been raised whether this would prevent a Government from abolishing private schools or from denying such schools tax relief.

This brings us to the core of the objections to the adoption of a bill of rights as proposed by the IPPR or to the incorporation into UK domestic law of the ECHR. There is no evidence to suggest that the UK judges would be less inclined to embrace the restrictions than their brethren in the European Court of Human Rights. There is indeed positive evidence to suggest that they would embrace them wholeheartedly.

It is not appreciated how dangerous would be decisions of the UK courts upholding the authorised restrictions in particular cases. These would form binding precedents. The list of these restrictions provides the courts with all the indications they would need on how to prefer the restrictions to the principles. Those listed under article 11, for example, may be used to justify censorship of attacks on politicians or other public persons, may give general protection to official secrets (in conflict with a subsequent article), may open the way to widespread interception of mail, phonetapping and other surveillance to ensure that freedom of expression is not threatening public order.

Two hundred years ago, Alexander Hamilton had somewhat similar reservations about the wisdom of inserting a bill of rights into the American constitution maintaining 'that the provisions against restraining the liberty of the press afforded a clear implication that a power to prescribe proper regulations concerning [the press] was intended to be vested in the national government.'

To repeat the obvious: the only way in which a judicial interpretation of the bill of rights can be reversed is by a contrary and subsequent judicial interpretation on the same matter. Once a series of consistent interpretations is imposed on an article, a code is built up which will be very difficult to unbuild. This is why we would be in a positively worse situation with an entrenched bill of rights. Under our present constitution, Parliament can always overrule judicial interpretation. Not so, under the proposed constitution.

What emerges from Charter 88 and the IPPR is, at first sight, no more than a statement of nineteenth century liberal principles: a Bill of Rights, the rule of law, electoral change, independent judiciary, devolution; plus freedom of information and reform of the House of Lords. Nothing much here to be alarmed about, oh my Bagehot and my Dicey long ago.

But a persistent error in recent days of those on the socialist left has been to underestimate the dangers of liberalism. On 15 January 1981 Tony Benn wrote in his diary 'Roy has made a terrible mistake in returning from Brussels'. But Tony mistook the mistake as twenty-nine Labour MPs joined the SDP.

Remember that the central purpose of the new constitutionalists is to replace 'the supremacy of Parliament' with a 'fundamental law which is prior to, independent of and the source of authority for the system of government'. And, as we have seen, that means, as night follows day, the positioning of the judiciary at the centre of politics and the strengthening of the conservative right. Liberals presumably know that this is the natural and inevitable result of their re-drafting of the constitution. This is no game played with and by students. This is adult, hard politics. For behind the front that presents itself as the foolishness and play acting of the House of Lords, or question time in the Commons, or television interviews and chat shows, or select committee interrogations, there is a real world. Most of us, most of the time, laugh

> At gilded butterflies, and hear poor rogues
> Talk of court news; and we'll talk with them too,
> Who loses and who wins, who's in, who's out.

But the losers are the homeless, the sick, the ill-educated, the mad and the prematurely dead.

There was a time when democracy was supposed to be about to take care of the evil consequences of man's inhumanity to man. The franchise would be greatly extended, the powerful rich would be made (at least) account-able and (at best) sent empty away. This was to be done through the instrumentality of democratic Government which would surely respond to the needs of the general public. We know now that it has not worked out like that. That kind of democracy did not happen. Instead what we have is a political system structured to sustain the powerful rich. A future Gibbon contemplating the characteristics of present-day society will find a fiscal system which progressively favours those with capital assets over those without, a House of Lords whose members can claim over £100 (tax free) for each day they attend, thousands of homeless persons who sleep on the streets or are huddled in bed and breakfast rooms, health provision which sharply distinguishes those who can from those who cannot afford to pay, a public appointments system which promotes nepotism and ensures that first, second and third preference is given to the socially acceptable, a judiciary drawn from amongst the most highly salaried members of the profession, an assured place among positions of power and influence for retired public servants, a medical profession which itself distributes merit awards out of the public purse to its members, leaders of state and private monopolies who are paid grossly inflated salaries. The list of privileges is endless. Such a capitalist plutocracy needs no dictatorial or totalitarian powers. Nor need the future Gibbon look for a secret conspiracy.

There are those who point to the apparent contradiction of Conservative Governments advocating the rolling back of State power while enforcing centralisation. But this is to confuse ends and means. These Governments have indeed been most active and full of energy. But their deliberate purpose is to weaken irreversibly the structure of government.

For over 150 years, the regulatory powers of government have grown progressively, as we learnt in our schooldays. In the middle years of the last century, the activities of central departments, local authorities and public bodies of many kinds reacted strongly to the laissez-faire tradition, so much so that the very existence of that classical doctrine has become suspect.

The supervision of lunatics from 1832 under the control of the Lord Chancellor; the regulation of employment in factories from 1833; the massive reform of the poor law in 1834 transferring powers from justices, overseers and boards of guardians to commissioners; the beginning of modern local government in 1835; the powers of the Home Secretary over the naturalization of aliens and the administration of prisons from 1835; the powers of the Treasury over the Post Office from 1839; wide powers for the Crown and revenue officers over customs, smuggling and seizure from 1845; powers given to the Treasury and the Board of Trade to deal with the railway boom from 1844; the great reforms in public health begun in 1848; control over harbours from 1851; the reform of patents law and administration from 1852; the comprehensive legislation concerning the superintendence of merchant shipping in 1854 by the Board of Trade; the regulation of telegraph companies from 1863; and the provisions of the Elementary Education Act of 1870 which form a bridge from the more regulatory functions of the State to the provision of services and the beginning of the Welfare State. These lists could be greatly extended.

Separate from these and yet so much involved as a sub-text was the growth of trade unions and their progressive advancement by the replacement of the old criminal illegalities and civil restrictions with new statutory rules (which the judiciary towards the end of the nineteenth and the beginning of the twentieth century sought to subvert).

The threefold growth in major local services between 1890 and 1912 culminated in the Lloyd George budget and the insurance provisions. Despite the economic depressions of the 1920s and 1930s progress was made in slum clearance and extended public health legislation. The Attlee Governments inaugurated the national health service, reformed the poor law and other social services, developed land use planning and through nationalisation greatly improved the production and distribution of coal, gas, electricity and transport. Conservative and Labour Governments during the middle decades of this century stimulated house building and encouraged the development of all levels of education. The relative reduction of public expenditure in the 1970s largely enforced by the general economic situation was followed by the unforced public expenditure cuts in the 1980s and the end of government in the public interest.

Throughout the span of years from 1832 to 1979, the administration of these numerous activities varied in efficiency and completeness, had its successes and failures, but by the mid twentieth century amounted to a substantial body of achievement. The primary beneficiaries were the general public for the main purpose was to further the public interest. In many matters – especially health, housing and education – those principally responsible for the development of these services were professional men and women in local authorities and other public bodies. Medical officers, surveyors and architects, education officers and schoolteachers, working in the public service, provided much of the driving force, supported in this and other fields by middle grade and senior civil servants in the Departments. One of the most remarkable and calamitous of the changes that have taken place over the last thirty years has been the decline in the status and the influence of these public officers.

Until recently, politicians spoke of the public interest with respect even when they were disregarding it. Public officers believed in it and many spent their lives in its pursuit. They saw themselves as guardians of the common good and resisted the demands of powerful private interest groups. Today that high standard of public service has been prostituted to the wishes of political masters.

The deliberate weakening of the structures of central and local government authorities and the abandonment of their role as protectors of the public interest is being effected in a variety of ways of which the most obvious are the privatisation of public utilities, the creation of separate hospital trusts and the marketing of health services, opting-out for schools, the passing of responsibilities from government departments to Next Steps agencies, the growing pressure on universities to become fee and loan financed institutions. Modern Conservatives do not begin to accept that government has a major role in protecting the public interest. They subscribe to the teaching of those in the USA inelegantly known as public choicists who take the tools of economics and apply them to the material of politics[2] and arrive at anti-governmental pro-market prescriptions.

Public servants are seen as concerned not with the altruistic provision of services but with advancing their own part of the bureaucracy as 'self-interested utility maximisers'. This of course is a popular view and takes strength from the element of truth it contains. But public choicists argue that it is the whole truth. Their view contrasts with those who believe that 'the public interest', however elusive in definition, does exist and stands over against private interests. In public law, one consequence of the adoption by judges and others of protecting the public interest is that public servants are subjected to scrutiny to ensure that their motives and purposes are properly directed. So also participation, consultation, and accountability form part of a structure designed to maximise involvement of the public in the political process. These may often work poorly, even corruptly, but that is their purpose.

All this is anathema to public choicists who consider these devices simply serve the interests of those who can best manipulate the system. And here again the element of truth intrudes. But again it is only a part of the truth. Politicians are seen as self-seeking as others, perhaps more so, and majoritarianism is rejected in favour of a constitutional democracy where limits on governmental power are imposed.

Officers and councillors in local government can also be seen, especially in the days when they could raise local rates without constraint, in the same light. The poll tax, under which we all paid the same amount for the services we received (just as we would in the market place), can be seen as an aspect of constitutional democracy, and the reversion to a property-based tax becomes (in choicist terms) a regrettable return to majoritarianism.

The development of opportunities for judicial review of Government action over the last 25 years has paid little regard to the public good. The public choicist sees it as an example of judges maximising their own self-interests. Most recently, the newly appointed Master of the Rolls and Lord Chief Justice have come out publicly in favour of a Bill of Rights. Sir Thomas Bingham claimed that the present situation weakened public confidence in the courts. He supported the motion in a debate that 'This house supports the introduction of a judicially-enforceable bill of rights.' Similarly we find leading 'human rights' barristers strongly advocating this extension of the jurisdiction of UK courts.

Nevertheless the American public choicists rely on a reformed Constitution which, inevitably in that country, depends on a Supreme Court. In the UK this leads to the proposals for a written constitution, complete with a Bill of Rights and on this the rightwing public choicists join hands with the UK liberals. Both are distrustful of majoritarian democracy, the former because they believe it lacks constitutional restraints on governmental power, the latter because they fear it might imperil the particular set of values which they espouse.

It is almost superfluous to emphasise that all devices which weaken central and local government by the same token weaken democratic accountability. Already privatisation in its many forms has deprived the House of Commons and elected local authorities of many of their opportunities for scrutiny.

None of the substantial social and personal problems of the late twentieth century is likely to be solved by the market economy and monopoly privatisation.

Today we are faced with problems more serious even than those of the mid-nineteenth century. They concern poverty and unemployment, homelessness, vagrancy, the decline of health care and provision for the old and mentally ill, pollution of the atmosphere, of rivers and beaches, the destruction of natural resources, dilapidated and underfunded schools, escalating rates of crime and of drug taking, AIDS and, beyond our shores, overpopulation, famine and the worsening economies of the poorest nations.

The scale of these problems is so great, both domestically and globally, that only the authority and resources of Governments can begin to solve them. And it is our tragic misfortune that the crisis has occurred at a time when, under the prevailing political and economic philosophy, public and collective action is denigrated. We are supposed to welcome free enterprise, open markets, deregulation, individualism, privatisation, profit-taking, capitalist adventurism, company takeovers, city deals. These activities are not only incapable of resolving the crisis. They are its cause. We are being urged to embrace as solutions the very practices that have created the problems. What is put forward as the way to a prosperous future will accelerate the decline for all but a few.

Today, collectivism and the pursuit of the common good are devalued. Labour leaders seem to have stopped describing themselves as democratic socialists perhaps because they wish to appear as social democrats for electoral purposes. The cult of individualism and the emphasis on individual rights is the cult of Thatcherism.

It is not in the nature of privately owned corporate power to have regard to long-term interests or the common good. Nor is it likely that the major industrial and commercial companies would agree to spend large sums needed markedly to reduce pollution of the atmosphere. And if they did agree, enforcement would be virtually impossible. Only Governments, backed by the force of law and an adequate inspectorate, can begin to reverse the current trends. Only Governments have both the means and the motivation to restore our standards of public health and housing, medical care, transport and education even to their former levels. Public provision and public enterprise at public expense can arrest the present decline. The private sector will never do so.

Weakening of central Government – especially privatisation – creates problems for a future Labour Government. So also does the growth in judicial review which has enlarged the powers of the courts to set aside the fulfilling by Ministers of statutory duties. The line is not always easy to draw. Where Departments deliberately try to extend their powers beyond those given by Act of Parliament – a rare but not unknown occurrence – they should be prevented. But frequently judicial interpretation of the proper limits of those powers is restrictive. There is a danger in the judicialisation of the political process. This is taken to extremes in those proposals for reform of the Constitution (like that of the IPPR) which would enable the courts to overrule legislation itself. For a leftwing government this could be highly damaging and is the political reason – others apart – for resisting such change.

Conservatism is the creed of those who wish to preserve in its essentials the distribution of power in society today. It believes in private capitalism, funded by the large financial institutions and serviced by employees with differing responsibilities from the most menial to the most influential. Responsibility lies with a board of directors who, as individuals, may or may not own much of the capital. It may pursue this purpose in a highly competitive market or in one that is protected by monopoly or cartel. It may be a small business, highly dependent on specialist consumers, or a multi-national agglomerate serving many and diverse interests. Those who direct its activities may be considerate to the work force or tyrannical, they may be worried, in their private lives, about the environment and support the Royal Society for the Protection of Birds, or they may have none of the finer instincts commonly attributed to men and women of their social status. They may, in a word, be goodies or baddies. But the corporation they serve is committed by the necessities of its industrial or commercial existence to obtaining the highest possible return on the money invested. And as such it cannot take account of other, more general, interests represented to it by the members of the public at large as beneficial to them but not to it.

Liberals are different, but they can never avoid the central dilemma of their faith. They want many good things to come to pass, like better housing for the working classes, a somewhat more equal distribution of wealth, good schools, less unemployment, contented trade unions, and jam for tea on Sundays. At the same time, they disapprove of State intervention, and above all, they are dedicated to 'the rights of the individual'. These two principles of their faith are then happily joined in a creed that makes the government the enemy of the individual. It follows that State power must be tightly constrained.

Socialists are different again. They believe humanity to be composed of social animals, a collection of individuals who are inseparable from the society in which they live. From conception until death they are an integral part of society. Their problems arise from this. This is the human situation, perhaps the human tragedy. In this society there are no natural rights, only those which society has conferred.

The proposed changes to the constitution, and the incorporation of a Bill of Rights, will enable private interests, of individuals and of corporations, to override measures designed to promote the general welfare. Only through the agency of accountable public institutions and the activities of accountable public servants, will the public interest prevail.

NOTES

1. The better view is that Dunning referred not to the power of the executive but to 'the influence of the Crown' which in 1780 was a somewhat different complaint. But no matter to present purposes.
2. See Patrick McAuslan 'Public Law and Public Choice' in 51 *Modern Law Review* (1988) 681 to which I am indebted.

WHY NATIONALISM?

Michael Löwy

The burning problems of our times – such as the growing gap between the South and the North, the need for general disarmament, the world capitalist crisis, the threat of ecological catastrophe – are obviously of an international character. They can hardly be solved on a local, regional or national scale. However, at the same time as the world economy is becoming more and more unified by multinational capitalism, a spectacular tide of nationalism is rising, in Europe and on a world scale, submerging everything on its way.

While some national movements are emancipatory and progressive, nationalism is very often a 'false solution' to the economic, social, political and ecological challenges of our times. Why then has it become so popular in so many countries and areas of the world?

There is no easy explanation for this upsurge, but it could be helpful to compare it with the parallel revival of religious feelings. The crisis of both existing models of (instrumental) rationality – capitalist accumulation and bureaucratic productivism – favours the development of non-rational (sometimes irrational) reactions such as religion and nationalism. Of course, both phenomena can also take progressive forms – as in national liberation movements, or in liberation theology – but the regressive tendencies (nationalist and/or religious intolerance) are quite formidable.

In many countries of the world religion tends to merge with nationalism, infusing it with greater power of attraction and an aura of 'sacredness': this is the case with Catholicism in Poland and Croatia (as well as, in a different context, Ireland), of Christian orthodoxy in Serbia and Russia, of conservative evangelism in the USA, of certain forms of Jewish orthodoxy in Israel, of Islam in Libya and Iran. In other cases, religion and nationalism are competing rivals or even forces in open conflict, as it is the case with Islamic fundamentalism and Arab nationalism in North Africa and the Middle East.

In any case, nationalism has its own roots and does not depend necessarily on religion in order to expand. How to explain its present rise? One could perhaps consider the nationalist wave as a sort of reaction to the growing internationalisation of the economy and (to a certain extent) of

125

culture, a struggle against the threat of homogenisation. It could also be understood as a compensatory movement, trying to counterbalance the decline of economic independence by reinforcing (sometimes to monstrous proportions) the ethical, political and cultural moments of the national identity.

A similar (but different) hypothesis had been suggested by Theodor Adorno in a conference in 1966 (on 'Education after Auschwitz'): if nationalism is so aggressive 'it is because in the era of international communication and supra-national blocs, it cannot really believe in itself, and has no choice but to become outrageously excessive, if it wants to persuade both itself and others of its substantive character.'[1] Of course, the argument applies to a much greater degree to the situation in Europe in the 90s than in the 60s.

However, this and other general interpretations, although useful, cannot quite explain the extraordinary diversity of the phenomenon, which takes very different forms in different parts of the world. One has therefore to examine the *specific nature of nationalism in each of its multiple contexts*, in order to be able to understand its moving forces.

Let us begin with *the region* where this new nationalist tide is particularly visible: Eastern Europe and the ex-USSR. An intelligent observer of Eastern European politics has remarkably well summarized the events in this part of the world:

> The last remnants of solidarity between the nonemancipated nationalities in the 'belt of mixed populations' evaporated with the disappearance of a central despotic bureaucracy which had also served to gather together and divert from each other the diffuse hatreds and conflicting national claims. Now everybody was against everybody else, and most of all against their closest neighbours – the Slovaks against the Czechs, the Croats against the Serbs, the Ukrainians against the Poles.

The most astonishing thing in this analysis is that it was *not* written a few weeks ago: it is a passage from the well known book of Hanna Arendt on the origins of totalitarianism, published in . . . 1951, which describes 'the atmosphere of disintegration' in Eastern Europe during the 20's, i.e. after the liquidation of the Austro-Hungarian Monarchy and the Tsarist Empire – the two 'despotic bureaucracies' referred to in the above quotation.[2]

Incidentally, a similar assessment can be found also in Rosa Luxemburg's notes on War and Nationalism from 1918: 'Nationalism is at the moment a trump. From all sides nations and semi-nations appear and claim their right to form a State. (. . .) At the nationalist Brocken it is now the time of the Walpurgis night'.[3]

In other words: we have been drawn, in a large part of Europe, *seventy years back* . . .

Let there be no misunderstanding: there is nothing regressive – on the contrary – when (today, as in 1920) multinational empires, which had become true 'prisons of peoples', crumble and the oppressed nations recover their liberty. To that extent, there is undeniably a *democratic moment* in the national revival which took place since 1989 in Eastern Europe and the USSR. Socialists and democrats cannot but rejoice when the Soviet tanks leave East Germany, Poland and Hungary, and the troops of the KGB quit the Baltic countries, leaving these people to decide for themselves their future, and freely choose unity, separation or federation.

Unfortunately, not everything is so pleasant in this picture: the best and the worst are inseparably mixed in these national movements. The best: the democratic awakening of spoliated nations, the rediscovery of their language and culture, the aspiration for freedom and popular sovereignty. The worst: the awakening of chauvinistic nationalisms, of expansionisms, of intolerances, of xenophobias; the awakening of old national quarrels, hatred against the 'hereditary enemy'; the growth of authoritarian tendencies, leading to the oppression of one's own national minorities; and finally, the upsurge of fascist, semi-fascist and racist forms of nationalism, in Russia ('Pamiat'), in Rumania, in Slovakia, in Croatia (neo-ustachi), in Serbia (neo-chetniks), in the former DDR (neo-nazis), and elsewhere as well. The eternal scapegoats of the past – Jews and Gypsies – are again being selected as responsible for all the evils of society . . .

Paradoxically, this negative and sinister aspect, this 'return of the suppressed', this resurrection of the ancient national *vendettas* appears nowhere in a more brutal and absurd form than in Yugoslavia – the only one of the so-called 'socialist' countries which had been able to escape from the control of Moscow and to establish a relatively egalitarian federation between its component nations. Anti-fascist solidarity between the various nationalities, rooted in the Communist partisan fight of World-War II, has now left the stage, to be replaced by a savage *bella omnia contra omnes*.

Of course, one can explain this paradox by several and complex economic, cultural, political, religious and historical causes – without forgetting the heavy responsibility of the Serbian Stalino-nationalist regime of Milosevic, who opened, by his policy of oppression against Kossovo's Albanians, the Pandora box of nationalisms in the country.[4] Nevertheless, there remains an irreducible kernel of pure irrationality in this explosion of hatred against the 'other' – whose most dreadful expression is the policy of 'ethnic cleansing' implemented by Serbian nationalist forces in Bosnia-Hercegovina.

It is impossible to predict, for the moment, if the 'Yugoslav paradigm' is going to be followed by others, and if the present conflicts between Slovaks and Czechs, Hungarians and Rumanians, Moldavians and Russians, Azeris and Armenians, Georgians and Ossetians, Russians and Ukrainians, etc, etc, will or will not take the form of a general confrontation; and if the dissolution of the ex-USSR will or will not lead to national wars (with nuclear arms?) that would make the present conflict in Yugoslavia look like a small incident. Anything can happen, and unfortunately the worst is a distinct possibility.

The reasons for this nationalist explosion, which is shaking practically the whole former 'socialist bloc', are, among others, the following:

1) The rebellion against decades of national discrimination and 'Great Russian' hegemonism. This is the most obvious motive behind national movements, both in the ex-USSR and in its former 'satellites'. There is no doubt that the annexation of the Baltic states during the Second World War, or the invasion of Hungary in 1956 and Czechoslovakia in 1968, left a very deep imprint in the national consciousness of these countries. Once the iron lid of Soviet occupation was lifted, it is understandable that a vast nationalist upsurge would take place.

But this does not apply to Yugoslavia, an independent state which had liberated itself from Soviet hegemony since 1948 . . .

2) According to the Czech historian Miroslav Hroch, 'where an old regime disintegrates, where old social relations have become unstable, amid the rise of general insecurity, belonging to a common language and culture may become the only certainty in society . . .'.[5]

This helps to understand the parallel between present events and those of the 20s, after the disintegration of the traditional Empires in Central and Eastern Europe.

3) The collapse of the socialist ideas, values and images (including the idea of 'proletarian internationalism'), as well as of working class culture, discredited by so many years of bureaucratic manipulation, and identified by very broad masses as the official doctrine of the 'ancien regime'. Politics, like nature, hates a vacuum. No other rival political ideology had such a powerful tradition and such ancient roots in popular culture as nationalism – often combined, as we saw, with religion. Liberal individualism of the Western kind, while attractive to the intelligentsia and the rising new class of business men, had little appeal to the broad mass of the population.

4) The desire of relatively advanced nations, regions or republics to cut loose from poorer and relatively backward areas, in order to keep their own resources for themselves, and to join, as quickly as possible, the Western European Market. This applies particularly to Slovenia and Croatia, to the Baltic republics, and in general to the Western parts of the ex-USSR (in relation to the Asiatic ones). A similar phenomena, by the way, can also be found in Northern Italy (the rise of the so-called Lombard Leagues).

To these main explanations, one has to add the manipulation of nationalist feelings by neo-stalinist or neo-liberal elites trying to keep (or to win back) their power: Azerbaijan, Russia, Serbia and Croatia are good examples of this process.

Of what help, in so chaotic a situation, confronted with such a confused maelstrom of territorial conflicts, historical claims, chauvinist exclusions and liberating uprisings, can the analytic and political instruments of Marxism be?

Marxism has the great advantage of a critical/rational, as well as humanist/universal, standpoint. But it will remain disarmed in confronting present developments, if it is not able to get rid of certain myths and illusions which belong to its own tradition.

Among the myths, there is one which is particularly obnoxious: the idea of a 'scientific' and 'objective' definition of the nation. Thanks to Stalin, this dogma wrought havoc in the four continents, transforming theory into a true Procrustian bed, imposed by decree of the Political Bureau (charged with verifying if this or that nation lived up or not to the 'objective' criteria).

Happily, most Marxists dealing today with the national question have understood quite well that the nations cannot be defined in purely objective terms (territory, language, economic unit, etc) – even if these are far from being irrelevant – but that they are *imagined communities* (Benedict Anderson), *cultural creations* (Eric Hobsbawm). Already in 1939 Trotsky insisted, in a discussion with C.L.R. James about the Black question in America, that 'on this matter an abstract criterion is not decisive, but the historical consciousness, the feelings and impulses of a group are more important'.[6]

As far as illusions are concerned, there is one which can be found in Marx himself and which haunts the reflections of the best Marxists from Rosa Luxemburg until our own day: the imminent decline of nationalism and of the nation-state, made anachronistic by the internationalisation of the economy.

An attenuated version of this hypothesis can still be found in 1988, on the eve of the most formidable nationalist wave in Europe since World War II. In his book, otherwise excellent, on nations and nationalism since 1780, Eric Hobsbawm risked the following diagnosis: 'while nobody can possibly deny the growing and sometimes dramatic, impact of nationalist, or ethnic politics, there is one major aspect in which the phenomenon today is functionally different from the 'nationalism' and the 'nations' of nineteenth- and earlier twentieth-century history. It is no longer a major vector of historical development'. In his opinion, 'the declining historical significance of nationalism is today concealed . . . by the visible spread of ethnic/linguistic agitation'. In other words: 'in spite of its evident prominence, nationalism is historically less important. It is no longer, as it were, a global political programme, as it may be said to have been in the nineteenth and earlier twentieth centuries. It is at most a complicating factor, or a catalyst for other developments'.[7]

One would like to subscribe to this optimistic view of things (from the standpoint of internationalist socialism), but one can hardly avoid the impression that the great historian is taking his desires for reality. One does not need to sympathize with nationalist ideologies in order to take into account their growing influence in Europe. It is difficult to predict what is going to happen during the next century, but now, and in the coming years, it is impossible to consider the role of nationalism in Europe (and elsewhere) as a minor or secondary factor.

Hobsbawm is more to the point when he shows the inadequacy of nationalist 'solutions', particularly in Eastern Europe. Unlike the nationalists, Marxists are convinced that national independence – although necessary, in many cases – is far from sufficient to solve the basic economic, social, ecological or political problems confronting the population. Particularly if we consider the new kind of economic (and therefore also political) dependence of the recently emancipated nations towards Western finance.

Western European liberals often consider this Eastern nationalist explosion – and its xenophobic manifestations – as the product of 'underdevelopment', of primitive semi-agrarian societies, of populations having lived too long under 'Communism' and lacking democratic experience. Some even pretend that nationalism is only a plot of ex-communists (as in Serbia, Bulgaria or Azerbaijan) to keep power. Western Europe is presented as a harmonious world, well beyond such irrational passions: reconciled, the nations of this democratic and modern part of the continent are quickly moving towards their integration in a united European Community.

This idyllic image does not quite correspond to reality. It is an illusion, if not a mystification, to claim that Western Europe is now 'beyond nationalism', or that it has, as Ernest Gellner recently wrote, achieved 'Stage Five' in the history of European nationalism, a 'relatively benign condition' where 'economic and cultural convergence jointly diminish ethnic hostilities'.[8]

National conflicts, nationalist feelings, and nationalist movements exist also in Western Europe, and are growing. They belong basically to two very different species:

1) the – usually progressive – movements for the rights of the national minorities and/or *oppressed nations*: the Basque and Irish are only the visible (and explosive) top of an iceberg, which includes Catalans and Galicians, Scots and Welsh, Corsicans and Greek-Cypriots – and several others.

2) *xenophobic and racist nationalism*, directed not so much against the old 'enemy from outside' (other European nations) but against the 'enemy from inside': the immigrant workers of Arab, African, Turkish, Kurd or Eastern European origin (as well as, often, the Jewish or Gypsy minorities). The political expression of this development is the surprising rise of nationalist parties and movements of semi-fascist, fascist or even nazi character (in France, Austria, Belgium, Germany, etc) – representing already 7 million voters in the European Community! – as well as the murderous aggressions of skinheads and other racist bands. In Germany

alone in 1991, there have been more than 1,200 aggressions by racist thugs against foreign immigrants (compared to 270 in 1990).[9]

It is true that racism is not identical to nationalism. But as Adorno already emphasized at the above mentioned conference in 1966, 'the awakening of nationalism is the most favourable climate' for the upsurge of racism and intolerance.[10] In its most radical and extreme forms, nationalism often turns into racism, by trying to ground national supremacy on pseudo-biological criteria.

The main targets of Western European xenophobic nationalism were until recently the immigrants from the South (particularly Africa and Asia); the next victims will be – or are already, mainly in Germany – the unfortunate immigrants from Eastern Europe, expelled from their countries by national conflicts or by the economic catastrophe resulting from the brutal introduction of a market economy. After the Arab, the African or the Turk, it is now the turn of the Pole, the Romanian or the Albanian to become the scapegoat for Western racist/nationalists.

Mainstream Western European parties refuse to endorse racism, but they share a sort of 'Western nationalism' which leads to the exclusion of immigrant workers from democratic rights (eg. to vote and to be elected) and to the closure, as tightly as possible, of the EEC borders to non-Western immigrants. Could it be that one day the European Community will rebuild the Berlin Wall a little further to the East, and re-establish the barriers of electrified barbed wire of the old 'Iron Curtain', this time on the Western side of the border?

As a matter of fact, the presence of the immigrants is only a pretext: they constitute no more than 2% of the European Community's population; moreover, they were already there 15 or 20 years ago, without provoking the same reactions. Why precisely now has this xenophobic wave taken place? The economic crisis, unemployment and the degradation of living conditions in the popular neighbourhoods are certainly among the main factors.

But there is something deeper taking place in the political culture of some popular layers: as in Eastern Europe, but in a different way, the decline of socialist and class values, so long identified with the USSR and the Communist Parties, make room for national/racism. From this standpoint, the rise of nationalist values has, in both parts of Europe, common roots. To this one has to add, in the West, the disappointment with the social-democratic management of the crisis, increasingly undistinguishable (with the exception of a few details) from the neo-liberal one. The failure of social-democratic governments (or coalitions including such parties) to confront the growing social inequalities, their adoption of the conventional (bourgeois) economic wisdom, and their involvement in various affairs of corruption (eg. in France and Italy) have paved the way for all sorts of xenophobic 'populist' movements. Thanks to the weakening of the socialist culture, capitalism appears more and more as a 'natural' system, as the only possible horizon, as the necessary form of production and exchange; as a consequence, economic and social problems like unemployment, poverty or urban insecurity are no longer attributed by significant sections of the population to the disfunctions of capitalism, but to the presence of immigrants and other 'foreigners'.

Progressive and reactionary forms of nationalism can also be found in the so-called Third World (a term which has lost any meaning, since there is no more any 'Second World'), i.e. in the dependent periphery of the imperialist world system.

Several important emancipatory and progressive movements of national liberation can be found today in Africa, Asia and the Middle East. But it should be emphasised that most of these movements – like those in Kurdistan, Eritrea, South Africa, Palestine, Timor, Sudan – are not directly opposed to Western imperialism as such but rather to local forms of national oppression. With the exception of the wave of popular protest in the Arab world against the Gulf War, anti-colonial and anti-imperialist nationalism seems to have lost much of its influence, to the profit of basically reactionary and/or xenophobic movements like Islamic Fundamentalism, ethnico-linguistic and religious Communalism (India, Sri-Lanka) and Tribalism.

Contradictory forms of nationalism co-exist also in Latin-America.[11] The classic example of reactionary nationalism is the 'patriotic' ideology of military regimes – as in Argentina, Brazil or Chile in the 70's and 80's – usually directed against the ghost of 'international communism' and its Latin-American 'subversive agents'. In the name of the 'Doctrine of National Security', every social protest, every leftist movement is denounced as being 'of foreign inspiration', or based on 'exotic doctrines alien to our national tradition'. This conservative brand of cold-war nationalism makes an extensive usage of national symbols (the banner, the national anthem) and patriotic rhetoric, but it accepts without hesitation US hegemony ('the American leadership of the Free World'). It may refer to geo-politics in order to claim a sub-imperialist role of regional hegemony – like the Brazilian military during the 70s – but this ambition leads very seldom to an open conflict with rival Western powers, as in the Argentinian war with Britain around the Malvinas/Falkland islands.

Middle-class populist nationalism, which had its peak during the 40s and the 50s (Peronism in Argentina, the Peruvian APRA, 'getulismo' in Brazil, etc) is in decline and has come to terms with foreign capital. The most obvious example is the present Peronist government in Argentina (President Menem), which has systematically broken all the links with the nationalist tradition of the movement and has followed very strictly the instructions of the IMF. In some cases, like Mexico, the crisis of the governmental populist movement (the PRI, Institutional Revolutionary

Party) leads to a split, and the formation of a new party. The Mexican PRD (Revolutionary Democratic Party), led by Cuauhtemoc Cardenas – the son of former president Lazaro Cardenas, who expropriated the US oil companies in Mexico during the 30s – aims at a renewal of the nationalist and anti-imperialist tradition of the Mexican Revolution.

Revolutions in Latin America always had simultaneously a *social* and a *national* content. This applies not only to the Mexican Revolution of 1910-11 or the Bolivian Revolution of 1953, but also to the more radical (i.e. aiming at a socialist transformation) revolutions in Cuba (1959-61) and Nicaragua (1979). Fidel Castro and his followers were inspired by the struggle and the ideas of José Marti, the Jacobin, nationalist and anti-imperialist leader of the insurrection against Spanish colonialism; and the fighters of the FSLN (Frente Sandinista de Liberacion Nacional) in Nicaragua considered themselves as heirs to Augusto Sandino's war of national liberation against the US marines (1927-32). The struggle for national independence and sovereignty, in confrontation with aggressive US imperial policies, was a decisive component of the Cuban and Nicaraguan revolutionary movements and of their popular support.

Today, the fight against foreign debt and the IMF policies has been the main focus of progressive national feelings and anti-imperialist mobilisations in Latin America, taking the form of rallies, strikes, protests and even mass riots. Thanks to the heavy requirements of the (strictly impossible) debt repayment, the IMF and the World Bank exert such a kind of direct control (without precedent since the end of Spanish colonisation in the 19th century!) over the economic and social policies of these countries that their independence is often reduced to a fiction. The 'advisors' and 'experts' of the international financial institutions dictate to Latin American governments their rate of inflation, their budgetary cuts in education and health, their wages policy and their tax structure. The popular struggle against such outrageous forms of dependency, and against the repayment of the foreign debt, is not only a 'nationalist', but also an *anti-systemic* (to use Immanuel Wallerstein's useful concept) movement, by its opposition to the logic of world capitalist finance. It has also a 'class' component, by its conflict with the local rulers – eager to comply with the policies of the IMF and of the foreign banks.

It is not surprising that in some countries, like Brazil, Bolivia or Peru, it is the labour movements, the unions and the leftist parties that lead the fight against the repayment of the foreign debt: national and social liberation are intimately linked in the consciousness of the most active sections of the movement. Lula, the leader of the Brazilian Partido dos Trabalhadores (Workers' Party) – 47% of the votes at the presidential elections of 1989 – called for an immediate suspension of the payment and the establishment of a public inquiry on the debt, in order to find out what happened to the money borrowed (mainly by the military regime which ruled the country from 1964 to 1985). He also called for a common initiative of the indebted countries, since none of them is strong enough to confront the creditors alone.

How far can a single country – even a powerful one like Brazil or Mexico – refuse the dictatorship of the World Bank and break the yoke of imperialist domination? Can Latin-American unity, under popular leadership, constitute an alternative to the US plans of economic integration? How to achieve national and social liberation in an underdeveloped country without the economic or military support of an industrial power like the USSR? How important are the contradictions between Europe, Japan and the USA and could they be exploited by liberated peripheric countries?

This and similar questions – which cannot be easily answered – are being debated among progressive, socialist and anti-imperialist forces, in Latin-America and elsewhere in the ex-Third World. They show that national liberation is still a key issue at the periphery of the system, but also that purely nationalist solutions are of limited value: the need for an internationalist strategy is perhaps better perceived now than in the past.

The example of Cuba seems to show that an independent country can, at least during a limited amount of time, survive in confrontation with a US blockade, a boycott by the world financial institutions and no support from the ex-USSR. But in the longer run, the future of Cuba will depend on developments in the other parts of Latin America.

During recent years, the various socialist, nationalist and anti-imperialist forces in Latin America – including, among others, the Brazilian PT, the Nicaraguan FSLN, the Salvadorean FMLN (Farabundo Marti Front of National Liberation), the Mexican PRD and the Cuban Communist Party – feeling the need of an international (or at least regional) coordination, have associated themselves in a united front, called the Forum of Sao Paulo, which meets yearly and discusses common perspectives. At the first conference of the Forum, in 1990, a document was adopted, which presented the broad outlines of a common strategy for national liberation in Latin America. First of all, it rejected the proposition of 'American Integration' proposed by US President Bush, denouncing it as an attempt to 'completely open our national economies to the disloyal and unequal competition of the imperialist economic apparatus, submitting entirely to its hegemony and destroying our productive structures, by integrating them into a zone of free exchange led and organized by the US economic interests'. The document opposes to this proposition of integration under imperialist domination, 'a new concept of continental unity and integration', based on the sovereignty and self-determination of Latin America, the recovery of its historical and cultural identity and the internationalist solidarity of its peoples. 'This presupposes the defence of the Latin-American patrimony, an end to the flight and exportation of capitals, a common and united policy towards the scourge of an unpayable foreign debt, and the adoption of economic policies in benefit of the majorities, able to combat the situation of misery in which millions of Latin-Americans live'.[12]

Next to anti-imperialist nationalism, a different sort of emancipatory nationalism has been developing in Latin America during the last years: the movement of the indigenous nations for their rights. The debate around the Fifth Centennial of Columbus's arrival in the Americas, and the Nobel Prize attributed to Rigoberta Menchu have given a greater visibility to this indigenous struggle for the defence of their communities, their land and their national culture against the oppression of the ruling oligarchies (usually of Spanish descent).

These Indian movements, associations or political parties (like the Tupac Katari Movement in Bolivia) – which usually are not limited to one ethnic group (Quechuas, Aymaras, Mayas) but unite all the Indian communities in each country – develop a thorough criticism of Western civilisation and its values (private property, individualism, commodity production), in the name of the pre-capitalist (and pre-Columbian) indigenous traditions, and their communitarian culture. Their struggle has at the same time, a national, social and ecological character.

While some organisations have a stronger ethnic component, and call for the restoration of the old Indian nations and empires, most of those movements fight for the recognition of the national and cultural rights of the indigenous peoples, in coalition with other oppressed groups and classes. One example of this is the continental-wide movement against the official celebrations of the Fifth Centennial, called 'Five Hundred Years of Indian, Black and Popular Resistance', which had as one of its main aims the solidarity with the struggles of the indigenous peoples. Of course, there are very great differences between the indigenous nations of countries like Guatemala, Peru and Bolivia, where they constitute the majority of the population, and the small surviving tribes of the Amazonian area. While in the first case the national struggle is intimately linked to the social one, and to the agrarian question (the struggle for land), in the second one it is rather a matter of protection against the ethnocidal logic of 'civilisation'.

The resistance of trade-unionists, ecologists and Indian tribes against the destructive development of agro-business may lead to common action, as happened recently in the Brazilian Amazon area, with the constitution of a Confederation of the Rain-forest Peoples, by initiative of the well known trade-union and ecological leader Chico Mendes (recently killed by land-owners).

Finally, there is a third form of progressive nationalism in Latin America (and the US as well): Black nationalism, which is particularly important in the Caribbean countries. Its historical roots can be found in the slave rebellions, and in particular in the Haitian Revolution of 1791, led by Toussaint L'Ouverture and the Black Jacobins. In a country like Brazil, where the majority of the population is black or coloured, there have also been slave revolts (like the Quilombo dos Palmares, a community of rebel slaves during the eighteenth century). In our days, the main form of Brazilian Black cultural resistance is religious, through the development of Umbanda, a synchretic cult composed of African and Christian elements.

What should be the attitude of Marxists in relation to national conflicts? Marxism is opposed to the nationalist ideology, but it does not ignore the importance and legitimacy of democratic national rights.

This is why, during conflicts between Western imperial powers and dependent countries of Asia, Africa or Latin-America, Marxists usually defend the rights of the peripheric nations, and struggle against all forms of imperial aggression (whatever their 'democratic' or 'juridical' cover) – but this does *not* mean that they should give any kind of support to reactionary military, religious or nationalist dictators of the Third World, like Gen. Videla, Ayatollah Khomeini, Saddam Hussein or General Noriega . . .

As an internationalist world-view, Marxism – to be distinguished from its multiple national-bureaucratic counterfeits – has the advantage of a universalist and critical position, in contrast to the passions and intoxications of nationalist mythology. On the condition, however, that this universalism does not remain abstract, grounded on the simple negation of national particularity, but becomes a true 'concrete universal' (Hegel), able to incorporate, under the form of a dialectical *Aufhebung*, all the richness of the particular.

Thanks to the concept of *imperialism*, Marxism is able to avoid the pitfalls of the Eurocentric (or 'Western') false universalism, which pretends to impose on all countries in the world (and particularly those on the periphery), under the cover of 'civilisation', the domination of the modern bourgeois/industrial way of life: private property, market economy, unlimited economic expansion, productivism, utilitarianism, possessive individualism and instrumental rationality.

This does not mean that socialists ignore the universal value of certain achievements of European culture since 1789, such as democracy and human rights. It means only that they refuse the false dilemma between a pretence 'Western' universalism and the narrow-minded worship of cultural differences.

For Marxism, the most important universal value is the liberation of human beings from all forms of oppression, domination, alienation and degradation. This is an utopian universality, in opposition to the *ideological* universalities which apologetically present the Western status quo as being the accomplished human universal culture, the end of history, the realisation of the absolute spirit. Only a *critical* universality of this kind, looking towards an emancipated future, is able to overcome short-sighted nationalisms, narrow culturalisms, ethnocentrisms.

Starting from this premise, how should Marxists react to the present European national conflicts (or to Third-World communal strife)?

First of all, Marxism proposes a capital distinction between the *nationalism of the oppressors* and of the *oppressed*. Without adhering to any nationalist ideology, Marxist socialism supports unreservedly the national movement of the dominated and rejects without hesitation the 'Great Power chauvinism' of the ruling nation. This distinction is more than ever justified and it operates like a precious compass to find one's bearings in the present tempest. But its use is made difficult by a well known characteristic of modern nationalisms: each oppressed nation, as soon as liberated (or even before), considers as its most urgent task to exercise an analogous oppression over its own national minorities. Frequently, during the present inter-ethnic conflicts, each side persecutes the minority belonging to the rival nation, while manipulating its own nationals on the other side of the border (Yugoslavia is a good example in point).

We need therefore a universal criterion in order to disentangle the web of the opposed and mutually exclusive claims. This criterion can only be that – common to socialists and democrats – of the right of self-determination (until separation) of each nation, that is, of each community which considers itself as such. Indifferent to the myths of blood and soil, and not recognising any purely religious or historical claims over a given territory, this criterion has the immense advantage of referring itself only to the *universal principles of democracy and popular sovereignty*, and of taking into consideration only the concrete demographic realities of any inhabited space.

This principle does not prevent socialists from defending the option which seems to them the most desirable or the most progressive at a given historical moment: state separation (independence), federation, confederation. The essential point is that the concerned nations and nationalities should freely decide their own future.

This rule – incorporated by Lenin into the Marxist vocabulary – is more than ever necessary. But, again, its application to the present national conflicts – particularly in Eastern Europe and the ex-USSR – is not always easy. In many cases the interpenetration of the nationalities is such, that any attempt to cut borders into this mosaic is fraught with perils. The dream of national homogeneity inside the state, which haunts almost all nationalisms, is a most dangerous perspective. As Eric Hobsbawm observes, in a sober historical reminder: 'The logical implication of trying to create a continent neatly divided into coherent territorial states each inhabited by a separate ethnically and linguistically homogeneous population, was the mass expulsion and extermination of minorities. Such was and is the murderous *reductio ad absurdum* of nationalism in its territorial version, although this was not fully demonstrated until the 1940s.'[13]

Let us return to our initial paradox: at this strange nationalist end of the century, the most urgent problems have, more than ever, an international character. The search for a way out of the economic crisis of the ex-'socialist bloc', the question of the Third World's debt, and imminent ecological disaster – to mention only these three major examples – require planetary solutions. Those of Capital are well known and perfectly organised on a world-scale: they have inevitably, in whatever place they have been implemented, the same double result: make the rich even richer, and the poor even poorer.

What alternatives exist to the totalitarian grip of 'really existing' world capitalism? The old pseudo-internationalism of the Stalinist Comintern, of the followers of various 'Socialist Fatherlands', is dead and buried. A new internationalist alternative of the oppressed and exploited is badly needed.

It is from the fusion between the international socialist, democratic and anti-imperialist tradition of the labour movement (still much alive among revolutionaries of various tendencies, radical trade-unionists, left-socialists, etc) and the new universalist culture of social movements like ecology, feminism, anti-racism, and Third-world-solidarity that the internationalism of tomorrow will rise. This tendency may be a minority now, but it is nevertheless the seed of a different future and the ultimate guarantee against barbarism.

NOTES

1. T. Adorno, *Modèles critiques*, Paris, Payot, 1984, p. 106.
2. H. Arendt, *The Burden of our time*, London, Secker and Warburg, 1951, p. 267.
3. R. Luxemburg, 'Fragment über Krieg, nationale Frage und Revolution', *Die Russische Revolution*, Frankfurt, Europäische Verlagsanstalt, 1963, p. 82.
4. See on this the remarkable essay by Catherine Samary, *The fragmentation of Yugoslavia*, Amsterdam, Notebooks for Study and Research, no. 19/20, 1992.
5. Quoted by Eric Hobsbawm in 'The Perils of the New Nationalism', *The Nation*, 4 November 1991, p. 556.
6. L. Trotsky, *On Black Nationalism and Self-Determination*, New York, Pathfinder Press, 1978, p. 28.
7. E.Hobsbawm, *Nation and Nationalism since 1780. Programme, Myth, Reality*, Cambridge University Press, 1990, pp. 163, 170, 181.
8. E. Gellner, 'Nationalism and Politics in Eastern Europe', *New Left Review*, No. 189, October 1991, p. 131.
9. *Bild am Sontag*, January 26, 1992.
10. T. Adorno, *op. cit.*, p. 106.
11. I am referring more extensively to Latin America because I am more familiar with this area of the Third World.
12. *Inprecor*, no. 6, July 1990, p. 6.
13. Hobsbawm, *Op. cit.*, p. 133.

RETHINKING THE FRELIMO STATE

John S. Saul

The sad trajectory of the Mozambican revolution has been devastating, almost beyond words, for Mozambicans. It has also been a sobering experience for those of us who have, over the years, supported – and sought to interpret – Frelimo's progressive development project in that country. 'Frelimo's progressive development project'? It is a sign of the times that there seems to be something distinctly old-fashioned about even phrasing the issue in these terms. 'Development project'? A misguided expression of modernist arrogance, surely. 'Progressive'? Scepticism about the appropriateness of 'socialist solutions' is so rife (even on much of the left) that this term, too, seems highly suspect. And what about 'Frelimo' itself? This is, apparently, the most suspect variable of all – to judge from much of the current writing about Mozambique.

Of course, it behooves all of us to understand better the sorry pass to which Mozambique has been brought under Frelimo leadership: from a country, admittedly backward, that nonetheless entered upon its independence in 1975 with high hopes to a country in tatters, possibly, now, the most desperately poverty-stricken in the world. Not so long ago, explanations of this disastrous trajectory began with the hard fact of South African destabilization. But increasingly – 'a paradigm shift', we are told by British Africa-scholar Gervase Clarence-Smith[1] – the centre of gravity of accepted explanation seems to have moved, the blame for failure now falling more and more onto the shoulders of Frelimo itself, and onto that movement's various errors of omission and commission.

A useful corrective? Certainly those of us who have been closest to Frelimo over the years are, at least in part, guilty as charged: can there be any doubt that we overestimated the scope of Frelimo's achievements and underestimated the seriousness of the weaknesses attendant upon its efforts? Yet I don't think it mere defensiveness to suggest the danger that the pendulum of explanation has begun to swing too far in the other direction, that the South African role in destroying Frelimo's undertakings now runs the risk of being underestimated rather than overestimated and that the Frelimo project now runs the risk of being caricatured, negatively, beyond recognition. As we will see in this essay, any such extreme rewriting

139

of Mozambican history, if left unchallenged, could prove very costly indeed, not least in spawning a temptation, on the part of Mozambicans and others, to learn precisely the wrong lessons from the virtual collapse of the Mozambican state.

Something more general is also at stake. The alacrity with which the most negative interpretations of Frelimo's role in Mozambique have been seized upon in many quarters reflects not merely a 'paradigm shift' in the study of Mozambique but a virtual sea-change in much of the discussion, even on the left, of African development prospects. Some aspects of this change are healthy. Concerns about 'democracy' – protean though the notion may be – will not so easily be ignored in future, for example. But some seem more to represent a failure of nerve, a loss of confidence, in the face of the grim fecundity of the 'New World Order' and of trends towards the recolonization of southern Africa. Beware an African Studies in retreat – whether to the benevolent logic of the market or to the 'moral economy' of the village – that casts more doubt than is necessary upon the possibility and/or wisdom of heroic purpose and revolutionary possibility. In discussing Mozambique, past, present and future, in the present essay, I will also seek to comment on the 'false solutions', both analytical and practical, that this broader trend thus places on offer.

I A Paradigm Shift?

The range of criticisms of Frelimo practices is, in fact, quite broad, finding perhaps the most dramatic form in South African Communist Party veteran Joe Slovo's assertion, at a New York symposium on 'The Future of Socialism', that Mozambique's attempted socialist project was 'both premature and wrong'![2] How are we to interpret this assertion? At one level it might be considered the mere application, by a long-time Communist, of a rather conventional Third International Marxism to the Mozambican case. After all, even at the highest point of 'fraternal relations' between Mozambique and the Soviet Union, the Soviets were never quite prepared to accord Mozambique any higher status than that of a 'state of socialist orientation' because of its relatively 'primitive' level of social relations.

Moreover, Slovo did not state clearly what he would have had the progressive leadership that found itself in power in Mozambique in the mid-70s actually do with that power – thus rendering his own position, without any further elaboration, a rather too comfortable and passive one. Of course, he is also correct up to a point: the 'backward conditions' Frelimo inherited ('the absolute level of undevelopment' as I have phrased the point elsewhere), as well as the country's underdeveloped class structure and its extreme international vulnerability, would indeed have presented very real problems to any fledgling revolution in Mozambique. And yet the temptation to attach more importance to 'necessary preconditions'

than to concrete political and economic practices in explaining the
strengths and weaknesses of an 'actually-existing socialism' can also lapse
into a singularly dismissive way of approaching the issue.

Slovo's position does not, in any case, represent the sort of 'paradigm
shift' other authors[3] have principally in mind when they use that phrase to
summarize a recent redefinition of the terms of analysis of things Mozambican. At stake for them is less a preoccupation with such absolute limits as
history had imposed upon Frelimo's ability to realize its aspirations than a
debate over the relative importance of several more immediate factors in
derailing the process of transformation in Mozambique. In Alex Vines'
words there is a move 'in academic analysis . . . away from the causality of
the Mozambican crisis being South African destabilization, with the
emphasis being shifted to a focus on Frelimo's agrarian policies as the roots
of the problem'. Or, in Clarence-Smith's more pungent phrasing, 'in effect,
Frelimo dug its own grave in the face of an apparently derisory enemy . . .
Renamo exploits all the anger and resentment that Frelimo has created in
the countryside through its policies'.[4]

In fact, it is only the more extreme versions of this approach[5] that argue
for a 'paradigm shift' in anything like such stark terms. If we look at the
most careful analyses of the war in Mozambique we find that a great deal of
weight is still given – correctly – to the impact of Pretoria's sponsorship of
Renamo and its ruthless destabilization tactics in Mozambique.[6] Thus,
William Finnegan, while quite alert to the flaws in Frelimo's own project,
emphasizes the importance of the fact that 'few (new governments in
Africa) have had the bad luck to live next door to a powerful foe ready to
exploit their every misstep'.[7] Even this formulation threatens to understate
the case, of course. For there is something remarkably cold-blooded about
the current tendency to develop an approach to Mozambique that reduces
South Africa's ruthless policy – 'the destruction of an African country'[8] – to
something like a residual variable. True, every historical situation is 'overdetermined', making it virtually impossible ever to hold enough other
strands of determination 'constant' to reach, confidently, some definitive
account of any one of them. But we ignore at our peril (both moral and
analytical) the conclusion of a US State Department report that once
described the war in Mozambique as 'one of the most brutal holocausts
against ordinary human beings since World War II'.[9]

Not that fully grasping the centrality of this reality need blunt the edge of
debate about the strengths and weaknesses of Frelimo's own broad project. It is here that we return to the hard fact that much of the texture of the
debate about Mozambique is more fundamentally critical of Frelimo's
undertakings than in the days when 'scholar-activists' supportive of the
movement (the Mozambican versions of Patrick Chabal's notorious 'red-
feet'[10]) were the chief contributors to the literature. A key point of
reference in this respect is the work of Christian Geffray,[11] his case-study

showing some of the ways in which, in one corner of the country, Renamo did use both the tensions that existed in and between local communities and the negative reaction of some rural dwellers against Frelimo's economic mistakes and administrative highhandedness to give some domestic political grounding to its activities.

Debate continues to swirl around the accuracy of Geffray's emphasis and the generalizability of his findings.[12] Moreover, Geffray himself would not use such data to blunt awareness of the extreme ruthlessness, even barbarity, with which Renamo has carried out what remains, essentially, a wrecker's role. Even so, such new material has served, as indicated, to sharpen the critical focus on Frelimo. It seems no accident that it is in a review of Geffray's book, prominently published (in the *Times Literary Supplement*) and provocatively titled ('Between Two Terrors'), that Peter Fry gives particularly vivid voice to a new orthodoxy in-the-making on matters Mozambican, contrasting the misguided development efforts of the old Frelimo with those 'who are supporting President Joaquim Chissano in his attempt to set Mozambique on a course of development in tune with the realities of the regional and international political and economic environment and, above all, with the aspirations of the people of Mozambique'.[13]

'In tune with the realities of the regional and international political and economic environment'. A rather jejune way to describe the pattern of Mozambique's resubordination to South African and global capitalist dictate that Chissano has been forced to accept and that we will outline further in section III of this essay. And what about 'the aspirations of the people of Mozambique'? In this regard, Fry makes great play of evidence supplied by Geffray as to Frelimo's overbearing approach to local tradition – epitomized by him in the term *abaixismo* (rough translation: 'down with-ism'). Yet Fry himself acknowledges that things are a bit more complicated than this when, at the end of his review, he qualifies his assertions, now invoking the need for 'debate on Africa's most fundamental problem: how to reconcile the desire for modernity and the need for economic development with the equally strong attachment to very different forms of social organization from those of politically and economically dominant spheres of the world'.[14] But what kind of politics follows from this kind of understanding? What kind of critique of Frelimo should it ground? We must dig deeper to find the sub-text that permits the easy swing of Fry and others to a new orthodoxy that emphasizes the negative nature of the Frelimo experience.

As noted above, the materials are available for a more careful reprise of the complex dynamics of the war's escalation, one that would demonstrate the ways in which the most assertive proponents of the 'new paradigm' school have overstated their case. Here it is more important to emphasize the extent to which a 'mood-swing' in the most current analytical approaches to 'progressive regimes' in Africa has provided the premises that help make such overstatement possible. As noted at the outset of this essay what is crucial is the growing hegemony of an approach – joined at a point where left and right seem increasingly comfortable to meet – that is sceptical about the role of the state, sceptical about socialism and, at least in some of its expressions regarding Africa, sceptical about the claims of 'modernity' itself.

Perhaps the strongest manifestation of this mood swing in African studies is to be found in the writings of those grouped around the influential French journal – left-leaning at its launching a decade or more ago – *Politique Africaine*.[15] Darbon, in discussing 'l'État prédateur', suggests that 'at the beginning of the 1990s, little remains of the hopes for development that had been placed on the state structures of the African countries. . . . The concept of the state as stimulus or promoter of development seems to have completely failed in Africa'.[16] Bayart takes the point a step further:

> The state is the dominant economic agent in Africa whether the regime is single-party, pluralist or socialist. Everywhere the state's integration into the world economy has proceeded apace. Everywhere there has been primitive accumulation, that is, over-exploitation of the peasantry. State accumulation is intimately connected with individual accumulation at all levels (including the highest) and in all countries (including the most 'socialist'). Power in whatever form is inevitably an instrument for the accumulation of wealth. . . . It is, therefore, otiose to seek to establish a conceptual difference between the private and the public sector. Both are the instruments of a dominant class striving to establish its hegemony.[17]

That said, it also bears noting that the critics save their strongest fire for a state that presumes to intervene in the name of socialism. Thus Jean Médard (in his *Politique Africaine* article, 'L'État patrimonialisé') writes of the special temptation both liberals and socialists face of seeing the state as 'the demiurge of development', based on an unlikely hope: 'to realize its role, it would be necessary that the state be a pure instrument of the technocratic rationality of its leaders, who themselves would have to be animated by commitment to the 'general weal' and sufficiently detached from society to remodel it 'from outside' with a great degree of independence'.[18] But it is for socialists in particular that he reserves his deepest scorn: 'within a socialist framework development is even more difficult since, if a capitalist framework at least has the merit of favouring growth, the socialist framework suffocates it. And even if we know enough not to confuse growth with economic development, we also know that there cannot be development without growth'![19]

It will be obvious that Médard's conclusion rests on a vision of the benign workings of the unfettered market-place in Africa that is difficult to square with available evidence regarding the actual experience of capitalist accumulation in Africa. Not that Médard suggests the transition to capitalist growth to be, necessarily, a smooth one. But in his outlining of the impediments to such growth he highlights not contradictions that might be thought to be inherent in the logic of capitalist accumulation itself but rather those springing from the manner in which capitalism's functioning is held back in Africa by the workings of quasi-traditional patron-client relations.[20] The celebrated trajectory of Goren Hyden – in his quest for an effective means of 'capturing' the peasantry – from enthusiasm for the efforts of Tanzania's 'demiurgic' state to an equal and opposite enthusiasm for the free run of the market is a related case in point.[21]

But Manfred Bienefeld has, in any case, underscored the extent to which many analysts much further to the Left than Hyden have come to espouse 'individualistic resolutions' to development problems, manifesting extreme suspicion of any state's claim to represent 'a general interest' and ready to 'discount the relative dangers and inflate the expected benefits of deepening an economy's entanglement with the international market and of increasing reliance on internal markets'. And this in spite of the fact that, in Bienefeld's view, 'the present African crisis was most clearly foreseen by those looking at Africa from a dependency perspective in the 1960s'. In the process Bienefeld neatly parries Bill Warren's much-cited assertion – remarkably close to the orthodoxy of the World Bank, Bienefeld notes – of 'the historically progressive and economically efficient nature of recent capitalist development in the Third World'.[22] Note, then, that it is on premises much like those Bienefeld here criticizes that Clarence-Smith grounds his own critique of the Frelimo state's original project. Any effort by Mozambique to break its links with South Africa, he suggests provocatively, would be 'like asking somebody to kill the goose that lays the golden egg'. And like Médard he seems to take for granted that development of 'Mozambique's economy along capitalist lines' is a virtual guarantee of 'growth'![23]

One further strand to today's ubiquitous critique of the state is also worth noting here, one that may appear to be rather contradictory to the point just mentioned but is often held in uneasy tandem with it nonetheless. Recall, for example, Geffray's influential analysis of Frelimo's practice, cited above. Central to his argument is a critique of the movement's failure to take the layered complexity of Mozambique's local, 'quasi-traditional' society seriously. Ultimately, he seems to go so far as to cast doubt upon the very legitimacy of Frelimo's attempt to change that society at all. As O'Laughlin summarizes his argument, 'Geffray tends to assume that in Nampula there is a homogeneous peasantry, sharply differentiated from townspeople and living within a traditional world dominated by traditional cults, rules and practices. The clearest voices in this world view are those of the lineage elders'. And Frelimo (O'Laughlin paraphrases Geffray as suggesting) should, among other bows to the integrity of local societies, 'honour the authority of traditional leaders who are not on the side of the Portuguese'.[24]

The implication: there is a certain 'modernist' arrogance in Frelimo's decision to do otherwise.[25] O'Laughlin thinks very differently: 'Looking at

15 years of African independence, Frelimo saw this dualism as divisive, anti-democratic and responsible for maintaining economic backwardness in the countryside. I agree', she says. [26] In short, if genuine democratic empowerment is to occur – if, as one example, the emancipation of women in rural Africa is to be facilitated – the structures of the quasi-traditional world *must* be challenged. To think otherwise is to be 'politically naive. Permit people to respect and honour religious figures and title-holders, to be sure, but the underlying question of how local governance and political power is to be organized cannot be conjured away'. Her conclusion: 'The problem is that dignity and authority were enmeshed in a system of local governance which any socialist political strategy would have to alter'. [27]

As we will see below, O'Laughlin does not view this argument as an excuse for 'well-intentioned' left authoritarianism or even as the occasion for any white-washing of Frelimo's activities. Indeed, she interprets the failure of Frelimo's rural strategy as 'less the "revenge" of traditional society [as Geffray seems to suggest] than the negative fall-out from weaknesses in Frelimo's own application of "modern", socialist politics'. [28] It should also be clear, however, that O'Laughlin's is an increasingly unpopular way of conceiving things – at a time when most observers are so eager to distance themselves from any guilt by association with the notion of 'the state and/or party as modernizing agent' that they would dismiss her formulations more or less out of hand. Not that most such observers are actually all that 'relativist' and 'post-modern' in their own approach to 'quasi-traditional' societies, of course. It is merely that, like Peter Fry, they are comfortable to square this particular circle by leaving any 'progressive' breaching of the supposed integrity of such societies to the workings of 'impersonal market forces'!

Needless to say, there are some valuable insights in much of the literature we have been discussing. Thus, Geffray merely overstates an otherwise important insight when he argues that the Mozambican government too often saw rural populations merely as 'an arithmetical collection of desocialized individuals . . . curiously just waiting for Frelimo to provide them with social organization'. Médard, in his description of the 'demiurgic state', also evokes something real regarding the all too common arrogance of ostensibly progressive elites, not least in Mozambique. And Bayart's firm emphasis upon the need to facilitate the empowerment of civil society in order to offset the African state's abusive propensities is also to the point.

But can society 'reappropriate the state'? Can a 'more "equal" relation between state and society' be established? Bayart does suggest that 'civil society can only transform its relation to the state through the organization of new and autonomous structures, the creation of a new cultural fabric and the elaboration of a conceptual challenge to power monopolies'. Nonetheless, there remains a certain Manichean quality to Bayart's emphasis on the 'epistemic gulf between state and society', [29] one that can picture the state forever seeking to 'capture the peasantry' but cannot quite envisage the peasantry (and other popular classes) becoming capable, in any foreseeable future, of capturing the state. Indeed, for Bayart, 'Africa's potential for democracy is more convincingly revealed by the creation of small collectives established and controlled by rural or urban groups (such as local associations) than by parliaments and parties, instruments of the state, of accumulation and of alienation'.[30]

Yet 'the state' – some state– is not about to disappear from the world in which Bayart's 'small collectives' seek to find their feet, and chances are that if the state is not itself being transformed into an agent of transformation – thwarting overall societal disintegration, qualifying external dictate and widening developmental possibilities, stemming abuses of power, private and public, facilitating and defending fledgling popular initiatives – his 'local associations' will themselves have only limited prospects of being allowed the space to develop. Bayart's is a fall-back position of very modest aspiration then, even if many might consider it a 'realistic' one. And, of course, he is correct to think that the state itself is unlikely to be transformed unless – the paradox is real – the 'civil society' in formation has become strong and democratically assertive enough to force the state to hold to a positive course. But this is merely to suggest that the simultaneity of the need both for leadership *and* for mass action inherent in a process of socialist transformation frames a contradiction that cannot be made to disappear – and demands the construction of an on-going political process that takes both terms of this equation seriously. As we will see in the following section, Frelimo – the party, the state – at least momentarily embraced this difficult challenge and it is this that made its project so distinctive in Africa and – not least in the nature of its failure – so instructive.

As anticipated above and in sharp contrast to this approach, the 'new paradigm' emerging in the literature on Mozambique speaks less of the dilemmas facing Frelimo (and of the errors the movement has made in confronting them) than of the fundamentally misguided nature of its entire state-ridden project.* William Finnegan, in one of the best of recent books

---

* Note, too, one added complication here: root-and-branch criticism of Frelimo's 'statist' project is made both by observers who see Frelimo as having been too socialist and others who see it as not actually having been socialist at all! Thus, Adam and Moodley can blithely reduce Frelimo's original project to one of 'rhetorical socialism . . . hardly taken seriously by its proponents themselves', concluding that 'the elite therefore adjusts ideological interpretations as arbitrarily as they adopt them . . . because a collective ideological commitment hardly existed in the first place',[32] a position more or less echoed (albeit from the opposite end of the political spectrum) by Michel Cahen.[33] And even so sensitive an observer as William Finnegan is able to remark, in a parallel manner, on the 'breathtaking ease' with which Frelimo now moves to 'switch tracks' to 'some form of capitalism'.[34]

'Breathtaking ease'? Finnegan can only make this remark against the grain of the evidence of his own powerful book, the best part of which describes the terrible pounding Mozambique

on Mozambique,[31] goes much further than many such critics in acknowledging that 'the "Marxism-Leninism" and "international pro-letarianism" of Frelimo were as rigorous as any ruling-party ideology on the continent and had clearly made sense as a framework for national liberation and development in the early days of the revolution'. Yet even he can conclude that 'the end of the Cold War also seemed to highlight the superficiality of Western concepts like communism and capitalism when transplanted to Africa'. In fact, it is really communism/socialism he wishes to quarrel with. 'Capitalism' may be a 'western concept' too, but Finnegan has no qualms about asserting, more or less simultaneously, that for Mozambique 'some form of capitalism [has] seemed to become the only economic and political model with a future'! 'Marxism', on the other hand, 'was, *pace* Samora Machel, a European product' that really made no sense under Mozambican conditions.

One must, of course, give due weight to Finnegan's concern – so central to the current literature on Mozambique – at 'the social and economic distance between the elite, whether it calls itself revolutionary or an aristocracy, and the great mass of illiterate peasants'. Nor is he wrong to argue that 'vanguardism has inherent weaknesses – it fosters passivity and authoritarianism – and the victories won by a vanguard in the name of the people rarely end up empowering the masses'. But communism, socialism, Marxism . . . all to be regarded as irrelevant notions? This would be sobering enough coming from Finnegan. Even worse is the fact that many Mozambicans have themselves now been beaten into accepting some such conclusion.[36]

Yet – unless one shares the unreal premises of a Clarence-Smith or a Peter Fry regarding the likely fecundity of capitalism in Africa – can this really be cause for celebration?[37] Surely there is a need in contemporary Mozambique for a socialist perspective that can make sense of the country's present situation vis-à-vis an ascendent regional and global capitalism and make sense, too, of the social forces that continue to fray Mozambique's own social fabric. Equally important is the need to interrogate the demise of Frelimo's project from such a perspective if the real lessons of its failure are ever to be learned by those who must eventually seek to re-focus the energies of the poorest of the poor in order to reverse the terrible 'liberation' that global capitalism has inflicted upon Mozambique. These,

---

had endured for daring, in the first instance, to struggle against its subordination to global capitalist dictate. In so arguing, such critics choose to ignore the testimony of virtually all those who actually examined the Frelimo state closely enough in its early years to have a studied opinion on the subject. For as one such analyst (Bridget O'Laughlin) has recently put the point, 'If we abstract from this history, we tend to see only the defensive measures of the 1980s and forget the optimism, sense of reconciliation and broad mass participation in activities organized by Frelimo, in both rural and urban areas, during the first years after independence.'[35]

in any case, are the unregenerately old-fashioned premises that frame the following two sections of this essay.

II Evaluating the Frelimo State

We begin, then, by taking seriously the progressive opening represented in Africa by Frelimo's original socialist project, sharing Dan O'Meara's sense that 'as a political movement, Frelimo had proved itself, and would prove itself again and again, capable of a domestic and international political creativity and imagination unique in Africa.'[38] But there is also a need for a comprehensive critique both of Frelimo's project and its practices.[39] For the movement's own failures played some role in producing the present unhappy outcome, whatever the precise weight one might ultimately give them when measured against the impact of other factors, South African destabilization in particular. Of course, not everything now being said by the new generation of Frelimo's critics was profane knowledge to committed observers of Mozambican developments even in the heyday of Frelimo's maximum credibility. However, there is little doubt that when Frelimo came to power in 1975 it proved all too easy to overestimate both the clarity of its vision regarding the modalities of societal transformation and the symbiotic nature of its link to the popular classes – notably the peasantry.

My own first attempts to make sense of the history-making possibilities that seemed open to the Frelimo leadership as it came to power in the mid-1970s turned around the notion (developed out of the work of Hamza Alavi) of the 'overdeveloped', relatively autonomous, state that was up for grabs in the fluid circumstances of Africa's initial transition to independence. Although the degree of the 'post-colonial state's' autonomy remained subject to debate – and the task of transforming it much more difficult than might have been predicted – the concept seemed a helpful one. Certainly, it gave added resonance to my own conviction that the nature of the still forming group and/or class (I referred to it as a 'petty-bourgeoisie-in-the-making', Colin Leys as the 'state-party apparat', Patrick Chabal simply as the 'revolutionary leadership'[40]) that began to take shape around this state was of considerable significance in defining development outcomes. Even more concretely, this formulation anticipated that struggles within this group – such as had already occurred within Frelimo circles in exile in the late-1960s when the hegemony of a cadre of left-leaning leaders was consolidated – would be of considerable importance.[41]

It is important to be very precise about what is being claimed here since it seems necessary to lay to rest a canard that has served, ever since it was first articulated by Gavin Williams some years ago, to caricature this emphasis on the importance of 'petit-bourgeois politics'. At that time,

Williams wrote: 'Since the state is governed by the petit-bourgeoisie, and since their politics is indeterminate, the state may turn in any direction, depending on the ideology of those who come to control it. Like many members of the African "petit-bourgeoisie", Saul appears to think that "what we need is a good ruler, with a progressive ideology".'[42] This is, quite simply, a *reductio ad absurdum* of my argument. Just because one grants some active role to this 'group', it is not to be construed as having been removed from, and placed above, history, the production process, or the broader class structure. Moreover, nothing in the arguments surveyed by Williams suggest that it should be considered as being so isolated.

Such a line of analysis did indeed suggest the importance of the fact that guerilla war had produced in Frelimo a leadership cadre, a fraction of the petty-bourgeoisie, drawn towards a progressive/socialist project. But it also made quite clear that the extent to which the potential for consolidating such a project might be realized depended crucially on three variables: the strength of the forces pressing the leadership to diverge from such a project; the nature of the links the leadership would actually forge with those popular classes in whose name it professed to speak; and the capacity of the leadership to develop clear and effective policies for realising the kind of socio-economic transformation it envisaged. Unfortunately, on the latter two fronts the Frelimo leadership's project can be found wanting. Not flawed, *pace* the new critics, so much in the ends ('development', 'socialism', 'anti-imperialism') that it sought as in the means chosen to move towards those ends. This is, at any rate, the judgement underlying the argument that follows.

The constraints on their activity were real enough, of course, ranging from the drag of 'historical backwardness' (the grim legacy of Portugal's primitive colonialism and an exaggerated economic dependence on South Africa, and the shortfalls in education, literacy, health standards and the like that were dramatic even by African standards) to the brutal fact of South Africa's destabilization itself. Moroever, the apparent 'relative autonomy' of the newly independent state proved to be a decidedly mixed blessing. Although Samora Machel spoke eloquently at the very moment of independence of the need to transform, root and branch, the inherited Portuguese colonial state, its old-fashioned, hierarchical and highly bureaucratized structures soon began to entangle the incoming Frelimo team and, no doubt, helped encourage a certain high-handedness in its practices.[43] Did this entanglement also begin to tempt the 'state/party apparat' to develop a 'class interest'? That this might have been so is one principal theme of Joe Hanlon's influential analysis of the Frelimo state's first decade, *Mozambique: The Revolution Under Fire*, for example.[44]

Yet the primary weakness of the Frelimo state was not, in the first instance, its parasitic and exploitative nature. A high level of commitment to a transformative project did move the 'state/party apparat' for many years and both conspicuous consumption and corruption remained relatively unimportant during that time. The pull towards 'high-handedness' was another matter, however. For a second danger of excessive reliance on a state apparatus that remained 'relatively autonomous' was more immediately ominous than any pull towards parasitism. Perhaps if one reads, for 'autonomous', such words as 'ungrounded', 'suspended', 'free-floating' it is possible to get a sense, at least metaphorically, of the nature of the problem: *viz.*, that the Frelimo state remained suspended above the society whose liberation it sought to facilitate (Médard's demiurge!) and dangerously compromised by the great difficulty it would ultimately have in rooting its project in an active popular base.

Not that the tension, alluded to in the previous section, between 'leadership' and 'mass action' could merely have been willed away. Frelimo did offer a vision sufficiently coherent, in the first instance, to promise the moulding of a new, nation-wide Mozambican identity. It was also one linked closely enough to the cause of poorest of the poor to promise policies (notably in the spheres of health and education) that could transform such people's lives in positive ways. Not relying naively on mere spontaneity to produce this result, the party used the state to help create organs of potential empowerment for women, workers and peasants. Make no mistake: this project bore the stamp, in many particulars, of 'enlightened leadership', leadership that sought to help various 'progressive' classes and categories to 'name' themselves much more self-consciously.

Nor need this active role in helping draw to the surface of society certain self-definitions (e.g., 'women', 'workers', and 'peasants') rather than others (e.g. 'races', 'tribes', and 'regions') be considered to be, inherently, an arrogance. It only became so to the extent that Frelimo proved incapable of acknowledging to itself the paradox inherent in its role and risking the democratic implications of the task of empowerment it was setting itself. Here Frelimo's decision, in 1977, to pronounce itself a vanguard party became a key moment. This dictated the winding down of the messy and somewhat unpredictable – but often promisingly democratic – politics that were occurring in the *grupos dinamizadores* of the period; in addition, by further encouraging the laying of the firm hand of a fairly undemocratic centralism across the local assemblies, unions and women's organization that it had itself willed into place Frelimo came, in time, to render many of its own progeny still-born. Perhaps we can also argue the even more formative importance of another decision, one that antedated the embracing of the 'vanguard party' model *per se*: that is, the decision, inscribed in the very foundation of a one-party state, to forego pluralism in the name of revolutionary purity.[45] Of course, it is much easier to say this now, with the benefit of hindsight, than most of us found it possible to say at the time. Still, the fact remains that from the very beginning the Frelimo leadership was unwilling to put at democratic risk its own 'essential' role in the transformation it wished to set in train. And the costs of adopting the model of revolutionary leadership it did were to prove very high indeed.

Nor is it obvious that such costs need have been paid. Democratic leadership can, in principle, succeed in sustaining itself without the collapse into vanguardism and mere fiat that came to haunt Frelimo's practice. But so to succeed would require what O'Laughlin (as cited above) has termed 'socialist methods of political work', methods that would find the party both more sensitive to the nuance of local context and also capable of struggling, competitively, to win popular allegiance to the nobility and efficacy of its project against the pull of other poles of popular identification. This was possible, O'Laughlin insists, even in the Mozambican countryside, where peasants are alert to a diversity of possible strands of potential self-identification – including many 'modernizing' ones, both economic and political, that reach far beyond Geffray's confined world of quasi-traditionalism.[46] As we will see, quasi-traditionalism in its purest expression becomes most potent only as a fall-back position for peasants when other means of security and/or progress seem unavailable. But such was the hardness – externally evoked, internally generated – of Frelimo's style that the more positive possibilities of 'mobilization' that O'Laughlin alludes to were all too seldom realised.[47]

Incapable of rooting itself entirely effectively in a mass politics, the Frelimo state had become instead a 'developmental dictatorship' (in Eboe Hutchful's evocative formulation).[48] This fact must be central to our analysis – but so, too, must the fact that this was a developmental dictatorship *of the left*. My point: we lose far too much if we permit Bayart and others to collapse the distinction between 'left' and 'right' in this context into one overarching abstraction and to see all African states as belonging to one genus: the profoundly suspect, necessarily exploitative African state. We must, in short, keep open the space to assert that the weaknesses to which a 'developmental dictatorship of the left' is prone are rather different from those that afflict a 'developmental dictatorship of the right'. For it is only by specification of the weaknesses of the former – and not from any more generalized brand of 'state-bashing' – that useful lessons can be learned from the Mozambican experience.

The chief lesson? That even the most benignly left-wing but quasi-dictatorial leadership will have difficulty in sustaining its transformative project unless it allows itself (and/or is forced) to be held accountable to real rather than merely notional democratic pressures from below. Of course, it may well be argued that the costs of an undemocratic political practice in Mozambique would have been less had the Frelimo leadership not made mistakes on other policy fronts. The area of economic policy is particularly noteworthy in this regard. As I have argued elsewhere, the adoption of a model of 'primitive socialist accumulation' is by no means the fated requirement of a left regime in the context of underdevelopment. In principle, Frelimo could have adopted a different approach – what I have called 'the socialism of expanded reproduction' – that built on a more effective interchange between industry and agriculture, urban and rural, and better addressed the most pressing and immediate material requirements of peasants (and others). Instead of producing a 'crisis of reproduction' for the peasantry, such a strategy might have provided the material foundation for the peasants actually embracing as their own Frelimo's modernizing and socializing project.[49]

Not that this failure can be delinked from the movement's own undemocratic practices. Had Frelimo been a bit less confident that it knew what was best for the peasants it might not have adopted so readily an economic strategy that exacerbated their 'reproductive crisis', nor moved quite so aggressively (at least in some areas) to 'socialize' from above – via the communal village programme – their way of life. Significantly, at the one moment at which decisions about economic strategy seemed to bow to democratic input (in the run-up to the Fourth Congress, when both the need to address the reproductive crisis and to adopt a more flexible approach to the use of market mechanisms in the countryside were forced onto the agenda by popular protest), the Frelimo state came closest to striking the kind of balance between leadership and mass action that best promised both economic advance and political support. By then, however, the war of destabilization had escalated to such a point that the pursuit of a more measured approach to rural development had little chance of being implemented. Soon, as capitulation to the IMF and the World Bank loomed large for the Frelimo leadership, the subtleties of pursuing a more flexible and realistic socialist strategy had given way to full-scale retreat before the logic of capitalism.

But how had Frelimo come to abandon 'the peasant line' and democratic practices that had seemed so much a part of its liberation struggle against the Portuguese? In part this paradox may be more apparent than real, for the school of liberation struggle, even if it did serve to radicalize the Frelimo leadership's outlook in important and progressive ways, was probably also a much harder one than many of us realized at the time. It bred a certain ruthlessness alongside the commitment it evoked and, in Frelimo's case, also a cockiness, bracing but dangerous, about the efficacy of revolutionary will in blowing aside apparently insuperable obstacles. Moreover, it is also easy to forget (as Colin Leys and I have noted elsewhere) 'the climate of the times during the "thirty years war" for southern African liberation (1960–1990), a climate that shaped much of the discourse both of the liberation movements themselves and of their supporters around the world. Can there be any doubt that the Left during those years of relative success (both within the region and beyond) too often took the righteousness of its cause for granted, allowing the subtle narcotic of "correctness" to dull its democratic sensibilities?'[50]

For the Frelimo leadership, however, there was also the Soviet factor, a factor so central, militarily, to the triumph of the Mozambican struggle and one given further credibility by the Soviet regime's own apparent success in the building of 'socialism'. But linking its star to the Soviet Union was, for Frelimo, a fateful choice.[51] For the costs to Frelimo's project of Soviet tutelage can now be seen more clearly than ever to have outweighed the benefits. And yet it was not difficult to see, even at height of Frelimo's powers, that the movement was learning precisely the wrong lessons from what passed for Marxism in Eastern circles: lessons about the most overbearing of vanguardisms,[52] the most inflexible of primitive accumulation-driven economic strategies, the most unnuanced of class analyses, and the most unilluminating and disempowering versions of Marxist methodology.[53] Here was one kind of Marxism – *one kind*, one wants to insist to him – well worthy of Finnegan's scorn. Of course, one must not overstate the case. Frelimo was not merely a prisoner of this 'Marxist-Leninist' embrace. Sometimes its preachments merely meshed – all too comfortably – with the Frelimo leadership's own worst instincts. And sometimes the Frelimo leadership's own sense of itself and the nature of its revolution enabled it to win more helpful insights from the revolutionary tradition. This said, however, it remains true that the impact of Soviet-style 'Marxism-Leninism' was yet another reason for the difficulties Frelimo had in identifying the subtle tactics and strategies necessary to realizing its goals.

Meanwhile, the world was closing in on the Frelimo state. Might a combination of less overweening self-confidence and a sharper set of analytical tools have enabled Frelimo to neutralise some of that onslaught that Botha and Reagan had in store for it? Certainly, had the regime had greater success in fortifying itself domestically – by consolidating, democratically, its popular base and by finding the keys to greater economic advance – it would have been that much less vulnerable to attack. On the other hand, once Reagan assumed power the odds against finessing western hostility and advancing a radical project lengthened precipitously. Perhaps Mozambique could have found room for manoeuvre by ducking some of the fights in the region – it committed itself fully to ZANU's war in Zimbabwe and gave what limited backing it could to the ANC – that were to prove so costly in rousing first Rhodesia's and then South Africa's merciless retaliation. But even to put the question in these terms is to underscore just how cruel was the environment of choice in which Frelimo sought to plot its course in the 1970s and 1980s. Moreover, Mozambique was target for South Africa and its allies not merely for whatever role it played in the continuing battle for southern Africa. The symbolic and practical significance of the socialist option (warts and all) that it had chosen might well have been excuse enough for the roll-back mentality that moved its enemies to counter-revolutionary activity. To forget this, even in the current climate of shifting paradigms and of rethinking 'the state', 'socialism' and of so much else, would be to blame the victim indeed.

III The State of Recolonization

Perhaps the best testimony as to how much has been lost with the virtual collapse of the erstwhile 'Frelimo state' is provided by a clear description of what that collapse has left in its wake. The Frelimo state was, indeed, a 'left-developmental dictatorship', one weakened (fatally or not we will never know, since it was not left to its own devices) in its purpose by both its dictatorial propensities and by other deep flaws in its strategic vision. But, in potential at least, it bore the promise of providing a protective inter-mediary between the Mozambican people and a global/regional economy that, left merely uninflected, held out no positive prospect for them. It also bore the promise of ensuring a context within which the realization of a better life – a promise the mass of the population was by no means indifferent to – was at least a plausible one for Mozambicans. Are they offered a better promise now that the (admittedly flawed) Somoran project has been smashed and the 'Frelimo state' as formerly defined is no more?

Not that getting a lead on the state of the state in contemporary Mozambique is easy to do. Its writ does not run all that broadly because of the war and the social chaos that now defines so much of Mozambican society. Still, there is a state (and still a Frelimo party ostensibly at its helm) – even though what is left standing in Mozambique seems something remarkably close to the most extreme model of the state's external determination conjured up in the 'bad old days' of dependency theory. Thus Marshall writes of an 'erosion of Mozambican sovereignty' and suggests that 'control has shifted out of Mozambican hands in an alarming fashion'.[54] This is particularly marked, most observers agree, in the free run of decision-making that the IMF and World Bank have now claimed for themselves. Certainly, these bodies make no bones about the thrust of their agenda: basic to the Structural Adjustment Programme has been, in the words of the World Bank, 'the recognition that the closer integration of the Mozambique economy is essential, with domestic industrial and agricultural producers being exposed both to the incentives and disciplines of international markets'.[55] And 'the IMF, for its part, could see the crisis only in terms of excessive state control of the economy, excessive control of foreign exchange and too few exports, with measures of privatization and deregulation as the obvious remedies'. Moreover, neither the IMF nor the World Bank will brook much challenge.[56]

Is this what Peter Fry had in mind when, as quoted earlier, he hailed Mozambican President Joaquim Chissano for 'his attempt to set Mozambi-que on a course of development in tune with the realities of the regional and international political and economic environment'? Surely we need to compare this version of events with the forlorn flavour of a remark I myself heard Chissano make in a Maputo speech in 1990:

> The US said, 'Open yourself to . . . the World Bank, and IMF.' What happened? . . . We are told now: 'Marxism! You are devils. Change this policy.' OK. Marxism is gone. 'Open market economy.' OK, Frelimo is trying to create capitalism. We have the task of building socialism and capitalism here.
>
> We went to Reagan and I said, 'I want money for the private sector to boost people who want to develop a bourgeoisie.' Answer: $10 million, then $15 million more, then another $15 million. You tell me to do away with Marxism, the Soviet Union and the GDR and give me [only] $40 million. OK, we have changed. Now they say, 'If you don't go to a multi-party system, don't expect help from us.'[57]

What could more starkly reveal just how supine Mozambique has been forced to become vis-à-vis western dictate?

Several observers have pointed to an additional dimension to this picture. Thus Hanlon, in his most recent book,[58] provides impressive chapter and verse regarding the powerful grip of the World Bank and IMF on Mozambican decision-making. But he also emphasizes the extraordinary role that is increasingly being played by aid agencies, both foreign-governmental and private, in dictating policy outcomes. While manifesting, via food aid and other programmes, the 'human face' of structural adjustment, aid agencies (World Vision and Care are two whose role he explores in particular detail) have policy agendas (the need for privatization is a common theme). Moreover, Hanlon comes close to suggesting that, in usurping its role over a broad front, such agencies actually become, to a significant degree, the state!

The palliatives offered by 'aid' to the contrary notwithstanding, the costs of buying this structural adjustment package have been high for many Mozambicans. Oppenheimer, for example, writes that 'price rises caused by sweeping currency devaluation and commercial speculation together with underproportional wage actualization and restraint in public sector spending contributed to the lowering of already precarious standards of living of large parts of the population'.[59] And Judith Marshall's various writings have further documented the 'social impact' of such programmes, notably in terms of the erosion of advances in the area of health and education that were once thought to be the most notable accomplishments of the Mozambican revolution.[60] At the same time, it remains far from clear that, having been forced to swallow the pill of structural adjustment, Mozambique can now expect the kind of growth that a Clarence-Smith might foresee as flowing from the capitalist option. Experience of capitalist development strategies elsewhere in Africa is not so very promising in this respect. Nor are the early returns from Mozambique particularly favourable. Thus, one economist's recent analysis concludes, after a careful sifting of the evidence, that 'prospects for growth and development are poor; unemployment is rising; inflation remains high; the balance of payment deficit is worsening; and the astronomical external debt is rising.'[61] Indeed, a second analysis of recent economic trends in Mozambique (by Kenneth Hermele) suggests that a likely future for the country is 'a weak and dependent form of capitalism, which basically will serve the South African economy with labour, transport routes, markets and raw materials', a situation that (in Merle Bowen's phrase) would be 'all too reminiscent of the colonial era'.[62]

Another dimension of the impact of opening Mozambique so dramatically to the benisons of the global capitalist economy also bears noting. For the flip side of increased deprivation for many Mozambicans is the crystallization of a distinctly novel level of socio-economic privilege for others. In Oppenheimer's words, we find 'a rapid social differentiation process breaking up an economically inefficient and poverty-bearing, but relatively egalitarian, social order. . . . Consequently, social exclusion became a wide-spread phenomenon. Abject poverty now co-existed with ostentatious consumption'.[63] Moreover, this new world of 'social exclusion' and differential opportunity ('opportunity' compounded of novel private sector activities and of access to jobs and other spin-offs from the large aid-giving industry now ensconced in Mozambique) creates a milieu, political and social, very different from that which existed in the past.

Thus, the fluidity that may once have marked Mozambique's petty-bourgeoisie-in-the-making and rendered it a potential seed-bed of 'revolutionary leadership' seems increasingly a thing of the past. For this group is now crystallising its self-interest and 'classness' around the new structure of privilege in Mozambique at quite a rapid rate. And as this happens so, in turn, the opportunism that characterises petty-bourgeois politics elsewhere in Africa becomes, increasingly, the norm within Frelimo itself. The old unity of common social purpose that once bound Frelimo together seems lost forever, replaced, increasingly, by a jockeying for position that has seen the invoking even of racist appeals in the heat of battle for political advantage (the trumpeting of a narrowly defined 'African nationalism' by the prominent long-time Frelimo leader Armando Guebuza, for example[64]).

True, Hanlon does suggest that within ruling circles there was some attempt, at least in the early rounds of negotiation (1985–6) with the international bankers, to safeguard elements of the old progressive agenda.[65] In this he finds a remnant of the old 'Frelimo state' that is well worth defending. Indeed, he has criticized some in the international solidarity network who feel the need, increasingly, to direct their assistance to Mozambique to initiatives at the grass-roots and within civil society – in order to help revive, in the longer term, the social base for a renewal of progressive politics in Mozambique. But this, Hanlon insists, is to play directly into the hands of the right wing aid agencies with their own agenda of undermining the state and hastening the pace of market-driven privatization. In arguing his case, Hanlon seems little inclined to make requisite distinctions between initiatives designed to spawn collective forms of popular empowerment and those cast in more privatizing terms. True, Hanlon's point has some resonance: recall our earlier insistence – against the thrust of Bayart's argument – on the need to facilitate a positive role for a non-parasitic state if a meaningful process of transformation is to be sustained. Yet to prove his case he would have to identify more convincingly than he does the militant attributes (in terms of both policies and personnel) of the present state that merit defending in this way.[66]

Sadly, it is no longer easy to do so in Mozambique. Nor is it any easier to paint a positive picture when one turns to examining the workings of the new, post-destabilization Mozambican state at the local level. True, the continuing chaos spawned by war makes it difficult to generalize about the reality on the ground in any case. Formally, however, the present Frelimo leadership is said to be learning a rather dubious lesson from Renamo's own manipulation of displaced chiefs to impose its order on areas it controls. For Frelimo has now begun to dismantle what were, in spite of their weaknesses, incipient structures of grass-roots participatory de-mocracy at the level of local government in order to facilitate 'a return to some form of chiefly role . . . in which rehabilitated chiefs are mandated to govern over rural populations and to collect taxes on behalf of the government . . . as an expedient way of reasserting state authority and increasing state revenues in the rural areas'. For Roesch, echoing Bowen's summary (above) of another aspect of contemporary Mozambican prac-tice, this revival of a pattern of indirect rule not so very different from the Portuguese mode of governance also has to 'be seen as part of the process of recolonization in Mozambique'.[67] Recall, too, O'Laughlin's warning, cited earlier: 'I think it would be a fundamental error to conclude that war in Mozambique shows that Mozambican peasants need colonial-style regulos!'

More informally, the pattern of grass-roots politics as practised by local populations faces a 'retreat to tradition' that it is equally difficult to be sanguine about. For beyond the various barbarities that the collapse of civility and emergence of the rule of the gun and the panga have thrown up in rural Mozambique, there are other revealing developments. Take, for example, the extent to which, 'in the context of the much eroded authority of the state, an intense competition between Renamo, Frelimo and local forces has occurred for spiritually-empowered agency, and that such agency has been part of "progressive", "traditional", and "reactionary" programmes alike'.[68] Studies of such phenomena, Ken Wilson notes, highlight the proliferation in war-ravaged Mozambique of the truly hor-rendous brands of 'cultic violence' and 'ritualized destruction' launched by Renamo but also 'the practice of magic and ritual by Frelimo' and others (like the influential Naprama movement) in order to find an effective way 'to counter Renamo ideologically'. This, it must be emphasized, is a world of 'spirit possession', ancestor worship and mystical chiefly powers, where, among other magical possibilities, bullets are expected by some believers to turn to water.

True, it does make some sense to understand such 'religious traditional-ism' as 'the Mozambican peasantry's attempt to reconstitute a new system of meaning and social order out of the war-shattered wreckage of Frelimo's post-independence experiment and the colonial-cum-traditional society which Frelimo sought to transform'.[69] But is it merely a 'western', rational-ist bias that suggests the recent analysis of Eboe Hutchful to be relevant to any attempt to make sense not only of the pattern of violence in rural Mozambique but also of this ambience of ideological response to it?

> . . . in Africa, no less than in the Soviet Union and Eastern Europe, developmental dictatorships had degenerated in the process of 'orientalization', in which strong states had clamped themselves on weak and subordinated civil societies. Beneath the political facade of orientalism, however, society had survived, resilient and remarkably unreconstructed. In the face of this nonresisting resistance, the historical project of the autonomous, bureaucratized political leaderships had wilted and decayed. The final outcome of the peaceful capture of the enervated state and bureaucracy in Eastern Europe is a potent lesson that could be repeated in Africa, and elsewhere in the Third World. But to those (particularly in the West) who would, as a result of these revolutions and a weariness of 'high politics', romanticize 'civil society' in the abstract, the contradictions revealed within East European society by the lifting of strong state power should prepare them to tolerate in Africa also what *Time* has aptly described as the 'return of the demons'.[70]

Again, we must avoid 'blaming the victim'; the cruel cynicism of the South Africans in helping bring Mozambican society to this sorry pass cannot be underscored too often. But it is sad indeed that Hutchful's formulation can seem even minimally plausible as an accurate post-mortem on what is left standing in the wake of Frelimo's efforts to help effect the Mozambican people's liberation.

Social regression seems, in fact, to inform the new Mozambican polity at every turn. For the unleashing of other 'demons' will almost certainly be one key ingredient of the newly competitive politics that a liberalization of the Mozambique's political system is likely to entail. Frelimo in its heyday may well be criticized for having underestimated, in the name of a new national purpose, the ethnic, regional and racial diversities/inequalities that are part and parcel of the Mozambican reality (although it is also the case that those who criticise the movement's insufficient sensitivity to possible popular resentment at the underrepresentation in its ranks of, say 'Africans' or 'northerners' are generally less than clear about what a more subtle progressive politics on this front might have looked like). But the decay of Frelimo's project now finds ethnic, regional and racial parties threatening to crowd out most other political expressions on the electoral stage[71] – unless Frelimo itself can retain just enough credibility to keep alive the sense of achieved nationhood that is the one surviving feature of its original high purpose. Yet, as noted earlier, even Frelimo seems increasingly to be riven by developments that reflect the lowest common denominator of petty-bourgeois politics in Africa – with implications that may prove very bleak indeed.

In the urban areas the superimposition of structural adjustment on a situation of war-induced social breakdown (the fall-out, most notably, from the precipitous movement of vast numbers of displaced rural dwellers to Maputo and other centres) is also a volatile one. Crime rates have escalated exponentially, for example. True, there have also been some signs of the rebirth, from the bottom up, of a more progressive politics in such settings. Judith Marshall, writing in 1991, emphasized the import-ance of a wave of strikes in Mozambique that seemed directly caused by reaction to the grim impact of the structural adjustment programme on the lives of ordinary Mozambicans. And she found considerable promise, too, in the fledgling activities of a trade union movement newly 'autonomous' from single-party control, alongside a number of other mass-based organ-izational initiatives also beginning to find their feet within 'civil society'.[72] Perhaps it is to this kind of development, even more than to the staging of multi-party elections, that one may look for much of the long-term promise of the freeing of Mozambique's political system from Frelimo's unqualified and too often over-bearing domination.

In the short-run, however, the brand of resistance offered to the politics of structural adjustment by trade unions and other such popularly-based organizations within civil society may not immediately produce any more positive results. In fact, in her recent analysis of contemporary Mozambi-que Merle Bowen follows Jonathan Barker in suggesting that the kind of state crystallizing out of Mozambique's present volatile set of circum-stances is quickly becoming the instrument of a 'triple alliance' of elements newly privileged by economic liberalization: 'international financial capi-tal (World Bank and IMF), private capital (foreign and domestic) and (progressive) small farmers'. And, if put under pressure, those who act on behalf of this alliance may soon feel they have no alternative but to abandon any concomitant commitment to a fledgling liberal democratic system in order to control the social contradictions spawned by the economic orthodoxy they prefer.[73] At that point, Bowen suggests, 'the most serious threat to ordinary Mozambicans in the approaching era of reconstruction may be the need for an increasingly repressive state to guarantee the smooth performance of the "triple alliance".'[74]

Trading a 'left-wing developmental dictatorship' for a 'right-wing de-velopmental dictatorship'? There is some evidence that this will indeed be Mozambique's fate. Sadly, however, even this sorry denouement – a capitalist-driven rehabilitation of social order – to Mozambique's failed revolution may prove too much to hope for. How much more likely, in light of what has been argued above, is a demon-driven politics and an 'un-steady state'[75] to match: if Frelimo fades away (or becomes, at best, ever more of a shell of its former self); if warlords continue to stalk the land; if the politics of race and region and religion comes to predominate . . . Then, even were a Yugoslavian/Somalia situation to be avoided, any 'dictatorship' that emerged from this fire-storm with a brief to restore 'law and order' could prove to be very nasty indeed – and anything but 'developmental'.

*   *   *

The costs of Frelimo's failure have been great, however future historians may ultimately judge the relative importance of the three factors – the drag of 'historical backwardness', the impact of external intervention/destabilization, the weight of Frelimo's own errors of omission and commission – that have produced the sorry denouement to Mozambique's socialist project. As the last section of this essay has demonstrated there should be very little comfort to be garnered from the decay of Frelimo's original project, however strongly one may feel inclined to decry its various weaknesses. Nor, needless to say, is the future a promising one. The question was posed earlier in this essay whether there is good reason to expect the rebirth of a left practice that can 'promise to reverse the terrible "liberation" that global capitalism has inflicted upon Mozambique'. Unfortunately – I insist that it is unfortunate, paradigm-shifters to the contrary notwithstanding – such has been the extent of the defeat of Frelimo's revolutionary undertaking that socialist advance is not on the agenda in that country for the foreseeable future. Indeed, it may be that, for some time to come, the very most that can be hoped for is that not all Mozambicans will learn the wrong lessons from what has befallen them in recent years. There are some small signs that this is the case. If so, then (to paraphrase Frelimo's antique motto) the struggle really can be expected to continue.

NOTES

*The present essay is in effect, prolegomenon to a longer manuscript on Mozambique, now in preparation and tentatively entitled *What is to be learned? Rethinking the Mozambican revolution*. The essay itself was first presented, in draft form, at the Fall Workshop of the Canadian Research Consortium on Southern Africa, Queen's University, Kingston, Ontario, Canada, December 5, 1992. I am especially grateful to Manfred Bienefeld for helpful comments on that earlier draft.

1. Gervase Clarence-Smith, 'The Roots of the Mozambican Counter-Revolution', *South African Review of Books* (April/May, 1989), p. 10.
2. In his verbal submission to the symposium, faithfully recorded by the present writer, October 12, 1990; Slovo's position, coming from an ANC activist, might also be considered somewhat ungracious given the price extracted from Mozambique for contributing for as long as it did to the broader struggle for southern African liberation, although one also knows that the Mozambican government was itself less than gracious to Slovo and others in 1984 during the period of its all too zealous implementation of the conditions of the Nkomati Accord as they bore, negatively, on the ANC-in-residence in Mozambique.

3. Clarence-Smith, *op. cit.*, and, more recently, Alex Vines, *RENAMO: Terrorism in Mozambique* (London: James Currey, 1991), p. 74.

4. Clarence-Smith, *op. cit.*, p. 9.

5. As advanced, for example, by Jean Copans in his 'Preface' to Christian Geffray, *La cause des armes au Mozambique: Anthropologies d'une guerre civile* (Editions Karthala, 1990) and by Clarence-Smith himself (*op. cit.*).

6. Required reading on this subject is Robert Gersony, *Summary of Mozambican Refugee Accounts of Principally Conflict-Related Experience in Mozambique: Report Submitted to Ambassador Jonathan Moore and Dr. Chester A. Crocker* (Washington: Department of State Bureau for Refugee Programs, 1988). Equally relevant – and just as sobering – is William Minter, *The Mozambican National Resistance (Renamo) as Described by Ex-Participants* (Research report submitted to the Ford Foundation and the Swedish International Development Agency, 1989). On this subject, see also Otto Roesch's paper – prepared for the Queen's Workshop at which the present essay was itself first presented – entitled 'A New Paradigm? Rethinking Renamo's War' (as well as other of Roesch's writings, as published regularly in *Southern Africa Report (SAR)* and elsewhere) and my own essay, 'Development and Counterdevelopment Strategies' in John S. Saul, *Socialist Ideology and the Struggle for Southern Africa* (Trenton, N.J.: Africa World Press, 1990).

7. William Finnegan, *A Complicated War: The Harrowing of Mozambique* (Berkeley and Los Angeles: University of California Press, 1992), p. 70.

8. The phrase is that of Margaret Hall (in the title of her article 'The Mozambican National Resistance Movement (Renamo): A Study of the Destruction of an African Country', *Africa*, 6 [1], 1990). Hall sets up her own careful analysis of developments inside Mozambique – including an unsparing critique of 'the structural weaknesses of the Mozambican state' – by suggesting she will focus 'on the internal processes destabilization *has set in train*' (emphasis added).

9. Gersony, *op. cit.*

10. As defined in his 'People's war, state formation and revolution in Africa: a comparative analysis of Mozambique, Guinea-Bissau and Angola', *Journal of Commonwealth and Comparative Studies*, 21 (198).

11. *Op. cit.*

12. For a further elaboration of this point see Otto Roesch, *op. cit.* Much the best critique of Geffray's own work is Bridget O'Laughlin, 'Interpretations Matter: Evaluating the War in Mozambique', *Southern Africa Report*, 7, #3 (January, 1992).

13. Peter Fry, 'Between Two Terrors', *Times Literary Supplement* (November 9–15, 1990), p. 1202.

14. *Ibid*.

15. Many related themes are beginning to find their way into the English-language literature, *viz.*, James Manor, *Rethinking Third World Politics* (Burnt Hill, UK: Longman, 1991) – a book to which *Politique Africaine* authors Jean-François Bayart and Jean-François Médard make important contributions in any case.

16. Dominique Darbon, 'L'Etat prédateur', *Politique Africaine*, 'Special 10e anniversaire: L'Afrique Autrement', #39, p. 37.

17. Bayart, 'Civil Society in Africa' in Patrick Chabal (ed.), *Political Domination in Africa: Reflections on the Limitations of Power in Africa* (Cambridge: Cambridge University Press, 1986), pp. 115–16; see also Bayart's own *L'Etat en Afrique* (Paris: Fayard, 1988).

18. Jean Medard, 'L'Etat patrimonialisé', also in *Politique Africaine*, #39, pp. 25, 26.

19. *Ibid.*, p. 34. Médard refers in this context to a second paper of his, one I have not read but the title of which epitomizes, I suspect, its content: 'Le socialisme en Afrique: l'autopsie d'un mirage'.

20. Médard also notes, in a rather more satisfied tone, that at least this same logic does help to hinder – or at least further distort ('l'Etat prédateur est lui-même prédaté, l'Etat parasite est lui-même parasité') – the malign workings of the 'demiurgic state'; Médard cites in this regard Bayart's notion of the 'revenge of civil society' (against 'l'ambition totalisante de l'Etat'!)

21. Contrast, in this regard, Hyden's *Beyond Ujamaa: underdevelopment and an uncaptured peasantry* (Berkeley: University of California Press, 1980) with his later *No Shortcuts to*

Progress: African development management in perspective (Berkeley: University of California Press, 1983).

22. Manfred Bienefeld, 'Dependency Theory and the Political Economy of Africa's Crisis', *Review of African Political Economy*, #43 (1988), pp. 81, 82.

23. Clarence-Smith, *op. cit.*, p. 10.

24. O'Laughlin, *op. cit.*, pp. 27, 28.

25. For a manifestation, more generally cast, of this kind of left-leaning 'bad conscience' regarding the claims of 'modernity' see Jean Copans, *La longue marche de la modernité africaine* (Paris: Editions Karthala, 1990).

26. *Op. cit.*, p. 28. O'Laughlin sees the roots of this 'dualism' in the colonial power structure as being far more important than any roots it might be thought to have in any more time-honoured 'tradition'. In addition, 'in most of Africa after independence, this legal and administrative dualism was maintained, although the boundaries between the two systems and movement between them was made more flexible'. Her conclusion: 'I think it would be a fundamental error to conclude that the war in Mozambique shows that Mozambique peasants need colonial-style regulos.' We will return to this point in section III, below.

27. *Ibid.*, p. 31.

28. *Ibid.*, p. 33.

29. Bayart, *op. cit.*, p. 120. The rather melodramatic formulation within which this phrase is found is also of interest: '. . . because they more readily lend their services to the state than to its challengers. African intellectuals (with few exceptions) have failed to provide civil society with the original conceptual instruments required for its advance. Even when they have had the courage to offer themselves to the leadership of the resistance, they have in no way been able to transcend the epistemic gulf between state and society.'

30. Bayart, *op. cit.*, p. 125.

31. Finnegan, *op. cit.*, from which the several quotations in these two paragraphs are drawn.

32. Heribert Adam and Kogila Moodley, 'Interstate Relations Under South African Dominance', in Wilmot G. James (ed.), *The State of Apartheid* (Boulder: Lynne Reiner Publishers, 1987).

33. Michel Cahen. *Mozambique: La Revolution implosée* (Paris: Éditions L'Harmattan, 1987).

34. Finnegan. *op. cit.*, p. 240.

35. O'Laughlin, p. 27; Judith Marshall evokes the promise of this period particularly effectively in her book *Literacy, State Formation and People's Power: Education in a Mozambican factory* (Bellville, SA: CACE/UWC, 1990).

36. As I have written elsewhere on this subject (in 'From Thaw to Flood: The end of the Cold War in Southern Africa', *Review of African Political Economy (ROAPE)*, #50 [March, 1991]). 'The burden of the past (and the ideological oversimplifications of the Cold War era) rests heavily on a leader like Joaquim Chissano, for example, who can now summarize the situation by suggesting that "Marxism was creating problems for us" – proceeding to elide "Marxism" with official Soviet-style "Marxism-Leninism" in such a way as to leave himself almost no conceptual middle-ground for blunting the charge of the most unadulterated of free-market nostrums' (p. 155. The same might be said of Finnegan.

37. To be fair, Finnegan is himself little inclined to join in any celebration of the capitalist future he sees as unavoidable for Mozambique; as he puts the point, 'Without some extraordinary natural resource, such as oil, it is not at all clear that a severely underdeveloped country, firmly on the periphery of the modern world system, has even a fighting chance of development'. Moreover, he adds ominously, 'in Mozambique's case its dependence is not on the developed North. More directly and more profoundly, it is on South Africa' (*ibid.*, p. 241).

38. Dan O'Meara, 'The Collapse of Mozambican Socialism', *Transformation*, #14 (1991), p. 82.

39. It bears noting that O'Meara's own essay (*ibid.*) is itself a powerful and measured contribution to such a critique.

40. See my paper 'The Nature of the Post-Colonial State: Further Reflections' and also Colin Leys. 'State and Class in Post-Colonial Africa: Comments on John Saul's Theses on the Post-Colonial State', both presented to a panel entitled 'Bureaucratic Bourgeoisie or

Power Elite? – On Power in Africa', African Studies Association annual meeting, Philadelphia, 17 October, 1980. See also Patrick Chabal, *Amilcar Cabral Revolutionary leadership and people's war* (Cambridge: Cambridge University Press, 1983), especially chapter 7. 'People's war in lusophone Africa: a comparative perspective'.

41. See John S. Saul, 'The Context: Colonialism and Revolution', being chapter 1 of Saul (ed.), *A Difficult Road: The Transition to Socialism in Mozambique* (New York: Monthly Review Press, 1985).

42. Gavin Williams, 'There is no theory of petit-bourgeois politics', *Review of African Political Economy (ROAPE)*, #6 (May – August, 1976).

43. See Edward Alpers, 'The bureaucratic legacy of Portuguese colonial rule in Mozambique', paper presented to the 1986 Conference of the Review of African Political Economy, Liverpool, U.K., September, 1986.

44. Joseph Hanlon, *Mozambique: The Revolution Under Fire* (London: Zed Books, 1984); as it happens Hanlon's own argument on this point is crossed in his text by several other, seemingly contradictory, emphases.

45. For further discussion of these decisions, and the general premises underlying them, see my essay 'Development and Counter-Development Strategies in Mozambique', *op. cit.*.

46. Jonathan Barker, in his book *Rural Communities Under Stress: Peasant farmers and the state in Africa* (Cambridge: Cambridge University Press, 1989), has effectively reminded us there is no single 'peasant response' to their world. There is, to begin with, a considerable range of diversity within 'the peasantry' – along lines of class, region, farming pattern and the like – that makes generalization risky. But even when considered in more general terms, what can be affirmed is that peasants are open to respond to a wide range of stimuli and to make them their own.

47. 'Hardness', yes, but also *'falta dos quadros'* – the relative lack of trained, skilled and confident cadres below the top leadership level (this fact being itself a reflex of Mozambique's low level of overall development) – helped blunt the edge of Frelimo's positive impact vis-à-vis the populace in the countryside, and elsewhere.

48. Eboe Hutchful, 'Eastern Europe: Consequences for Africa', *ROAPE*, #50 (March, 1991).

49. See my chapter, 'The Content: A Transition to Socialism?' being chapter 2 in *A Difficult Road* and, for the impact of this 'reproductive crisis' on the Mozambican peasantry, also Otto Roesch's doctoral dissertation, *Socialism and Rural Development in Mozambique* (University of Toronto, 1986). Not that the performance of the Mozambican economy was so terribly weak during the first five years of independence. In this sphere balancing off the impact of policy weaknesses against the impact of external shocks – flood and drought, international terms of trade (including rising oil prices) and, in the end, destabilization – is particularly difficult.

50. Colin Leys and John S. Saul, 'Liberation without Democracy: The Swapo Crisis of 1976', paper presented to the Inaugural Research Seminar of the Canadian Research Consortium on Southern Africa, Montreal, November 6, 1992, p. 30.

51. Consider, however, the cruel dynamics of the Cold War context of the time; the Frelimo leadership felt it had some good reason to think that, as a regime seeking to evade the writ of global capitalist domination, it actually had little real choice in this regard.

52. There can be little doubt, for example, that Frelimo learned far too much about police methods from the East Germans and others.

53. No benefit of hindsight is necessary here. I made much the same points about the costs of Soviet influence in my chapter, 'The Content' (cited above) and also in earlier writings.

54. Judith Marshall, *War, debt and structural adjustment in Mozambique: The social impact* (Ottawa: The North-South Institute, 1992).

55. This 1987 World Bank statement is quoted in Marshall, *ibid.*, p. 9.

56. Marshall (*ibid.*, p. 8) is here summarizing the account of IMF negotiations with Mozambique found, in fascinating detail, in Joseph Hanlon, *Mozambique: Who Calls the Shots?* (London: James Currey Publishers, 1991); Marshall herself recounts a briefing from Jacinto Veloso, Mozambique's Minister of Cooperation, in which 'we were told quite matter-of-factly that the international donor community had effectively frozen all grants, loans and credits to Mozambique until such times as Mozambique was prepared to accept an adjustment program with the IMF' (p. 8).

57. Quoted in my article. 'Mozambique: The Failure of Socialism?', *SAR*, 6, #2 (November, 1990).

58. Hanlon, Mozambique: Who Calls the Shots? (*op. cit.*).

59. Jochen Oppenheimer, 'Development Cooperation in the Context of War and Structural Adjustment: The Case of Mozambique', paper presented to the conference of the Canadian Association of African Studies, Montreal, May, 1992.

60. See, most notably, Marshall, *op. cit.* and her numerous reports from Mozambique in the pages of *Southern Africa Report* in recent years.

61. Kim Jarvi, 'Structural Adjustment in Sub-Saharan Africa and the Case of Mozambique', unpublished paper (Toronto: York University, 1992). Moreover, in Oppenheimer's view (*op. cit.*), to the extent that economic decline was momentarily reversed in Mozambique this was 'as a result of a very high and, in the long run, unsustainable influx of external assistance'.

62. Here then, at the end of the day, is Clarence-Smith's 'goose that lays the golden eggs'! Bowen is quoting from Hermele's *Mozambican Crossroads: Economics and Politics in the Era of Structural Adjustment* (Bergen, Norway: 1990) and adds herself that, 'this trend has been reinforced by western governments who have readily accepted South Africa's self-portrayal as the stabilizing and modernizing force in the region' (in her 'Beyond Reform: Adjustment and Political Power in Contemporary Mozambique', *Journal of Modern African Studies*, 30, #2 [1992], p. 274.

63. Jochen Oppenheimer, *op. cit.*.

64. See, for example, David Ottaway, 'Black Nationalist Opposition Emerges: Frelimo's Rule, Racial Equilibrium Seen Imperilled in Mozambique', *The Washington Post*, 11 December, 1990 as, for more on Guebuza's politics, my article, 'Mozambique: The Failure of Socialism', *SAR*, 6, #2 (November, 1990).

65. Hanlon, *Mozambique: Who Calls the Shots*? (op. cit.), pp. 117 - 8, where he discusses Frelimo attempts to defend some expanded role for the state and also to make the World Bank and IMF take seriously the fact of on-going destabilization as a parameter for defining Mozambique's economic situation. But Hanlon also notes that a meeting with World Bank officials in November, 1985, 'was nearly the last time anyone talked about a "basic socialist framework"'.

66. There is a certain irony to Hanlon's emphasis here. One of his original contributions to the discussion of Mozambican politics was, as we have noted above, to emphasize – even to overemphasize – the extent to which those who staffed the Frelimo state were taking on many of the attributes of a bureaucratic bourgeoisie. Now, at a point when this process is much further developed, his new book scarcely mentions the implications of this fact for thinking through the pros and cons of supporting the actually-existing state that is in place in Mozambique.

67. Otto Roesch, 'Mozambique Unravels? The Retreat to Tradition', *SAR*, 7, #5 (May, 1992), p. 30.

68. K.B. Wilson, 'Cults of Violence and Counter-Violence in Mozambique' (unpublished paper, n.d.); see also Vines, *op. cit.*, a number of case-studies by various authors currently being edited by Wilson himself at Oxford for future publication and, inter alia, Margaret Hall, *op. cit.*.

69. Roesch, *ibid.*.

70. Eboe Hutchful, *op. cit.*, 'Eastern Europe: Consequences for Africa', pp. 57 - 8.

71. See Ottaway, *op. cit.*, amongst numerous other sources.

72. Judith Marshall, 'Resisting Adjustment in Mozambique: The Grassroots Speak Up', *SAR*, 7, #1 (July, 1991)/

73. For an exemplification of some of the contradictions inherent in the relationship between economic liberalization and political democratization in present-day Africa see Marcia Burdette, 'Democracy vs Economic Liberalization: The Zambian Dilemma', SAR, 8, #1 (July, 1992); see also Issa Shivji, 'The Democracy Debate in Africa: Tanzania', *ROAPE*, #50 (March, 1991).

74. Bowen, *op. cit.* p. 279; the 'triple alliance' model introduced here by Bowen (p. 258) is drawn from Barker's *Rural Communities Under Stress*, cited earlier.

75. On this possibility see the essay entitled 'The Unsteady State: Uganda, Obote and General Amin' in my *The State and Revolution in Eastern Africa* (New York: Monthly Review Press, 1979).

AFTER PERESTROIKA

K. S. Karol

I find it difficult to speak calmly of 'real problems and false solutions' in the former USSR. The theme arouses too many passions for it to be reduced to economic and social factors alone. Even at its most critical of the Soviet experiment, the Western Left has always had to define itself in relation to the Revolution of October 1917, which was the product of a common socialist culture. Despite the polemics, the hope that both branches of the tree would one day unite never disappeared totally. With the coming to power of Mikhail Gorbachev, that hope became much more substantial from 1985 onwards. Resolved to democratize society, the new leader made a brave attack on the dogmas of a Marxism-Leninism that had become anachronistic. If Gorbachev could succeed in his attempt, it did seem that this time the USSR would be able to transform itself, if not into a truly socialist society – the heritage of the past was too burdensome for that – at least into a transitional society which would no longer give socialists and communists of the whole world cause to blush. The scale of the project – and of its likely repercussions – explains the disappointment felt by the left when it failed. Twice betrayed by his supporters in 1991, Mikhail Gorbachev has been removed from power, and the USSR has ceased to exist. It has splintered into fifteen Republics, two of which are already at war with one another and three of which are being torn apart by civil wars, whilst the other ten are embroiled in chaos. The CPSU, which had as many as 19 million members, has vanished into thin air almost overnight, like a *groupuscule*. How could this happen? Can we speak of a new 'Russian Revolution'?

A Latin proverb states that 'Times change and men change with them'. It is well known that the propensity for change increases in troubled times, but it seems to me that certain Soviet citizens have broken a few records in this domain. I would like to give a few examples.

After the publication of my *La Chine de Mao* in 1967, I was persona *non grata* in the Soviet Embassy in Paris for twenty years. As the third year of 'perestroika' began to dawn, Ambassador Iakov Riabov, a member of the Central Committee and a former secretary of the CPSU in Sverdlovsk, began to invite me to meals and conferences in order to explain to me that

166

Gorbachev's aim was to perfect a society which was already in many respects exemplary. Seeing that I was sceptical, he suggested that I should go to Moscow to meet Boris Yeltsin, his old comrade from Sverdlovsk who had recently been promoted to alternative membership of the Politburo. The appointment was set up for the end of September 1987. Unfortunately, the Central Committee torpedoed the project; in the meantime Yeltsin had fallen from grace. It was only a year later, in June 1988, that I met him at the XIXth All-Union Conference of the CPSU, when I personally heard him demand his 'political rehabilitation' on the grounds that he was a good Communist who had been unfairly removed from the Politburo. His appeal was proof that times had changed, for in the past no dismissed leader had a chance to demand his rehabilitation in this way. Who could have predicted that this ultra-loyalist would, only two years later, become one of the most bitter enemies of communism, and that he would ask Russia's Constitutional Court to condemn the CPSU – to which he owed his entire career – as a 'criminal organization'?

I find my second example even more intriguing: it concerns Eduard Shevardnadze who, in October 1988, granted me a long and uninhibited interview in Paris. Whilst he did not try to avoid any of my questions, I had the feeling that he was giving the stock answers expected of a Soviet Minister who was quite sure that he had an answer to every problem. His vision of the conflict-free world that would emerge thanks to improved Soviet-American understanding, seemed unrealistic to me. But he swept aside my objections by stating that he had more faith in humanity than I did. The next year, he received me again, this time in an impressive ministerial office in Moscow which was richly decorated with portraits of Lenin and Gorbachev. As the conversation was off the record, he spoke to me openly of his worries about Georgia where, after a bloody military intervention against a peaceful demonstration in Tbilisi in April 1989, the nationalist tide was rising very fast. Shaking his white head in pain and indignation, he read me a letter from a relative in the Kutaisi region describing how the crowd had torn down Lenin's statue. We met again in Rome and in Paris in 1991, when he was no longer a minister. His comments were, inevitably, those of a disillusioned man, but the refrain was still the same: peace and democracy above all.

In March 1992, Eduard Shevardnadze went back to his native Georgia to attempt to reestablish peace. He had been asked to come to the help of the newly democratic Georgia because the elected President, Zviad Gamsakhurdhia, an ultra-nationalist dissident, was terrorizing the country. Kamsakhurdhia was driven out at gunpoint, and Shevardnadze was appointed president of a provisional Council of State. Less than six months later, in August 1992, the pacifist Eduard Shevardnadze was sending tanks to take Sukhuimi, the capital of Abkhazia, which had remained more loyal to the values of the former USSR and was demanding more independence.

Having removed the bust of Lenin from the Government Palace, the triumphant invaders posed for photographs with their trophy. Not having a crane to remove Lenin's statue from the main square, they shelled it with mortars. I have to admit that, when I saw these photographs in the Moscow press, I was very perplexed. I knew that Georgia had been poisoned by Zviad Kamsakhurdhia's fanatical xenophobia and anti-communism. But who would have believed that Eduard Shevardnadze himself would have been so badly affected by the same poison as to approve the sacking of Sukhuimi and to deny Abkhazia the right to a truly autonomous existence?

One could compile a whole anthology about the conversion of less important figures, especially intellectuals. *Verba volent, scripta manent*, and, thanks to *glasnost*, all these people wrote a great deal. Like the chorus in a Greek tragedy, they initially sang in harmony with Gorbachev, and were grateful for being able to express themselves democratically. But in the second act, they had already begun to distance themselves from their leader and were outdoing him with their denunciations of the entire Soviet past. The leitmotiv had become: 'We want unqualified democracy', which implied that every trace of socialism had to be rejected. Pretending to ignore the chorus at his back and avoiding polemics, Gorbachev stubbornly went on recommending 'a socialist option' within a Communist perspective. Disliked by his party, which had not wanted *perestroika*, and abandoned by his democratic allies, Gorbachev was losing ground and seemed very vulnerable, despite his undeniable prestige on the international stage.

This shift to the right – curiously enough, in Moscow it was described as a shift to the left – gathered speed when the walls began to come down in Eastern Europe. Gorbachev certainly gained more international prestige by refraining from interfering in the internal affairs of those countries. But if he had taken into account his own country's political calendar, he would surely have slowed down the process of the 'decommunization' of the East to ensure that the reunification of Germany, for example, did not take place a few months before legislative elections were held in Russia and in most of the Republics. Having failed to play his trumps at the right moment – and he had a lot of trumps in his hand – he had to watch powerlessly as electoral gains were made by a loose coalition of anti-communist forces brought together by 'Democratic Russia' and nationalists demanding independence in the Baltic lands. Although isolated and enjoying little support, he did at least cling to certain principles for longer than his comrades. Even after the terrible ordeal of the coup of August 1991, he reasserted when he returned to Moscow that: 'I am not a weather vane. I will not abandon my socialist principles and I will continue to fight for the renewal of the Communist Party of the Soviet Union.' This was too much for even the last handful of loyalists. Stupified by his 'scandalous' declaration, they used it as an excuse to jump happily on to Boris Yeltsin's victorious bandwagon.

Are we to conclude that Moscow is particularly fond of weather vanes? Thousands of Russian proverbs tend to suggest the opposite. Since time immemorial Russians have warned against those who turn their coats at the first puff of wind. An old peasant saying even advises young girls not to trust divorced men: 'He left his first wife, and he will leave you too'. The high-ranking divorcees of the CPSU are sometimes asked why they suddenly broke up with 'their lifelong Party'. Two answers are worth recalling: those given by Leonid Kravchuk, the president of the Ukraine, and by Gennady Burbulis, Boris Yeltsin's right-hand man and the 'idealogue' who now sits in Mikhail Gorbachev's office in the Kremlin. It should be recalled in passing that both men played a decisive role in organizing the 'summit of Slav Republics' that was held in Bialwierza Forest in Belorussia in December 1991. The summit hastened the break-up of the former USSR.

For Leonid Kravchuk, it is all so simple. As Party Secretary in the Ukraine, he had been responsible for ideological work and energetically fought the nationalists. He did not know that the CP had been destroying his country for a long time.[1] Once he had seen documentary evidence of its crimes, he dropped the red flag and picked up the beautiful blue and gold flag of the Ukraine. What were these documents that had previously been inaccessible to a leader of Leonid Kravchuk's status, to one of the most important leaders in the former USSR? No one knows. Not that it matters greatly: his answer is at least concise and coherent, and it served as a rallying cry for all the refugees from the CP who, under the leadership of Leonid Kravchuk, are now defending the independent Ukraine. One of my friends in Moscow adds: 'It takes a real statesmen to tell lies as big as the mountains of the Caucasus without batting an eyelid'.

Writing in *Izvestia*, Gennady Burbulis gave a very different answer.[2] Twelve years younger than Kravchuk, this forty-five-year old philosopher used to teach 'scientific communism' in Sverdlovsk, and slowly, but surely made his way up the Party hierarchy in the wake of Boris Yeltsin. In order to get himself elected to the People's Congress in 1989, he demanded 'All power to the Soviets'. 'It was a mistake', he now admits, but he claims not to have made any other mistakes. A fanatical defender of private property, he claims to have always preferred a market economy to collectivism. Gennady Burbulis did not need to read the mysterious documents that persuaded Leonid Kravchuk to change sides so suddenly; even when he was in Sverdlovsk, he would rather have taught the liberal doctrines of Friedrich von Hayek than the 'disastrous egalitarian utopia' of communism. Forced to conform to the demands of totalitarianism, he practised an Orwellian doublethink until such time as he was able to say out loud what he had always thought in secret. Such statements absolve him from any need to reply to his many enemies, who cannot forgive him, among other things for his involvement in the 'Bialowierza plot', which sealed the dissolution of the Soviet Union, and who bring out recordings of his old lectures in Sverdlovsk at every possible opportunity.[3]

Gennady Burbulis's answer suits large number of intellectuals and members of the *nomenklatura*, who would like to have it believed that they too were forced to say the opposite of what they had always thought. Identifying with Kravchuk, who knew nothing, or with Burbulis, who always knew, serves the same purpose: it allows the elite of the CPSU to change sides with a clear conscience. In order to situate this society's 'real problems', we have to look at the real intellectual outlook of the Soviet 'power elite' over the last decades.

I deliberately use C. Wright Mills's definition because it seems to me more pertinent than either that of the Trotskyists (bureaucracy) or that of Milova Djilas (the new class). C. Wright Mills's elite is made up of men and women who are, in material terms, much better off than ordinary people and who also have the ability to take decisions affecting the destiny of all. The USSR's 'super-rich' were of course much less wealthy than their equivalent in the United States, and Moscow's 'celebrities' enjoyed much less celebrity than their trans-Atlantic counterparts. Yet after the Khrushchev period, social stratifications in the land of the Soviets became very pronounced, as society became increasingly hierarchical, even though this blatantly contradicted its official doctrine. Those at the top of the social scale were not only irremovable; they were also able to guarantee their children a place in the sun. Their major concerns were no less egotistical than those of their Western counterparts, but, given that there was no private ownership of the means of production, they were unable to increase their wealth and power beyond a certain point. Greedy and completely unscrupulous, they appropriated a bigger slice of the national cake year by year. They did so at the expense of the national economy. By 1956, credits for education and health had simply stopped rising, and the USSR has therefore been outstripped by most Western countries, even in the essential sectors in which it once showed other countries the way. One could list other areas in which the USSR has fallen behind, but let us simply note that if Burboulis and Co. did not believe in the 'egalitarian utopia' they used to teach, their pupils had even less faith in it, as they could see the gap between the power elite and mere mortals growing bigger day by day. On the one hand, there were the *zolotyie dietki* ('the gilded youth'), and on the other there were the *sieryie kryssy* ('the grey mice'). Each group lived in a world that would not change for generations to come. It comes as no surprise to learn that, for a great number of privileged Soviet citizens, the values of Western capitalism were, when it came down to it, more attractive than the values of their communist grandfathers. The social situation of this power elite quite naturally determined its behaviour, its appetites and the tastes it borrowed from the capitalist world. The conviction that democracy can exist only when there exists a property-owning bourgeoisie and 'kulaks' was not born overnight. They had been coming to that conclusion throughout the previous period, less clearly than Gennady Burbulis suggests, but quite definitely nonetheless. And they obviously did not imagine that the new bourgeoisie and kulaks required by democracy would be chosen at random from amongst the people. Total-itarianism prevented them from openly demanding that role for them-selves, but they knew perfectly well that they would be given it, especially if they could retain power.

In 1990, the journal *Sociolguitcheskie issledovania*, which is not widely distributed and which tends to take a christian-democratic line, published, to my great surprise, an extract from Trotsky's *The Revolution Betrayed*.[4] In that book, Trotsky argued that, if it was not overthrown in time by the people, the soviet bureaucracy would try to transform itself into a property-owning class. It seems to me that, when that book was published, very few readers took that prophecy seriously. It was seen as an expression of bitterness or even sectarianism on the part of the exile in Mexico. Even in 1990, the extract published in Moscow did not stimulate discussion, so improbable was the future envisaged by Trotsky. It was only after the 'democratic' victory of August 1991 and the irresistible rise to power of Boris Yeltsin that things began to change radically. On the first anniver-sary of the 'three glorious Moscow days', the victors are, like Gavriil Popov, who resigned as Mayor of Moscow, now explaining at great length that 'the *nomenklatura* of the CPSU without the CPSU have taken complete control in order to promote reform, but above all to profit from it'.[5] A revolution, he says in substance, finds expression in the overthrow of a ruling class – as in France in 1789 and as in Russia in 1917 – but this time the same class has remained in power. To complete that pertinent observa-tion, we might add that the class in question is looking for ways to transform itself so as to base its power on a different system of property ownership.

This is undeniably new, and the process is just beginning: Mass privatiz-ation will not begin until Autumn 1992, when there will be a no-holds-barred fight for every factory, large or small, for land, if possible, and for everything else! Sergei Alexiev, the star of the democratic camp and a man above suspicion, writes quite openly in *Moscow News* that government plans for privatization will allow the nomenklaturists to acquire most of the national heritage 'because their old party loyalties have enabled them both to keep the power they had in the previous period and to maintain the many connections they established during the long years in which they worked together.'[6] Gavriil Popov advises the democrats to be patient and to form an opposition, but he also advises them to grab a share in power wherever they can, and to take their share of the cake without any delay.

Others are talking of the *nomenklatournyi capital* ('nomenklatura capital') which will be the earlier 'quasi-capitalism's' legitimate heir. After a whole year of pro-capitalist 'ideological bombardment' – capitalism is now being referred to by its true name, and not as 'normal society' – public opinion is, they think, ready for this radical reform. The Russian man in the street is traditionally a sceptic, and he is well aware that this has nothing to do with ideas and that it is purely a matter of power and money. If it did not cost him anything, he would no doubt accept the situation ('I wouldn't object if they paid me more now that they are capitalists than they did when they were communists'). But whilst the privatisers make no secret of their ambitions, the task may be beyond them, strong as they are, simply because 'they cannot pay more.' Quite the contrary. Hence the climate of fear in Moscow and throughout the country; people are afraid of popular revolts, coups and other calamities. The transition from 'real socialism' to capitalism will not, in other words, be straightforward and the present power elite is creating more problems than it can resolve in its attempt to change its spots. Hence its great internal divisions, and hence the changes of tack when it applies its policies. In order to understand this curious battle, we must first look at the avatars of the 'shock therapy' introduced by the Yeltsin-Burbulis-Gaidar team at the beginning of 1992.

Nascent capitalism in England, in other European countries and in the United States undoubtedly led to increased wealth. Karl Marx, its most severe critic, paid tribute to its ability, which was unlike anything that had been previously known, to revolutionise the means of production and to create new markets. But the former USSR is not a virgin land where capital can play a similar role. It is already an industrialized country with an enormous productive potential, and it is in crisis because of the corruption of the elite and because the central command structure created in the era of industrialisation is no longer adapted to an economy of that size. That is why Gorbachev wanted to introduce a 'socialist market' – the definition of which left something to be desired – which would, in his view, free producers from the constraints of rigid planning and oil the wheels of the system. Unlike the reformers in other Communist countries, he came to believe, after some initial hesitations, that priority should be given to political reform, arguing that the roots of the problem lay in the Soviet citizen's alienation from politics and work. Having failed to introduce shopfloor democracy in 1987, he resolved to free the state from Party control and to democratize it by calling elections. The Congress of People's Deputies was elected in 1989 and Soviets (parliaments) were elected in every republic, region and municipality in 1990. It is therefore somewhat of a paradox to hear orators in these assemblies – especially in Russia – accusing the former President of having blocked reforms during his six-year rule. If that were true, how could they have become deputies in a country in which there had been no free elections for seventy years?

The truth is that Gorbachev's 'liberal' critics hold it against him that he did not immediately dismantle the two pillars of the centralised economy: Gosplan (the central planning body) and Gossnab (the state distribution body). It should be recalled that 87.7% of the Soviet state's revenue comes from the profits made by state and cooperative enterprises, and that it would have been suicidal to kill the goose that laid the golden eggs in the name of market-economy dogma. Experience proved, moreover, that granting factories total accounting autonomy and encouraging the development of the private sector was enough to provoke the illegal accumulation of wealth at the expense of the profitability of the economy. Even in Gorbachev's day, the first millionaires, who came from the nomenklatura and the mafia of the underground economy, were beginning to demonstrate 'the power of their money.' They were not, however, entirely sure of their future: the President was threatening to fight corruption and had even promulgated a decree (which was never applied) allowing the KGB to undertake investigations without a court warrant. The President had a lot on his plate as a result of the rise of demands for independence and, wishing to put first things first, he turned a blind eye to what seemed to be temporary economic anomalies. In 1991, he organized a great national referendum on a 'New Union of Republics'. The outcome was satisfactory (57% in favour), but it did not put a brake on the centrifugal forces. In the meantime, the managers of the big factories were founding commercial banks – which were in fact financial holding companies – whose parasitic operations astonished even western specialists in speculation. *Pravda*, the central organ of the CPSU, published advertisements for the first 'raw materials and commodity exchanges', using a slogan that was familiar from the past: '*Enrichissez vous*'. Then, during the short-lived coup of August 1991, the 'Moscow rich' financed the defence of Boris Yeltsin's 'White House' and constantly shouted his praises from the rooftops in the hope of reaping political dividends.

In these conditions, the victory of the democrats was almost automatically transformed into a victory for the radical wing of the marketeers, who were anxious to make the transition to capitalism 'with a single leap across the precipice', to use an expression that has been in vogue in Moscow since 1990. How were they to prepare to make that leap? The liquidation of Gosplan and Gossnab had sounded the death knell for the old system, but had not thereby established a western-style economy. The state might well proclaim that it no longer wished to intervene in the economy, and might well take its inspiration from the precepts of Ronald Reagan and Margaret Thatcher, but that did not turn Russia into the United States or Great Britain. It was therefore decided to proceed one stage at a time, and to begin – on the advice of the International Monetary Fund and in the expectation of receiving its help – by balancing the state budget. No sooner had Boris Yeltsin reached the heights of power than he

asked the thirty-five-year old Yegor Gaidar and a few other young economists to apply the 'shock therapy' that had already been tried out in Poland
for more than two years, beginning in January 1992. According to those
who dreamed it up, this therapy would work like chemotherapy. In order
to block the spread of cancerous cells, chemotherapy also temporarily
stops the growth of healthy cells; that is the price the body must pay to rid
itself of the illness and to return to normal. When applied to the economy,
the therapy consists in ceasing to subsidize non-profitable sectors so that
'healthy cells' of private entrepreneurs can multiply and get the country
out of its crisis. In Poland in 1989, the 'liberal doctors' promised that the
worst of the treatment would be over within six months. In Russia in 1992,
it was known that this was far from being the case and that Poland was
sinking into a depression. The Yeltsin-Burbulis-Gaidar team nevertheless
promised in its turn that the situation would stabilise within six months and
would then begin to improve.

The miracle did not take place. For a variety of reasons – the size of the
country, the anarchic proliferation of 'commercial banks', the impos-
sibility of ensuring the partial convertibility of the rouble – 'shock therapy'
did even more damage in Russia than it had done in Poland. This wild form
of capitalist accumulation is purely destructive and does nothing at all to
increase 'the wealth of the nation'. I have before me an interview with
Russian Vice-President Alexander Rutskoi published in *Moscow News* on
23 August 1992. He draws up a balance sheet for the 'therapy' with a few
figures that do not require comment: 'Since the beginning of the year,
industrial output has fallen by 18%, national revenue by 18%, agricultural
output by 27%, and foreign trade by 27%. In order to reach the 1990 level,
we have, according to my calculations, at least eight years of very hard
work ahead of us.'

How are we to explain such a rapid collapse on such a large scale?
Without going into details, we can identify a few decisive factors: a) the
removal of subsidies and of almost all price-controls resulted in an increase
in the cost of living that is unprecedented in the country's history; prices
rose by 30, 40 or even 60 times the original figure (officially, according to
Gaidar, they rose by 18 times); b) very few factories in Russia – even
profitable ones – can do without state credit facilities, for the very good
reason that, despite the recommendations of the plan, their clients often
pay them late. The decision to do away with those facilities at a time when
prices were spiralling resulted in widespread non-payment and in a fantas-
tic level of debt on the part of all factories. According to official statistics,
the total owed was 39 billion roubles in January 1992, but it had risen to
3,200 billion in July, and most factories did not even have enough roubles
to pay wages; some put their staff on unpaid leave; others invented their
own currency or paid wages in kind, resorted to barter and God knows
what else. c) Russia imposed reforms on the other republics because

Russia alone controlled their common currency – the rouble. Despite that, the Republics were not slow to establish their own banks and to establish their own economic priorities. In these conditions, the very idea of balancing the budget was ludicrous, particularly as the CIS's economic ministers did not even attempt to coordinate their policies, realizing that it was a case of 'every man for himself'.

Taking their cue from an unfortunate slogan launched by Boris Yeltsin in an attempt to stimulate enterprise ('take all the freedom you can') everyone who was in a position to plunder national assets was, in the meantime, doing so with great imagination and no scruples. In a country where the mere possession of foreign currency had until very recently been an official crime, all restrictions and controls were removed overnight. Russia's central bank estimates the outflow of capital at 15 billion dollars since the beginning of 1992.[7] The statistics do not, however, tell us what proportion of those dollars belong to legal exporters who have decided not to repatriate them, and what proportion belongs to speculators who are investing their loot in tax havens in the Bahamas. The distinction between the two sectors is, besides, somewhat vague, as the top managers and the new entrepreneurs tend to work in partnership rather than to compete, and often come from the same social background. To the best of my knowledge, only Armenia has banned its ministers and top bureaucrats from becoming involved with private businesses. The relevant law will not come into effect until January 1993, but the other republics do not seem to be in any great hurry to follow Armenia's example. In the meantime, the Russian minister for energy states, as though he were talking about someone going off with boxes of matches in his pocket, that, according to his estimates, two million tonnes of oil are being exported without licences every month. One does not have to be a great intellectual to guess that fraud on this scale – and oil is only one example – is only possible because of the connivance of the administration and the private sector, which are getting rich by doing one another favours.

Within the space of a few months, the Russian economy had been 'dollarized' on a scale that has never been seen even in eastern Europe, which has years of experience of these things. In Moscow, the dollar soared from 60 roubles in January to 300 roubles at the end of September 1992. At this absurd rate of exchange, which suits the logic of the speculators, the average Russian wage (5,000 roubles per month) is at the level of the poorest countries in the world – Haiti and Burma. 'Dollarization' is helping some to get rich illegally and is impoverishing the majority. The smart districts of Moscow and St Petersburg are now full of the 'new poor', but the imperturbable commentaries on 'The Voice of Russia' explain that similar contrasts can be found everywhere – in New York, London, Rome and Lisbon – and that it is quite natural to find them in the big cities of the former USSR too.[8]

Not all the power elite would endorse such cynical comments. It is already seen as a miracle that the people did not rise in revolt during the first winter of 'shock therapy', but it would be decidedly dangerous to gamble on its continued passivity. Public opinion polls show that less than 10% of the population is satisfied with the radical reforms, whereas 70% are unhappy with them, and 6% 'already want to take to the barricades.' In the Moscow region by-elections of July 1992, more than 60% of voters abstained, and the democrat candidate received only 5% of the votes cast. Boris Yeltsin saw which way the wind was blowing and summoned the ministers and top bureaucrats to the bedside of Russia's sick economy. Former Prime Minister Valentin Pavlov is still in prison as a result of his involvement in the August 1991 coup, but his closest collaborators – Tchernomyrdin, Bartchuk and Khaya – are now back in the Kremlin. Victor Gerachenko has been made director of the National Bank. He is a 'second-generation Soviet banker', and succeeded his father as director of the former USSR's Gosbank. All this confirms the existence of the CPSU nomenklatura's 'many connections' and of the many shared interests that transcend the noisy public disputes. It should be remembered that during the stormy session of the Supreme Soviet that followed the coup, Boris Yeltsin pointed an accusing finger at Gorbachev, who had tried to protect certain ministers. 'Read this report aloud,' he shouted, handing him the stenographic record of the last meeting of the Council of Ministers. But that was in August 1991, and Gorbachev had to be humiliated. In August 1992, the former president counts for nothing on the political scene, and there is nothing to prevent Yeltsin from rehabilitating 'comrades' or 'gentlemen' who do, after all, know more about the economy than young Yegor Gaidar and the other 'boys in pink shorts', to use Vice-President Rutskoi's early description of Gaidar's team.

Another example, this time relating to the coup, shows how fluid and murky Russian politics can be. The guiding light behind the dangerous adventure of August 1991 seemed to have been the KGB chief Kruitchkov, acting with the help of Defence Minister Yazov, who deployed his tanks in the streets. But on the anniversary of the coup, General Mikhail Moiseev, former head of the General Staff, broke his silence and told the press that he had not been aware of anything and that Marshal Yazov had enlisted the help of only two top-ranking military men: General Pavel Gratchev, who brought his paratroopers from the Far East to Moscow, and Air Marshal Yevgeny Chapochnikov, who supplied the aircraft for the operation.[9] All in vain, as at the last moment, the paratroopers remained in their barracks. The final outcome is still astounding: Air Marshal Yevgeny Chapochnikov is now Commander in Chief of the CIS's armed forces, and General Pavel Gratchev is Russia's Minister for Defence. The two men who took part in the plot have been promoted, whereas the honest Moiseev has been dismissed. Where is the logic in all that?

A friend in Moscow said that this is a westerner's question. 'According to your logic', he told me, 'Yeltsin should not have become president of the Supreme Soviet in 1990 because he could initially count on only 30% of all deputies. When the time came to elect a president by universal suffrage, it would have been logical for him to choose his running mate from his own camp and not from the CPSU. But our logic, and especially Boris Yeltsin's logic, is based upon the art of behind the scenes negotiations: you have to win over likely "comrades", tame the waverers and buy the hard-liners. General Moiseev's revelations do nothing to embarrass Yeltsin; on the contrary, they show that he did buy some plotters and did keep his word. Doesn't he boast of having outwitted them?'

My friend in Moscow is not pro-Yeltsin – far from it. He does not see him as a charismatic leader ('He's not clever enough') and does not believe that he will emerge victorious from the new battles that are looming on the social front. Caution suggests that we should not make too many predictions about those battles, but it is time to examine the opposing forces.

The almost simultaneous break up of the 'Democratic Russia' electoral pact and the CPSU is not really surprising. Both were conglomerates bringing together men with different opinions, some because they were opposed to the government of the day, others because they were bound together by the rites and customs of a party that lost its ideological soul long ago. Because of its mixed composition, the new government – which was made up of 'radicals' from the *nomenklatura* and some democrats – helped to fragment the political scene still further. On 28 October 1991, Boris Yeltsin announced his intention of founding his own political party, but quickly realised that the project was unrealistic. It would have required the formulation of at least a programme, if not a doctrine, and the President of Russia has a definite aversion to such commitments. It should of course be recalled that the Yeltsin-Gaidar government did not in fact present a programme to the Supreme Soviet, and that its 'shock therapy' proposals were put forward only in a 'letter of intent' sent to the IMF in a bid to obtain credits. Within the former CPSU, now split into six mini-parties, discussion centres mainly on the rules of the game – the perennial problem of 'democratic centralism' – with a view to a possible but unlikely reunification. The Party's old leading lights – Ryjkov, Ligachev and Polozkov – have kept out of the debate and are, it is said, no longer on speaking terms. It is not surprising that only a tiny fraction of the population – estimated at 300,000 people, which is not very much for a huge country with a population of 150 million – should take a more or less active part in political life. There are of course parliamentary groupings in the Supreme Soviet and in the Congress of Deputies, and very bitter debates do take place, but it is hard to say just how representative the deputies are, given that they were elected long before the break up of the USSR. There are more opinion polls than there were, but they cannot replace the parties which, in democratic countries, allow governments to keep a finger on society's pulse. The Kremlin's strategists still hope, however, that the seething cauldron will eventually produce two 'non-extremist' forces which, like the Republicans and the Democrats in the USA, will be able to form a two-party system. A first small step in that direction was taken when the terms 'left' and 'right' began to be used in their correct senses; Mrs Thatcher's admirers in Moscow no longer say that they are on the 'left' and admit, like their fellows in the rest of the world, to being on the 'right'. The two parties which may, it is thought, form a future government have been established within the last few months; their names were previously unknown, but they are more open about their intentions than the old parties. Let me briefly describe them.

The mathematician Constantin Borovy, who is one of the richest men in Russia, made his fortune (estimated at hundreds of millions of dollars) by founding the first 'raw materials and commodity exchange' in central Moscow in 1990. The name is deceptive, as the exchange is in reality no more than a gigantic auction room where companies and even private individuals can sell or exchange their commodities. I admit that I have never quite understood just how it works, and I am not alone in that. When he was invited to New York by Wall Street's 'big wheels', Borovy disappointed those gentlemen, and either could not or would not reveal the workings of his highly profitable invention. But Constantin Borovy is now too rich and powerful to have to confine his interests to business. The highly ambitious Constantin Natanovitch may well have presidential ambitions, but given the prevailing climate of antisemitism, his Jewish patronymic is a serious handicap. He has therefore contented himself with founding a political party in partnership with the famous eye surgeon Sviatoslav Fedorov, who is a 'real Russian'. The last-named also distinguished himself as a reformer within the CPSU – I can recall his speech to the XIXth All-Union Conference of the CPSU – without neglecting his own business interests. He has built a major hotel complex in the grounds of his eye clinic. It is intended for foreign patients who will pay in hard currency. He has also opened Moscow's first big casino ('It's a place where you learn to take decisions', he says). His fortune is estimated at 100 million dollars, which certainly qualifies him to be co-President, with Borovy, of the 'Economic Freedom Party'. Both millionaires support Yegor Gaidar, but not in the same way as the other members of his government who, they say, are 'still building communism'. Their party would like to play the role the Republicans play in the United States, and like that party proclaims that every citizen should be able to go into business and get rich. In the Russian version of the old American myth of the shoeshine boy who became a billionaire, the 'Economic Freedom Party' cites the example of 41-year-old Valery Neverov, the 'honest academic' who was decorated by the Mayor of Moscow for being the best

USSR 'businessman of 1991', and keeps quiet about the sharks and mafiosi who are exploiting the anarchic market. Neverov, a professor of physics at the University of Tioumen in Western Siberia, made fabulous profits in his 'Hermes' oil exchange by buying at Soviet prices and then selling on the world market at forty times that price. This was semi-legal, as the state has accepted the right of oil-producers to sell 20% of their output in order to modernize their wells and to improve the work force's living standards. In practice, these deals have made the middlemen rich, and allow the directors of the oil fields to try out their brand new Mercedes on the dusty roads of the region. Having once spent some time in Western Siberia, I can well imagine the results, and I can quite understand that the people are not exactly enthusiastic about this kind of modernization. The 'Economic Freedom Party' does not agree; in its view, young people and active members of society have been gripped by 'business fever'; and it is flooding the press with adverts, and preparing to launch both a daily newspaper and a television channel.

The opposition to this 'big capital' party is provided by the equivalent to the American Democratic Party (to go on using the initial analogy): the 'Civic Union', which claims to be a centre-left party. It is prepared to cooperate with its 'Economic Freedom' rival over certain points (and in all matters concerning the development of the private sector), but is putting forward a more cautious overall strategy for the transition to a market economy.[10] The Civic Union is led by key figures like Alexander Rutskoi, the Vice-President of Russia, and Arkady Volsky, the chairman of a powerful lobby of state industries. The last-named is not afraid to describe 'shock therapy' as 'pure idiocy', openly admits to having prime ministerial ambitions, and recommends the adoption of the current Chinese model. He points out that, since 1979, China has had an annual growth-rate of 10% and that it attracted 30 billion dollars worth of foreign investment in 1992. The figures dazzle Russians, who are not really concerned about what lies behind the facade of 'China's success'. But are they capable of the same performance, or of imposing hyperexploitation on the workers? What is more, the Chinese regime rejects all forms of democracy, which means that when it cites China as a model, the Civic Union shows, say its critics, its own authoritarian instincts. General Rutskoi, one of the Union's founders and a hero of the war in Afghanistan does in fact have a somewhat 'Bonapartist' profile, and still has strong links with the army. In the present climate, the case being made against him – on the basis of assumptions rather than facts – does not seem to alarm many Russians, and his popularity continues to grow, and to outstrip that of Boris Yeltsin. In fact, the Volsky-Rutskoi duo is simply prioritizing a revival of industrial and agricultural output under the aegis of the state, and wants to delay privatization by introducing it in stages so as to avoid the clearance sales being held by the present government.

Arkady Volsky, who was director of the ZIL car factory before being given responsibility for the industrial sector in the Central Committee of the CPSU, is described by his enemies as 'a managing agent acting for the former USSR's military-industrial complex'. The description is meant to be pejorative, but it is in fact an involuntary tribute to Volsky's power. It is no secret that the USSR concentrated its best technologies, its best research laboratories, and its best engineers and technicians in the defence industries. Those who work in them, at any level, still have the accommodation, holiday homes, creches, hospitals and thousands of other facilities that go with the job. What private industrialist would agree to take on all that? One has only to ask that question to realize that the Civic Union is opposing doctrinaire privatization on pragmatic grounds, and that its hand is not short of trumps. The 'idiotic' policy of the radical reformers would result in the decline of the military-industrial complex's factories (mainly because of the brain drain) and, in the long run, in their paralysis. Even during the great arms race, these factories devoted some of their capacity to civilian needs (Aeroflot's planes have always been manufactured within the military-industrial complex, as have fishing boats, to take only two examples). Arkady Volsky maintains that his policies would allow the conversion and modernization of this vast sector and would make it capable of producing quality goods for both export and the home market. He is obviously counting on assistance from foreign capital for his ambitious project, but intends to carry it out under state leadership. In his view, the other essential precondition for its success is the reestablishment of the value of the rouble and of links between industries, which cannot rely upon the various 'exchanges' of Borovy, Neverov and Co. For his part, Vice-President Ruskoi, who is in charge of the agricultural sector, is arguing the case against those who say that the land should be sold to individual farmers and maintains, with figures to prove his case, that such an operation would cost 4,500 billion roubles, which cannot possibly be found, and that rural productivity would be even lower than it is now.[11] In short the Civic Union is arguing for a mixed economy in which the public and cooperative (*kolkhoze*) sectors would play the dominant role for a long time to come. This is essentially a technocratic programme and, in a sense, a social-democratic programme (it gives an important role to welfare), but its influential authors prefer to describe it as 'civic' or simply 'democratic' so as not to bring down the wrath of those who regard any mention of 'the social' as a reminder of the pernicious 'communist utopia'. Since the fiasco of 'shock therapy', Boris Yeltsin has been ready to listen to the arguments of the Volsky-Rutskoi team, particularly as he is now navigating a storm without a compass, the power elite can hear the mounting rumble of discontent from a base which is poorly organized but which feels that it has no place in this new 'democratic society'.

The images that reached us from Moscow after the aborted coup of August 1991 gave the impression of a generalized anti-communist uprising: the crowed tearing down Dzerzhinsky's statue, and besieging the CPSU Central Committee building and other Party offices. But a year after the event, Gavriil Popov revealed, in the series of articles mentioned earlier, that these 'enraged democrats' had been brought to Moscow from the surrounding area and that, even so, they did not represent an uncontrollable force. All it took to make everyone go home quietly was, he says, a presidential decree banning further manifestations of public disorder. We also know that the monuments spared by the upheavals of August 1991 are still there and that in St Petersburg, even Felix Dzerzhinsky's statue is still in place outside the headquarters of the former KGB. Although their anti-communist diatribes are becoming louder, Yeltsin, Burbulis and the rest of them have no intention of closing Lenin's Mausoleum, because, it is said, to do so would offend popular sensibilities. But how can they revile the Bolsheviks from morning to night without offending those same popular sensibilities?

The answer lies, in my view, in the loss of all historical memory of the October Revolution in the former USSR. Stalin was largely responsible for its destruction because he reduced an entire history to the personality of Lenin – and his own personality – and physically liquidated all the other protagonists. It took decades for the victims, starting with Nicolai Bukharin, to be rehabilitated under Mikhail Gorbachev (and Bukharin was rehabilitated for opportunistic reasons, or in other words to allow Gorbachev to claim his heritage). Communists in the USSR were taught a version of history which could be – and was – easily manipulated.[12] I am obviously not concerned here with an historical debate, but with a factor which may help us to understand the behaviour of an ex-communist elite which is trying to turn itself into a property-owning class. General Volkogonov said that: 'The last obstacle standing in the way of my departure from the CPSU was Lenin', and he was obviously not the only one who could have said that. Many others had to find at least one good reason to justify their careers within the Party, and Lenin was apparently the best reason of all because he was an intellectual – and intellectuals now enjoy great prestige – and because he founded a great state, which is not bad either. Aside from openly anti-Soviet dissidents – and there were not many of them – almost no one questioned Lenin's role. Generalized attacks on the Bolsheviks, on the other hand, had already begun to be made during *perestroika*, when any street violence or even mere reference to the working class, were denounced as unacceptably Bolshevik. I recall the indignation of a professor and deputy who read in *Pravda* that, after the anti-Armenian pogrom in Baku, a CP leader in Azerbaijan was considering forming workers' militias to combat racist disorder. 'This is a return to Bolshevik methods', he exclaimed, even though he was anti-racist and pro-Armenian. For the Russian elite, everything that is not strictly parliamentarian has gradually become 'classist', 'marxist' and above all 'Bolshevik'.

There must be a logic – and I think that it is indeed a 'classist' logic – to this fearful simplification, which reminds one of the reactions of the Western bourgeoisie when it felt itself threatened by the labour movement. On the other hand, whilst it is in historical terms absurd to make a distinction between Lenin and his Party, the fact is that statues and images of the old leader have always been ubiquitous in the USSR, whereas the Bolsheviks have not been part of the political landscape for fifty years. The good people of Moscow therefore have nothing good to say about the Bolsheviks, so as not to be accused of having violent intentions and, in my view, because the entire history of October seems as remote to them as the history of Herman Cortès's conquest of Mexico. For the last forty-seven years, the event that founded the USSR has not been the October Revolution, but victory over the Nazi invaders in the 'Great Patriotic War of the Russian people'. That became the source of the identity of anyone who claimed to be a Communist, but it was also the source of pride of every Russian. At the victory banquet held in the Kremlin in June 1945, Stalin made a famous toast to 'the great Russian people'. It became engraved on the memory of a whole generation, and seems to have been handed down to their children.

The Soviet people have lost their fatherland overnight. 'We used to be a great country, respected throughout the world, and now we are no more than fifteen wretched states begging for Western aid.' This heartfelt cry from the very 'patriotic' general Alexander Lebed is echoed throughout the country. The other Republics hung out flags when they gained their independence. Not the Russians, who had most to lose from the changes that were occurring. Despite the predictions of certain prophets, they did not become rich when they shrugged off the 'burden of aid' to the other former Soviet Republics. What is more, twenty-five million Russians are living outside their own country in 'fraternal republics' which do not even recognize their national identity. They are simply the 'Russian-speaking population', second-class citizens who, in the Baltic countries for example, do not even have the right to vote. And as if that were not enough, they are suffering because of inter-ethnic conflicts which, in theory, are no concern of theirs, but which are forcing them to flee in haste from first Azerbaijan, and then Chechen-Ingush, Tadzhikistan and Abkhazia. All these refugees have relations in Moscow, St Petersburg and even distant Sakhalin. Their families are too poor to help them, but share their indignation at the way they have been treated.

The slogans of October 1917 referred to 'the fraternal union of the proletariat', but it certainly does not apply to this situation. Stalin's 1945 toast seems tailor-made. Hence a phenomenon which is to say the least unexpected: from year to year, the generalissimo's popularity has been rising in the polls. In 1990, only 8% expressed support for Stalin. In 1991, 18% did so, but support for him suddenly rose to 49% in 1992. If we are to believe the figures, which seem to me to be an exaggeration, one in two Russians mourns 'the great Stalin' and would like to have a new leader of the same mettle.[13] It is not the power elite that is nostalgic about Stalin, nor is it the supporters of the potential two-party system; it is the working people who constitute the natural base for a left opposition. One of the organizers of the first demonstration to be held against Yeltsin's policies in Moscow, told me of his consternation at seeing groups of workers, including young people, marching into Manezh Square carrying portraits of Stalin. Seeing the television cameras homing in on these groups, he begged them to get rid of the portraits, but to no avail. He has now become accustomed to seeing old portraits of Stalin at meetings organized by right-wing 'patriots' whose ranks include monarchists with portraits of the Tsar, as well as at those organized by the Party of Labour, which is on the left and which is fighting for social justice. For the power elite, this is a heaven-sent opportunity; it can describe the opposition as 'red-brown' and imply that the collusion of today is a continuation of the collusion that supposedly always existed between Communists and Nazis. This is enough to give a heart attack to anyone who knows anything about the struggle to the death between the anti-Bolshevik fanatics of the Third Reich and Stalin's Russia, not to mention Red Army veterans, who do not exactly recall playing cricket with their 'ideological allies' during the war. With its overstated denunciations of the 'red-browns', the present government is poisoning the political atmosphere, and destroying the threshold of mutual tolerance that is an essential part of democracy.

Whilst it swears that it has the best of intentions, the West is also constantly stoking the flames. IMF advisers who know nothing about the Soviet economy demand the application of their 'universal' neo-liberal recipes and then say at the end of every quarter that the Russians do not deserve the aid promised because they are still not practising hard line capitalism. In Washington in June 1992, Yeltsin signed a truly unequal agreement on nuclear disarmament which will deprive Russia of the greater part of its strike force, whilst the Americans will not agree to give up the weapons that the Soviet military most fear. What is more, Moscow and the big provincial cities have been invaded not only by American businessmen, many of them shady, but also by a cohort of preachers from various Protestant churches. For many Russians, this is unbearably humiliating, and worse than any past humiliations. It will not take much to make them conclude that the American capitalist 'professors' who are telling Yeltsin and Gaidar what to do, are the root of all evil. The clear social divide that is emerging is not an extension of the old quarrel between slavophiles and westernisers; it is a dispute between those who are being forced to live on their devalued roubles – the majority of the population – and those who are prospering thanks to their green banknotes. Some people in the Kremlin – notably Burbulis, Poltoranin and Kozyrev – are claiming that the wolf is at the door, and denouncing 'the plots of the enemies of the market economy.' The more cautious Boris Yeltsin is attempting to adjust his fire by making direct attacks by decree on the omnipotence of the dollar – which, in the absence of any alternative economic strategy, is no more than wishful thinking – but this does reveal his 'patriotic' sensibilities and his awareness of the danger that threatens. For if certain Cassandras in Moscow are to be believed, Russia has lost is bearings and if it continues to go down the road it is following, the result will be a devastating civil war.

Such fears are not unfounded but, being incapable of thinking in apocalyptic terms, I prefer to believe that the rift in Russian society, which is the result of social conflict, will not lead to a bloody confrontation. The rise of nationalism and nostalgia for Stalin are no more than the froth on a wave of popular discontent (and are holding back a more effective expression of that discontent). But with time, as the various strata of the working class begin to defend their real interests, the present protests, which are both disorganized and contaminated by demagogy, will be drowned out. That is why I attach such great importance to the actions of the independent trade unions, which may appear to be corporatist but which do allow social subjects to organize around specific aims. Experience showed during the miners' strike of 1989 that Russian workers have a great capacity for self-organization and that once they begin to take action, they refuse to listen to patriotic false prophets bearing portraits of Stalin. Of course they are 'groups in fusion', as defined by Sartre, and will not become lasting movements capable of making their presence felt at the national level. But we know that a strike, and especially a victorious strike, marks consciousnesses and creates the premises for new actions and demands. It is no accident that the miners had only to threaten to cease to work in 1992 to win a 1,000% wage rise. For the moment, however, industrial workers are suffering less than other wage-earners in the public sector such as teachers, health-service workers and lowly bureaucrats. To say nothing of the misery of old age-pensioners, who have been hardest hit of all by the 'shock therapy', who have been reduced to poverty and who are usually a burden on the inadequate budgets of their relatives. For all those who are immune to 'business fever' – and many of them are struggling for reform – the trade unions are the only hope, and the Party of Labour is quite right to try to win their support. The road ahead is of course as long as the road that once lay ahead of the early labour movement in Britain, but I can see no other 'right solution' to the Russian crisis.

It would be wrong for me to forget Gorbachev at the end of a text which began by talking so much about him. In my view, the former president fluffed his exit from the Kremlin because he was either unable or unwilling to denounce aloud the 'Bialowierza plot' which destroyed the USSR; the stance he took against 'shock therapy' was also too ill-defined, and suggested that he was resigned to it all. And whilst he continues to speak of his 'socialist option' and even to attend the Congress of the Socialist International, the content of that 'option' has become almost impossible to determine. The fact remains, however, that the Russian opposition is wrong to blame *perestroika* for the present crisis, as it is simply not true that the ancien regime could have gone on functioning much longer. What is more, Yeltsin and his supporters are once more afraid of Gorbachev, having sensed that they are unpopular and realized that he is a strong personality who might still have a role to play. But their attempts to discredit him thanks to the absurd tactic of putting the CPSU on trial in the Constitutional Court may rebound against them by arousing sympathy for a victim of the arbitrary exercise of power. The left opposition would be making a serious mistake if it turned away from (or remained indifferent to the fate of) a leader whose thinking may be confused, but who does aspire towards something resembling social democracy at a time when most of the power elite is openly fighting for the worst of all possible capitalisms. Last but not least, not being an advocate of 'all or nothing' I think that the victory of Arkady Volsky's technocrats might be a good thing, and might help to improve Russia's terrifying economic position. Were that to happen, a degree of political sanity might also be restored.

Paris, 15 October 1992.

Postscript: 20 December 1992

Over the last two months, Russia has been through some serious ordeals which could have degenerated into civil war. But having come within an ace of disaster, it has found a compromise solution and has simply changed government. Victor Chernomyrdin, the new prime minister is a tech-nocrat, a top manager who formerly worked in the gas industry, and has links with Arkady Volsky's Civic Union. It seemed to me in October that this would be the inevitable outcome and I therefore do not wish to make any substantial changes to my article. In order to bring it up to date, I would like to imitate the end of certain films and indicate what has become of my 'main characters'.

BORIS YELTSIN. Having lost his majority in the Congress of People's Deputies, the country's highest legislative body, on 10 December he attempted an anti-parliamentary coup but he had the support of neither the army nor a substantial section of the population. His coup was therefore no more than a bluff, and *The Guardian* soberly concluded that he had been 'ham-fisted'. Valery Zorkin, the president of the Constitu-tional Court, needed all his skills to enable the ebullient Russian leader to save face and to persuade the deputies to accept a compromise that left the President's powers intact. Yeltsin did, however, emerge from the trial of strength with a tarnished reputation, and that can only be a very good thing for Russia's young democracy.

GENNADY BURBULIS. In order to appease the deputies' anger, Yeltsin sacrificed his eminence grise, the former professor of 'scientific communism' who, according to his critics, had considerable influence over the President. At all events, it was Burbulis who encouraged him to threaten and insult deputies, and it is only natural that he should pay for the fiasco.

EDUARD SHEVARDNADZE. Being the only candidate in the presidential elections held in Georgia on 11 October, he was 'democratically' elected with 95% of the vote. He is also Prime Minister and has been granted special powers for a period of three years. On 23 November, he was baptised Gueorgui, meaning 'protector of Georgia' in an orthodox church in Tsbilitsi, and told the press that he had an icon of the Holy Virgin in his office. Being bogged down in the war in Abkhazia, which has united all the Muslim peoples of the Caucasus against him, he certainly needs divine protection.

LEONID KRAVCHUK is still riding high on a wave of nationalism, but the breakdown of the Ukraine's economy has forced him to sacrifice his faithful prime minister Vitold Fokin. Leonid Kutchma, the new prime minister, is, like his counterpart in Moscow, a top manager who previously worked in heavy industry. Chernomyrdin sums up the situation as follows: 'Once you could go shopping with a pocketful of money and come back with a basketful of groceries; now you go out with a basketful of roubles, and you come back with scarcely enough to fill one pocket.' In the circumstances, Kravchuk will probably have to tone down his demagogic talk of independence and try to work more closely with Russia and the other former Soviet Republics.

ALEXANDER RUTSKOI. During the session of the Congress of Deputies, Russia's Vice-President distinguished himself as one of the opposition's most effective leaders. He even went so far as to demand that Boris Yeltsin's entourage should be brought before the courts because of their political adventurism, which has done the country incalculable harm. His connections in the army no doubt did a lot to ensure its continued loyalty to Parliament. Defence Minister General Gratchev even dragged himself from his hospital bed to swear to the deputies that he was loyal to the constitution. He also made a point of saying that the army 'has not forgotten its comrades from the Afghan campaign'; this was a nod in the direction of General Rutskoi, who was a hero of the said 'campaign'. According to political observers in Moscow, the Rutskoi-Travkin ticket (Travkin is another refugee from the Yeltsin camp) stands a good chance of defeating Yeltsin in the next presidential elections.

RUSLAN KHAZBULATOV. The Speaker of the Supreme Soviet was the great strategist in the trial of strength with the Russian President, who was once his main protector. Yeltsin appointed him for two reasons. Khazbulatov is a Chechen, and his appointment to a high office of state symbolises the multinational nature of the Russian Federation; what is more, he is an academic and an economist who has never been part of the apparatus of the CPSU. What Yeltsin did not expect was that the Chechen would prove to be a real statesman who could impose his will upon a parliament in which outbursts of Russian xenophobia are not unknown. Curiously enough, he has also become a *bête noire* for the ultra-liberals, who have not forgiven him for telling Congress that there are many models for a market economy and that Russia should look for its own model and turn for inspiration to Sweden rather than the United States. Replying to Khazbulatov, Yegor Gaidar argued that, given the state of affairs in Russia, it was too early to be discussing Swedish and American models, as Sweden and America were amongst the richest countries in the world. But Sweden began to introduce its great social reforms in 1936, when the country was not all that rich. And the Labour Party founded the Welfare State in a Great Britain that had been ruined by the war. The grievances expressed to Congress by deputies were ample proof that the Russians were not ready to wait for some hypothetical general prosperity before they too had the right to a modicum of social justice. Khazbulatov also has to be given credit for his ability, during the December sessions, to neutralise the highly vociferous group of pseudo-patriots and Stalinist *revanchistes*. Jonathan Steele is perfectly correct to write (*Guardian*, 16 December 1992): 'Mr Khazbulatov has lived up to his reputation as Russia's most powerful politician.'

CONSTANTIN BOROVY. At the beginning of November, the founder of the 'Economic Freedom Party' fought a by-election in the Krasnodar constituency in Southern Russia so as to be able to participate in the session of the Congress of Deputies. The fact that he won less than 5% of the votes cast and came a long way behind a local leader from the former CPSU, may have convinced him that his dream of winning a majority for a party which openly describes itself as 'bourgeois', is unlikely to come true in the near future. Krasnodar's voters in fact failed to turn out in such numbers that the election was inquorate and will have to be rerun with different candidates. The test of elections showed that, like the other 'post-Communist' countries of Eastern Europe, Russia is already suffering from abstentionism, a very painful illness for new regimes, and one which is adequate proof that its citizens are disappointed by the ruling democrats' failure to keep their promises. Borovy was a victim of a very general phenomenon, but he naturally blames everything on the unfortunate heritage of 'real socialism'. His Party held its first Congress in Moscow at the beginning of December, and promises to fight the Chernomyrdin government.

VICTOR CHERNOMYRDIN. The new Prime Minister supports the theses of the Civic Union of Arkady Volsky, Rutskoi and Travkin. His task seems impossible: how can he reduce inflation and halt the downturn in production in a country which is, to cite Valery Zorkin, President of the Constitutional Court, ruled by 'totalitarian cliques of mafiosi'? For the moment, all we know is that Chernomydrin will prioritize the protection of national industries rather than the various joint-ventures, many of which are speculative, and that he will reintroduce the planned distribution of raw materials to get factories back to work and to ensure that airports are not paralysed by fuel shortages. He also wants to improve conditions for those social groups which have been worst affected by the crisis so as to 'put an end to the impoverishment of the population.' These measures do not yet represent a programme, much less a new and socialist-oriented economic model. But the fact that power is in the hands of a man who is not a dogmatic 'liberal' and who enjoys the trust of both President and Congress should, logically, mean that Russia will, given time, recover. Most deputies have a great deal of influence in their constituencies and have important positions in their local or regional Soviet. If they collaborate with Chernomyrdin and actively commit themselves to the new reforms, the state will gradually begin to function again, and that is a sine qua non if the present chaos is to end. The heritage of 'Gaidarism' is however, so oppressive that it is too early to draw conclusions.

NOTES

1. CF *Argumenty i facty* (Moscow), December 1991. In another interview in which he keeps it all rather vague, Leonid Kravchuk maintains (*Izvestia* 25 December 1991) that he knew nothing about Stalin's anti-peasant policy in the 1930s or about the repression that took place in Ukraine after the war.
2. *Izvestia*, 20 August 1992.
3. In the course of a quiz show, the film maker Nikita Mikhalkov asked television viewers 'Who said that?' and played them a tape of a delirious panygeric of 'real socialism'. Most said it was Mikhail Suslov; others thought it was Andrei Zhdanov. The speaker was in fact none other than Gennady Burbulis. The programme was immediately banned, and was spared only thanks to the intervention of Vice-President Alexander Rutskoi. It was, however, shown very late at night.
4. Cf *Sociologuitcheskie isseldovania*, I, 1990.
5. Cf the series of four articles published by Popov in *Iszvestia*, 21, 24, 25 and 26 August 1992.
6. Cf. *Moscow News* 16 August 1992 (Russian edition).
7. Cf the interview with the Bank's director Victor Guerachtchenko *Literatournia Gazeta*, 2 September 1992.
8. As far as corruption in the higher spheres is concerned, not only the press but even leaders say things that make one's hair stand on end. On 8 October 1992, Praesidium-member Mikhail Gurtovoi, told *Niezavissmaya Gazeta* that: 'no matter which ministry you go to, the deputy ministers and the main specialists are no more than travelling salesmen for western companies and spend their time placing orders on their behalf.' Ministers themselves have also been accused of taking over official flats and datchas, and of having bought them in great haste with money coming from bribes. Asked about this by *Argumenty i fakty* (October 1992) deputy minister Mikhail Poltoranin was non-commital: 'I own a datcha, which I built together with my sons. As far as other ministers are concerned, I can guarantee the honesty of those I know very well. I cannot say anything about the others.'

9. His comments were broadcast on the 'news hour' programme broadcast in Russian between 10 and 11 am on 18 September.

10. The *Graydenskiosivch* (Civic Union) emerged from a merger between four parliamentary groups: Arkady Volsky's Civic Union, Alexander Rutskoi's Democratic Russia, Nicolai Travkin's Free Russia, and *Smena* Change).

11. Rutskoi estimates the cost of equipping a modern farm to be at least 20 to 30 million roubles. Given that there are 152,000 would-be farmers, this does give a total of 4.5 billions. Even so, this would represent only a very partial privatization of agriculture.

12. I had occasion to deal with this problem in my *Solik*, which is based on my own wartime experience of the USSR. The book was published in France in 1983, long before the beginning of *Perestroika*.

13. The polls published in the Russian press are sometimes based upon readers' letters, and those who write to the press are not a representative cross-section of the population as a whole. It is also possible that the newspapers are deliberately exaggerating Stalin's popularity so as to warn their readers about the danger of neo-Stalinism. But even if we divide 49% by two or three, that still leaves a lot of people.

Translated by David Macey.

THE LEFT AND THE DECOMPOSITION OF THE PARTY SYSTEM IN ITALY

Stephen Hellman

Due to its domination by the largest and most interesting Communist Party in the West, the Italian left always moved according to its own rhythms, though it was never immune from the problems that afflicted the workers' movement and progressive forces everywhere. The PCI's distinctiveness earned it considerable attention, and no small amount of admiration, at times because it was successful and innovative (think of the heyday of Eurocommunism in the mid to late 1970s), and at other times simply because it *was*. The existence of a large, flexible, and open organization like the PCI – with the added bonus of Antonio Gramsci as a former leader – served as an inspiration to militants and intellectuals across Europe in their struggles against the obtuseness and lack of imagination of their own leaders, whether of the social democratic or the Brezhnevite variety.

Distinctive to the end, the PCI formally dissolved itself in 1991 while it still controlled more than a quarter of the seats in the Italian parliament. Other CPs, like the French, might cling to a practice and an identity that had failed to keep up with changing times, rendering such parties marginalized onlookers even before the dissolution of the USSR. The PCI's new leader, Achille Occhetto, surrounded himself with renovators and tried radical therapy in an effort to reverse the decline that had afflicted the party for over a decade. Convinced that this decline would continue if the party simply reacted to events, Occhetto felt that a break with the past was needed to lay the groundwork for a recomposition of the entire left. And only such a total reshuffling of the political cards, he believed, would create the conditions for a new, progressive aggregation of forces able to force the Socialists out of their collaboration with the Christian Democrats and finally drive the DC from power.

Occhetto understood a key aspect of the dynamics of the Italian political system, but could not control the course of events even within his own party, let alone within Italy as a whole. As a result, the new Democratic Party of the Left (PDS) was born weak and divided, leaving the left more feeble and fragmented than ever. And while Occhetto correctly foresaw that the PCI's disappearance would break down old alignments, things did

190

not go as planned as other factors intervened to push the party system in unexpected directions. Despite its fluidity, there is much in the present situation that should give any progressive person pause: forces that are at best ambiguous are on the rise, and questions that are at best secondary are dominating political discourse. At the same time, precisely because it is so fluid, the situation is by no means unremittingly bleak for the left.

In one sense, the course of recent events in Italy is highly positive. The squalid Christian Democrat-Socialist collaboration that has been the centre of gravity of the political system since the late 1970s is in serious trouble. The DC is crumbling in its Catholic strongholds, and the PSI's existence as even a medium-sized party has been called into question by a barrage of scandals that has unleashed unprecedented numbers of protest votes. But these votes have not gone to the left. The protest has been captured by the regionalistic populists of the Northern Leagues, which made a breakthrough in the 1992 general elections, obtaining nearly 10 percent of the vote nationwide, and twice that in the North. The Leagues have shaken off the ethnic, anti-southern bias and outright separatism of their earliest days, but they remain ill-defined and untested politically.[1] At the same time, their growth not only continues in their northern strongholds but shows signs of expanding into other areas of the North-Centre of the country.

How did the left, and the country, arrive at this situation? What are the options, and the dangers, that they face? In a situation in which events are breaking so rapidly, it would be pointless to attempt to provide a complete chronicle of events, and silly to make too many predictions. What is not only possible but absolutely necessary, however, is to outline the most important aspects of recent developments on the left, and within the party system as it slides between decomposition and, possibly, reaggregation. This will at least provide us with a vantage point from which to assess the way the political situation is unfolding.

Italian Communism on the Road to Dissolution

The PCI's final agonies showed, among many other things, the poverty (and simplicity) of commonly-used analytical categories on the left (and elsewhere). Because it never easily fitted preconceived models of what a Communist Party *should* resemble, or what the more orthodox CPs actually *did* resemble, people used to argue that the PCI was 'not really' a Communist Party, or that it was simply the 'functional equivalent' of social democracy. Although this assessment – delivered with contempt or admiration, depending on the analyst's standpoint – was persuasive in many respects, it was also a rather simplistic shorthand. That the PCI was not a typical Communist Party was apparent from its size and behaviour, which in important respects did resemble the mass parties of the Second International. But that it was also a *real* Communist Party was equally evident.

That the PCI was something quite different from a social-democratic party became fully evident when it tried to break with its past. The last (20th) Congress of the PCI, which became the founding congress of the Democratic Party of the Left (PDS), was to have been akin to Italian Communism's Bad Godesberg, 30 years after German Social Democracy's break with orthodox Marxism and its alteration in the direction of a catch-all *Volkspartei*, or people's party. The Italian Communists had never been as proletarian as the strongest Socialist Parties, and they had moved away from Marxist orthodoxies from the 1960s onward. Still, when the leadership tried to take the last step and sanction formally what had been in effect for a long time, the reaction was ferocious.

How do we explain this situation? From the end of the 1960s onward, the PCI really had no clear strategy other than to avoid isolation and eventually to be accepted as a partner in government. What it *did* have was a strong social presence, a solid organizational and electoral base, and enough flexibility and openness to hold its own and avoid the self-destructive impulses of other Communist Parties (the Spanish and French come immediately, and unflatteringly, to mind). As time passed, these qualities showed their limitations. Capitalist restructuring, along with the party's own floundering, took their inevitable toll, and the siren call of change became irresistible. Not to adjust to altered conditions promised a slow, but steady, decline into irrelevancy: between 1976 and 1987, the party's popular support slipped inexorably downward, from 34.4 to 26.6 percent. In addition to electoral decline and political isolation, the PCI was saddled with a cumbersome bureaucratic structure that could not keep pace with changing times and increasingly represented an intolerable financial drain on the party's diminishing resources.[2]

Yet significant change also entailed serious risks – more serious, it turned out, than many had assumed. Precisely because the party for so long had been an amalgam of tendencies and sensibilities with no clear programme, its identity and traditions served as a bonding agent that held together conflicting, sometimes incompatible, groupings. Its traditions and identity had changed over time, but until the 1980s they had generally done so at a glacial pace.[3] The slowness of its evolution was criticized as much by those who wanted the PCI to engage with the new forces in Italian society as it was by those whose aim was to jettison the past and assume a Labour or Social-Democratic identity. Above all, however, because of the party leadership's instinctive understanding that the PCI *was* its identity, this evolution took place slowly to allow the entire party to move in unison. To break the vicious circle of continuity and stagnation meant opening the possibility of fragmentation and dispersal. A dangerous undertaking at any time, this was especially risky in the conditions in which the PCI found itself at the end of the 1980s, as events quickly revealed.

The immediate cause of PCI secretary Occhetto's 1989 decision to change the party's name and symbol was, of course, the collapse of the Soviet empire in Eastern Europe. His dramatic decision was announced just days after the Berlin Wall fell, by which time many people on the left had already concluded that the label 'Communist' no longer had any *raison d'être*. But his decision touched off a firestorm of dissent in the PCI, paralysing the party for a year and a half: the change was announced in November, 1989, and it took two party congresses before the PDS was finally born in Rimini in February, 1991. This internal struggle was so intense and lacerating that it paralysed the party's initiatives in the political and social sphere. As the PCI tore itself apart, the novelty of Occhetto's *svolta*, or turnaround, wore off, and the benefits the new party was to have reaped by freeing itself from a cumbersome (and sometimes embarrassing) past never materialized.

The left would undoubtedly have opposed the *svolta* on its merits, but the opposition was especially furious because many people felt betrayed by Occhetto. After taking over the leadership of the PCI in 1987, i.e. long before the collapse of the USSR and its empire, Occhetto initiated a series of far-reaching changes in the party. In 1989, at the PCI's 18th National Congress, he obtained 90 percent support and appeared to have re-launched the party with a programme that called for an overhaul and opening-up of its structure and internal practices, all the while keeping its historical name and symbol.

Yet barely eight months after embarking on what was supposed to be the construction of a new PCI – and winning over the left wing in the process – Occhetto shattered the 18th Congress's equilibrium. The proposal of a complete break with the past and the creation of a party with a new name, symbol, structure and programme drove most of the left, and others as well, into the opposition. Occhetto had wanted to move swiftly, but resistance proved so strong that extensive, and exhausting, debates were required to head off a catastrophic schism. The fiercely-contested 19th Congress (1990) was originally supposed to put an end to the PCI and launch a new party. But internal resistance forced the congress to focus exclusively on the *principle* of founding a new party. And while the 19th Congress ended with two-thirds of the PCI accepting the change, a third remained hostile.

With a split involving much of the PCI's left wing appearing a very real possibility, Occhetto had to try to minimize the damage. Only the right wing, representing a fifth of the membership, seemed willing, in the name of coherence, to let the dissidents leave. A massive exodus of dissidents would, of course, have greatly facilitated the new party's march to the right.

No matter which way he turned, Occhetto encountered serious problems. One of the major reasons for the *svolta* was the assumption that, free of the baggage of the past, a new party would appeal to a reservoir of progressive noncommunist forces that was presumed to exist in Italy. (Prominent intellectuals had for some time posited the existence of a 'submerged left', and a network of leftwing 'clubs' sprung up in the late 1980s.) However large this latent constituency might have been, the drawn-out, inward-looking debate – necessary to deal with internal dissent – quickly dissipated the outside world's interest and stymied the party's effectiveness.

Emblematic of the new party's divisions and its difficulties in projecting a convincing image was the embarrassing way it was born. Confident that his centrist majority was 'self-sufficient', Occhetto enraged both the left and the right at the founding congress playing each off against the other on various votes, first isolating the left on organizational questions, and then joining with the left to defeat the right on the Gulf War, which was underway at the time. At the very end of the congress, Occhetto discovered that he did not have as much freedom to manoeuvre as he had thought. In the voting for the first secretary-general of the PDS, he was openly opposed by the left, and quietly sabotaged by the right, whose abstentions deprived him of the absolute majority of votes required by the party statute. The congress ended with no party secretary and Occhetto in hiding. Only after he publicly apologised for his high-handedness and made explicit overtures to the right was he finally elected secretary. The message clearly was that the party leadership could take nothing for granted, and that the factions were forces to be reckoned with.

Divisions within the party

From the mid-1950s on, a number of ideological tendencies had evolved and coexisted within the PCI; though not allowed to organize, they were, as a rule, openly tolerated.[4] Broadly speaking, the left retained an ill-defined but consistently-expressed conviction that capitalism had to be transcended. It was suspicious of institutional mediation, favouring social mobilization and confrontation. It was especially suspicious of suggestions that the party assume a governing role. And while extremely critical of the USSR, the left tended to be less Atlanticist than the rest of the party. In contrast, the right emphasized building political coalitions, and its fa-voured interlocutors were the historic parties of the left, the Socialists (PSI) and the much smaller Social-Democrats (PSDI).[5] The right consis-tently called for the PCI to assume a governing role, and it frequently diagnosed 'emergencies' that required the party's presence in power to save Italian democracy. Over time, the right's sympathies for mainstream Western traditions and alliances led it to advocate a complete break with the communist tradition and the acquisition of a modern Labour or Social Democratic profile, earning its followers the labels *laboristi* or, more often, *miglioristi* (meliorists). It always privileged relations with the PSI above everything else, even when the Socialists seemed dedicated to a permanent embrace with the DC. The right's leading figure has for some time been Giorgio Napolitano, who commands great personal respect among all wings of the party.

These original tendencies became more blurred in the 1970s, after party secretary Enrico Berlinguer proposed his 'historic compromise' strategy. This advocated Catholic-Communist collaboration – a theme dear to the left of the party. But it also called for a rapid entry of the PCI into national power: in practice, Catholic-Communist turned out to mean a DC-PCI condominium. Berlinguer saw the PCI and DC as the representatives of Italy's healthy, popular forces, and he held the PSI in contempt for its lack of a mass presence and constant vacillations. This scornful attitude toward the smaller PSI was always present in parts of the PCI, but it became widespread under Berlinguer. It was of course not lost on the Socialists, who were groping for a new identity under Bettino Craxi during the same period. Berlinguer's vision eventually won over many of his comrades, and had an especially strong impact on a new generation of Communists – and there were many of them – who came to the party and rose in its ranks in the 1970s.

In addition to the evolution of Italian Communist ideological and political tendencies, the 1970s also saw the further enrichment of discourses within the party as the PCI absorbed new ideas and forces from an increasingly complex and secularized society.[6] It absorbed some of these new issues in incomplete and often contradictory fashion, especially when the new clashed directly with older entrenched positions (e.g. environmentalism and opposition to nuclear energy). The lack of previous attention to certain issues also rendered the PCI vulnerable to intellectual fashions: when a handful of ranking feminists came to subscribe to Luz Irigaray's very distinctive ideas, these soon became official policy for the entire party. Though many feminists (and others) found the language and practice of Irigaray's supporters obscure or sectarian, the 'politics of sexual difference' actually became enshrined in the PDS's founding statute. Thus, as the party's fortunes turned downward and its organization stagnated and shrank in the 1980s, internal alignments crystallized around both classical and new issues. By the late 1980s, a mixture of fairly coherent ideologies coexisted with a variety of far more diffuse sensibilities. The ensemble was lively, but highly fragmented. It was primarily held together by the common tradition that was about to be eliminated.

Real world political divisions do not usually follow strictly philosophical and ideological fault lines. The 'centrist' tendency around Occhetto is radically different from the Berlinguer 'centre' that dominated the party for over a decade. Indeed, the *svolta* badly divided the *berlingueriani*: many were attached to the PCI's historical legacy and convinced that Occhetto's actions were ill-judged and improvised. They were, however, excited by the idea of the party in government, and recognized that a break with the past would hasten that eventuality. In the end, the *berlingueriani* split, with numerous older leaders joining an opposition comprised largely of people with far more radical temperaments than their own, whom they had fought for most of their political lives.

At the same time, while many leftists within the party joined the opposition to the *svolta*, others backed the secretary, at times enthusiastically, but more often with serious reservations.[7] Some of the most radical feminists had sided with Occhetto, for he and his collaborators had been open to their concerns. But they and others in the majority were extremely uncomfortable with the institutional implications of the *svolta*: the rush to change the party's name was seen as a naked bid for approval by the governing parties. They were also unhappy with the new Occhetto-migliorista alliance. Still, many leftists were firmly convinced that a break with the past was needed for a genuine restructuring of the Italian left, even though this meant furling the flag of Italian Communism. They were also determined to offset the influence of the reformists within the majority. Occhetto tried to keep a door open to the left, not only to avoid a split, but because many of his own supporters were distrustful of what they perceived as the right wing's infatuation with the Socialists and, worse yet, with Bettino Craxi.

Many on the PCI left were also taken aback at the composition of the opposition, which, as we have seen, threw together disgruntled *berlingueriani* along with the bulk of the historic left, usually identified with Pietro Ingrao. The Opposition also included some of the most radical elements of the PCI's old left wing such as the ex-Manifesto group (expelled in the late 1960s but readmitted a decade later) led by Lucio Magri and Luciana Castellina as well as the more militant ecologists and other new movement activists who were convinced that institutional mediations would suffocate the grass-roots initiatives they favoured. But the opposition counted as well on Armando Cossutta and his considerable rank-and-file following. The *cossuttiani* favoured social mobilization and an oppositional role for the party. They were also throwbacks to an old pro-Soviet line that had been marginal in the PCI since the 1970s, and that had been in an especially awkward position throughout Gorbachev's period of rule. They never obtained more than 3 or 4 percent support at party congresses, but everyone knew that their passive support was extensive, especially at the grass roots. Cossutta was an embarrassment, but the opposition – and, later, *Rifondazione*, needed his 'troops'.

Combinations of the many viewpoints within the party crystallized into the 'motions' that supported or opposed Occhetto at the 19th Congress of 1990 and then at the 20th Congress in 1991, which became the 1st Congress of the PDS. These far from compact groupings make up the factions that dominate the PDS today. Even after the departure of nostalgic old-style communists and the most socially radical elements for *Rifondazione*, the left that remains within the PDS remains a mixed bag. The largest left-wing faction has taken the name 'Democratic Communists', and is led by a number of elder statesmen, including, most prominently, Ingrao, the 77-year-old historic leader of the PCI left. But this group includes, in addition to classical leftists in the PCI tradition, ex-*berlingueriani* who represent a broad range of ideological positions but are fiercely anti-Socialist. The left suffered its most serious setback with the schism: although the bulk of the group remained in the PDS, many of Ingrao's followers departed. Not long afterward, the ex-Manifesto group also exited for *Rifondazione*. It had remained in the PDS with the goal of building bridges to *Rifondazione* and other elements outside the new party. When it became clear that the Democratic Communists would concentrate their efforts on the PDS's internal struggles, Magri and his comrades made their exit.

The centrist majority of the PDS is the most heterogeneous of all PDS groupings. Its major fault line, not surprisingly, has been the issue of under which circumstances it would entertain the idea of entering a national government. Occhetto, concerned about the total disrepute into which politics-as-usual had fallen, was hesitant after the general elections to commit the PCI to anything that might appear as a bailout of a weak government. In contrast, despite his well-known antipathy for Craxi and the PSI, Massimo D'Alema, considered number two in the PDS, was more inclined to negotiate terms with a weak governmental majority that needed all the support it could muster – until the League's spectacular success in limited local elections late in 1992. Since the PDS held up relatively well against the newest wave of protest votes for the Leagues, most centrists concluded that it would be suicidal for the party to associate itself with a discredited political class. (The PDS/PCI had also been implicated in the scandals, but on nothing like the scale of the DC or PSI.)

The reformists, whose influence increased within the majority after the foundation of the PDS, had the ground cut out from under them at every turn in 1992. Their consistent obsession with the Socialists cost them dearly during the general election campaign, as Craxi rebuffed their overtures. Craxi showed that he was less interested in a serious alliance with the reformists than with doing everything possible to make life difficult for the PDS. He was not above trying to woo unhappy *miglioristi* away from the PDS altogether. When a reformist broke with the PDS to become the 'independent' mayor of Milan with Socialist votes, Craxi's credibility sank to zero among his former suitors in the PDS, and Napolitano and his faction were humiliated. Following the elections, as the PSI was buried under an avalanche of indictments and scandals, and as the governing parties fell into increasing public disfavour, the PDS's right wing was further isolated internally. Some of its members even began to recognize the political stupidity of insisting on a governing role under prevailing conditions. By the middle of 1992, with most trends running against them, the miglioristi had been pushed out of the majority.

With the established parties increasingly discredited and political debate shifting toward a discussion of electoral reform, the centrists and reformists of the PDS went hunting for allies to create the sort of progressive bloc that would have wide enough appeal to stand a chance in a winner-take-all competition. The reformists, predictably, sought out the Socialists with whom they had always been closest. The centrists also made overtures to dissident members of the PSI, but Occhetto announced a far more ambitious goal: a complete recomposition of the left that included elements of the PSI, the smaller lay parties of the centre left, left-wing Catholics and Greens and other exponents of new social movements.

Rifondazione comunista

That Armando Cossutta and his coterie would refuse to join the PDS when it was created was a given. But until almost the eve of the PDS's foundation it was unclear how many former followers of Enrico Berlinguer, and above all how many of those from the Ingrao left would follow the *cossuttiani* and other dissidents out of the party. At the final reckoning, the schism was quite contained. Ingrao's unwillingness to rule out a split, and Occhetto's concessions, might well have wasted precious time. But the worst-case scenario was avoided. Moreover, in spite of historic trade-union firebrand Sergio Garavini's prominence in the opposition, and then in *Rifondazione*, the exit of union leaders from the PDS was minimal. (Garavini became the secretary of the new party, and Cossutta became its president.)

Rifondazione would thus not be a miniature, more militant version of the old PCI, as many dissidents had hoped. Instead, it would become more of a grab-bag of everyone on the left who was unhappy with the PDS, dominated at the base by ex-Communists. Alongside the *cossuttiano* rank-and-file were ex-Manifesto people, several *ingraiani* and *berlingueriani*, and a smattering of militant feminists, greens, and gays, who felt that the PDS would devote itself to institutional manoeuvring rather than aggressive social struggles. These were not the ex-comrades with whom Cossutta had most looked forward to working. Democrazia Proletaria, itself an eclectic ex-New Left group that combined workerism, feminism, and environmentalism with a long record of hostility toward the PCI (but also the Soviets), dissolved itself and joined *Rifondazione*, adding its 4 deputies to the 7 who initially broke with the PCI

Following the schism, a struggle over the legal right to the PCI's name and symbol did not help the image of either *Rifondazione* or the PDS. More than nostalgia was involved, for the use of a very well-known symbol on the official ballot might attract an avalanche of votes. (Such considerations had helped convince Occhetto to include a miniature version of the old PCI symbol in the PDS's new logo.) Similarly, since the PDS had inherited a large amount of valuable real estate from the PCI, huge sums of money were involved. The courts eventually gave the PDS title to the PCI's property, but allowed *Rifondazione* to contest the 1992 elections with a symbol very similar to that of the former PCI.

Rifondazione's real challenge to the PDS was in the support it attracted. Within a few weeks of the Rimini congress, the group claimed over 110,000 members.[8] D'Alema called these numbers wildly inflated, but, surveying the state of the PDS's left wing, Ingrao noted, 'We have to recognize that the majority of our base no longer exists.'[9] By the end of 1991, *Rifondazione* claimed 150,000 members in 600 local organizations, and PDS recruitment drives were encountering problems in areas (Turin, Rome, parts of Tuscany) where *Rifondazione* was strong.

Rifondazione's fortunes initially appeared mixed, with several embarrassing reminders of its own internal divisions. The abortive coup that nearly toppled Mikhail Gorbachev in August, 1991, led Cossutta – whose antipathy for Gorbachev was common knowledge – to remark that he was glad to see Gorbachev deposed. When the coup failed and Gorbachev effectively abolished the CPSU, Cossutta was put in a difficult situation. He acknowledged that the CPSU had been a 'disaster' for some time, but said it was nonetheless 'a tragic error' to dissolve it.[10] Cossutta's prominence hurt *Rifondazione*'s public image, but the large number of members he could speak for gave him vital leverage: nearly a third (5 of 17) of *Rifondazione*'s Coordinating Committee are *cossuttiani*.[11] More embarrassment followed the next year, when the *cossuttiani* joined with some of their ex-Communist comrades to block Luciana Castellina's promotion to the editorship of the party newspaper. This was a blatant settling of (very) old scores: some of the more sectarian elements of the PCI (and now *Rifondazione*) apparently could never forgive someone who had broken ranks with the old party and criticized it – and the Soviets – so severely from the left from the late 1960s onward. Garavini reacted angrily to this particularly vindictive form of factionalism, and hinted that he might be forced to resign if this was the way the new party intended to settle political differences. Thanks to his intervention and the equally angry reaction of others in *Rifondazione*, Castellina eventually did become editor.

Despite some initial missteps, *Rifondazione* had several things going for it in the early 1990s. The first was its limited, but compact, organizational base and reasonably strong presence throughout the country, save in historically 'white areas'. In the 1992 vote, *Rifondazione* was in the 7 – 9 percent range in areas of historic working class and/or Communist strength. This showing hardly makes it a major political power, but it also means that it cannot be dismissed out of hand. Even more decisive in *Rifondazione*'s relative success is the fact that this is clearly a party with clean hands that does not accept the status quo. The term 'protest vote' can

easily be misused, but it certainly applies to at least a part of the support
that *Rifondazione* has been able to attract. *Rifondazione*'s problems, in
some ways, are those of the rest of the left: it is host to a variety of views
that are in profound tension with one another; at least some of these are
totally contradictory. But as long as it remains a small opposition party,
these tensions can generally be avoided. Its fate under an electoral system
that forced alliances within broad ideological blocs would be far less
certain, which is one reason that *Rifondazione* is one of the strongest
supporters of proportional representation.

The Unravelling of the Italian Party System

Perhaps the only positive aspect to the sad spectacle of the PCI's hastening
its own demise was that in doing so, the PCI also speeded up the
disintegration of the Italian party system and whatever realignment of
political forces will eventually emerge.

Of all the capitalist democracies, the Italian party system has probably
been the most immobile throughout the postwar period. Despite profound
social transformations and some of the most tumultuous and extended
social mobilization anywhere in the West, Italians, in maddeningly predictable fashion, trooped to the polls and returned the same parties to
parliament – and to power. This immobilism was, with considerable truth,
attributed to the Cold War. With the largest Communist Party in the West
dominating the opposition and with the 'governing area' totally
hegemonized by Christian Democracy, the DC became the key player in
every one of Italy's postwar governments.

Cold War logic might explain why the party system polarized around the
PCI and the DC, but it doesn't tell us how the system could reproduce itself
so faithfully for so long. Between 1953 and 1987, Italian elections provided
lots of spectacle but only occasional drama. This happened because the
polarization took place within a context that combined a permissive system
of proportional representation, well-entrenched Catholic and 'red' subcul-
tures, and the lavish use of state resources for clientelistic and patronage
purposes. The most extreme illustration of predictability involves the party
that was the fulcrum of the system: in the five elections between 1963 and
1979, the DC's vote fluctuated less than a single percentage point (38.3 –
39.1).

The dramatic moments occurred when the DC was forced to broaden or
consolidate its coalition, which it always managed to do at others' expense.
In the 1960s, the DC brought the medium-sized (15 percent) Socialists
(PSI) into the ruling coalition and reactionary elements within the secret
services tried, but bungled, a *coup d'etat*. The Socialists lost much of their
credibility and a third of their votes over the next several years, as they
remained in a coalition that clearly had no intention of carrying out serious

reforms. In the mid-1970s, following a long period of social mobilization, the PCI obtained nearly 35 percent of the vote, and almost managed to force the Christian Democrats to end its exclusion from power. But the Communists were then hung up between government and opposition by DC manoeuvring and their own fecklessness. This brush with national power helped legitimize the PCI, but it also tarnished the party's reputation for having 'clean hands' and being unlike the other parties. It was also becoming painfully evident that the Communists did not really have a programme or broader project.

At the end of the 1970s, the Socialists once more came to the Christian Democrats' rescue, though they extracted a much higher price for their collaboration this time around. Thus, by the 1980s, the PCI was again isolated in the opposition: with its vote below 30 percent (and falling) and the PSI back in government, the PCI could no longer block DC-led coalitions. Italian politics in the 1980s was marked by a constant and public battle between the DC and PSI over the considerable political spoils the Italian system, with its massive state-run holdings, offers to those who hold national power. The distortions generated by this system are perhaps nowhere more evident than in the fact that the left opposition, through much of the 1980s, was one of the strongest proponents of privatization (strictly regulated, to be sure), while the DC tried to sabotage or delay serious reform proposals. The laws of the market are brutal, but they at least hold out the occasional hope of dynamism and growth; when the alternative is to turn a chunk of the economy into the fief of a party faction under the direction of political hacks, even leftists began to conclude that the market might be preferable.

The DC and PSI thus remained committed to a symbiotic, ugly, relationship. The extraordinary electoral stability of the past had given way to more volatility, but the marginalization of the Communists and the small size and fragmentation of the new political forces that did spring up appeared to make the DC-PSI tandem even more irreplaceable.

The system had shown signs of weakening in the 1980s, but it only began to unravel when Occhetto undertook the conversion of the PCI into the PDS at the end of the decade. We have seen how divisive and costly this transformation proved to be in political terms. Electorally, the price was also high: in the 1992 general elections, the PDS got just over 16 percent, and even when its vote is added to *Rifondazione comunista*'s 5.6 percent, the total is still more than 4 points less than what the PCI had obtained in 1987. If we recall that Proletarian Democracy (1.7 percent in 1987) dissolved itself to co-found *Rifondazione* with the dissidents from the former PCI, we see that the 'hammer and sickle left' lost nearly 6 percent between 1987 and 1992.

The PCI's abrupt exit from the scene obviously catalyzed the changes that had been underway for years. With the 'red menace' gone, the 1992 elections saw the DC fall below 30 percent for the first time. The governing coalition barely managed to scrape together half the seats in parliament. And, as we have seen, the Socialists were literally disintegrating by late 1992 following the failure of their broad strategy and their involvement in kickback scandals.

Who were the winners in this debacle? *Rifondazione* certainly exceeded all but the most optimistic expectations in garnering nearly 6 percent of the vote, though Proletarian Democracy's contribution to the total meant that not all these votes came from the former PCI. Another 6 percent of the vote went to several small lists with a progressive colouration (Greens, remnants of the Radical Party, etc.).

But the biggest winner of all unquestionably was the Northern League, or *Lega Nord*, which obtained nearly 10 percent of the vote nationwide by running against the Roman bureaucracy and the entire DC-led system. An amalgam of three regionalist movements under the hegemony of the Lombard League's charismatic leader Umberto Bossi, the *Lega Nord* was contesting national elections for the first time in this form.[12] The *Lega*'s support is very unevenly distributed, with its high points (over 25 percent) found in the Catholic North-East that used to be the DC's area of social as well as political dominance. But it surpassed 14 percent almost everywhere in the North, and has made an amazingly strong showing in some of the most advanced and urbanized areas of the country. It has gained most at the expense of the DC, but the League made inroads into the vote of *all* parties (which helps explain why the PDS plus *Rifondazione* combined still fell almost 5 percent short of the PCI's old vote).

Moreover, events following the elections showed that the League was anything but a flash in the pan and that the general elections had understated its potential. The kickback scandals broke during the electoral campaign, and as the evidence (and indictments) mounted against the PSI and DC over the course of the year, the *Lega* kept rising in opinion polls. In partial local elections held late in the year, the League became the largest party in important northern cities and their provinces (Mantua and Monza), scoring between 30 and 40 percent in these areas and making significant advances in areas where it had been much weaker just a few months earlier. By early 1993, local League governments with external PDS support were beginning to take shape in some northern centres.

The League's dramatic advances energized the debate over institutional reform that had been dragging on for years despite signs of increasing public outrage against the spoils system dominated by the traditional parties. In 1991, a referendum was held to limit to one the number of personal preference votes on ballots – the buying and trading of which were notorious among powerful economic (and criminal) power blocs within the ruling parties. The referendum took place against DC and PSI hostility: a maverick Christian Democrat led the petition campaign, while

Socialist secretary Bettino Craxi arrogantly announced that he would go to the seashore on voting day. He asked his followers to do likewise, for a turnout below 50 percent invalidates a referendum. Two-thirds of the voters ignored Craxi's advice, and 96 percent of them voted to limit preferences.

But DC and PSI foot-dragging continued into 1992, reflecting their desire to hang on to a system of power, as well as their disagreement over the shape political reforms should take. The Leagues' inroads into Catholic strongholds and grass-roots pressures had forced the DC to begin making cosmetic changes to its image, and to start to change its tune on reforms. As for the PSI, neither the general elections (where their losses were limited), nor the kickback scandals (denounced as a conspiracy against the party), nor increasing signs of rebellion within the party moved the Socialist leadership to act. Only when Craxi himself was officially accused on forty counts of corruption-related charges and PSI support began to dissolve later in the year did the Socialists begin to show signs of responding to the situation.

The (Unlamented) Collapse of Italian Socialism

Background: The Craxian strategy.

Even as scandals undermined the last vestiges of Socialist credibility, Bettino Craxi continued with an all-out defence of his party and the system of party power in Italy, as well as of his choice of alliance with the Christian Democrats.

Following the PSI's re-entry into government in 1979, it appeared for a time that Craxi would be able to hammer away at the DC all the while sharing power with it. His first stint as prime minister (1983 – 86) gave the Italian Republic its longest-lived government, despite DC efforts to sabotage him at every turn – 'snipers' within his own coalition put him in a minority 163 times during this period. More importantly, his tenure at the head of the government seemed to bear out claims that he and his party represented the country's dynamic, modernizing forces, whereas the DC (and the PCI, which he wanted to keep in the opposition until it was cut down to size) were vestiges of old-style politics, locked into obsolete structures and mind-sets.

The Craxian strategy paid off at the polls: in 1987, following his two terms as prime minister, the Socialists climbed to over 14 percent; when he took over the party in 1976, the PSI had just under 10 percent. Perhaps even more importantly, the Communists had gone from 34.4 to 26.6 percent in the same period. Craxi's Mitterrandian dream of eroding the PCI and having the Socialists dominate an eventual left alternative was a long way from being realized, but he had carried his party in the desired direction, projecting a decisive image while the PCI floundered.

But however much Mitterrand may have dropped the leftist baggage he carried into office, he built his legitimacy in clear opposition to the centre-right coalition that governed France until he displaced it. Craxi mouthed left-alternative platitudes while pushing the construction of an alliance with the PCI off into the future. He continued to criticize the Communists for not changing enough, for not being sincere democrats, and, above all, for not renouncing their past and calling themselves Socialists. Occhetto's *svolta* should have been cause for joy in the PSI, but Craxi's constant criticism of the process showed that he really was not interested in building bridges on his left.

After the DC finally wrenched the prime ministership out of his hands in 1987, Craxi kept his party in the government. As the 1980s wore on, the modernizing challenge he had launched at his larger coalition partner was muted as the two parties' relations increasingly degenerated into a public struggle for the enormous levers of patronage and clientelism available to those who govern Italy. Finding the centrist power-brokers of the DC more to his liking, Craxi made common cause with them, helping to isolate and ultimately defeat the leader of the Christian Democrats' left-wing faction at the end of the 1980s.

The 1980s: toward a symbiotic spoils system.

The squabble over the division of political spoils has been a hallmark of Italian politics, but it became more acute in the 1980s for a number of reasons. For one thing, the DC was weaker and therefore more vulnerable to political blackmail from coalition partners it desperately needed. As one Socialist leader put it, why should the DC control 80 percent of the institutions with only 30 percent of the vote?[14] Moreover, precisely because it lacked the subcultural roots and organizational traditions of the country's two largest parties (even though these were rapidly eroding), the PSI relied heavily on expensive mass media and communications investments to offset what it saw as the others' advantages. Perhaps most importantly of all, whatever broader political vision Craxi originally had possessed soon gave way to nothing more than a venal fight over political booty; in the process, his party dropped the last remnants of its 'competitive alliance' with the DC and became a full-fledged participant in what the Italians call *lottizzazione*, the apportionment of patronage according to political weight, but with the express purpose of obtaining for the PSI far more than 15 percent of the levers of power.

By the 1992 elections, the extent to which the Socialists had become mired in the spoils system was evident in the regional distribution of their vote. This party, born in the industrial heartland of the North and until recently still able to boast considerable support in the Milanese working class, now was weakest in the North, where the Leagues cut deeply into its (and the DC's) voters. It was strongest by far in the patronage-riddled South, where it had become the second largest party, and where its control of resources had obviously paid off. Predictably, its organizational base shifted southward as well, as local party bosses grossly inflated their membership rolls to increase their weight at party congresses. It is telling that the PSI effectively abandoned its claim to represent Italy's rising strata: Craxi's idea of modernization now seemed to be limited to changing Italy into a presidential regime – with himself as the choice for president. His ambitions changed from wanting to be the Italian Mitterrand to seeing himself as the Italian de Gaulle.

None of these developments seemed to bother those in the leadership around Craxi. Though their commitment to change might be cynical and self-serving, the Christian Democrats at least came out of the 1992 elections with a sense that the ruling parties could not arrogantly continue past practices while repeating that they were the solution to Italy's problems; Craxi did just that. Of course, for the DC, the sting of the Leagues was particularly strong (they lost 5 percent compared to the PSI's 1 percent), but there is more to it than that: the DC lost most heavily to the Leagues in many of its historical Catholic strongholds, and hence could not avoid drawing the conclusion that it was in deep trouble. As a party that had lost any semblance of its mass character years before, the PSI no longer had such antennae.

Only repeated scandals, aggravated by Craxi's insistence that the judicial inquiries were a plot against the PSI, finally galvanized internal dissent and made it go public. By the middle of 1992, some of those who had always felt that the Socialists should have looked to the left for political allies, to the PCI and, above all, to the new PDS, began to speak out openly against his leadership. One of the fiercest early critics was Ottaviano Del Turco, leader of the Socialist faction in the largest union confederation, the CGIL (his relatively autonomous power-base enabled him to speak out with impunity). As the scandals mounted, and the PSI began to crumble in the North and even suffer reversals in the South, a sense of political survival finally drove some of Craxi's erstwhile collaborators to turn against him. But even after being apprised of the charges pending against him, Craxi continued to hold onto his post and promise a fight to save his good name.

These acts made his (by now inevitable) resignation far more drawn-out and lacerating than it should have been, with incalculable, and probably irreversible, damage to his party. The question on many people's minds was how much would be salvageable of the PSI after 15 years of Craxi, during which the party had been irrevocably altered. If a new leadership instituted a thorough purge of corrupt elements, would anything other than a few healthy shreds be left? And how many leaders would be able to carry out a renovation free of the taint of corruption and collusion, since for so many years, the only way to rise in the party had been to show loyalty to its maximum leader?

'Transverse Alliances' and the Politics of Honesty and Electoral Reform
Following the 1992 elections, the Italian Parliament established a Commission for Institutional Reform to review a system that, by common agreement, needs a serious overhaul. Given the malfunctioning of Italian institutions and increasing invocations of a Second Republic, the degree to which serious political discussion and struggle has focused on the electoral system is striking.

It is striking, but it is not surprising, for three reasons. The first of these is that an extremely large and heterogeneous array of political forces that has little else in common does agree about the need to break the grip of *partitocrazia*, or 'partyocracy', the suffocating presence of the parties throughout society and the economy. The electoral system is seen as a direct and rapid way to weaken party bureaucrats and power brokers. The second reason is that, with the decline of the historically dominant governing and opposition parties,[15] the party system has fragmented to a point where few people continue to defend PR for its ability to reflect diversity. PR was rightly seen as a guarantee against marginalization by the left during the height of the cold war,[16] and it permitted the preservation of disparate voices as well as the rise of numerous new forces. But even many former supporters of PR acknowledge that times have changed, and they are appalled at the proliferation of very small lists. Only 3 of the 16 lists that won seats in the Chamber of Deputies in 1992 gained over 10 percent of the vote, and 10 lists were below 5 percent. The third reason, which was decisive in making the DC (and the PDS) abandon their preference for some modification of PR and embrace the principle of a single-member plurality system, is the astonishingly rapid rise of the Leagues, reflecting Italians' disgust with the existing state of affairs. As long as there were no real threats to its dominance, the DC could wince at its losses and continue as always; when the Leagues started breathing down its neck in the 1992 general elections, and when it was actually outpolled later that year, the DC was forced to act. Anything less than a radical break with the past is now framed as perpetuating the old, rotten, system.

As has been the case in Italy for more than a decade, those leading the movement for reforms have generally come from the fringes of the major parties, or from outside them altogether. They have also followed tradition by using referenda as a means of public agitation and as a way to force action on a recalcitrant legislature.[17] But in contrast to previous occasions, this time the movement has set loose forces that directly threaten the established parties, and above all the DC. A maverick, middle-of-the-road Christian Democrat, Mario Segni, was the animator of the referendum-based assault that is far from over. After the 1992 elections, he created a 'reform movement' for honest government that consciously evokes the Popular Party of Luigi Sturzo, which was the original forerunner to the DC. Nervous Church and DC officials began to worry openly that Segni might be establishing a new moderate bloc.

The moderates' success was such that at least two similar 'alliances' have begun to take shape on the left; each cuts across existing political divisions to enlist the support of leaders and members from a mix of parties. And this comes in the wake of an earlier 'transverse' phenomenon: the 'Network' List led by the ex-Christian Democrat former mayor of Palermo, Leoluca Orlando, whose strong anti-mafia stance brought him popularity (and eventually drove him from the ruling party). The Network obtained 2 percent nationwide, and was strongest in the South, particularly Sicily. But the Network's second most prominent figure is Diego Novelli, the former Communist mayor of Turin, who opposed the end of the PCI and refused to join either the PDS or *Rifondazione comunista*. Instead, he cast his lot with Orlando and helped broaden the anti-mafia appeal into a more generic call for government by honest people. Although weak in most of the North, the Network captured nearly 5 percent of the vote in Turin in 1992, and it rose much higher in opinion polls following the kickback scandals.

These are very recent events, and the established parties do not appear inclined to fade from the scene without a fight, so it is obviously far too early to produce a death certificate for the Italian party system. Italian parties have always demonstrated remarkable resilience, and the DC, in particular, has already rushed to embrace reforms it could no longer avoid. Still, things will never be the same again, for the volatility and fragmentation that have appeared in the past few years are without precedent in postwar Italian history. To use the fashionable social-scientific terms, there is no question that a major decomposition and dealignment of the party system is underway. To date, however, there are far more 'morbid symptoms' in evidence than there are clear signs of what a fundamental *re*composition or *re*alignment would look like if it occurred.

The most tragic morbid symptom is the direct aftermath of the PCI's transformation into the PDS. These events show that analyses can be correct, but real organizations exist under real conditions and are bounded by real possibilities. For all of the criticisms that can be made of his impetuous and bumbling leadership style, in reality Occhetto faced a hopeless task. He felt he had to break with the past, but the conditions simply did not exist for a new departure. New political movements and organizations do not automatically spring into life as old ones wear out. With no broad social movements to feed a new political force, the transformation Occhetto hoped to carry out merely euthanized the old party and then revealed that the leadership of the new party really did not have a very clear idea of what it wanted.

Institutional arrangements are certainly important, but the rush to embrace institutional solutions such as the reform of the electoral system surely has to qualify as another morbid symptom. It is ironic – and it should give one pause – that in Britain the stampede appears to be in the opposite direction, toward PR.[18] In the Italian case, there is naivete in the rush to embrace the single-member district, and especially in the belief that voting for individual candidates will force them to be responsible to the electorate while undercutting the role of party machines, for this is the argument used most frequently by supporters of the first-past-the-post system.

Moreover, while the single-member system (especially the two-ballot, runoff variant used in France) once appeared to be a promising way to force the left to unite against a moderate bloc dominated by the DC, recent developments have rendered this scenario problematic, not to say obsolete. The collapse of the Socialists and the meteoric rise of the Leagues complicates whatever neat left-right, government-opposition tendencies may have existed in the Italian party system. Recent events have created potentially troubling scenarios involving *three* major political groupings. And as anyone familiar with single-member plurality ballots knows, three-way divisions are not where such systems show themselves to best advantage. Would the PDS and DC band together to block the Leagues across the North, where the Leagues could well be the largest single party? On the other hand, if Bossi continues to sound more like a populist and less like an anti-southern racist, would progressive forces consider joining with him in a broad front to force the DC into the opposition? This is already taking place in some local governments in the North, to the dismay of those (including many of the left of the PDS and in *Rifondazione comunista*) who consider Bossi to be a demagogue at best and a racist at worst. The uncertainty is so great, and the protagonists so numerous, that it is unlikely that a 'pure' single-member system will emerge out of what is sure to be a tortuous series of compromises.

Discussions of this nature are highly speculative, and the real point is that they focus on institutional engineering and political alignments rather than the common programmes or projects around which political forces, new or old, might coalesce. This is lamentable, but it is, as they used to say, no accident. Despite all of the changes that have begun to take place on the Italian left, truly substantive discussions of what the left ought to stand for and how, specifically, it will change conditions for the better have been in short supply. As the rise of the Leagues shows, once the old rules break down, there are many ways to attack the status quo. It will be sad, and possibly tragic, if, having helped create a fluid and potentially promising situation, the left proves unable to help find a way out of it.

NOTES

1. The newness of the phenomenon has led to understandable confusion even in naming it. Several different regionalistic organizations formed in the 1980s. The most successful of these was the Lombard League, but similar organizations were created in Piedmont and the Veneto. Each was known by its title, e.g. Lega Lombarda, Liga Veneta, and collectively they were known as 'the Leagues'. In 1992, they formed a single list under the new title of Lega Nord, or Northern League. It has thus become common to refer to them in both the singular and plural, and I will follow this convention throughout.

2. For this period, see: Grant Amyot, 'The Italian Road to Reformism: The PCI and Occhetto's New Course', in R. Catanzaro and R.Y. Nanetti, eds., *Italian Politics: A Review, Vol. 4* (London: Pinter, 1989); Martin J Bull, 'La svolta di Occhetto e la crisi del Pci', in Catanzaro and Filippo Sabetti, eds., *Politica in Italia Edizione 90* (Bologna: Il Mulino, 1990); Frank Belloni, 'Il Partito comunista italiano in bilico tra la dissoluzione e l'ignoto', in Fausto Anderlini and Robert Leonardi, eds., *Politica in Italia Edizione 91* (Bologna: Il Mulino, 1991); Gianfranco Pasquino, 'Programmatic Renewal and Much More: From the PCI to the PDS', Johns Hopkins Bologna Center Occasional Paper No. 66 (June, 1991); and S. Hellman, 'The Difficult Birth of the Democratic Party of the Left', in S. Hellman and G. Pasquino, eds., *Italian Politics: A Review, Vol. 7* (London: Pinter, 1992).

3. These issues are discussed at length in S. Hellman, *Italian Communism in Transition: The Rise and Fall of the Historic Compromise in Turin, 1975 – 80* (N.Y.: Oxford Univ. Press, 1988).

4. For discussions of left-right differences and battles in the PCI, see G. Grant Amyot, *The Italian Communist Party: The Crisis of the Popular Front Strategy* (London: Croom Helm, 1980), and S. Hellman, 'Italian Communist Party Strategy and the Problem of Revolution in the West', in Shlomo Avineri, ed., *Varieties of Marxism* (The Hague: Martinus Nijhoff, 1977), pp. 195 – 225.

5. The PSDI was formed in the late 1940s following a split with the PSI, which was perceived as too close to the Communists. It never had a significant presence in the working class and became a consistent junior partner in DC-dominated coalitions throughout the postwar period. Its electoral support oscillated between 3 and 6 percent.

6. In the crucial decade 1968 – 1977, membership increased from 1.5 to 1.8 million, with an average of roughly 100,000 new members each year. As these figures suggest, the turnover was extreme in this period, raising many problems, but underscoring the rejuvenation that took place. By the end of the 1970s, more than half of all Italian Communists had joined the PCI within the past ten years.

7. Several of them jokingly called themselves *malpancisti*, from the term *mal di pancia*, which means 'bellyache'.

8. *Panorama*, 7 Apr. 1991, p. 53; *La Repubblica*, 22 March 1991, p. 4.

9. D'Alema is quoted in *l'Unità*, 20 March 1991, p. 5. For Ingrao's quote see *La Repubblica*, 22 March 1991, p. 4.

10. *La Repubblica*, 27 August 1991, p. 14.

11. The others were 10 *ingraiani* and 2 former members of the Pdup, which was linked to the Manifesto: *La Repubblica* 5/6 May 1991, p. 17.

12. See note 1. Bossi had previously been elected in the Lombard League to the Senate, where he was its only representative.

13. The turnout figure is high for a referendum. For details, see Patrick McCarthy, 'The Referendum of 9 June', in S. Hellman and G. Pasquino, eds., *Italian Politics: A Review, Volume 7* (London: Pinter Publishers, 1992), pp. 11 – 28.

14. Quoted in Economist Intelligence Unit, *Italy: A Country Report*, No. 3, 1988, p. 9.

15. A classic measure of electoral volatility and dealignment, the combined vote of the top two parties since the high point in 1976 has declined precipitously: 73.1 (1976); 68.7 (1979); 62.8 (1983); 60.9 (1987); 45.8 (1992).

16. One of Italy's bitterest political battles took place in 1953 over an electoral law that would have given a minimum of two-thirds of the seats in parliament to any coalition obtaining a majority of popular votes. Dubbed 'The Swindle Law', this rule failed to go into effect in the 1953 elections by a few thousand votes and was then withdrawn.

17. Despite the notoriety of the referenda to abolish divorce (1974) and abortion (1981), most of Italy's referenda have been organized by progressive forces to try to repeal or amend laws regulating wage escalators, judges' liability, nuclear energy, hunting, pesticides, life sentences, law-and-order legislation, etc. A half-million valid signatures can force a referendum unless the courts rule it out of order, and drives to collect the signatures often become highly effective single-issue campaigns. These are *abrogative* referenda to abolish specified laws, and their threat is often sufficient to provoke parliamentary action. If parliament significantly changes or replaces the law in question, as has occurred five times in the past, the referendum is avoided.
18. For a good sense of the debate, see Peter Mair, 'The Question of Electoral Reform', and Michael Dummett, 'Toward a More Representative Voting System: The Plant Report', both in *New Left Review* 194 (July – August, 1992): 75 – 97; 98 – 113.

WHY DID THE SWEDISH MODEL FAIL?

Rudolf Meidner

'From Marx to Market' is not only the title of a well-known book[1] or a play on words: the slogan can also be used as a telegraphed history of the Swedish labour movement.

The late 19th century pioneers of the movement were strongly influenced by German marxists and had as a concrete goal the transfer of the means of production into collective ownership. Their modern followers have abandoned – as have most socialists in Western democracies – the issue of ownership as the essence of socialism. The market economy is now generally accepted as the arena for the exchange of privately produced goods and services – albeit with restrictions and modifications in the interest of a fair distribution of wealth.

A Brief History of Swedish Social Democracy[2]

Of course, such a slogan cannot do justice to the Swedish labour movement's 'long march' through history and its many intermediary way stations. True, the first Swedish social democrats were marxists and their successors one hundred years later have a noticeable weakness for the market. But the marxist elements of the social democratic ideology were eliminated at an early stage and 'nationalization' was forsaken by the first social democratic government in the 1920s. It disappeared from the agenda when the government appointed a commission to investigate the topic of nationalization – an infallible method for burying ideas once and for all.

Instead, the Swedish social democrats started to build up a welfare society within the framework of capitalism, leaving the owners of capital to take care of producing goods but assigning to the state the responsibility for a fair distribution of the production results. Nationalization was replaced by 'functional socialism' which means that socializing some of the functions of ownership is preferred to undertaking wholesale socialization. Class hegemony gave way to the classless society, labelled as 'the people's home', a famous expression coined by the popular Swedish Prime Minister

211

P.A. Hansson in 1928, according to which all Swedes should feel and be treated as members of a family:

> In the good home equality, consideration, co-operation and helpfulness prevail. Applied to the great people's and citizen's home this would mean the breaking down of all the social and economic barriers that now divide citizens into the privileged and the unfortunate, into rulers and subjects, into rich and poor, the glutted and the destitute, the plunderers and the plundered[3].

This speech symbolized, as a Canadian observer puts it, 'the breakthrough of Swedish reformism', in so far as the idea of a people's home implied the conviction that socialism could be achieved through welfare reforms[4].

The scene changed for a short period in the 1940s, not as a result of changing ideologies but due to the need to adjust the Swedish economy to war-time conditions. Sweden, formally neutral but surrounded by threatening German armies, had to introduce regulations, rationing, price and investment controls: in short, a planned war economy. The experiences of this period – which eliminated the high pre-war unemployment – influenced the thinking of the authors of the 1944 Post-War Programme which was to be the blue-print for the forthcoming social democratic government[5]. The war economy had demonstrated the possibility of achieving the maximal use of all productive resources (albeit to some extent for unproductive purposes). Why, leading figures of the party asked, should state intervention not be used as a tool of achieving full employment also in peace time, especially as most economists foresaw heavy unemployment in the transitional period after the war.

The Post-War Programme indicated the high water mark of state interventionism in the modern history of Swedish social democracy. It advocated nationalization of basic industries and financial institutions, it recommended central planning of investment and assigned to the government a leading role in restructuring the country's industry. Most importantly, the programme allotted to the state the responsibility for achieving and maintaining full employment. Leading social democrats, among them Gunnar Myrdal, talked about the 'harvest time' of Swedish Socialism. Instead it turned out to be the last time that leading members of the party used the term 'socialism'.

Nor were socialism, state interventionism or planning to be the characteristics of labour's actual post-war policy. Sweden entered the post-war period with full production capacity and could benefit from the immense demand for commodities in a ruined Europe. As an exporter of scarce investment goods and raw materials Sweden benefited from the European restoration process. The Swedish engineering and forestry industries boomed, and unemployment problems did not appear. The opposite and unexpected occurred: a shortage of labour and with it, the threat of inflation.

The Swedish economy's performance in these years, with high growth rates, a well-balanced foreign trade and full employment, deprived the radical proposals of the Post-War Programme of much of their topicality. Why should industries be nationalized if the private owners could run them efficiently and with high profitability? Why should the government intervene in the economy if the market forces could resolve the structural problems and successfully guarantee full employment? Why should the government build up a planning machinery for an economy which was working well without planning? And finally: was it worthwhile to take on an ideological fight with the bourgeois opposition which campaigned vehemently against all kinds of planning?

Most of the socialist ideas of the Programme faded away as the market delivered the achievements which the socialists had aimed at: economic growth, which could be used for major social reforms, rising incomes, high employment. Many socialists came to the conclusion that social demo-cratic ideology had come to and end[6]. A de-radicalized labour movement took the lead in developing Sweden into a welfare society which aroused admiration and envy all over the world.

The Full Employment/Inflation Dilemma

There were, however, shadows in the rosy picture of the 'golden years' of post-war Sweden. It became obvious immediately after the war that shortage of labour – at that time a new experience for politicians and labour – caused wage increases exceeding productivity gains and, conse-quently, cost – push inflation. The government reacted by introducing various kinds of incomes policy measures, among them a government-inspired wage-freeze in 1949/50 which turned out to be a total failure. These experiences indicated that full employment and price stability were conflicting goals, and that the government had to make a political choice instead of forcing the responsibility for price stability upon the unions.

It was only natural that a number of economists employed by the LO, the dominant confederation of blue collar workers, tried to find a solution to this dilemma which had become a serious threat to the union movement. Full employment is an imperative condition of union strength. Yet wage restrictions in periods of high profitability when firms can pay higher wages cause distrust amongst the rank and file towards the union leadership. The trade-off between full employment and price stability was the point of departure for the development of a union proposal for a stabilization model which, in its final shape, became the central part of 'The Swedish Model' as a whole[7].

The proposal can be seen as a form of modified Keynesianism. Total demand, exercised through fiscal and monetary measures, should be high – but not high enough to ensure the full use of all productive resources and all skills in each branch and in each region. Beveridge's definition of full employment as the situation where there are permanently more jobs than those to fill them was, we LO economists argued, at the same time a good definition of inflation.

To avoid inflation, total demand must fall below the level where practically all labour can be absorbed. 'Islands of unemployment' should be eliminated, not by increasing general demand but by selected and targeted labour market policy measures such as retraining, mobility – promoting allowances, wage subsidies for disabled workers and public work for older and immobile labour. From the very beginning, active labour market policy was a central component of the non-inflationary full employment proposal which was presented and intensively debated at the 1951 LO Convention[8].

We were aware of the risk that powerful unions which are guaranteed full employment are strong enough to jeopardize the stabilization policy through aggressive wage claims. However, we rejected the idea that unions should be disciplined by unemployment. Our preference was for collective self-discipline imposed by the unions' own wage policy. This was conceived within the framework of an ideology based on the notion of solidarity, promoting a wage structure which reflected the kind of work and skill rather than the profitability of the firm.

It was obvious that union rivalry and militancy could be mitigated by a consensus between the affiliated unions on common goals and methods of wage policy. In the mid-50s the Employers Confederation (SAF) invited the LO to participate in central wage negotiations which came to characterize Swedish industrial relations over the following two decades. Many observers in and outside Sweden have considered the centralized Swedish bargaining system as the essential part of the Swedish Model. In my view, the model was originally aimed at solving the full employment/inflation dilemma, with active labour market policy and the wage policy of solidarity as complementing ingredients. The fact that Swedish wage negotiations came to be carried out centrally certainly facilitated the government's stabilization endeavours. Yet such centralization should mainly be seen as a consequence of the 1938 Saltsjöbaden agreement between labour and capital. Through this agreement the two parties laid down rules for their mutual relations, but they also demonstrated their autonomy vis-a-vis the government[9].

The stabilization dilemma is important because full employment, the goal with the highest priority for labour, must be reconciled with the need of price stability. In the words of Gunnar Myrdal, inflation is a deadly threat to socialism; and Gösta Rehn, one of the architects of the LO model, coined the slogan that socialists must 'hate inflation'. The development of the Swedish economy in the 1970s and 1980s has verified these warnings: the failure of the stabilization policy has been a decisive reason for the

shrinking popular support for the social democrats, for the enfeeblement
of the unions and for the continuous decay of the Swedish Model as a
whole.

Is Equality Counter-Productive?

Full employment is only one pillar of the Swedish Model, the second one
being equality. If Swedish socialists are fanatical about full employment,
they are also passionate about equality. The two wings of the Swedish
labour movement aimed to achieve equality by means of different but
complementary methods. The party-in-government was seen as responsible for developing a universal welfare system, based on generous transfer
payments and a comprehensive public sector which offered almost free,
i.e. tax-financed social services. An equalizing wage policy, aiming at a
solidaristic wage structure, was the unions' main objective.

As has already been mentioned, the policy for full employment had its
limits in the inherent risk of inflation. That is why full employment had to
be achieved by non-inflationary methods. There were analogous restrictions for universal welfare and for the wage policy of solidarity. The
welfare system must not run into conflicts with efficiency. Solidaristic wage
policy, which eliminates the use of wage differentials as incentives for
labour mobility, implies the risk of labour market rigidity. These potential
conflicts were not unforeseen by the proponents of the welfare state, nor by
the supporters of the wage policy of solidarity. In fact, remedies for solving
possible conflicts were incorporated in the model at an early state.

There is, in fact, no clear evidence that the welfare state is necessarily
counter-productive in terms of economic efficiency. Comparative studies
of countries with different levels of public expenditures for non-military
purposes do not confirm the hypothesis that highly developed welfare
states show lower growth rates than other countries. Sweden, which had a
record level of public expenditures and correspondingly high taxes did not
lag behind most other welfare states in Western Europe for the whole 1960
- 1990 period[10]. The high rate of absenteeism in Sweden is frequently
interpreted as abuse of the generous health insurance system but at a closer
look it can partly be explained by the fact that groups prone to absenteeism
(women, handicapped persons), who normally are not fully integrated in
the labour force in other countries, make up a substantial part of the
Swedish labour force. Nor can it be proved that the generous rules for early
retirement in Sweden have resulted in an abuse of the system: the share of
early retirees in Sweden is, in fact, lower than in most other European
countries with corresponding provisions.

The argument that universal welfare can negatively influence productivity and growth can also be questioned from another angle. High public
expenditures may look like a heavy burden for the tax-payers, but what is

frequently overlooked is the fact that a considerable part of public expenditures are investments in human capital and consequently highly productive. Child and mother care is everybody's right and prevents illness: a one year parental leave (longer than in any other country in Western Europe) gives the mother a period of privacy and respite (and can – though that is rare – also be used by the father); rehabilitation of persons with industrial injuries facilitates reintegration into the labour market. These active measures are substantial and economically useful elements of Swedish welfare policy.

There is, however, an area of the public sector where criticism can be justified. Health care, the care of children and the aged, education on all levels and social welfare are in Sweden carried out by public authorities. In the 1960s and 1970s public service, particularly health care, expanded immensely. Between 1960 – 1980 the number of public employees almost tripled and account now for one third of the Swedish labour force – an international record. The explosive expansion of the public sector has resulted in the formation of large organizations in metropolitan areas, in some cases with thousands of employees in single units. Economies of scale, with analogies from the private sector, were applied in building hospitals, schools and homes for the aged, frequently with bureaucracy and inefficiency as consequences.

In recent years national and local governments have made large efforts to improving efficiency in the public sector, for instance through the introduction of market mimicking arrangements in the delivery of public health and education[11]. The non-socialist parties seek a solution in the privatization of public services – a proposal which the social democrats vigorously rejected.

The wage policy of solidarity[12]

Whereas welfare has been the responsibility of public authorities, a second way to achieve equality was through the wage policy of solidarity itself. Solidaristic (originally called socialist) wage policy, which constitutes the ideological heart of the Swedish union movement, means two things. First, equal work should be equally paid, regardless of the profitability of the firm, the size or location of the workplace. What matters is the kind and nature of work, and the skills which are needed to perform it. The second aim of the policy is the equalizing of wage differentials, but not their total elimination. Different wages should be paid for different kinds of work. It is obvious that both components of the solidarity wage policy presuppose accurate job descriptions and norms of job evaluation.

Critics of the wage policy of solidarity have argued than an equalized wage structure impedes labour mobility. A number of studies have shown that wage differentials must be substantial to play the role of incentives in the labour market. Yet, in a full employment economy the use of such differentials as instruments of labour allocation would be irrational and expensive. The risk of inflationary wage spirals would be high. There is a structural effect of the solidaristic wage policy on labour mobility which may be more important than the alleged effects of large wage differentials. The equalizing of the wage structure squeezes out unprofitable firms unable to pay market wages. Redundant labour must be absorbed by more profitable firms or assisted by active labour market policy measures such as training, retraining, rehabilitation, etc. It is easy to recognize the close interconnection between wage policy and labour market policy in the model or, expressed in more blunt language, between union and government policies.

A more serious problem stems from the fact that wage restraint exercised by well-paid groups in profitable firms leaves unused capacity to pay wages in the hands of the capital owners. The union proposal to transfer parts of this kind of 'forfeited' wage increases into collective wage-earner funds was an attempt to solve the dilemma illustrated by the graph below in which the firms are ranked according to their profitability (and ability to pay wages). Firms unable to pay the 'normal' wage (set in the central negotiations) have to rationalize their production or, if they have exhausted that potential, will be squeezed out from the market – in both cases with labour redundancy as a consequence. It is then the responsibility of the labour market policy to find new jobs for the redundant labour.

The right part of the graph illustrates the fact that profitable firms have the potential to pay higher wages than those claimed by the unions. The remedy proposed by the LO in the wage-earner funds was to skim the excess profits and transfer them from the capital owners into the collective ownership of the employees[13]. The capitalists understandably disliked this idea. Nevertheless, it was a logical part of the Swedish model.

The Swedish Model Defined

Let me summarize what has been said about the different goals, restrictions and methods of the social democratic economic and social policy, and show how they form parts of a coherent and consistent model. The values of highest priority are full employment and equality. Both come into conflict with other goals, notably price stability and efficiency. The conflict between full employment and price stability can be solved by a policy which combines restrictive general demand management and selective labour market policy. Equality pursued by a system of universal welfare, by a large public sector and by a wage policy of solidarity has to be

Consequences of wage policy of solidarity for firms with different ability to pay wages.

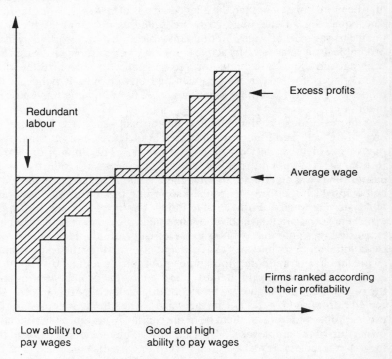

compatible with the goals of efficiency and economic growth. The table below illustrates the main components of the model.

It is obvious that the model sustains those elements of socialist ideology which point beyond the limits of a capitalist market economy. Experience has taught us that the free market forces guarantee neither full employment nor equality. To give the highest priority to these goals means challenging the principles of the capitalist system which is based on the profitability of privately owned capital.

The formation of a large public sector as the guarantor of the universal welfare implies that a substantial part of the economy is withdrawn from market rules and that social needs are separated from people's purchasing power. The wage policy of solidarity separates wages from profitability and cushions the market. The union proposal for wage-earner funds has rightly been considered as a union attempt to share the fruits of capital accumulation with the capital owners.

Schematic sketch of the Swedish Model

Objectives	Full employment	Equality
Restrictions	Price stability	Efficiency
Instruments	Combination of restrictive general measures and selective labour market policy	Universal welfare Large public sector Wage policy of solidarity Wage-earner funds

The Swedish model, formulated in the version we have presented here, is reformist in the sense that private ownership and free markets are accepted to a large extent, but it is socialist in so far as fundamental values of the labour movement are built into it. The model is based on a firm socialist ideology but recommends at the same time practical methods to attain the goals. The model combines visions and pragmatism of the traditional Swedish brand. It comes close to what Ernst Wigforss, a leading ideologist of the Swedish labour movement, called 'provisional utopias'.

The achievements

Now, what are the achievements of the Swedish Model or, to put it less ambitiously, of the social democratic governments after the war? Full employment was maintained practically for the whole period. At the same time, the labour force participation rate rose to a peak European level, primarily because of the almost total integration of women into the labour market. By drawing on the whole population in the active ages, the input of labour is higher in Sweden than in any other European country – in spite of longer vacations and other leaves of absence.

The universal welfare system developed into a network which meets all social needs – from the cradle to the grave. In the 1980s public expenditures reached a peak of 55 per cent of GDP and had to be financed by Western Europe's highest taxes. The public sector expanded immensely to employ one third of the labour force.

The wage policy of solidarity contributed to the compression of wage differentials[14]. The gap between male and female wages narrowed considerably, as a result of special clauses in the centrally negotiated contracts which favoured low paid workers. At the beginning of the 80s, Sweden showed the most egalitarian wage structure amongst Western countries. This was achieved through a labour market policy which relieved the unions of the responsibilities for employment problems caused by wage claims for the low-paid in declining firms and branches. Social democratic governments also accommodated the unions in another way: excess profits – which make wage restraint in profitable firms hazardous for the local unions – have been at least partly neutralized by payments into different funds, (among them the union-administered wage-earner funds – albeit in a rather symbolic shape, as we shall see).

No wonder that the Swedish Model was seen as a model for the left in Europe which was put on the defensive by neo-liberalism and by the collapse of the centrally planned economies in Eastern Europe. The Swedish system, build on the co-operation between strong labour and employer organizations and the government, with an economy that had managed to reconcile market principles with socialist values such as full employment, equality and solidarity, was hailed as the prototype of a 'Third-Way' society. The decline and disintegration of the Swedish Model is thus a matter of concern not only for the Swedish labour movement, but for the left as a whole. How can it be explained?

We can rule out the notion that the electoral defeats of the social democratic party in 1976 and again in 1991 are the cause of the Swedish model's decline. In the 1970s the labour movement was still so dominant that the non-socialist coalition government 1976 – 1982 was unable to alter the traditional welfare policy in a substantial way. Full employment was accepted as a central goal and the welfare system remained intact. When the social democratic government was replaced by a new bourgeois coalition in 1991, the model was already in a process of erosion and decay. The political shift can be seen as a formal confirmation of an ongoing process rather than its cause. The weak points of the model as it was put into practice, can be traced back to the early 1970s.

Weak points of the economic policy

The essence of the Swedish Model, as outlined in the report to the 1951 LO Convention, was the notion that full employment and economic stability could be made compatible. We argued that anti-inflationary full employment policy had to be based on two pillars: a restrictive general economic policy which does not guarantee full employment, and selective labour market policy measures which absorb redundant labour.

Swedish governments have frequently neglected the first part of the recommendation and tolerated periods of excess demand in the product and labour markets. The destabilizing effects of this inflation-prone policy were obvious already in the 1970s but became fatal in the 1980s: profits skyrocketed, speculation pushed property values to unsustainable heights, growth came to a stand-still and Swedish competitiveness faltered.

It is inappropriate to blame the unions for reacting aggressively in a tight labour market nor can the market forces be faulted for acting according to market principles in a situation of excess profits and high liquidity. Profit-maximization is the maxim of the free market and the capitalists did only what the textbooks prescribe. To ensure economic stability and to combat inflation is the responsibility of the national government – but the government had neither the courage nor the strength to play this role. Gunnar Myrdal's warnings came true: inflation mercilessly undermined the basis of the Swedish Model.

The first victim of the government's inability to control inflation was full employment. To be sure, unemployment was kept low in the booming 1980s, a remarkable success for Sweden, compared with mass unemployment in most Western European countries. Yet early in 1991 the threat of continuous inflation induced the social democratic government to drop full employment as the primary goal in favour of price stability. This made it easier for the non-socialist government elected later that year to tolerate an unemployment level which, one year after its inauguration, increased to Western European levels.

The conflict between equality and efficiency is not as sharp as the full employment/inflation dilemma. Not even critics of the universal welfare system allege that the large public sector is responsible for the Swedish economy's low rate of productivity growth. The public sector is attacked on ideological grounds by conservative groups who favour privatization. But even in the social democratic party one hears an appeal for greater efficiency which is often euphemistic language for poorer service.

The system of public transfer payments is under attack. Recently the bourgeois government and the social democrats, now the leading opposition party, have concluded an agreement aimed at shifting responsibility for sick pay and work injury insurance system from the public sector to the unions and employers' organizations – a move from universal welfare to a system which was introduced by Bismarck a century ago. If increasing unemployment can be seen as an adjustment to Western European conditions, the dismantling of the universal welfare system brings Sweden closer to Bismarckian Germany.

The wage policy of solidarity in a deadlock

Another important component of the model has been in a process of disintegration: the wage policy of solidarity. The policy which for decades had been a successful instrument for the compression of wage differentials has lost much of its earlier impetus. Since the beginning of the 1980s the wage structure has remained almost stable. The low-paid groups, amongst them women, no longer improved their relative position on the wage scale. There are several reasons for this break in a long trend.

The first of these has to do with the LO's own policy failures. When the LO formulated the aims and methods of the solidaristic wage policy in the 1950s two principles were laid down: (a) wage differentials should be narrowed but not eliminated; and (b) remaining wage differentials should reflect differences in the kind of work, not the profitability of the firm. The implementation of the second principle assumed norms, based on some kind of job evaluation. The LO was successful in its campaigns for lifting wages for the low-paid groups. It failed, however, to achieve consensus within the union movement on a practicable and solid normal system which could be used as a guideline for wage setting. Various attempts to find such norms came to naught and the unions focused on the equalization of the wage structure.

The principle of wage equalization fitted in well with the homogeneity of the labour force in the area of Fordist mass production which was dominant in the first decades after the war. As technology and work organization changed, however, firm-specific skills and incentives for 'learning by doing' could no longer be handled satisfactorily by the traditional soli-daristic wage policy. The LO was ill-prepared for these developments, which implied the need to adjust the wage structure to post-Fordist work organization. A recent proposal to broaden the concept of 'solidaristic wage policy' into a 'solidarity of work' policy, thus coupling wage and work, can be seen as an attempt to modernize the wage policy of solidarity – or rather to bring it back to the original intentions of the 1951 LO report.

The withdrawal of the employers' confederation (SAF) from the cen-tralized wage negotiations in the early 80s was a second obstacle to the pursuance of the wage policy of solidarity[15]. It is easy to see that this was a heavy blow to the LO's wage policy which presupposes the co-ordination of wage claims posed by affiliated unions. The decentralization of the negotiations to the branch level makes it much more difficult for the LO to keep to its principle of solidarity with the low-paid groups. The question is: why did SAFs withdraw from the central bargaining table?

The main reason the employers give is that central contracts have tended to become too complex and clumsy for the flexibility required in modern work organizations. Management prefers decentralized bargaining, even down to the firm level, which allows for larger wage differentials. (It should also be noted that Swedish multinational companies now have more employees outside Sweden than within the country and are accustomed to methods of wage setting which differ from the Swedish ones). The conflict between the unions' and management's view on the role of wages policy stands out more clearly than ever: the Swedish unions continue to aim at an egalitarian wage structure, while for the employers, wage differentials are instruments for managerial control.

Whilst these reasons are frankly admitted by the Swedish employers, their break with a long tradition of central bargaining may also have deeper ideological causes. The central wage negotiations in Sweden can be seen as a product of the Saltsjöbaden peace agreement of 1938 which became the basis for co-operation between the peak organizations SAF and LO. It was the tacit understanding of the agreement that state intervention in labour market matters should be avoided. The union-initiated wave of legal labour reforms in the 1970s, and especially the union proposal to transfer profits into collective wage-earner-funds, were inter-preted by the SAF as the abrogation of the Saltsjöbaden contract. The peaceful, almost friendly relations between LO and SAF in the first decades after the war, which impressed foreign observers of the Swedish scene, were replaced by militancy on both sides. The climate became too harsh for central bargaining.

Yet, a third factor undermining wage solidarity was the changing composition of the union movement. As long as the LO totally dominated the union movement the wage policy of solidarity was the leading ideology. With the increasing strength of white collar unions, other actors – politically neutral, with a higher degree of autonomy from their central confederation (TCO) and with different wage policy aims and strategies – showed up in the bargaining arena. The homogenous union movement became fragmented and conflicting interests debilitated LO's fight for an egalitarian wage structure. When LO requested its well-paid groups to accept modest wage increases and to exercise solidarity with their low-paid colleagues, they looked at the members of white collar unions who were not subjected to the same restraint. Although blue and white collar organizations have friendly relations, with few conflicts around demarca-tion, they frequently run into competitive situations in the area of wage determination.

A fourth and final reason for the demise of the wage policy of solidarity was that the support both of an accommodating labour market policy and of profit-squeezing arrangements could not be maintained. Certainly, no such support is available at present. The non-socialist government has renounced all responsibility for labour redundancy resulting from wage claims too high for inefficient firms. The LO wage earner proposal which aimed to squeeze excess profits was vehemently opposed by all non-socialist parties and, of course, by SAF. In 1983 the socialist government reluctantly accepted the principle of collectively owned wage-earner funds but it watered down the original intentions so much as to make the funds a largely symbolic gesture.

At this point the story of the wage earner fund issue, its passage from an overtly socialist union proposal to a number of toothless share holding funds of a rather conventional type, may be briefly recalled.

Wage earner fund schemes had been discussed in Western Europe in the early post-war years. The German DGB put forward the idea of national wage earner funds in the mid-fifties, aimed at correcting the inequitable distribution of wealth which followed with the rapid restoration of the German economy after the war. In the Netherlands the unions proposed in the sixties a similar fund scheme with its origin in the government-inspired incomes policy during the first post-war years. When the Danish unions in 1971 published a report suggesting a wage earner profit and investment fund the focus was mainly on economic and industrial democracy.

All these initiatives and debates had little influence on the Swedish labour movement. Its attention to collective savings was given to the introduction of a general pension system which was successfully accomplished in 1960 after a long and arduous campaign. When the idea of wage earner funds cropped up in Sweden in the 1970s the main motive was different from the motive in other countries. As has been already mentioned, the wage policy of solidarity, which for decades had been the very basis of Swedish unionism, implies the need for restrictive wage claims for well-paid groups, even if they are in profitable firms. It follows that an 'unused potential for wage increases' in profitable firms accrues to the capital owners as extra profits. The fact that wage restraint results in higher profits is a dilemma inherent in the wage policy of solidarity but it became more accentuated and obvious as Swedish export trades boomed in the beginning of the seventies.

The 1971 LO convention commissioned the confederation's executive board to initiate a thorough examination of the problem and to report back to the next convention in 1976. A small working group of experts was set up in 1973 and presented two years later a proposal which was intended to achieve three tasks: (1) complementing the wage policy of solidarity in such a way that modest wage claims would not enrich the owners of highly profitable firms; (2) counteracting the ongoing concentration of private capital; and (3) strengthening employees' influence at the workplace through co-ownership.

The solution which the working group report offered was a scheme for collective profit sharing, i.e. the establishing of a number of wage earner funds, financed by profit-related payments in the form of shares, and administered by union-dominated boards. The proposal was discussed intensively in the union movement, mainly in a large number of rank and file study circles which reacted in a surprisingly positive way. Many active unionists hailed the wage earner fund issue as an important step on the road towards economic democracy. The original motive – to lend support to the wage policy of solidarity – was overshadowed by the broader anti-capitalist aspects of the proposal which had a vitalizing effect on the union movement.

The LO leadership which originally had taken a rather neutral position vis-a-vis the working group report, was influenced by the positive, even to some extent enthusiastic reception by the union elite and decided to present the report with minor changes to the 1976 LO convention. It was adopted by acclamation followed by the singing in unison of the *Internationale*. An issue had been created capable of mobilizing and activating the union movement.

This only marked the beginning of an intensive and lengthy debate on the LO proposal. The fierce opposition of all non-socialist parties and business organizations forced the labour movement to make repeated retreats. When the social democratic government finally in 1984 introduced wage earner funds it was the first time that a Western country had realized the idea of employee-owned funds. But the scheme had been changed beyond recognition from the original LO proposal. Five small regional funds were established, mainly financed by an excess profit tax. The fund capital was used for purchasing shares in the stock market. The scheme was intended to be annulled after only seven years and the total assets of the funds amounted at the end of the period (1991) to less than five per cent of the total value of the Swedish stock market. None of the original tasks has been achieved and the whole scheme must now be considered a rather symbolic gesture. The strong Swedish labour movement had proved its inability to encroach upon private ownership, the very core of the capitalist system.

In the tumultuous campaigns arranged to fend off 'socialist aggression', the original motive for wage-earner funds was totally neglected: to solve the dilemma that wage restraint in profitable firms leaves the latter more profit than would accrue to them in a normal market. This problem is still unsolved. The question 'Cui bono', put by a Volvo worker under wage restraint to his shop-steward, remains as yet unanswered. A good answer from his point of view – but a bad answer from the perspective of a national wage policy – is local wage drift which posed a serious threat to the principle of solidarity throughout the eighties.

The internationalization of the Swedish economy

So far we have focused on the internal problems which have contributed to the decline of the Swedish Model: the government's inability to combine full employment and economic stability; the dismantling of the universal welfare system, and the increasing difficulties besetting the wage policy of solidarity. Another way to describe the same course of events is to say that the labour movement has lost its hegemonic position, and has failed to mobilize the working class for the defence of the model which was based on the movement's traditional values. The Swedish system, balancing private ownership and social control, has broken down because real power has shifted from labour to the owners of capital.

Of equally decisive importance for the fate of the Swedish Model is the internationalization of the Swedish economy. Large Swedish companies, favoured by governments and by the wage policy of solidarity, have grown into multinationals, expanding their employment more in their foreign subsidiaries than in the Swedish mother firms. Some of them have transformed themselves into transnationals – companies owned by Swedes but located outside the country. Ironically, a few of them have expanded thanks to social democratic policies. Thus Tetrapac, the world-wide packing industry, had its origin in the Swedish agrarian regulation system which permitted the dairy industry to act as a monopoly, thus guaranteeing the use of the company's milk pack by all Swedish households. IKEA had its domestic basis in furnishing the million apartments which were built as part of the social housing program in the 1950s and 1960s. Domestic mass consumption has been the precondition for many Swedish firms which moved out from the country as the home market became too small. They are products of the national Swedish welfare model but act as ungrateful internationalists. Swedish capital, liberated from all legal restrictions, is moving out of Sweden to get closer to foreign markets or simply to find cheaper labour. And the resulting loss of jobs in manufacturing industries has not been compensated for by an increase of jobs in private service trades or in the public sector.

The continuous outflow of Swedish capital, especially after the de-regulation of foreign exchange controls in the latter part of the 80s, is only part of the internationalization of the Swedish economy. With or without formal membership of the EC, and economy of Sweden's population size (9 million) and high export share of GDP (30 per cent) is integrated in the Western European economy to such an extent that the scope for national priorities is utterly limited. Recent events have demonstrated Sweden's dependence upon international financial markets: the Swedish currency was one of the targets of international (and national) speculation and the central bank could defend the Krona only by increasing interest rates to absurd heights – an infallible method for depressing the economy and causing unemployment further to rise. The fight was in vain: in November 1992, the Swedish Krona was devalued.

Two scenarios

There are two main scenarios for the future of the Swedish Model, which, of necessity, must be presented in a rather simplified form. The first one is an extrapolation of the erosion which has been going on for more than a decade. The unique features of the model will vanish, one by one. The hegemony of the reformist labour movement for more than 60 years can then be interpreted as a short period of Swedish history when the country was transformed from a remote agrarian economy into a modern, highly industrialized welfare state.

History, traditions, ideological strength and the leadership's ability to mobilize the working class and to find allies in other classes gave the social democrats the leading role in this process. It could be that in these few decades Sweden came closer to the ideal of a classless society than any other country.

Internal and external factors have, however, hollowed out the basis for the model. The attempts to realize the concept of a classless society within a framework of an internationalized market economy will be brought to an end, not because the model was a failure, but because the conditions have changed. Social democracy has fulfilled its purpose well in a singular phase of Swedish history but must step down as a driving force as Sweden becomes just a small part of a large block of capitalist states. There is no room in this scenario for a specific Swedish profile.

There is another possible scenario, brighter but less likely to materialize. The increasing opposition to the concept of a super-national, centralized European organization can force its architects to modify their original plans. National states may in that case be in a better position to adhere to their own commitments and priorities.

If Western Europe is continuously hit by mass unemployment, an alternative model which aims at full employment and equality can attract attention in other countries. The precondition is that the Swedish labour movement is strong enough to restore the original model, to eliminate unemployment, to stop the dismantling of the welfare system, to find generally accepted norms for the wage policy of solidarity, and to support its wage policy by some kind of collective capital formation. I do not conceal my own preferences. The concept of a society which is built on moral values is, in my view, too promising to be extinguished by inhuman market forces.

NOTES

1. Brus, W. & Laski, K. *From Marx to the Market*, Clarendon Press Oxford 1989.
2. In connection with the centenary of the Social democrat Party in 1989 a history of essential areas of the Party's activities was published and is available in English: Misgeld, K., Molin, K. and Åmark, K., Creating *Social Democracy – A Century of the Social Democratic Party in Sweden*. Penn State Press, University Park 1993. Among recent books in which the development of the modern Swedish labour movement is analyzed are the following. Hamilton, M.B., *Democratic Socialism in Britain and Sweden*, MacMillan Press, Basingstoke 1989. Tilton, T., *The Political Theory of Swedish Social Democracy*, Clarendon Press Oxford 1991. Pontusson, J. *The Limits of Social Democracy*, Cornell University Press, Ithaca 1992.
3. Quoted from the English transition in Tilton, op. cit.
4. Olsen, G.M., *The Struggle for Economic Democracy in Sweden*, Avebury, 1992.
5. *Arbetarrörelsns Efterkrigsprogram* (The Post-War program of the Swedish Labour Movement), Stockholm 1946.
6. Tingsten, H., *Den svenska socialdemokratins itéutveckling*, (The development of the Swedish Social Democracy's ideology) Stockholm 1941.
7. Some of the early contributions to this debate are collected in Turvey, R. (ed.), *Wages Policy under Full Employment*, William Hodge 1952.
8. *Trade Unions and Full Employment*, A Report delivered to the 1951 LO Convention, Stockholm 1953. For a survey of the Swedish labour market policy see Standing, G., Unemployment and Labour Market Flexibility: Sweden, ILO, Geneva 1988.
9. *Saltsjöbaden 50 År* (The Saltsjöbaden Agreement in 50 years), The Swedish Center for Working Life, Stockholm 1989.
10. Korpi, W., *Halkar Sverige efter?* (Does Sweden lag behind?, Carlssons, Stockholm, 1992.

11. Saltman, R., & von Otter, C., *Planned Market and Public Competition.*, Buckingham: Open University Press 1992.

12. A recent analysis of the Swedish bargaining system and the role of the wage policy of solidarity is given in Martin, A., *Wage Bargaining and Swedish Politics*, Trade Union Institute for Economic Research, Stockholm 1992. (See also Swenson, P., *Fair Shares: Unions, Pay and Politics in Sweden and West Germany*, Cornell University Press, Ithaca 1989.

13. Meidner, R., *Employee Investment Funds*, Allan and Unwin, London 1978. Meidner, R., *Wage Earner Funds*, in S'zell, G., (ed.), Concise Encyclopedia of Participation and Management, Walter de Gruyter, Berlin 1992.

14. Hibbs, D.A. & Locking, H., *Wage Compression under Solidarity Bargaining in Sweden*, Trade Union Institute for Economic Research, Stockholm 1990.

15. Pontusson, J. & Swenson, P., *Markets, Production, Institutions and Politics: Why Swedish Employers have Abandoned the Swedish Model*, Paper prepared for Eighth International Conference of Europeanists. The Council for European Studies, Chicago, March 1992.

BORDERS: THE NEW BERLIN WALLS

Saul Landau

By the 1990s only the uncurbed passage of labour from one market to another remains as an impediment to realizing the ultimate meaning of freedom for the transnational entrepreneurs. Advances in technology and communications have permitted capital to move unobstructed throughout most of the world. From board rooms in Tokyo, New York and London, loans, credits and investments were transferred to cities in Africa, Asia and Latin America to finance new factories or agribusinesses – or to speculate. International agreements cleared the path of centuries-old obstacles that impeded commodities' free passage across national borders – at least for the time being.

Current frontiers, the encumbrances to workers' travel, derive not only from historic settlements, wars and treaties, but also from ideologies and sentiments of racism and nationalism, constructs that distinguished a worker or petty merchant in one country from his counterpart in another. Ideologies that divided workers or prevented competition at one historical period, continue to function in the 'new global village', frustrating the creation of a global and mobile labour force, which would allow capital to reduce further the socially necessary cost of labour.

Even as improved transportation allowed for increased mobility, social attitudes and laws obstructed people of darker skin or different customs from working inside national borders. Over centuries, in the age of empire, a virtual pigmentocracy was established and it set the standards and rules of residence and citizenship within the North American and West European nations – with implicit or explicit bias against people from the South and the East. Eurocentric axioms continue to provoke fear among members of the working and middle classes that hordes of 'uncivilized' immigrants will pollute, dilute or in some form pervert the direct line of western culture that runs from Greeks and Romans through Europe of the Reformation and Enlightenment and into the present; all held together by a White Christ and Moses that people of darker hues cannot truly share.

In the 1990s, as notions of 'global village' are taught in classrooms around the world, the idea of free labour passage from one country to another remains elusive, if not downright politically combustible. Social and political forces in several European nations and the United States threaten violence if large numbers of workers from poor countries continue to migrate to take on the most menial tasks in the developed nations. Thus, as borders disappear for capital and goods, formally at least, they remain quite intact to control the passage of labour.

The fence that separates the United States from Mexico doesn't deter most of the millions of Mexicans and Central Americans who have learned how to scale it, tunnel under it or cut holes in the barbed wire. Each year they pick the Americans' food, clean their houses, care for their children, build and maintain their homes and offices, and even dig their graves. A large number are deported every year, or choose to return to their homeland on weekends where they maintain their families and permanent residence. In fact, the day, week or month labourers, like those who stay for years, are little recognized participants in the social and economic life of both countries: citizens of the poor country, aliens in the rich one.

From the 1970s on, the new Hispanics, the generic category for Spanish-speaking Mexican, Central American and some Caribbean people, have become part and parcel of the US economy and culture. Yet, opinion polls show that sizable sectors of the white, Afro-American and even resident Spanish-speaking public do not want the newcomers living permanently in the country. These fears are abundantly communicated to legislators who translate them into action. Although millions of people from the South do cross the forbidden line, many millions more cannot.

Some Southwestern and Western border residents as well as uniformed members of the Border Patrol have taken to shooting those trying to elude the border barriers. In 1990 and 1991, vigilante patrols killed and wounded several people crossing the Rio Grande in Texas. In December 1990, a twelve year old Mexican boy scaled the fence that divides Mexicali and Calexico, California. He claimed he only wanted a better view of a fight that had developed on the US side of the border. He saw the INS truck approach and retreated to the fence. The border patrolman's dum-dum bullet ricocheted through the lad's insides as he dropped to the ground on the Mexican side. One Mexican observer said the scene reminded him of incidents he had seen on television of East German border guards shooting people attempting to ascend the wall to the West.

As television during the Cold War years feasted on spies coming in and going out into the cold, the increasing migratory labour force faced less glamorous lines separating the world of abundance from that of scarcity, those with possibilities from those in hopelessness, people of the South in need of work from those in the North who had it. For millions of people living in the South, the Berlin Wall was a dubious symbol. For them, the struggle between East and West, communism and freedom, good and evil, hardly related to the partitions they encountered: the borders that closed their access to jobs.

By the 1990s, there was no violence at the site of the torn-down Berlin Wall. But a different kind of violence erupted throughout Germany and other parts of Europe. In some cities neo-Nazi, skinhead gangs murdered 'guest workers' – with the collaboration of sectors of the police. In Italy border guards 'set an example' for would be immigrants by brutally beating Africans and Albanians seeking refuge and work. In 1992, in France and other northern European countries right wing political parties gained strength by using xenophobia as their central issue.

Racism was hardly new to Europe and the United States, but the coincidence of recession and waves of immigration produced a combustible equation. Borders in the 1990s no longer maintained political security against penetration by East or West of each other's territories, but protected the affluent North from the desperate and disparate South. However, the anti-immigrant frenzy, along with headline-creating riots and the frenetic demands to erect race and class-based barriers obscured a deeper dynamic: the restructuring of labour into a mobile and global force.

The neglected immigration prism

In the 1990s, immigration has again become an acceptable prism through which to view world events. After the end of the Second World War the movement of labour was a low research priority compared to the dramatic possibilities inherent in the Cold War equation. Nevertheless, underneath the fog generated by Cold War crisis mongers, a powerful shift was occurring in the nature of the world's labour force.

Well before the Soviet Union and its Bloc disintegrated, scores of millions of people living in rural and self-subsistence environments were shaken like ripe apples on a tree into the world's pile of wage labour. Women comprised the majority of this new labour force. They, their mothers or grandmothers were driven from villages often by the very troops who were supposedly 'freeing' or 'protecting' their country from communism, or by international banks promoting 'development'. Their own governments behaved as collaborators in the massive uprooting of their citizens. Like a modern enclosure movement, powered by war, technology and 'development' policies, a new wave of displaced people emerged as potential labourers. For centuries, their families had lived as peasants on the margin of global capitalism. Men, women and children migrated from Africa, Asia and Latin America – and Southern and Eastern Europe as well – to find themselves occupying the lowest rungs of the labour ladder in the affluent West, or the oil-rich areas of the Persian Gulf. The immense acreage on which peasants grew subsistence crops for millennia was turned into agricultural plantations, subsidiaries of food-exporting, agri-business corporations.

The US Mexican border marked one segment of the North-South partition line, which Mexicans began crossing in large numbers in the 1950s when US growers needed a cheap labour force for newly irrigated desert lands of California, Arizona and Texas. These 'wetbacks' (the pejorative term derives from the fact that Mexicans had to cross the Rio Grande river to enter Texas or New Mexico) served as an avant-garde of the developing mobile labour pool. By the 1980s Mexicans were joined by Central Americans, Chinese, Southeast Asians, Filipinos and Pacific Islanders who infiltrated the porous borders and port cities of the United States to make garments and semi conductors, wash dishes and pick vegetables – enterprises that had room for low wage immigrants willing to work in substandard conditions and without Green Cards.

For many decades US workers had struggled with employers to have a union as a bargaining agent on issues of wages and working conditions. The vulnerable immigrant is afraid not only to join a union, lest he be expelled from the country, but has no leverage without a union to bargain on any questions of wages or conditions. US citizens and permanent residents will not, indeed cannot abide the conditions that desperate Salvadorans or East Asians feel forced to accept. When there was economic boom, the displacement of blacks and resident Hispanics by green-cardless Salvadorans was less abrasive than under bad times.

In addition, after a decade of using cheap immigrant labour, entire sectors become dependent on that work force. Should the INS enforce the law and deport the busboys and dishwashers in Los Angeles and Washington D.C., as examples, the restaurant industry would face a serious crisis. What began as a temporary displacement of one low wage workforce by a lower one quickly became institutionalized.

Causes of the new immigration

The reasons for the mass migrations in the contemporary world have been as diverse as high and low intensity wars, new technology, land erosion, 'development' plans of the IMF and the lures of a commercial paradise contained in the US television and movie shows exported to the third world.

Some of the immigrants came to the United States because they were environmental refugees, meaning their land was depleted, poisoned, deprived of water or simply insufficient in size to support successive generations. Others were ejected from their villages, towns and even their countries by greedy oligarchs or transnational food companies – backed by military dictators. Often small farmers could not afford the technology required to compete with agro giants. In some countries, peasants became victims of 'development' policies sponsored by multi-lateral agencies and governments. Still others were escaping the ravages of wars that sometimes lasted for decades. Indeed, a case could be made that World War III, between the rich and poor parts of the world, was well underway when World War II – a conflict between wealthy nations – ended.

The colonial or imperial powers fought virtually one continual war against revolutionary, independence, and anti-colonial movements. Simultaneously, third world nations and tribes fought each other, often over capriciously conceived territorial lines drawn by colonial administrators. When possible, the imperial powers delegated repression to proxy armies trained by or under the tutelage of Special Forces or CIA operators.

The ongoing wars in the South impinged on the civil society of the North only when extraordinary sacrifices were required – in Korea and Vietnam for the United States; Vietnam and Algeria for France. These imperial wars had unforeseen immigration effects on the imperial homeland. The CIA's Vietnamese, including some tribes people, or Central Americans running from a dirty war sought refuge in the United States – which had to provide a home at least for a small percentage of these victims of foreign policy adventures. From 1959 through 1993, the US government waged almost continual low intensity war against Cuba, one tactic of which was to welcome any Cuban 'escaping' from communist tyranny, while simultaneously denying visas to Cubans who wanted to emigrate legally – thereby forcing the desperate ones to hop on rafts to cross the shark infested Caribbean or to hijack planes.

The wars, however, overshadowed a larger process that was turning Southeast Asia, the Caribbean and Central America from rural-based peasant societies into urbanized and 'modernized' nations. 'In an absent minded way,' wrote Samuel Huntington in 1968, 'the United States in Vietnam may well have stumbled upon the answer to "wars of national liberation"'. The effective response lies neither in the quest for a conventional military victory, nor in esoteric doctrines and gimmicks of counter-insurgency warfare. It is instead forced-draft urbanization and modernization which rapidly brings the country in question out of the phase in which a rural revolutionary movement can [succeed].'

The 'reciprocity' of US wars in the Third World is ironic, as 'leftist rebels' and right wing 'freedom fighters' both arrived at the shores of the United States. Indeed, distinctions became meaningless. There were 'refugees', like anti-Sandinista Nicaraguans and the first waves of CIA Vietnamese, and 'economic migrants', as the later 'boat people' and the early groups of Salvadoran migrants in the United States were branded. These categories obscure the facts of history: wars produced huge migrations of people. US involvement in these wars meant that those fleeing war (winners or losers) would try to come to the United States because it was the richest country and afforded the most opportunity to poor people. Huntington did not anticipate that his brand of 'modernization', when applied throughout the rest of the Third World, would also bring leaders of 'the countries in question' to a point where they would be forced to export their own populations to survive.

Just as economic pressure reaches its highest point inside third world nations, the cry is heard in the developed world to stop further immigration of people of colour. Those holding anti-immigration sentiment do not necessarily relate the arrival of the new comers to failures of US foreign policy, or to flaws in the 'development' strategy of the IMF and World Bank. Americans have been noted for their historical amnesia. Indeed, in 1993, when professors mention the wars in Southeast Asia and Central America, students' eyes tend to glaze over as if these events belong in the realm of a hazy past. Yet, often sitting in the same classroom are Vietnamese or Central American students whose very presence resulted from a US foreign policy 'mistake',

In both regions policy makers assumed implicitly that a US-designed order could be imposed through high (Vietnam) and low (Central America) intensity conflicts. The wars failed to realize the objective, but they did beget several million refugees – one of the unforeseen consequences of intervention. From the mid 1970s through the early 1990s, the United States took in Vietnamese, Laotians, Cambodians, Afghans, Nicaraguans, Salvadorans and Guatemalans displaced by wars.

Vietnam

By the time that US forces withdrew from Vietnam, in 1973, South Vietnam's most lucrative enterprise was providing services to the Americans stationed there. The importation of enormous quantities of US manufactured goods overwhelmed whatever economy had existed previously. When the war ended Vietnam no longer had the independent capacity to feed its population. After the initial flight of Vietnamese on the CIA payroll or intimately linked to the US-backed government came refugees fleeing not so much from communism but from a country that could not provide for them.

The first wave of almost 130,000 Indochinese (primarily Vietnamese) reached the United States in the spring of 1975. These people were generally well-educated, French-speaking, and Catholic, members of the Southeast Asian elite who were connected with war-time US military and business interests. Some were Vietnamese associated with the Phoenix Program (a CIA-directed operation that relocated – or killed – Vietnamese suspected of being sympathetic to the Viet Cong into government controlled zones). Some of these CIA operatives were torturers and killers. But also among the first wave of immigrants were doctors, lawyers, military officers, business men and civil servants who brought their children to America and began lives with their new sponsors, Americans volunteering to help the new arrivals over the trauma of their exit and difficulties of assimilation.

Subsequent waves of 'boat people', as they became known in the late 1970s and early 1980s, were considerably less well-educated or connected with American society. Instead of calling them displaced people because of the wreckage of war, the escaping Vietnamese were promoted as refugees fleeing communism and welcomed with some resettlement aid and services. The flood of refugees from Indochina to the United States served simultaneously as a painful reminder of a failed policy in Vietnam and as a propaganda tool to show how people were escaping from communism. In fact, many of them were 'economic refugees' seeking to make a better living than could be eked out of post-war Vietnam.

Among the unintended consequences of the war in Southeast Asia were the fate of the progeny of US troops. These children, singled out by their physical features and American first names, were ostracized along with their families from Vietnamese society. Several thousand such youths, along with siblings and parents (usually their mothers), have been resettled in the United States since 1988. One example should suffice to illustrate their vicissitudes.

Lo didn't consider migrating to the United States until she gave birth to a girl in Vietnam who shared the Anglo features of her father, a US soldier. Despised in Vietnam, the two boarded a boat in 1983, and after surviving a terrible odyssey at sea, arrived in the United States. In 1991, both mother and daughter cleaned hotel rooms in Washington, D.C. and boast of becoming 'American'. Both are seeking an American man to marry. Lo began to cry when she thought about Danang, her home, and her family. Her daughter shrugged when the subject arose. 'I don't like Asians,' she said.

This sentiment echoed nativist resentment against the 'boat people', who were 'taking our jobs away'. In Galveston, Texas and Monterey, California, organized campaigns against newly-arrived Vietnamese fishermen 'unfairly competing' with the locals, led to violence. In other areas as well the later waves of Indochinese refugees stretched the United States' good-will capacity. Government officials decided they had paid enough for the mistake of Vietnam and admissions of Vietnamese in the 1980s was decided yearly; government funding for resettlement was reduced and meted out erratically.

Central America

The United States intervened periodically in Central America to prop up puppet governments or bring down democratic and revolutionary regimes. But until the 1980s the interference in Central American affairs had not produced a massive exodus of refugees into the United States itself. When the CIA began its military support of the government of El Salvador and simultaneously its sponsorship of the counterrevolutionary war against Nicaragua in 1981 it produced impossible conditions, especially for people in areas of actual combat – which spread significantly over the next decade. With US-sponsored wars occurring in their countries, large numbers of Central Americans saw little opportunity to survive economically. Some Nicaraguans were or professed to be political refugees escaping Sandinismo and were granted asylum. Salvadorans, fleeing from a right wing government, were at first branded 'economic migrants', although their country was in the throes of an even more devastating civil war.

By the end of the 1980s remittances from workers in the United States to families throughout Central America, Mexico, the Caribbean and the Philippines had become props to maintain national economies, the difference between national solvency and bankruptcy. Filipinos send home some $3 billion a year from the United States alone. Salvadorans and other Central Americans remit more than $2 billion yearly.

In El Salvador, the remittances began to make an appreciable difference to the dollar balance in the government treasury. Indeed, President Jose Napoleon Duarte pleaded with Ronald Reagan, during a 1982 visit to Washington, not to deport the newly arrived Salvadoran labourers, explaining that their remittances to their families provided El Salvador with desperately needed millions of dollars in foreign exchange.

The millions who have migrated are a third world export of last resort. During the Persian Gulf War alone, India lost more than $2 million in remittance income derived from its labour in the area. Philippine Airlines estimated their loss at $800,000 a day from cancelled flights to the Gulf. Pakistan, Bangladesh, Sri Lanka and several of the North African states also had sizable labour forces throughout the region, as they do in other parts of the world.

Central American immigrants settled in communities where their kin already lived. Most of the new arrivals continue to be smuggled into the United States from Mexico by 'coyotes' who provide transportation, fake visas and lodging for undocumented immigrants who pay between $2,000 and $5,000 for passage to the United States. Almost forty percent of the approximately 2 million Central Americans in the United States live in Southern California. Los Angeles has now become the largest Salvadoran city outside of San Salvador. But other immigrants live in tent colonies in the canyons and gullies between Los Angeles and San Diego. Each day they seek work picking fruit or as construction workers. Self-segregated by nationality, the refugees exchange news of their home countries while lookouts peer down from the bluffs to watch for INS officials.

Although the conditions under which the newly-arrived live in California ravines or field barracks are atrocious, their counterparts in large cities hardly enjoy ideal living conditions. In the Mount Pleasant neighbourhood of Washington, D.C., where up to 100,000 Salvadorans reside, men share single rooms, often using the 'hot bed' system – one sleeps while the other works – which the Chinese immigrants invented in San Francisco in the 1920s. Salvadorans make up 50 – 70 percent of the total Latino population in the Washington area. Restaurants, child care, house work and the construction industry provide employment for those without working papers.

In Washington, D.C. in 1990 a policewoman shot a Salvadoran man on the street in the Mt. Pleasant neighbourhood. She claimed he had drawn a knife when she confronted him in a drunken state. The Salvadoran men around him at the time said he was too drunk to do anything. The shooting incident was only a spark that lit an already combustible pile of grievances. Afro-Americans and Hispanics alternately fought police and each other. Throughout three days of rioting, some members of each group cast racial aspersions on the other, while simultaneously Central Americans and Afro-Americans expressed solidarity with each other against police, landlords and insensitive city officials.

Behind the interracial tension there were concrete issues. The Salvadorans provided a welcome low-wage labour force for entrepreneurs. Between the late 1970s and the late 1980s, a period marked by extensive expansion, Afro-Americans fared worse as Hispanics took some of their traditional jobs in construction, restaurant and hotel servicing and home and child care. With the 1991 recession, the Hispanics, voiceless and undocumented, were the first to be marginalized by the slumping economy. It is little wonder that the uprooted, war-weary and unemployed would take to the streets and in doing so add another ripple to America's evolving racial/ethnic history. Like the Los Angeles riots of 1992, the Washington blow-up indicated that a crisis might well be brewing around the issue of continued immigration while mounting numbers of coloured Americans receive diminishing services and no aid for their chronic state of unemployment.

The new US population

Counting Hispanics, people of colour will become the majority in the United States before mid 21st Century. In the late 1980s new and contradictory patterns began to emerge with the new labour force. Watsonville, California, located on the Monterey Bay, in the Pajaro Valley, was for decades the home of food processing plants. In 1990, after winning a prolonged strike against four canneries and processing plants – for $6.25 an hour and modest health benefits – the workers found themselves victims of plant relocation. Three of the four major factories were purchased by a British transnational and moved to Irapuato, Mexico, ironically the birthplace of some of the 'illegal' workers in Watsonville.

But the story doesn't end with the relocation of the factories. In the Irapuato area the farmers ceased growing corn and beans, the traditional staples, and began planting strawberries and broccoli for the nearby plants to freeze and export to the United States. Corn and beans were then imported from the United States at a higher price to feed the work force, whose daily wage was about $4.00.

In addition, children as young as thirteen were recruited to work full-time shifts and management paid no health or other benefits to the work force. In Mexico, the food processing plants had no expensive environmental regulations to meet. There was no oversight of farming methods; so the locals who sold their crops to the factory used nearby river water to irrigate their chemically fertilized and toxically-sprayed crops. The nearby tannery and slaughterhouse dumped chemicals and animal remains into the river.

In Watsonville itself the unemployed workers had no redress. Unions found themselves ill-equipped to confront the relocation issue. In Irapuato the unions were corrupt and dealt with management, so the newly employed workers there also lacked means to protest the low wages and poor conditions. In both places wage labourers were experiencing the meaning of the new world order. This kind of transformation of the workplace and environment offers chilling prospects for the future, especially in the event that a NAFTA agreement is reached.

Immigrants with a business culture and education often find that the United States remains a land of opportunity and, once having taken advantage of the possibilities, fall into the familiar language of racism that has been part of US culture since the 17th Century. A pecking order based on class and nationality often develops.

A Korean man in New Jersey boasts of his ability to provide his children with private schooling, nice clothes, stereos, and a large house. His family moved from the 'slums' of northern Virginia, where he berated 'Those Vietnamese!'. 'Why are they here?' he shouted in his thick Korean accent. 'They don't work, they're dirty and they don't speak good English!'

One Mt. Pleasant resident held forth on the newly-arrived Salvadorans. Twenty years ago black men could find work washing dishes and doing day construction. Black women could clean houses and take care of white children. No more. 'The Salvadorans got it locked up. No wonder. They come here and take our jobs because they work for dirt wages and take all the shit the boss gives them. They live like pigs in a sty, seven to a room and can't even speak English.'

Raul and some of his Salvadoran co-workers at the Chinese restaurant in Alexandria, Virginia denounce their adopted home and talk nostalgically about how wonderful life was in San Miguel, El Salvador before the war, before they had to emigrate, illegally, to find work to support their families. They were lucky because they arrived in the 1980s, when jobs were plentiful.

For the Salvadorans: 'They [Afro-Americans] don't like to work hard. We have to work because our families down there [El Salvador] will starve if we don't send the money. Here there is work. There we had no work, no land, lots of war. When I make enough money I'll return and buy some good land and live like a king.'

The new immigrants are part of a diverse population of more than 15 million people of colour (counting Hispanics) who have arrived in the United States since 1965, a dramatic contrast with the relative trickle of Third World immigration during the first twenty years after World War II, a period marked by a racially and ideologically restrictive immigration policy, dominated by the McCarran-Walter Act. The McCarran-Walter Act established a preference system, 'to best preserve the cultural and sociological balance of the country.' The State Department would grant visas only to immigrants who had relatives living in the United States, provided they passed political loyalty tests. The Act restricted Southern and Eastern Europeans, Asians and Africans, on the presumption that they were less assimilable than Northern Europeans. Congress opened a few holes in the McCarran-Walter law by creating 'separate doorways' to allow into the United States anti-communist refugees from Eastern Europe in 1952.

These 'doorways' allowed the President some minor immigration compensation for his foreign policy setbacks. In contrast to many of the pro-Nazi and extreme right-wingers who entered under this programme, members of radical and working-class movements who had dominated US immigration before World War II were kept out. The Hungarian uprising of 1956 left thousands of US-inspired 'freedom fighters' in a precarious state until they were allowed in under emergency immigration provisions. The Cuban revolution of 1959 produced an exodus of refugees most of whom had two things in common: they were white and anti-communist. By 1970 more than 500,000 anti-communist Cubans had settled in the United States. The first waves of Cubans received warm welcomes in the United States, in contrast to the largely poorer and darker-skinned Marielitos of 1980.

The McCarran-Walter Act corresponded to a country still racially segregated by law. Immigration patterns changed colour lines during the days of the New Frontier and the Great Society. The Hart-Cellar Act of 1965 repealed the national origins quota and facilitated family reunification by reserving three fourths of all new visas for family members wishing to join relatives residing in the United States. The Act was crafted to encourage a new round of European immigration, since most families in the United States had come from Europe. But it also benefitted residents of English-speaking territories in the Western Hemisphere and made new Asian migration more viable as well.

In the wake of the collapse of communism Congress made provisions to allow up to 700,000 skilled immigrants from Eastern Europe. The ex-

Soviet systems thus ended up bearing the cost of educating engineers and scientists who would ultimately migrate to the West. One of the effects of this influx of high tech immigrants was to drive down salaries of US technicians. Indeed, the arrival of hundreds of thousands of East European specialists coincided with the recession of 1990 and exacerbated the already difficult employment situation in certain high tech industries. IBM, once the company that crowed about its no layoffs policy, dropped tens of thousands of its employees in the early 1990s, many of them engineers and high-skilled professionals.

President Bush carefully avoided linking the new immigration policy with the layoffs that were occurring. In his new world order, 'immigration is not just a link to America's past, it is also a bridge to America's future,' Bush said as he signed the Immigration Act of 1990, allowing major increases in the number of immigrants each year. The bill, President Bush said, puts 'an end to the kind of political litmus test that might have excluded even some of the heroes of the Eastern European revolution of 1989.' Under the law, new immigration of skilled workers – engineers, architects, doctors, etc. – will increase by 400,000 the number of immigrants who will be accepted from 1990 through 1993, reaching a total of 2.1 million. The only 'defectors' still welcomed and aided are Cubans who are still considered political refugees, fleeing from Communism.

But new immigration policy doesn't mean erasing borders. Quite the contrary. In Western Europe and the United States, the welcome mats in the 1990s are reserved for the rich and skilled. Even Canada, long one of the freest of nations on the immigration question, tightened its restrictions on non-skilled foreigners.

The world's workers and the nature of their work

Massive uprooting of people has been an on-going process for centuries as capital continues to try to rationalise its quest for the local labour force on a global scale. But the crisis nature of Cold War ideology shrouded this process underneath ideological wrappings. It also masked a crisis of more durable proportion caused by the uprooting of tens of millions of people. Families, villages, towns and entire cities were altered or relocated. By 1990, migrating labourers abounded in the United States and the Caribbean Basin, Europe and the Persian Gulf. During the 1990 Gulf War hundreds of thousands of Filipinos, Indians, Pakistanis and Sri Lankans in Kuwait, Saudi Arabia and other Emirates became displaced workers when their jobs were adversely affected by the war. Indeed, Indian brain surgeons and ditch diggers alike had maintained Kuwaiti society from top down. Where the labour market beckoned, workers arrived, the United States being the most attractive place. In turn, the economies of the labour-exporting countries became dependent on the earning from their new export.

Maria from El Salvador now lives in suburban Washington, D.C. where her mistress has taught her how to operate the automatic dish washer, while the mistress herself plants flower bulbs in her manicured garden. Before the war in El Salvador, Maria planted flowers and corn and fed the animals on her small plot. The course of the war in the 1980s forced Maria's family off their land. In San Salvador, the capital city, swollen by refugees from the countryside, some of Maria's relatives found work. But her family in the poor urban barrio depends on her $300 a month remittance. They write to her that she has made the difference in their lives between suffering and minimal comfort. In the evening, Maria often babysits and does day end household chores before going off to her room where sometimes she weeps from loneliness.

Ninoy stoops to pluck the berries from the California ranch controlled by a trans-national company in Europe. Like Maria, he also grew up on his family farm, where generations of the Ramos had lived until they were forced to move. Like his Salvadoran counterparts, Ninoy sends his monthly remittance to the house in the Manila slum where his family now resides. He does not write to them about his crooked back, a result of bending over day after day.

In December, 1992, outside of a suburban Washington, D.C. bowling alley, Salvadoran, Nicaraguan and Guatemalan men waited to pick up Christmas day jobs until the alley's owner got a judge to prohibit the men from gathering. 'It was like an axe falling on me,' said one of the prospective labourers when a policeman shooed him away. 'This was supposed to be the land of opportunity, but there's nothing but cold here.'

In New York City, Caridad found work sewing buttons on blue jeans in a dusty garment centre factory. She earned $6.00 an hour, provided she met the daily quota. By skimping and scraping, not eating lunch, sharing a room with three other women and depriving herself of all but bare necessities, she not only survived but managed to send a monthly cheque of $250 to her family in Nicaragua. One day in late 1991 she arrived for work, but the factory door was shut. On it was a sign in English only that one of her fellow sewers finally interpreted. 'CLOSED. NO MORE WORK.'

In the late 1980s and early 1990s scores of textile factories owned by US entrepreneurs opened in Honduras and El Salvador, some of them encouraged by US Embassy staff. The stitchers made $.40 cents an hour doing the same work that Caridad performed for $6.00. Eventually, Caridad and some of the other women who once made jeans found other work in the New York area, baby sitting, house cleaning or making beds in hotels. Some, however, took a quicker route to an income and became prostitutes or drug dealers, parts of criminal gangs of their own countrymen.

In 1990, San Francisco, California police arrested an eighteen year old Salvadoran man – we'll call him Jesus Diaz – on a downtown street for selling rocks of crack cocaine. The young man spoke almost no English and reported that he had come to the United States only four weeks prior to his arrest to find work. His native village had been partly destroyed by the decade-long war and he later admitted that he was not anxious to do military service in El Salvador. But he had sought work in several California cities to no avail. Indeed, he discovered that hundreds of Salvadoran men waited on street corners in hope of being hired – but on most days the pick-up truck that carried men to do daily yard work or farm work did not arrive.

As the police interrogation proceeded, the young man refused to name those who recruited him, pleaded guilty to a charge of selling crack and received a three year prison sentence. Police estimated that in the two weeks he hung out on the busy street he sold upwards of $10,000 worth of the illegal drug. A veteran police sergeant said that there were hundreds of Jesus Diazes throughout the San Francisco Bay Area and other cities who could not find work and were therefore easily recruited to sell drugs.

The deal Jesus made was that if caught he would serve the three year sentence, would be given $2,000 as long as Jesus kept his lips sealed about the names of his recruiters, Salvadoran army veterans from his home town.

Across the Bay, in Oakland, California police investigated the stabbing death of a newly arrived Mexican youth by a Cambodian teenager. Both belonged to rival gangs that were fighting over control of a piece of territory – a street corner, in this instance. In Long Beach, California Mexican and Cambodians blazed away at each others' homes with sub-machine guns. In New York City Vietnamese and Chinese gangs blew each other away in Chinatown.

In other cities blacks are pitted against Hispanics, Asians against blacks or sometimes one ethnic or racial group declares war on rival factions. These gang wars or street wars to control a corner, a block or a neighbourhood are based on the economic reality of global migration in the 1990s. It is not only true in the United States but in Germany and other European nations as well.

The increase in crime in the United States over the past two decades is partly related to the fact that the economy and social order is ill-equipped to integrate the numbers of immigrants into the legal economy. Drugs and its concomitant partner, gun-running, inevitably produce a crime ladder, one which impacts on the middle class. Just as dealing in illegal drugs requires gunmen, so too does it beget other kinds of law breaking. On the other side, there are crazed crack addicts who rob and sometimes kill for one rock. And the immigrants involved often target one another. The Cambodians win a corner from the Mexicans not because they hate Mexicans, but so that they can control drug traffic, gambling and prostitution. At one side there are groups like the 'Jamaican posses', bands of poor youth who come to the United States or Canada as security agents for drug dealers, and who like their Columbian counterparts, develop a psychopathology of murder as a tool of intimidation.

The IMF and World Bank 'development'

For much of the developing world the 1980s were marked by budgetary rule by the IMF. Economists from the Fund practically eliminated spending on health, education and social services. The IMF demanded that borrowing countries eliminate subsidies for food staples, remove protection for local crops, devalue local currencies and in all ways reduce labour costs, under the pretext that such conditions would be irresistible to foreign investors.

By being forced, bribed or cajoled into accepting the IMF-World Bank premise, that the state apparatus was a wasteful impediment to development, third world governments, one by one, delegitimized the very core of their development alternative. Instead of having the state provide some cushion for the most desperate segment, the multilateral agency intellectuals insisted that government officials had to trust in the equilibrium-seeking 'free' labour market, so that the longer-run national good could be pursued. The effect of two decades of those development policies was to destroy national autonomy in most third world nations by eviscerating their national budgets.

The IMF formula pushed Third World governments initially to integrate themselves into the world economy as exporters of cheap agricultural and manufactured goods, and labour. Third World nations competed against each other to attract foreign capital by reducing wages and offering tax- and regulation-free environments.

When the price of export commodities dropped or failed to keep pace with imports – which occurred in predictable cycles – the non-oil producing South became ever more dependent on exporting their most abundant commodity: labour. Some hard-pressed countries found a means not of developing, but at least surviving by exporting labour and using the remittances as a form of catastrophic national economic insurance.

'Haiti's long term future will be urban,' a 1983 World Bank report concluded about that poor country's population movements. 'This migration will sustain the development of assembly industries, cottage industries and other urban, labour-intensive activities consistent with an export-led growth.' What the Bank report omitted was that the act of transforming rural people into migrant wage labourers in their home country was also a step toward making them into immigrant labour for the United States.

Similarly, in nearby Jamaica the multilateral lending institutions prevailed in a struggle to force the Jamaican government to discard notions of self-sufficiency in favour of the export oriented growth pattern. In the 1970s, Prime Minister Michael Manley had encouraged unemployed slum-dwellers from Kingston and other over populated urban centres to take up subsistence farming by offering small plots and other services. Manley also tried to limit imports, while simultaneously building infrastructure in health, education and roads. These policies, while supported by the Jamaican electorate, did not resound happily in the international lending community.

After his 1976 re-election, as bauxite prices dropped, depreciating Jamaica's revenues, Manley confronted Jamaica's balance of payments problem. The IMF loan package effectively reversed the very programmes on which he had won his election and re-election. By 1979 Manley and his Party felt compelled to reject the IMF solution as incompatible with the development programme he had pledged to fulfil. Manley lost his 1980 re-election bid to Edward Seaga who pledged a supply side solution for Jamaica's woes. Despite support and aid from President Reagan and David Rockefeller, massive loan infusions from the multilateral agencies and bilateral aid from the United States, all totalling over $4 billion, Seaga's Jamaica did not attract significant amounts of private capital and its export-oriented strategy failed to provide the necessary income to make its economy viable.

When Seaga left office in 1989 Jamaica's debt had risen to $10 billion (for a population of 2.2 million) and its balance of payments situation had worsened. The supply-side advocate discovered that if even a semblance of democracy exists the Prime Minister's movement in bringing drastic monetarist reforms is curtailed by constituent pressures. So, Jamaican unions who helped elect Seaga could not be disregarded after his election unless Seaga was willing and able to turn toward military or police rule.

The result of Jamaica's inability to recover from its downward cycle has meant that Jamaicans continued to leave the island in large numbers for the United States, Canada and Great Britain. More Jamaicans live abroad than on the island. This safety valve probably helped stem the outbreak of violent rebellion as it did on neighbouring islands where similar conditions prevailed and the US government allowed for some escape clause.

New industries did spring up in the Caribbean region, but mostly in so-called 'free enterprise zones'. In Kingston and other island capitals young women, recently arrived from the countryside, laboured in dim light and heavy air over sewing machines or semi-conductor tools. These women frequently travel to other Caribbean islands, following the trail of the factories which close down without notice and relocate on other islands even at the vaguest hint that a union organiser was nearby or that the government wanted to regulate health or safety features.

Throughout Asia, Latin America and the Caribbean, young women forced from their farms and villages found work at small parts electronics assembly, textile manufacturing, apparel, toys and other products for Western markets. Besides reducing labour costs, foreign employers sought young women in patriarchal societies because they were turned quickly into obedient, disciplined and adept performers of tedious jobs. The young women and girls, without the opportunity to join unions, had no vent for grievances about low wages or poor work conditions without the risk of being fired.

The superintendent of a Maquiladora electronics plant in Ciudad Juarez, on the US Mexican border, explains: 'We like to hire girls who don't have too much experience because they aren't spoiled. We shape them to our needs by appealing to their feminine sensibilities. Then you can trust they won't fly off the handle, making unrealistic demands or joining unions. We like to think of our company as a family where everyone knows their duties.'

The role of US culture in stimulating labour migration

If wars and IMF-designed economic policies were in and of themselves insufficient to promote a steady flow of labour from the Third World, the US culture industry provided additional incentive. Included among the varied meanings of freedom was the right of US capital to penetrate other countries' markets. In this vein, entertainment conglomerates placed their technically superior TV shows, slick advertisements and other shiny pieces of commercial culture into Third World homes and public theatres.

With the distribution of radio and television sets throughout the Third World, western culture arrived en masse in the form of entertainment. The magical qualities of the hi tech programmes and special effects of the Hollywood films offered more than an evening's diversion or vicarious sensations: inside each show there was etched an implicit definition of the beautiful, i.e. the good. Virtue and nobility were identified with the American way of life. The deliberate and organic life style of the village became implicitly boring and therefore inferior.

Inherent in the form and content of Hollywood movies and network television shows is the idealised American way of life – from sexual behaviour through dress and car fashions to family interaction. The appearance of incredible affluence stands out as the invariable component in the perfectly produced episodes of police and family dramas and inane sit coms. This message became crudely translated to mean that in America there continues to exist the great Horatio Alger possibilities, the myth of Anyman as potential millionaire – or super hero or great lover – available only in the land of the free.

The images bespoke of possibilities that the majority of the world's people could never attain – the two car, middle class family living in a suburban split level with a boat mounted on a trailer and all three kids going to Grade A universities.

Hollywood and US television productions assume fashion as gospel, in clothes, gadgets and diet. In turn, the imported culture raised demand among Third World middle and even working classes for imported food, consumer goods and entertainment. The seed of yearning was planted: big city life in America was exciting, if not always safe.

The results of this three-way intervention – war, development and technology – in Third World societies helped to forge a new set of social, political and economic ties between the United States and nations of Asia, Latin America and the Caribbean. The anti-communist idiom was like the seed cover for the kernel of US exports: 'freedom' to join the growing pool of migrant wage-labourers – freedom from all previous obligations.

The material results of 'development' left little of permanent value in scores of countries. But considerable damage was done. Dams diverted rivers, often to the disparagement of the surrounding farmland and the larger environment. In some areas people starved or had to move because development projects depleted their trees and water. Most of the major infrastructural projects brought labour forces from one place to another, wasted resources and destroyed the environment. Or, the projects simply remained unfinished.

Often, when a dam or bridge was built or the project ran out of money, the recently recruited labour was left unemployed and without benefits. Once unemployed, the worker fell from the column of suffering to the column of disaster. Forced to leave the country of birth or seek work in criminal sectors, the former peasant had unknowingly joined the mobile work force of the world.

He or she could not look to reformist governments or progressive labour unions to redress grievances or provide sustenance. By the late 1960s and into the 1970s reformers were replaced by generals who, in the name of order and stability, dropped notions of social equity from the official vocabulary and unabashedly obeyed the orders of the giant lending institutions. Repressive military regimes destroyed or weakened labour unions. So, already low wages dropped lower, and consequently reduced the socially necessary cost of labour.

This story of changing patterns of world labour over the last forty-five years has now become apparent as the Cold War vocabulary changes into rhetoric of 'new world orders' to justify interventionism. Despite its epic lack of success by the middle 1980s, the principles of 'free market' and 'free trade' had become axiomatic in most Third World state policy. This meant that Third World labour would remain cheap and abundant at the core and the periphery and that Third World land and resources would be available to any bidder. The notion of substantive human rights had all but disappeared from official language. Ironically, the words freedom and prosperity were substituted for rights, to justify economically beneficial arrangements for global capital.

Conclusion

When historians study the Cold War in future generations they may conclude that the movement of wealth from the South to the North, which includes the movement of labour, was one of the understudied dynamic processes of the period. Just as the post-World War II era, through the late 1960s, saw the ascendancy of human rights as a universal doctrine that allowed labourers and the poor to make claims for justice and equity, so did the era of the 1980s see the reassertion of the strength of capital, under the euphemism of freedom. By the 1990s, terms such as labour rights in policy and business circles became the equivalent of mating with alien species.

The gains western labour made during the 1960s in wages, benefits and other 'expenses' that capital was forced to pay, were reduced beginning in the late 1970s and then further cut in the 1980s. What the Reagan and Thatcher 'revolutions' accomplished was precisely the reduction of the socially necessary costs of maintaining and reproducing a labour force.

This was but the last stage of a process that involved the virtual destruction of the world's peasantry. Although the elimination of the peasant as the basic provider of the world's food did not begin in the postwar period, in the Third World it made its most epic moves in that era. The human consequence of this transformation is material for the greatest human tragic drama of the end of this century.

The combined push of bank and corporate-based development, organised by the IMF and World Bank, the unending wars fought mostly under the anti-communist ideological umbrella and the aggressive push of US technology and culture acted as a triple force for change in the Third World. By 1990 the Third World population with some exceptions had become a global labour force without even symbolic protection. Those aspiring for independence and social justice had to redefine strategies. When Soviet leaders announced they would no longer play Cold War – that is, behave as if they were a socialist super power competing with the capitalist United States for the great battle over social systems – the Third World was deprived of the one country that had been willing to write the equivalent of insurance policies for some revolutions, and act as arms and fuel supplier for others. Socialism no longer stood as a social system, backed by a major power, to threaten the reign of capitalism – except as an idea, and then one that had been discredited in the major media and through the cultural apparatus of the West.

From Washington, triumphant language obscured the reality of the phenomenon that had occurred. 'Freedom' in the former Soviet Union and Eastern Europe meant increased suffering for the vast majority along with the transplanting of institutions of free speech and politics that translated in reality into parliamentary bickering and procedural confusion. Capitalism's 'victory' in 1990 did not materialise into what members of Solidarity in Poland had thought of for the decade of the 1980s as justice.

The end of the Cold War initiated the era in which capital could dictate its terms as never before to the world's labour supply and claim nearly unimpeded access to much of the world's resources. The removal of the Soviet Union from the arena of international competition meant the powerlessness of international labour – until new forms of resistance consolidate.

One of the ironies of the period was the ambiguity of national borders. On the one hand, capital and labour flowed across them with few obstacles. On the other hand, people deemed to be aliens – not included in the needed labour flow – became feared enemies who would deprive the indigenous work force of jobs and contaminate the blood of the body politic.

Those people allowed, if not forced, to pick and package the food supplies for tens of millions of US and European households were also seen as undesirable residents. The boundary that provided no impediment for the food to enter from Mexico to the United States bore a 'keep out' sign for those Mexican labourers deemed unnecessary.

No longer do border guards shoot people as they come from former communist countries into the West; the symbolic dividing line has vanished. In the 1990s, walls have lost their ideological disguises, but have acquired racial and ethnic spikes that promise to grow more menacing. In 1992 1.8 million immigrants came to the United States, 'far too many for us to absorb,' complained an INS official. 'And if this keeps going there will be a crisis.'

Indeed, neither the economic nor social structures of the United States and the other advanced countries can adjust to the constant influx of low wage workers of different colours and ethnic backgrounds. There is little reference in official addresses to the welcoming greeting given by the Statue of Liberty, but at the same time Western economies gear up for higher 'productivity', which amounts to lowering wages while increasing the amount each worker produces – a job ideally suited for the world's migrating labour force since they are the neediest and most unprotected of all workers. All this portends ethnic and racial strife amidst class conflict as the grim formula for the future.

IN DEFENCE OF UTOPIA

Daniel Singer

'Anywhere out of this world'

Baudelaire

'Be realistic, ask for the impossible'

May 68 slogan

Each period has its bogeys and its significant dirty words. One of the favourite insults at present seems to be the term Utopian, meaning in the best of cases foolishly Quixotic, though used most often as a nightmarish adjective soaked with all the blood of the *gulag*.

In the concise Oxford dictionary Utopia is defined as '(Book published by T. More in 1516 describing) imaginary island with perfect social and political system; ideally perfect place or state of things [=nowhere, f Gk *ou* not + *topos* place]'. My old copy of the *Encyclopedia Britannica* calls it 'an ideal commonwealth whose inhabitants exist under perfect conditions' and enumerates a long list of visionary writers and their works from Plato and his *Republic* through Francis Bacon and Tommaso Campanella to William Morris and H.G. Wells. The *Larousse* adds two utopias *à rebours* – the Brave New World of Aldous Huxley and Orwell's 1984. All three dismiss 'utopian' with varying degrees of contempt: the first as typical for 'an ardent but unpractical reformer'; the second as applicable to 'a visionary reform which fails to recognise defects in human nature'; the French as wishful thinking ('taking its desires for reality').

My aim here is not to examine the historical evolution of the image of an ideal society.[1] Nor is it to repeat the Marxist criticisms, inaugurated by Engels, against vain attempts to alter society radically, based not on the real contradictions of that society but on the imaginary projections of an ideal against which the reality must be judged and condemned. My purpose is much narrower. It is to stress that in the current context the absence of a vision of the future, of a project, of a radical alternative cripples and paralyses the potential movement from below and may divert it in dangerous directions. It is to ask why the Establishment, which has always tried to do so, is now so particularly successful in persuading the people that its regime is eternal, that there is nothing beyond its horizon.

249

In a sense, the problem we are facing is not new. It is as old as socialism itself and the inevitable duality of its struggle, which can be summed up in shorthand: a socialist movement has to fight within the framework of existing capitalist society and provide solutions which ultimately lie beyond that framework. If it concentrates too much on that future it runs the risk of sectarian isolation. Yet if it limits itself to struggle within the system, it loses its original *raison d'être*, the search for a radically different society. Naturally, the Establishment has always tried to present its reign as final and the Fukuyamas with their end of history are not a latter-day invention. The relevant question is why, in peddling such wares, our Establishment is more successful than its predecessors?

Part of the explanation, at least, is linked with the collapse of the Soviet system and the identification, for so long and by so many, of the socialist dream with stalinist and post-stalinist reality. It is important to repeat that the Soviet experiment began in conditions of backwardness unforeseen in Marxist projections; that when the Bolshevik Revolution failed to spread, primitive accumulation in Russia produced a despotism both bloody and Byzantine; and that there were a good many on the socialist left to condemn its crimes, the more so since they were committed in the name of socialism. It is important to say, but insufficient, because the attraction of the first victorious workers' revolution was such that millions of people believed that what was being forged in the Soviet Union was socialism. Particularly before the last war, eminent visitors could genuinely proclaim: 'I have been over into the future and it works' (Lincoln Steffens) or assert that the USSR was 'a land where utopia was becoming reality' (André Gide).

The confusion was further confounded by the fact that Stalin, while trampling the principles, was careful to preserve the vocabulary. The Soviet Union was a 'proletarian dictatorship' even if the workers exercised no power whatsoever. 1936, the year of the great purges and of terror at its highest, was also the year when 'the most democratic' constitution was promulgated. And after the war the countries of Eastern Europe became 'people's democracies' when the people were deprived of any say in matters concerning their fate. This yawning gap between theory and practice, expressed in Orwellian newspeak and perpetuated by Stalin's successors, was a major factor in demoralisation, in the popular resentment and, ultimately, in the total rejection of socialism.

The dream was lumped together with reality and this enables current propagandists to put the blame on utopia. In Russia in particular, people like Mr Yeltsin's right-hand man, Gennady Burbulis, yesterday teacher of Marxism-Leninism, today preacher of the capitalist gospel (after all, what matters is the preservation of power!) used to describe the Soviet Union as a Marxist paradise and now brand it as Marxist hell, but seem to have no doubt about its socialist nature. Actually, it is absurd to attribute the sufferings of the Soviet people to the utopian ambitions of their masters. Did Stalin dream of equality? Did he try to tackle the social division of labour, to abolish the hierarchical order, to dismantle the mighty state? Were Brezhnev or Chernenko driven by the goal of socialist revolution? To ask such questions is to raise a laugh. And yet the verbal association between socialism and the stalinist system does the trick. For some time to come, the very idea of moving in a direction other than that of a capitalist society will be treated as dangerously utopian and associated in Russia with barbed wire and in Eastern Europe with the Soviet tank. For how long may depend on the pedagogical capacity of 'really existing capitalism'.[2]

Nevertheless, the destruction of the Soviet legend cannot, on its own, explain the current distaste for utopian projections, especially if we keep in mind that, while the neo-stalinist system collapsed spectacularly in 1989, the myth itself was shattered a third of a century earlier. Stalinism was a curious mixture of terrible oppression and almost religious belief. The traumatic shock came in 1956, when Nikita Khrushchev, the keeper of the shrine, told the faithful that their dead demigod was stinking. People of the younger generation can hardly imagine the grief and prostration the 'secret speech' provoked amid Communists and sympathisers. A new period had begun. In eastern Europe, the ruthless believers were succeeded by more pragmatic time-servers. In the western world it was the age of disenchantment. After the invasion of Hungary a few illusions were still left, but once the Soviet tanks had entered Prague not even the faithful party-liners seriously claimed that the future was being forged in the East. Therefore, a quarter of a century later, we must seek some additional reasons to explain why the search for a different society is so unfashionable in the West. We must look at the weakness of the western Left: the submission of Social-Democracy and the bankruptcy of Communism.

Social-democracy is now a misnomer. It has lost not only its original meaning, but also the one it acquired after the Bolshevik Revolution. In theory, at least, the Social-Democrats, too, were committed to the socialisation of the means of production, the transfer of power to the working people, the withering away of the state, in short to the abolition of capitalist society. Only they claimed that this could be achieved gradually, without a break and within existing institutions. Admittedly, their anti-capitalist zeal could be described as lacking passion, yet they felt compelled to claim they were dreaming of a different world. Then, in the conflicts of the Cold War and the thirty years of unprecedented capitalist expansion, all pretences were dropped. The French Socialists, when François Mitterrand was elected President in 1981, were probably the last ones to suggest that one could 'change life' by changing society. Two years later they were kneeling in front of the golden calf and became high priests of financial orthodoxy. By now Europe's Socialists may differ from America's Democrats by their attitude towards the state or their connection with labour unions, but they are no more 'utopian' seekers of a different society than, say, Bill Clinton.

Western Communists, for a time, did have this utopian dimension. Indeed, they were convinced that they were part of an international army which, on the Russian front, was actually forging the future. But those days are long gone. After the invasion of Czechoslovakia even the obedient parties like the Portuguese or the French ceased to present Russia as an example. To accuse the much more independent Italian CP (or PCI) of having stuck to the neo-stalinist model is, therefore, totally unjustified. The real indictment is that, having discarded the model, it put nothing in its place. Partly because it did not examine the roots of the Soviet crimes, i.e. the nature of the regime, it did not analyse either the fast changing structure of western capitalism and the socialist answers these changes required. And so, when the Berlin Wall collapsed, the PCI was ideologically bare and tried to recover its poise through exorcism, by putting on new robes and calling itself PDS, the Democratic Party of the Left. By now a prisoner of the ruling ideology, it found itself with a potential movement, a tradition, a heritage and no perspectives whatsoever – in historical terms, an actor doomed to leave the stage.

But why should the western left bother about a global alternative? Among currently unfashionable words 'total', cleverly confused with totalitarian, and *weltanschauung*, the conception of the world as a whole, treated as the path to the *gulag*, come quite close to the top. It is natural that, shaken by the protest movement of the sixties and threatened by the economic crisis of the ensuing decade, the Establishment should have condemned any attempt to link separate revolts into a coherent whole as the greatest sin. But this process also provides the obvious answer to the question above. Our system, like any other, has its inner coherence. Its social sciences, particularly economics, are exercises in formal logic, never questioning the basic premises on which the argument, and the society, rest. An opposition not seeking a radical alternative has a similar posture and is reduced either to mere protest or to tinkering with the existing structure. The political scene is full of illustrations.

Take, for instance, the debate over the integration of Western Europe connected with the ratification of the Maastricht Treaty. In France, in the verbal battles preceding the referendum, the Socialists were perfectly consistent when they shared the pro-Maastricht platform with representatives of the moderate Right. Having surrendered to capital at home in 1983, they were pursuing the same line on a European scale nearly ten years later. (Equally coherent was the conversion to Europe of the British Labour Party, which stopped pretending that it might one day implement policies so radical that they would clash with the neo-liberal framework of the European Community). Indeed, those who had to do a great deal of explaining were the left-wing opponents of Europe's capitalist integration, preaching either a *non* or a plague on both your houses.

If they wanted to remain true to themselves, they had to stress that their negative attitude towards the Europe of big business had no jingoist connections; that they were ready to give up shibboleths of sovereignty to build things together with the working people of other countries; that the bourgeois nation-state was for them, at best, a provisional platform for starting radical changes which could only succeed by spreading; that only a Europe building a different society could have the will and the means to stand up to the United States. In other words, not to be confused with reactionary nationalists, left-wingers had to show that their opposition to the capitalist construction was based on an alternative conception, the vision of the United Socialist States of Europe, which would not be states for much longer. The same can be said of most topical problems: privatisation, the role of the state, the control of international finance or western intervention throughout the world. The voice of the Left is so desperately weak in all such debates, because socialists seem to have lost the capacity to think in terms of a different project.

Yet is it still possible to build such projections after the terrible Soviet experiment and the dramatic collapse of great expectations? Yes and no. In a sense, a project is now more indispensable than ever. After all that has happened, people may still be driven by their conditions to rebel, but they will not enter a coherent movement, will not join a potentially hegemonic bloc capable of long term action without knowing the goal and the route to be travelled, the end and the means. It will not be possible to sell them 'pie in the sky' or to dismiss their demands on the grounds that Marxist classics refused to indulge in such speculation. The classics of Marxism, after all, did not live through the Stalin era.

The precedent, however, points also in the opposite direction. The main lesson of the abortive attempt is that when people are deprived of their power of decision, even in terrible moments in the heat of battle, the provisional absence of democracy tends to become permanent with tragic consequences. Never again will the movement be conceived as an armed battalion within a society requiring barrack-room discipline. Socialism, to echo Rosa Luxemburg, cannot be a Christmas present for those who voted well; it is by definition, a conquest from below. Hence, it cannot be built thanks to a blueprint drawn at the top and imposed from above. The vision of a different society must be elaborated collectively and in the open. It must take into account the spectacular changes in the capitalist world and answer all the awkward questions (eg whether the greatly altered working class is still the main agency of historical change). Even so, the project itself is bound to be flexible, provisional if socialist construction is seen as a conquest by the working people, advancing stage by stage and changing themselves as they change society.

The utopian dimension must be seen in this context. I have always thought that one of the main attractions of Marx's thought was the complex combination of historic necessity and political will or, to put it crudely, that the revolutionary transformation was both the result of the development of the productive forces and an upheaval, the 'world upside down'. What, linked together, was an asset became a drawback when torn apart. On one side, you had the search for a shortcut without awareness of economic reality and, on the other, the belief in the mechanical progress of productive forces which, on their own, were to give birth to a socialist society.

Of the two, the cult of growth, which has brought humankind to the verge of self-destruction, did probably more harm to socialism. The emergence of ecology as a separate force is one striking illustration of the failure of the socialist movement to fulfil its task.[3] But productivism had another consequence, too. The crucial preoccupations of Marxism were reduced to a liturgy used on rare festive occasions. The Soviet Union invented a new way of extracting surplus but not any different patterns of production and consumption. Stalin's slogan – to catch up and overtake America – remained the goal of his successors and when, instead of gaining, they began to lose ground in this race, they were totally bewildered. One reason for Mikhail Gorbachev's utter failure to take the system on the road towards 'democratic socialism' was that his vision of a socialist society was nothing more than prosperous capitalism with a degree of social security.[4]

All this does not imply that the state of economic development is irrelevant. The romantic rebellion against the horrors of capitalism has inspired fruitful analyses and passionate indictments.[5] The search for socialism, however, cannot be confused with the quest for paradise lost. It is forward looking even when it rejects the idea of technological progress as neutral and not socially determined. The snag is that the only modernity we know is capitalist and the two terms, therefore, tend to be confused. The confusion is particularly ambiguous in the fashionable discussions where 'post-modern' problems are treated as if property relations, class conflicts or the hierarchical division of labour were things of the past, almost irrelevant to the new age. Nationalism, racism, foreign intervention are put on the agenda as moral issues unrelated to their social context. Even work is treated as if all that mattered was the organisation of leisure, leaving labour to be exploited in capitalist production.

These are clearly digressions, abstract discussions ignoring, intentionally or not, the true nature of 'really existing capitalism'. The true difficulty for socialists is that they must view various aspects of modernisation – the size of the plant, technological innovation, the organisation of labour – not only as they affect working people immediately, but also as they will affect them in the future when they, the associate producers, will run the self-managed society. Thus, the socialists must at once condemn capitalist modernity and seek within it potentialities for another mode of development. Their project will inevitably be utopian in the sense of untried, venturing into uncharted territory. This dimension, nevertheless, is badly needed to stretch the normal exercise of politics – the confrontation between what is and what can be done – beyond the artificial frontiers set by the establishment.

Indeed, the most difficult task for the socialist movement is to preserve a permanent link between its current defensive struggle and that vision at once distant and crucial. The assumption that socialism must be universal, covering the whole globe, obviously does not mean that all revolutions will take place simultaneously; the fact that it must abolish the production of commodities does not imply that the market will vanish overnight; and the notion that the state must ultimately disappear will not prevent that state from being used in the meantime to eliminate classes and inequality. Hardly anybody now conceives the revolutionary process as the seizure of the Winter Palace followed by an inexorable march towards a classless society. Even in the best of cases, if the revolution were to happen in an advanced economy like that of the United States, the transition would be long and the road full of pitfalls. The end of capitalism, to borrow a concept [6], is not the end of the reign of Capital. But it is imperative that all along the road we should know where we are heading, that we are advancing towards a world in which exchange value has been replaced by use value, social inequality has vanished together with classes and people have gained mastery over their fate; in short, not towards a post-modern but towards a post-capitalist society moved by its own, still unknown contradictions.

But why should we at all embark on such a long, dangerous and uncertain journey? Look at the capitalist world around you, plain to see now that it can no longer conceal its features by turning the light on its allegedly communist rival. Incidentally, the disappearance of that rival shows that the tremendous expenditure on arms in the last half century was not a burden imposed by the 'red peril' but an indispensable part of the existing economic system, though one yielding diminishing returns. The lengthening lines of the jobless confirm that capitalism, while stimulating the technological inventiveness of humankind, then turns its achievements not into a new life but into profits and unemployment. The gap between the rich and mighty on one side and the poor and outcasts on the other, far from narrowing, widens even in the privileged countries of advanced capitalism.

As to the distance between the haves and the have-nots on the world scale it has become indecent, exploitation combined with charity beating all records of hypocrisy. We impose our terms of trade, squeeze the third world beyond any possibility of repayment, precipitate the horrors of war and then rush to the rescue. And we show it all – obviously not the exploitation, but the starvation, death and the white knight in his tank – in full technicolour to the awed audience watching it throughout the world.

For, with our technological genius, we have invented instruments of communication and discovery which debase our understanding and prevent us from looking beyond the capitalist horizon.

Part of their ideological power lies in our own weakness, in our tacit acceptance that change can be merely marginal. It is time to wake up, to revive the slogan which, a quarter of a century ago, in May 1968, echoed through the streets of Paris, time to be realistic enough to ask for the impossible, for what our system, its high priests and pundits, its propaganda machine and its mass media have as their task to describe as impossible or, if you prefer, dangerously utopian. From Bosnia and its 'ethnic cleansing' or the former Soviet Union, where atavistic forces may be unleashed anytime by the explosive mixture of ideological void and economic collapse; from the fires in racist Los Angeles or Rostock with its xenophobia. *Ein volk*. . . . Most modern voices and ghosts from the past remind us that the barbarians are not at the gates, they are amongst us, ready to rule and to run amok once again, if we don't wake up soon enough and so not start building a different world, however utopian this may sound today.

NOTES

1. Among the fairly recent books on the subject see *Bronislaw Baczko:* Lumières de l'Utopie. Payot 1978 and M.Löwy and R. Sayre: *Révolte et mélancolie. Le romantisme à contre-courant de la modernité.* Payot 1992.
2. It will also depend on the extent to which the unapplied principles did penetrate the unconscious of the population in eastern Europe. Judging by the complaints of the technocrats there about the thirst of the population for social justice and equality, this factor is very far from negligible.
3. The other is, obviously, the emergence of Feminism as a separate movement.
4. Another reason was that the clique backing him wanted to consolidate its privileged position through private property and deserted him for Yeltsin, when he did not move fast enough in that direction.
5. On this aspect see Löwy and Sayre mentioned above.
6. From István Mészáros. A concept he develops in *Beyond Capital*, Merlin Press forthcoming.